JIHAD ON TWO FRONTS

ALSO BY DILIP HIRO

Non-fiction

After Empire: The Birth of a Multipolar World (2010)

Inside Central Asia: A Political and Cultural History of Uzbekistan, Turkmenistan, Kazakhstan, Kyrgyzstan, Tajikistan, Turkey and Iran (2009) (*Financial Times' Best History Book of the Year*)

Blood of the Earth: The Battle for the World's Vanishing Oil Resources (2007)

The Timeline History of India (2006)

The Iranian Labyrinth: Journeys through Theocratic Iran and Its Furies (2005)

Secrets and Lies: Operation 'Iraqi Freedom' and After (2004) (*Financial Times' Best Politics and Religion Book of the Year*) (*Long-listed for the George Orwell Prize for Political Writing*)

The Essential Middle East: A Comprehensive Guide (2003)

Iraq: In The Eye Of The Storm (2003)

War Without End: The Rise of Islamist Terrorism and Global Response (2002)

The Rough Guide History of India (2002)

Neighbors, Not Friends: Iraq and Iran after the Gulf Wars (2001)

Sharing the Promised Land: A Tale of Israelis and Palestinians (1998)

Dictionary of the Middle East (1996)

The Middle East (1996)

Between Marx and Muhammad: The Changing Face of Central Asia (1995)

Lebanon, Fire and Embers: A History of the Lebanese Civil War (1993)

Desert Shield to Desert Storm: The Second Gulf War (1992)

Black British, White British: A History of Race Relations in Britain (1991)

The Longest War: The Iran-Iraq Military Conflict (1991)

Holy Wars: The Rise of Islamic Fundamentalism (1989)

Iran: The Revolution Within (1988)

Iran under the Ayatollahs (1985)

Inside the Middle East (1982)

Inside India Today (1977)

The Untouchables of India (1975)

Black British, White British (1973)

The Indian Family in Britain (1969)

Fiction

Three Plays (1985)

Interior, Exchange, Exterior (Poems, 1980)

Apply, Apply, No Reply & A Clean Break (Two Plays, 1978)

To Anchor a Cloud (Play, 1972)

A Triangular View (Novel, 1969)

Editor

Babur Nama: Journal of Emperor Babur (2006)

JIHAD ON TWO FRONTS

South Asia's Unfolding Drama

Dilip Hiro

HarperCollins *Publishers* India

First published in India by
HarperCollins *Publishers* in 2011
A-75, Sector 57, Noida, Uttar Pradesh 201301, India
www.harpercollins.co.in

1 2 3 4 5 6 7 8 9 10

ISBN: 978-93-5029-169-6

Typeset in 11/14 Adobe Garamond at
SÜRYA

Printed and bound in Inida by
Manipal Technologies Limited, Manipal

CONTENTS

Map 1: SOUTH, WEST AND CENTRAL ASIA

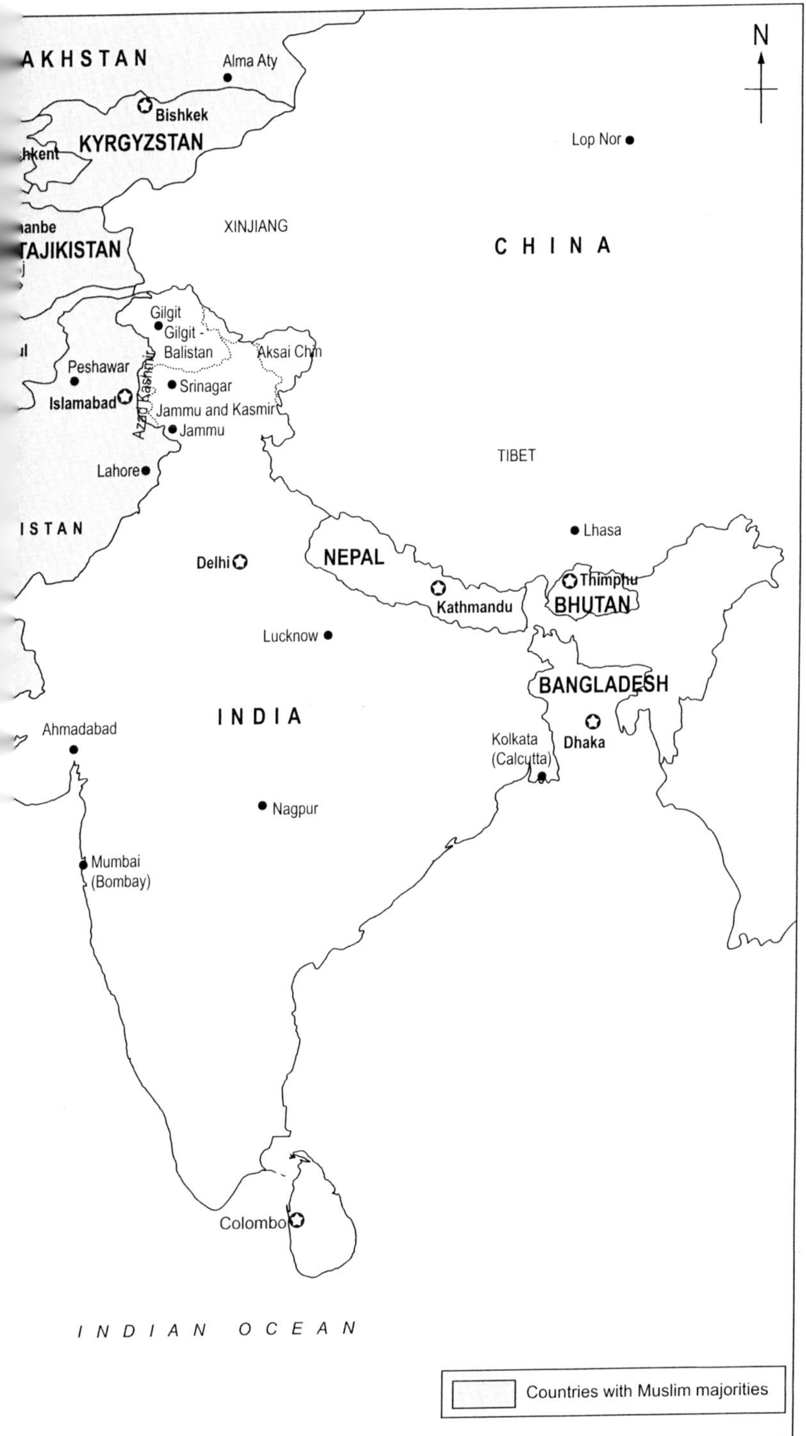
AKHSTAN
Alma Aty
Bishkek
KYRGYZSTAN
hkent
XINJIANG
anbe
TAJIKISTAN
CHINA
Lop Nor
N
Gilgit
Gilgit - Balistan
Aksai Chin
Peshawar
Islamabad
Azad Kashmir
Srinagar
Jammu and Kasmir
Jammu
TIBET
Lahore
ISTAN
Lhasa
NEPAL
Delhi
Thimphu
BHUTAN
Kathmandu
Lucknow
BANGLADESH
INDIA
Ahmadabad
Kolkata (Calcutta)
Dhaka
Nagpur
Mumbai (Bombay)
Colombo
INDIAN OCEAN
Countries with Muslim majorities

Map 2: AFGHANISTAN

Map 3: PAKISTAN

Map 4: PUSHTUN-DOMINATED AFGHANISTAN-PAKISTAN BORDER

Map 5: JAMMU AND KASHMIR

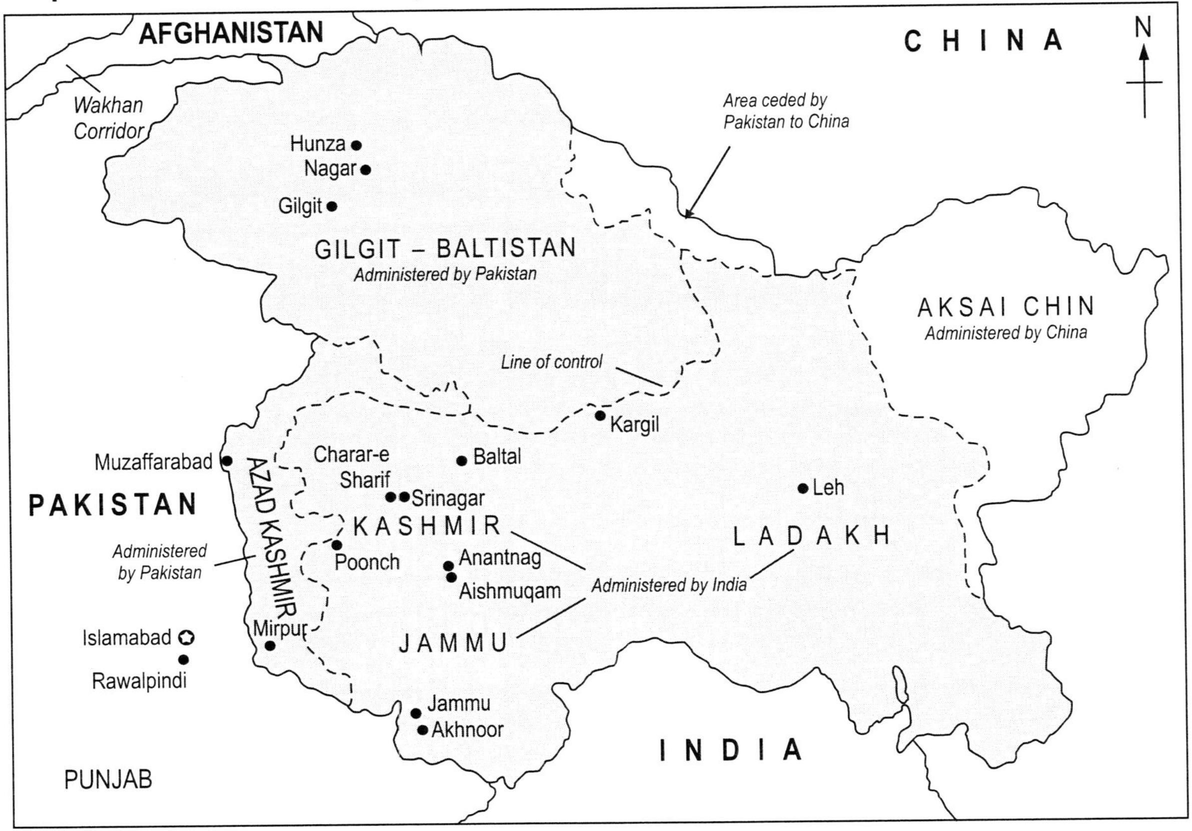

Map 6: INDIA

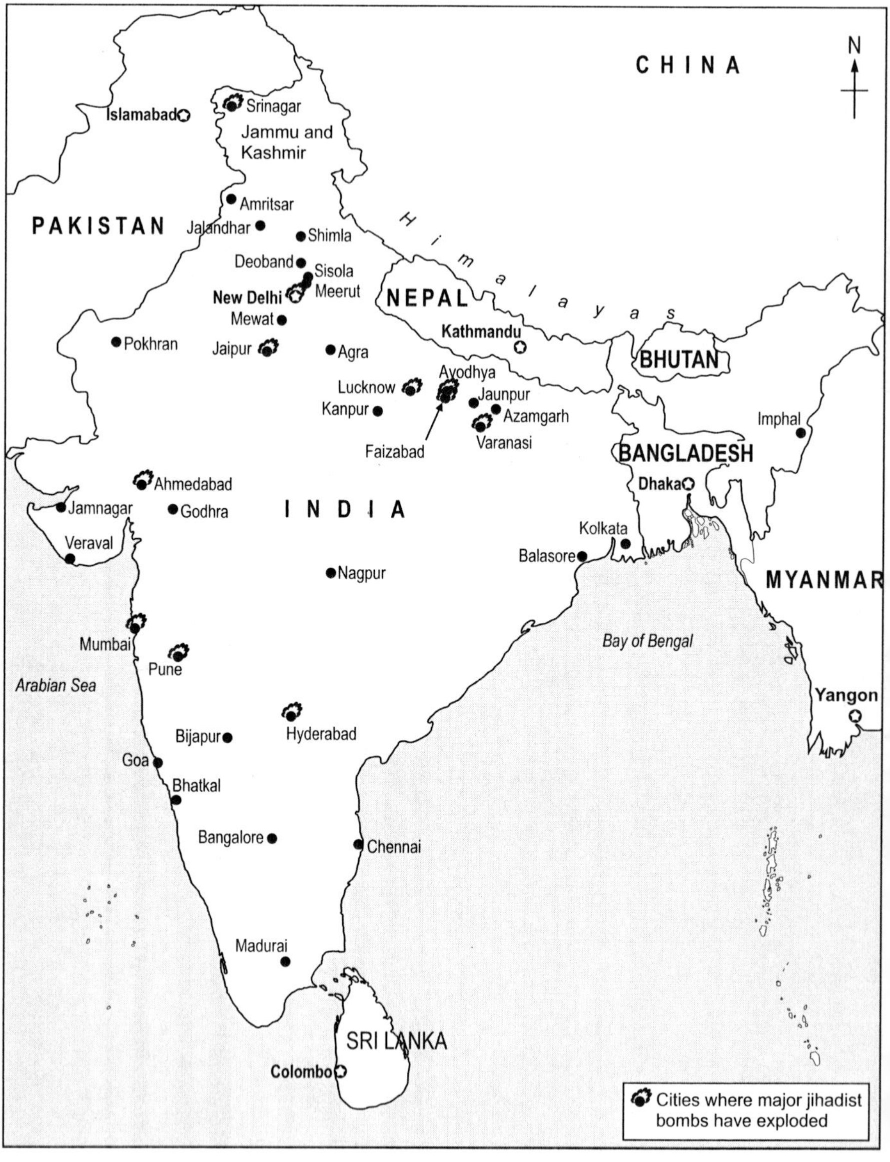

N
CHINA
Islamabad
Srinagar
Jammu and Kashmir
PAKISTAN
Amritsar
Jalandhar
Shimla
Deoband
Sisola
Meerut
New Delhi
Mewat
Himalayas
NEPAL
Kathmandu
BHUTAN
Pokhran
Jaipur
Agra
Ayodhya
Lucknow
Jaunpur
Kanpur
Azamgarh
Imphal
Varanasi
Faizabad
BANGLADESH
Dhaka
Ahmedabad
Jamnagar
Godhra
INDIA
Veraval
Kolkata
Balasore
Nagpur
MYANMAR
Mumbai
Pune
Bay of Bengal
Arabian Sea
Yangon
Hyderabad
Bijapur
Goa
Bhatkal
Bangalore
Chennai
Madurai
SRI LANKA
Colombo
Cities where major jihadist bombs have exploded

PREFACE

THIS BOOK IS about the ongoing jihad and the associated violence in South Asia.

An Arabic word, *jihad* means 'effort'. It is part of the Arabic phrase *jihad fi sabil Allah*, 'effort in the pathway to God'. Jihad is waged in various forms – internal and external – and degrees, war being the most extreme. In its internal form, jihad is the internal struggle of moral discipline and commitment to Islam by a Muslim. However, it is jihad's external form that has interested most chroniclers. Historically, the term 'jihad' has been used to describe an armed struggle by Muslims against unbelievers to advance Islam or counter danger to it. Many Islamic thinkers use the term 'greater jihad' for the struggle against one's base instincts, and 'lesser jihad' for the struggle against unbelievers. In this book jihad means 'lesser jihad'. A Muslim who wages jihad is called *mujahid* (plural *mujahedin* or *mujahideen*), or jihadist or jihadi.

A pre-eminent feature of Islam in South Asia is that the mystical philosophy embedded in it, called Sufism, has tens of millions of followers. Since Sufis do not run their own theological schools to train clerics, they do not compete with the main Sunni and Shia sects of Islam. So, irrespective of his or her sectarian affiliation, a Muslim can follow Sufi practices and rituals freely.

When Islam is used as a political ideology, it is called Islamism and its adherents are known as Islamists. Over the past decade or so, these two words have replaced the earlier terms, Islamic fundamentalism and fundamentalists. By that token, the adjective Islamist stands apart from Islamic, which has a much wider application.

Since modern Afghanistan evolved as an independent Muslim country almost a century before Pakistan, a narrative of its history appears in the book immediately after a description of the Sufi shrines in the region. With the emergence of Pakistan along its 1,610-mile (2,576 km) long eastern border, Afghanistan's history became interlinked with Pakistan's. The turmoil caused by the leftist military coup in Afghanistan in 1978 transformed Pakistan into a front-line state in the Cold War between Washington and Moscow. The end of the Cold War in the aftermath of the collapse of the Soviet Union in 1991, which signalled the victory of the United States, did not bring peace to Afghanistan. Age-old ethnic rivalries, mainly between Pushtuns and Tajiks, escalated into a civil war. Meanwhile, having succeeded in bringing about the withdrawal of the Soviet troops from Afghanistan in 1989, the veterans of the anti-Soviet jihad, working with the Pakistani military's intelligence service, turned to securing the exit of Indian troops from the Muslim-majority Kashmir.

The end result of these events has been the creation of a complex equation covering Afghanistan, Pakistan, Kashmir and India, which has the second largest Muslim population in the world after Indonesia – with the US as an important player, particularly after 9/11. Events in one country or territory (such as Indian Kashmir) impact on one or more of the other political entities, the common thread being the existence and activities of jihadist organizations. In this book I have narrated how and why we have arrived where we have in the region, while delineating the role each major participant has played against the background of its domestic and external conditions.

A word about place names, and the spellings of Arabic, Bengali, Dari, Hebrew, Hindi, Kashmiri, Persian, Pushtu, Russian, Sanskrit, Sindhi and Urdu words. A foreign word, written in italics at first mention, appears in roman at later appearances. There is no standard way of transliterating foreign words. In each case I have chosen one of the most widely used spellings in the English-language print media – except when the spelling of an author I cite is different from mine. There I have merely reproduced the published spelling in the quoted material.

The following terms signify religious or secular titles: allama, ayatollah, emir, hajji, imam, mahatma, maulana, maulavi, mirwaiz, mullah, qazi, and shaikh.

Last but not least, my sincere thanks to Heather McCallum, my editor at Yale University Press, London, for helping me to realize, in her inimitably gentle ways, the full potential of my book proposal.

The epilogue takes the analytical narrative to August 2011. It is not indexed.

London
August 2011

DILIP HIRO

INTRODUCTION

THIS BOOK HAS a dual purpose: to show that the interrelated jihadist movements in Afghanistan and Pakistan have infected India, and that they pose a serious threat to the Pakistani state. Since the founding of Pakistan in 1947, its history has been moulded by independent India as well as Afghanistan. The chronicles of these countries – with a staggering combined population of 1.5 billion – are inextricably linked. This overarching fact has determined the arcuate shape of the present book, with Afghanistan and India as springers and Pakistan as the keystone.

Currently, the region is suffering from varying degrees of destabilization caused by Islamist terrorism, which originated and thrived in Afghanistan as a counterforce to the large presence of Soviet troops in the 1980s. After the expulsion of Soviet forces from Afghanistan in 1989, the jihadists from Pakistan, assisted by the newly formed Al Qaida, focused on liberating the predominantly Muslim Kashmir from the Hindu-majority Indian government. By gaining the upper hand in the irredentist movement in Kashmir, dominated so far by secular Kashmiri nationalists, they caused a backlash in India. The fortunes of the Hindu nationalist Bharatiya Janata Party (BJP) rose, with its emboldened zealots demolishing a sixteenth-century mosque in 1992, an incendiary act. That inflamed the already fraught relations between minority Muslims and majority Hindus, and started a cycle of violence and counter-violence between the two communities which has yet to run its course.

Following 9/11 and the subsequent overthrow of the Taliban regime by Washington, Afghanistan became a battlefield between the resurgent Taliban and United States-led North Atlantic Treaty Organization (NATO) troops. There is as yet no end in sight to that conflict. The Pakistani government is engaged in a bloody struggle with extremist Islamists entrenched in the tribal belt abutting Afghanistan, while jihadists in India, working in collusion with their counterparts in Pakistan, have killed hundreds of Indians in bomb attacks in major cities since 2005.

The forging of close links between India, Israel and America over the past two decades has increased jihadists' hostility towards Delhi. Intent on destabilizing India, they aim to exploit the existing fault line between the aggrieved Muslim minority and the Hindu majority. Muslims are the most underprivileged community in India. Proportionally, more of them live below the official poverty line than Hindus, and fare worse than even outcast Hindus in education, health and jobs. They are grossly underrepresented in the Central parliament as well as in the private and public sectors of the economy. With the establishment of Pakistan in 1947, the most influential members of the community migrated to the new state, leaving their co-religionists short of effective leadership.

Sustained efforts by the Pakistan-based Lashkar-e Taiba (Urdu, 'Army of the Righteous'; LeT) have succeeded in creating a jihadist organization called the Indian Mujahedin (IM). Since 2005, the IM has claimed responsibility for major terrorist assaults on public transport, bazaars, cinemas and temples aimed at causing maximum loss of life and inflaming Hindu–Muslim relations.

At the macro-level, the IM, LeT, and Al Qaida share the malevolent aim of igniting a war between India and Pakistan, both nuclear-armed states. Between 1999 and 2002, the two neighbours came close to war, the casus belli being Kashmir. In May 1999, fighting between Indian and Pakistani troops in the Kargil region of the Indian-controlled Kashmir became intense. US president Bill Clinton intervened. Pressured by him, Pakistani prime minister Muhammad

Nawaz Sharif ordered the withdrawal of his troops. In May 2002, an assault by Kashmiri terrorists on military residential quarters near Jammu killed thirty-seven people. Delhi put its armed forces on the highest alert; Islamabad did likewise. One million soldiers faced one another across the international border. It took many weeks of active diplomacy by Washington to persuade the two sides to pull back from the brink of war.

In late 2008, extremist Islamist leaders watched with glee the abrupt rise in India–Pakistan tensions when – following a multipronged attack on targets in Mumbai in November 2008 – the Indian media named some of the forty-two alleged training camps for terrorists in Pakistan as targets for India's air force. Al Qaida intervened. A video warned that, were Delhi to carry out its threat, it would hit targets in India – an under-policed country where security is lax and soft targets abound.

To settle the Kashmir dispute, insists Pakistan, there must be a plebiscite to determine the will of Kashmiris, promised by the United Nations in 1948 and agreed by Delhi. India now argues that such an exercise has become redundant as there have been numerous elections in Indian-administered Kashmir, covering a little over three-fifths of the original princely state of Jammu and Kashmir.

Public opinion in Indian Kashmir has turned increasingly against Delhi. That has made the Central government more repressive than before – inflaming sentiment in Pakistan and increasing support for the LeT's commitment to liberate Indian Kashmir. The LeT's ranks are drawn mostly from the graduates of the Pakistani madrasas established with government aid during the rule of General Muhammad Zia ul Haq (1977–88). By the mid-1990s, there were ten thousand madrasas in the country. Today, in a typical district of Punjab, they account for a quarter of all schools.

After his coup against the democratically elected government of Prime Minister Zulfikar Ali Bhutto, leader of the Pakistan People's Party (PPP), Zia ul Haq consolidated his power by boosting minor Islamist groups and suppressing the PPP as a prologue to establishing a military dictatorship. He embarked on a blanket Islamization of Pakistani state and society with a plan to apply the Sharia in full by June 1990. Though he died in an aircraft explosion in 1988, a strong legacy of Islamization has remained.

Zia ul Haq's Islamic initiative got a boost when, following Moscow's large-scale military intervention in Afghanistan in 1979, Pakistan became a front-line state in the Cold War. Islamabad and Washington armed and trained tens of thousands of Afghan and non-Afghan mujahedin to destabilize the Marxist regime in Kabul. As a precondition for furthering the anti-Soviet jihad in Afghanistan, Zia ul Haq got the Ronald Reagan administration (1981–89) to suspend the US commitment to the non-proliferation of nuclear weapons. Islamabad forged ahead with its plans to fabricate an atom bomb with the help of China. A long-time ally of Pakistan, anti-India China was keen to aid Islamabad to build a nuclear weapon to counterbalance India's detonation of a 'nuclear device' in 1974. In early 1984, China exploded an atom bomb, assembled in Pakistan, at Lop Nor in Xinjiang province. The Reagan White House repeatedly lied to Congress about Islamabad's nuclear programme. Why? Because American law required the president to certify every year that Pakistan was *not* engaged in a nuclear-arms programme before generous US aid could be channelled to bolster the anti-Soviet jihad in Afghanistan. Though President George Bush Senior and President Bill Clinton later stopped aid to Islamabad after the Soviet withdrawal from Afghanistan, they continued to turn a blind eye to Pakistan's back-door entry into the Nuclear Club.

Fed up with the internecine fighting among the triumphant mujahedin factions in Afghanistan that erupted in the spring of 1992, Pakistan's Inter-Services Intelligence (ISI) directorate built up a fledgling organization called the Taliban. Set up originally by Mullah Muhammad Omar in 1994, it got a boost when the ISI helped it to recruit volunteers from among the two million Afghan refugees in Pakistan. The Taliban's capture of Kabul in September 1996 then unveiled an ultra-orthodox regime reflecting a mixture of conservative rural Afghan mores and elements of the puritanical Wahhabi doctrine of Sunni Islam. Mullah Omar came under the influence of Osama bin Laden, a Wahhabi.

The following year, Pakistani president General Pervez Musharraf recognized the Taliban regime and overtly helped it in several ways. It was only when, following 9/11, the George W. Bush administration threatened his government with dire consequences if it did not derecognize the Taliban that Musharraf reversed this policy. But the move was half-hearted. After the Taliban's defeat in December 2001, the semi-autonomous Federally Administered Tribal Areas (FATA) of Pakistan along its border with Afghanistan became sanctuaries for fugitive Al Qaida and Taliban leaders.

The ISI's revival of the Afghan Taliban in 2003–04 and Musharraf's alliance with Islamist factions at home emboldened jihadists. When one of Pakistan's jihadist leaders, Maulana Abdul Aziz Ghazi, threatened civil strife if the government did not promulgate the Sharia in the capital, Islamabad, forthwith, Musharraf had no option but to use military force to attack his armed followers in his mosque–madrasa complex in 2007. In response, Islamist militants, operating from FATA, the Swat Valley and elsewhere, mounted a jihad against military, police, and civilian targets. They also formed an umbrella organization, Tehrik-e Taliban Pakistan (Urdu, Taliban Movement of Pakistan; TTP). Low-intensity warfare ensued between the ISI and the TTP.

Despite this, the ISI's policy towards the Afghan Taliban remained unchanged. It continued to bolster the Afghan Taliban even when the latter intensified its attacks on NATO forces in Afghanistan. It did so to counteract the influence that India had acquired in post-Taliban Afghanistan through its generous aid programme complemented with the opening of health clinics and assistance with the training of Afghan officials. After all, Islamabad's military planners are aware that in the event of an all-out conventional war with India, their comparatively narrow country lacks strategic depth. The only way to overcome that critical drawback is to have Afghanistan as a firm ally.

The revived Afghan Taliban started setting up a parallel government in the countryside of the Pushtun-dominated southern and eastern Afghanistan from 2005 onward, funded and armed by road tolls and taxes levied on crops, including opium poppies, not to mention drug traders who supplied 90 per cent of the global demand for heroine. This coincided with the rising unpopularity of the incompetent and corrupt government of President Hamid Karzai – re-elected in 2009 in a poll marred by widespread fraud – protected by the ever-expanding Western forces led by the Pentagon.

Where appropriate, I have challenged the conventional historical narratives of the main players – Afghanistan, Pakistan, America, India, and the Soviet Union – with evidence. For example, the official chronicle says that Washington got involved militarily in Afghanistan only after the Soviet military intervention on 26 December 1979. The truth is that President Jimmy Carter authorized clandestine action against the leftist government in Kabul on 3 July 1979, almost six months earlier. Another example is the debunking of the conventional narrative about pro-Moscow India being tilted against Washington until the disintegration of the Soviet Union. I show clearly how *both* the White House and the Kremlin actively supported India against China throughout the 1960s and 1970s. Furthermore, at the appropriate points, I outline an alternative history. If, for instance, after December 1979 Carter had followed the advice of his pragmatic Secretary of State, Cyrus Vance, instead of the hawkish national security adviser, Zbigniew Brzezinski, the globe's chronicle would have been starkly different.

In the accounts that follow, I have embellished the conventional narrative of important events and actors with brief descriptions of how ordinary people in different parts of South Asia live. I have also, where appropriate, described the terrain – which in the case of Afghanistan has played a major role in shaping its history – and the strategic Khyber Pass as well as Peshawar and Quetta, not to mention Kabul and Kandahar. These elements are meant to create a more rounded view of the region than is usually on offer in conventional history books. Given the interconnectedness of the these neighbouring countries, some overlap between chapters is inevitable. I have, however, avoided duplication by mentioning different facts and insights about the same event in different chapters.

In the opening chapter, I recall my visit to the mausoleum of Sufi saint Nizamuddin Auliya in Delhi. My description of the singing of the qawwali music there provides a link to Pakistan since qawwali is an integral part of Pakistani culture, as is Sufi poetry. This leads to a brief history of Sufi Islam covering India, Afghanistan, Kashmir, and Pakistan. I bring to life the celebration of the death anniversary of Lal Shahbaz Qalandar in the Sindhi town of Sehwan Sharif, when up to half a million Pakistani Sufis assemble to sing and dance in his honour in the midst of wafts of hashish smoke and the scent of rose water. I then briefly deal with the Sufi orders in Kashmir and Afghanistan.

The narrative in this chapter highlights syncretism – coalesing of different forms of worship and rituals – an important aspect of Islam which, for several reasons, remains largely unknown in the Western world. Sufism and the jihadist ideology lie at opposite ends of the Islamic spectrum. Sufism could be a strong antidote to Islamist extremism if it were to be properly tapped and channelled. So far, however, neither the governments nor moderate Islamic leaders in Pakistan and Afghanistan have devised a strategy to do this. Nonetheless, the potential remains.

A brief chronicle of Afghanistan since 1848 in Chapter 2 illustrates its five major features, which together provide a key to understanding fully this strategic country. The single most important feature is Islam. The chapter shows how history keeps repeating itself in this mountainous land, with each major successive development impacting more widely than the previous one. Second, the divide between Pushtuns, concentrated in the south and south-east, and Tajiks, occupying most of the north, has remained virtually unbridgable. Third, every attempt to introduce socio-economic reform results in a reactionary backlash. The more radical the reform package, the more severe the reactionary blowback. Fourth, the origins of the current civil war in Afghanistan can be traced to late 1978 when the Marxist People's Democratic Party of Afghanistan split between moderates and hardliners, with the hawks seizing total power, rushing secularization and socio-economic reform at breakneck speed, thereby destabilizing the state and society. Fifth, Afghanistan and Pakistan became inextricably entwined in 1974, long before the Soviet military intervention in Afghanistan, with Pakistan's ISI directorate fostering and bolstering Afghan Islamists. In the course of illustrating this thesis, I describe rural life, which has remained unchanged for millennia.

The subsequent chapter relates how Soviet military involvement in Afghanistan led to increased activity by Pakistan's ISI among Afghan Islamists, who then became the Reagan administration's freedom fighters. In its overzealous campaign against the Soviet presence in Afghanistan, the Reagan White House not only overlooked mounting evidence of Pakistan's nuclear-arms programme but actively suppressed such documents acquired by the State Department. In Pakistan under Zia ul Haq, Islamization and nuclearization went hand in hand. The failure of the Soviet troops and their Afghan allies to stamp out insurgency gave impetus to Zia ul Haq's twin-track programme.

Chapter 4 describes how and why, following the departure of the Soviet troops from Afghanistan in early 1989, the leftist regime of Muhammad Najibullah lasted beyond the Soviet Union's collapse in December 1991. It finally fell in April 1992. The second civil war that erupted among the victorious mujahedin groups followed the age-old ethnic divide between Pushtuns and Tajiks. That provided an opportunity for Pakistan's ISI to bolster an altogether new organization called the Taliban. With the Taliban capturing Kabul in September 1996, Pakistan achieved its single most important foreign policy aim since its establishment in 1947: a proxy regime in Afghanistan.

Chapter 5 relates how Al Qaida and the LeT, a creature of

Pakistan's ISI, embarked on liberating Indian Kashmir from the Delhi government. Given the disaffection of Kashmiri Muslims in the strategic Kashmir Valley, the foreign-trained guerrillas succeeded in energizing the insurgency. The Central government reacted by increasing its military and paramilitary forces there. They used brutal methods to suppress the violent protest. The insurgency peaked in 1997. The unsuccessful attempt in December 2001 by Kashmiri Muslim terrorists, trained by the LeT and the newly established Jaish-e Muhammad ('Army of Muhammad'), to take hostage Indian cabinet ministers nonetheless highlighted the Kashmir dispute. In the more audacious and meticulously planned attack on targets in Mumbai in November 2008, the terrorists repeatedly mentioned the suppression of the Kashmiri Muslims and the visits of Israeli generals to the Valley.

In Chapter 6, I describe how India went through different phases in its relationship with Israel before normalizing relations in 1992. Since America played a crucial role in bringing about this change, I examine Delhi's relations with Washington. Until the 1962 China War, India followed a policy of strict non-alignment with the blocs led by the US and the Soviet Union. Afterwards, Washington and Moscow backed India against China until Reagan became US president in 1981. Then, because India refused to condemn the Kremlin for its Afghanistan adventure, relations between the two leading democracies soured. Since 1992, steady announcements of India's joint projects with Israel in defence and space have fuelled popular hostility in Pakistan towards India. Another contributory factor is the semi-clandestine linkage between Delhi and Tel Aviv in countering the separatist insurgency in Kashmir. The steady reinforcement of Delhi–Washington links received a boost during the presidency of George W. Bush when the US inked a civilian nuclear deal with India in 2008 even when the latter refused to sign the nuclear Non-Proliferation Treaty.

Chapter 7 shows that Pakistan's military leaders have a vested interest in keeping the Kashmir issue alive. I sketch a brief chronicle of the sixty-two-year-old dispute. In the absence of a satisfactory resolution, Pakistani generals have succeeded in maintaining a large army whose upkeep eats into the national budget for education and public health. The Kashmir issue helps to unify politicians of different ideological hues and ethnicities. It also justifies the narrative of Pakistan's history in school textbooks which is imbued with the glorification of the armed forces and a deep hatred of India and Hindus.

This process gathered momentum under the military rule of General Zia ul Haq. At this time, Islamization began permeating all spheres of life, private and public. Chapter 8 provides the details. Zia ul Haq's death in 1988, followed by civilian rule for eleven years, did not materially reverse this process. Nor did the subsequent military dictatorship of General Musharraf. As a result, a whole generation of Pakistanis, imbued with Quranic values, has grown up. It is the one that will determine the country's future. It cannot be suppressed or wished away.

Chapter 9 outlines the lower status of Muslims in India, socially, economically, and politically. They are the victims of widespread discrimination. This has been documented on the macro scale in the Sachar Commission report of 2007. The perpetrators of the illegal demolition of the historic mosque in Ayodhya in 1992 have yet to be charged. The same is true of those who carried out the anti-Muslim pogrom in Gujarat a decade later. My portrait of Sisola in Uttar Pradesh, a Muslim settlement of five thousand, captures the residents' living conditions and how they view their status locally and nationally.

In Chapter 10, I offer the background against which the Pakistani Taliban is challenging the state's powerful military, police, and intelligence apparatus. Overall, Pakistan's government has been increasingly unable to deliver such basic public services as education, health care, and rule of law to most of its citizens. Its economy is in dire straits. Its poorly funded education system is being superseded by a thriving network of madrasas, which disgorge hundreds of thousands of graduates annually with a deep commitment to Islam and jihad but lacking knowledge in math, science, and technology. Their religious education makes them easy targets for the recruiting agents of militant organizations like the LeT and the Pakistani Taliban.

Chapter 11 outlines developments in Afghanistan under the presidency of Hamid Karzai. I describe the physical conditions as well as the way of life in Kabul, which is now home to one out of eight Afghans. I provide details of the widespread graft that permeates the civil service, police, and judiciary from top to bottom, and illustrate the deeply corrupting influence of the drugs trade. My description of that industry covers all the links in the chain – from the growing of poppies to the delivery of finished heroin – and shows where the Taliban get their cut and its size. I also detail the flagrant vote rigging in presidential and parliamentary elections.

The focus of Chapter 12 is on the policies of the Barack Obama administration. It shows the advance that the Afghan Taliban – backed by a majority of Pushtuns in Afghanistan as well as Pakistan's ISI – has made in expanding its base. So far, it has matched the escalation in the fighting engendered by the American commanders in Afghanistan against the backdrop of dwindling public support for the war in the US. There are uncanny parallels with what the US administration did in the 1960s in Vietnam. Just as in South Vietnam, so now in Afghanistan, Washington has looked on helplessly as fraudulent elections for the presidency and the parliament respectively in 2009 and 2010 wiped away any legitimacy that the Karzai administration had.

Chapter 13 sketches the best and worst future scenarios for Afghanistan, Pakistan, Kashmir, and India. It also discusses the prospect of Pakistan's atom bombs or their parts falling into the hands of extremist leaders. It offers ideas for countering Islamist extremism, including rallying Sufi institutions and leaders to confront jihadists – by force, if necessary. Driven by their fanaticism, Sunni Islamist extremists in South Asia have targeted not only Christians and pantheistic Hindus but also Shias and Sufis, thereby staging jihad on two fronts – a strategic error which ought to be exploited by their adversaries.

The concluding chapter offers the reader an overarching analysis of this complex but interrelated socio-political phenomenon, covering a vital region in turmoil, which has the potential to threaten world peace.

1

THE SUFI CONNECTION

A TEMPERATE THURSDAY evening, late February 2010, the New Delhi suburb of Nizamuddin. Along a crowded, rutted side lane, past the milling throngs of pilgrims and stallholders selling savouries and round caps of cotton – often white, sometimes patterned – who part slowly for weaving motorcycles, auto-rickshaws, and an occasional car; past the well-kept shrines of Mirza Ghalib (1797–1869), the Urdu poet laureate of the Indian subcontinent, and Amir Khusrau Dehlvi (1253–1325), the originator of northern Indian classical music; and then treading on the unevenly cobbled floor of a narrow, covered bazaar – a series of holes in the wall stacked with cheap goods – with the dark, slender shopkeepers in long white shirts, tight pajamas, and low cylindrical caps selling red flowers, rose water, and gaudily printed religious texts in Urdu, Hindi, and English; you come to a robust threshold of the monument where an attendant takes charge of your shoes.

Beyond it lies the mausoleum of Nizamuddin Auyila. A Sufi saint of the Chishti Order – derived from Chisht, the town in western Afghanistan where it was established in 930 by Abu Ishaq Shami – Nizamuddin Auyila died aged eighty-two in 1325, when north India was governed by the sultans of Afghan pedigree. A succession of these rulers erected a complex around Nizamuddin's bare grave. At its centre now stands a square chamber surrounded by verandahs, pierced by arched openings, while its roof is surmounted by a dome springing from an octagonal drum. The dome, ornamented by vertical stripes of black marble, is crowned by a crest of lotus, a floral symbol sacred to Hindus. In due course, the mausoleum acquired a mosque along with a communal washing place for ablution before prayers, and an assembly hall.

On capturing Delhi in 1526, the Kabul-based Zahiruddin Muhammad Babur (1487–1530), the founder of the Mughal Empire in the Indian subcontinent, sought blessings at this shrine. In our times the high-powered pilgrims to the mausoleum, known locally as Nizamuddin dargah, have included not only the visiting Pakistani president General Pervez Musharraf but also the Indian prime minister, Indira Gandhi, a Hindu.

The only way to have a glimpse of the redoubtable saint is to enter the carpeted room of the caretaker, Sayyid Ausuf Ali Nizami. A well-built man of forty-five in a long silk shirt, white salwar and black fez cap over his chubby, moustached face, he sits behind a low writing desk. In a corner behind him hangs a brazenly disproportionate painting, captioned in English, of a small Amir Khusrau Dehlvi staring at Nizamuddin, who wears a mountainous turban and sports a beard so luxurious that it masks his facial features.

As dusk fell during my meeting with Nizami, a wiry old man in a lungi entered the sky-blue room with a metal plate bearing a stick of burning incense. The practice reminded me of my visits to Hindu temples and Eastern Orthodox Churches in Jerusalem and Bethlehem.

On one side of Nizamuddin's domed grave is a prayer hall for women. And on the other is a communal quarter where free meals are served, funded by those whose wishes have been fulfilled, thanks to the intercession of the holy saint.

Given that Friday is the day for believers' congregational prayers in a mosque, dargahs draw their crowds on Thursday evenings. In Islam as in Judaism, the day starts with sunset, so a Christian or Hindu Thursday evening is a Muslim Friday evening. On this Thursday, the mausoleum was a hive of activity, with women moving freely among men as children ran around unaccompanied. Men's white or beige long shirts and tight pajamas, pants and shirts or salwar kameez looked drab compared to women's yellow-and-red saris with ochre-coloured borders, partly covered by russet shawls, or pink or sky-blue salwar kameez and dupatta to cover their breasts.

To enter the inner sanctum, the pilgrim has to mount the steps leading to a marble platform: male devotees only. 'Ladies Not Allowed Inside', reads a sign at the entrance to the hallowed place.

Nizamuddin's tomb lies in a grilled enclosure. On that day it was draped in green silken sheets, overlaid with red ones, all profusely spattered with red flowers, being the offerings of devotees. The red strings tied on the marble trellis around the tomb symbolize wishes of the pilgrims backed by pledges of charity if the wish is granted by God. The reason for the need for the intercession of the Sufi saint is the belief that human beings are far too sinful to approach God directly. All around the inner chamber, men were standing next to the walls, with cupped hands raised in silent prayer. They beseeched the saint for the end to an illness, success in finding a job or winning a court case, or relief from the clutches of an avaricious moneylender.[1]

The sentiment prevalent among the devotees on this warm Thursday was well captured by Ahmad Shafeek, a shopkeeper: 'If the saint intercedes for me with Allah, my plan [shared only with the saint] will be successful.' Those who had their wishes fulfilled aired the news widely and helped elevate the status of the shrine; and those who failed blamed their own fate.

A straw poll of the pilgrims showed that most of them had come to receive the holy sage's blessing. A few added that they were also drawn by the qawwali, Islamic devotional music, that was being played in the forecourt. (Qawwali is a derivative of *qawwal*, meaning someone who repeats a *qual*, an utterance of Prophet Muhammad.) As for Nizamuddin Auliya, no devotee in salwar kameez or long shirt and tight pajamas – common among the working and lower-middle classes – had any idea who he was. The one exception was Faheem

Dehlvi, the dark-eyed, moustached publisher of an Urdu magazine, *Shama* ('Flame'), clad in Western pants and a shirt with a breast pocket holding a pen.

What about Sufism? The response to this question almost invariably was: 'I know nothing about it.'

HISTORY OF SUFISM

Islam spread among societies where existing religious practices involved either idol worship or a personality cult. This was as true of Arabia of the seventh century as it was of Java of the thirteenth. As a result, those who adopted Islam missed the psychic satisfaction they had derived from worshipping idols, or objects of nature, or even some superior human being – practices strictly forbidden by the Quran. Furthermore, Allah, as portrayed in the Quran, was a severe entity who aroused more awe and reverence than love or affection among believers.

To the bulk of new converts, Islam came across as a creed concerned primarily with precise and overt observance of the Quranic edicts and the pursuit of political power. Strict obedience to Allah's commands and rigid observance of religious rituals left many believers spiritually and psychologically unfulfilled. The debates about the finer points of the Quran and Sunna (Prophet Muhammad's practices), which deeply engaged the ulema, left other, largely illiterate believers cold and bewildered.

The Muslim masses sorely needed a humane, charismatic Islamic leader whose words and actions would infuse their new faith with warmth. In the early history of Islam, the tragic figure of the idealistic, uncompromising Imam Ali (598–661) was the personality from whom many of the fresh converts drew inspiration. Later, the martyrdom of his son Imam Hussein in 681 provided spiritual sustenance to this body of believers. After that, no equivalent figure emerged to satisfy the spiritual needs of the newly converted.

Some Muslims sought solace in undertaking ascetic exercises and arduous spiritual practices, believing that such means would bring them closer to the Deity. They were inspired by the example of Prophet Muhammad (570–632) who used to withdraw into a cave and undertake nightly vigils, as well as by the practices of Christian hermits. Like the adherents of the Eastern Orthodox Church, they came to believe that Allah, or the Ultimate Reality, could be apprehended only by direct personal experience. They therefore stressed meditation and contemplation of the Deity, and regarded active involvement in worldly affairs, or pursuit of political power, as a distraction from the path of seeking Allah within. Through their practices they injected warmth, piety, and altruistic love into Islam. They came to be known as Sufis – from the term *suf* (wool), linked to the patched woolen garment that they wore as a sign of their asceticism.

Hassan al Basri (d. 728), who lived as an ascetic, was the first known Sufi personality. The next renowned Sufi saint was Abu Ishaq Shami (d. 940). Over time, two kinds of Sufis emerged: ecstatic and sober. A glaring example of ecstatic Sufism is the Qalandar Order, popular in today's Pakistan. In the sober category, the Naqshbandi Order stands out.

The ecstatic Al Hussein ibn Mansour al Hallaj (857–922) declared: 'I am the Truth' – and was executed as a heretic. Among sober Sufis, Abu Hamid Muhammad al Ghazali (1058–1111) was the most prominent. His personal experiences led him to conclude that mysticism was a meaningful way of perceiving the Ultimate Reality, even though it did not enable the believer to learn anything about it beyond what was already revealed in the Quran. In other words, he tried to fit mystical experience within the bounds of the Sharia – Islamic law, consisting of the Quran and the Sunna. His greatest contribution to Islam was his *Ihya Ulum al Din* (Arabic, 'Revival of the Religious Sciences'), a manual for everyday existence that blended institutional observance with individual virtue. Ghazali integrated the legal system with a spiritual infrastructure originating in the Prophet Muhammad's mystic consciousness. In *Ihya Ulum al Din*, he urged the faithful to be aware of God's presence while undertaking not only prayers and fasting but also such mundane actions as eating, washing and sleeping. His work became the living manual for the Sufi orders, which arose soon after his demise in 1111.

The first major Sufi brotherhood with set rules and procedures was Qadiriya. It was founded by Abdul Qadir al Gailani (1077–1166), a resident of Baghdad. In the absence of any social organization outside the extended family, Sufi orders provided the only platform for social solidarity. A brotherhood consisted of aspirants (*murids*) or mendicants (dervishes) who took an oath of allegiance to the guide, known as shaikh, pir, or *murshid*. Women were admitted as associate aspirants.[2] The shaikh headed a hierarchy within the order which was linked by a chain of inherited sanctity (Arabic, *baraka*) or kinship to the founding saint. This chain went back to the early Sufi founders, such as Hassan al Basri, and through them to the House of the Prophet or to Prophet Muhammad himself. Sufi brotherhoods went on to establish their own convents.

A typical Sufi complex consisted of a mosque, an assembly hall for the Sufis to conduct their communal prayer, *zikr* (or *thikr*; literally, 'remembrance'), cells for the Sufis to live and meditate in, and a toilet. The zikr, recited loudly or quietly or just mentally, involves control of inhalation and exhalation – the essential elements of Buddhist meditation. Generally, the zikr formulas involve the recitation of different syllables of the Islamic creed – 'There is no god but Allah, and Muhammad is the messenger of Allah' – or some of the ninety-nine names or attributes of Allah. Then comes meditation, which lets the Sufis' own thoughts rise up.

Visits to a Sufi complex afforded the novices and servants the company of Sufis. Many Sufi orders devised a framework within which rich and colourful liturgical practices were spawned as the devotional rituals of novices. Next up the hierarchy are those who learn Sufism's social ethics. Finally come the older Sufis, living in seclusion, engaged in meditation and prayers. As a collective, they are known as *ikhwan*, 'brethren'. That is why Sufi orders are also known as brotherhoods.

The turbulence in the Islamic world, caused by the devastating invasions of Central Asia and Iran by the pantheistic Ghuzz Turks and Mongols in the eleventh and twelfth centuries, weakened the Muslim Turkic sultans. The resulting collapse of the official channels for redressing citizens' grievances led them to seek the help of the Sufi orders. Their involvement in the day-to-day affairs of the common folk became so widespread that by the mid-twelfth century Sufism began competing with mainstream Islam. By then, with the long-running Sunni–Shia dispute having been settled in Sunnis' favour, much intellectual energy was channelled into Sufi philosophy, its orders being generally free of sectarian influences.

Popular activity at the shrines led to an identification between ordinary Muslims and the Sufi orders. This engendered genuine reverence for the Sufi shaikh. By and large, Sufi saints conveyed their message of love and tolerance through popular modes of communication – poetry, music, and romantic tales of love, separation, and ultimate union. An added attraction for non-Muslims was the free food provided at many of the Sufi shaikh's retreats.

The overthrow of the Sunni Abbasids in 1258 by the invading Mongols led by Hulagu Khan created a further ideological and intellectual vacuum in which Sufism thrived. Sufi orders took on board both orthodox and dissident ideologies. They became involved in political–military campaigns. For instance, in 1453 Sufi dervishes participated in the successful seizure of Constantinople by the Ottoman Turks.

Celebrations were held to commemorate the saint's death anniversary called *urs* (Arabic, 'wedding night'), the temporal demise signifying the return of his soul to the supernatural source from which it had been separated during its earthly existence. Earlier Sufi shaikhs were frequently credited with miraculous powers. It was believed that their inherited sanctity, which survived their death, lingered around their tombs and could be invoked for personal welfare. Out of this arose the practice of saint worship. Unlike Hinduism and Buddhism, Islam does not believe that the spirit is eternal and indestructible. So this concept was un-Islamic.

Within Islam, relations between the ulema and Sufi shaikhs were tense. Sufi personalities based their claims to spiritual leadership on calls by God or Prophet Muhammad in a vision or a dream, and not on strict book learning, as was the case with the ulema. The latter, committed to implementing the Sharia, demanded obedience, whereas Sufi shaikhs preached tolerance. Today, anti-Sufi sentiment remains particularly acute among those Muslims who are the adherents of Salafi, Wahhabi, or Ahl-e Hadith (derivative of *Ahl al Hadith*: Arabic, 'People of the Hadith') ideology. A derivative of *salaf al saliha* (Arabic, 'the pious ancestors'), the Salafiya movement stressed the militancy and purity of early Islam. For their religious practices, those subscribing to Ahl-e Hadidh – sayings and deeds of Prophet Muhammad – philosophy referred directly to the Hadith ignoring the myriad interpretation issued by the ulema since the death of the Prophet. Wahhabis belong to a puritanical subsect within Sunni Islam that sprang up in Arabia in the mid-eighteenth century. Osama bin Laden, the leader of Al Qaida, was a Wahhabi; so too are the rulers of Saudi Arabia.

While the adherents of these ideologies collectively form only one-fifth of the 1.57 billion-strong followers of Islam worldwide, their impact on the events in the Muslim and non-Muslim regions increased dramatically due to the jihad they conducted against the Soviet troops in Afghanistan in the 1980s. During this decade-long campaign, they scoffed at the Sufi practices, especially saint worship, of their Afghan comrades in the seven-party Islamic Alliance of Afghan Mujahedin, or Afghan Mujahedin for short. They destroyed several Sufi shrines, notable for their blue domes, in the areas controlled by the Afghan Mujahedin.

While saint worship was heretical in Islam it appealed to most new converts drawn from societies steeped in this tradition. Thus, Sufism served as a bridge to pre-Islamic creeds, helping to win converts to Islam and retain them. An outstanding case of this is the Rishi Order in Kashmir.

THE RISHI ORDER IN KASHMIR

This brotherhood was established by Nouruddin Rishi (1378–1439), whose mentor was Lalleshwari (1320–92), a female Brahmin poet, popularly known as Lalla Ji, Lalla Ded, or Lal Vaid. She rebelled, preached the oneness of God, which clashed with Hinduism's pantheism, condemned the caste system, and came under the influence of Islam. She and Nouruddin became the precursors of the blending of the ancient Vedic Hindu philosophy and Sufi practices that has moulded Kashmir's language and culture. *The Wise Sayings of Lalla* continues to influence Kashmiris. Regarded as the patron saint of the Kashmir Valley, Nouruddin is revered by both Muslims and Hindus, who carry flowers to his shrine at Chrar-e Sharif, 21 miles (34 km) west of Srinagar, the summer capital of the state of Jammu and Kashmir (henceforth Kashmir).

Nouruddin preached that the reiteration of the Islamic creed could only be completed when the believer realized the reality of self. That is, it was through self-knowledge that a devout mystic attained knowledge of God. Aware of the customs and practices of the Hindu ascetics who abounded in Kashmir – considered ideal for meditation since the Buddhist era – the young Nouruddin retired to a cave to pray for years on end. He gave up eating meat, even though it is allowed by the Sharia. Influenced by his piety and syncretism, a majority of Kashmiris, then adherents of Hinduism, converted to Islam.

Among his leading disciples was Zainuddin Shah (d. 1448) – popularly known as Zain Shah – a convert from Hinduism. After serving Nouruddin for many years, he retreated to a mountain cave at Aishmuqam. Emulating the practices of Hindu sages, he led an ascetic life and remained a celibate. He became known among Hindus as Zanak Rishi. His mausoleum near Aishmuqam attracts many devotees today. Pilgrims cross the bridge over the Lidder River to walk up the hill to the bottom of a 130-step stoney stairway. While climbing to the shrine, which is built on a spur, they rub their hands over the stair wall and then place their palms over their foreheads and chests to imbibe the saint's holiness. At the top, an arched gate of wood, inlaid with Quranic verses, opens onto a cobbled courtyard, latticed windows, and green roof.

The mausoleum's inner sanctum, the Sufi saint's grave draped in green cloth, lies inside a cave, with a sturdy pillar holding up the roof. Unlike at Nizamuddin Auyila's shrine in Delhi, women – clad in salwar kameez of bright floral prints, representing the flowers of the Kashmir Valley – are allowed to pray on one side of the marble platform while men in salwar kameez or Western dress beseech the Rishi on the other side. Before leaving the revered site, a devotee dips a finger into a hole in the rock, filled with body oil on the edge of the tomb's enclosure, and rubs it into his or her forehead in the belief that it can cure all illnesses. To avoid showing their backs to the revered sage, the pilgrims walk backward.

Over the centuries, the Sufi saint's shrine in Kashmir has become more than a spiritual site. It is now a place for festive celebrations and such secular rituals as the first cutting of the hair of a newborn baby.

During the upsurge in political Islam in Kashmir that followed the success of the Afghan Mujahedin and their allies in forcing the Soviet withdrawal from Afghanistan in 1989, some Kashmiri Muslims adopted Salafi or Wahhabi versions of Islam. They railed against the practice of saint worship common among Kashmiri Muslims, who followed the moderate Barelvi school within the Hanafi tradition of Sunni Islam. (Sayyid Ahmad Barelvi [1786–1831], the founder of the Barelvi school, co-opted Sufi practices into the Sharia orthodoxy whereas the rival Deobandi school was vehemently against Sufi Islam.) But their condemnation had little impact on the traditional ways of Kashmiris.

Referring to the Salafi father of his friend, Basharat Peer, a native of Seer Hamadan village in southern Kashmir, writes: '[H]is father and his [Salafi] group campaigned against prayers at shrines arguing that making the saint an intermediary between creator and creation was un-Islamic. The village [had] so fiercely opposed them that they had to hide in friends' houses, lest a mob set upon them.'[3]

The Salafi teacher and his followers would have been aghast to witness the musical soirée at the Nizamuddin Auyila mausoleum in Delhi and to learn that music was a source of spiritual nourishment for the Sufi shaikh and the founder of the Chishti Order, Abu Ishaq Shami.

SUFI MUSIC

Every Thursday evening there is a several-hour-long qawwali performance in the carpeted forecourt of the mausoleum of Nizamuddin Auyila. In essence, a qawwali is the Sufi zikr (remembrance of God) performed to music in public, and is regarded as part of the journey to the Divine. A qawwali begins mildly and builds up gradually to such an elevated level of energy that it induces a hypnotic state among both musicians and listeners.

During my visit in February, eight musicians – long-haired and young or middle-aged, sitting cross-legged in two rows – performed at the far end of the forecourt. To their left were several rows of women, some of them heavily made-up and expensively dressed. To their front and right sat far more men, sitting cross-legged, most in salwar kameez or long shirts and tight pajamas, but some in pants and shirts.

The ensemble had a lead singer and an accompanist, with two others playing harmoniums (which have replaced the traditional sarangi, a bowed, short-necked string instrument), and another playing the tabla. They and others repeated the key word or verse from the Quran, and aided and abetted percussion by clapping their hands – a communal ritual in which the audience participated with rising energy as the evening progressed. On this particular evening the musicians took just one holy word – 'Allahu' – and rendered its myriad variations for hours while the listeners joined in, clapping and swaying their heads, enchanted.

The Chishti Order lays great stress on the importance of poetry and music, with musical soirées an integral part of the brotherhood.

It was Amir Khusrau Dehlvi of the Chishti Order who blended Hindu devotional music, called bhajan, with the musical tradition of medieval Persia (modern Iran and Afghanistan), which had spread to Central and South Asia, and produced qawwali. 'It was Khusrau Dehlvi who extracted the essence of the Hindu bhajan and dispensed with the deities whom Hindus praised in their music,' said Faheem Dehlvi in his interview.[4]

Qawwali's popularity extends beyond northern India to the Punjab and Sindh provinces of Pakistan. One of the most popular qawwalis in the Punjabi language in Pakistan is: '*Duma dum mast qalandar/ Ali da pahla number/ Ali Shahbaz Qalandar*' (Oh Qalandar, forever intoxicated/ Ali's number one/ Ali Shahbaz Qalandar). It invokes the name of the Sufi saint Lal Shahbaz Qalandar (1177–1274), buried in the Sindhi town of Sehwan.

SUFISM IN PAKISTAN

Born into the family of a Shia dervish in the Afghan town of Marwand, Lal Shahbaz's birth name was Usman Marwandi. He joined the Sufi order of Qalandars, peripatetic Sufi dervishes, who like dreadlocked Hindu mystics – called sadhus – preferred austerity and dressed in rags.[5] Like sadhus, he remained celibate. Travelling through West Asia, he arrived at the Punjabi city of Multan and then moved south, settling down in Sehwan, an important centre of Hindu worship and learning, in 1251.

Because of his fondness for red rags and his soaring spiritual being, the Sufi shaikh became known as Lal Shahbaz (Urdu, 'Red Falcon'). His retreat in Sehwan, built on the site of an ancient Shiva temple, included a theological school, where he was the leading teacher. His mystical version of Islam attracted thousands of non-Muslims. Well versed in Hinduism and Buddhism, he was fluent in Persian, Turkish, Arabic, Sanskrit, and Sindhi. Hindus considered him the incarnation of Bhrithari, a saint-king in central India in the first century BC, who abdicated in favour of his younger brother and became a yogi.

Before the partition of the Indian subcontinent in 1947, when Hindus formed a quarter of Sindh's population, they were frequent visitors to Lal Shahbaz Qalandar's burial place. Among them was my mother, Mohini, a native of Sehwan. As a toddler, I remember being taken to the holy site by her.

A shrine was built around his tomb in 1356 and upgraded in subsequent centuries to a white marble monument embellished with flashing neon lights. It stands out due to its glazed tiles, artful mirror work, and gold-plated door, the latter donated by Muhammad Reza Shah Pahlavi (1919–80) of Iran and installed by Prime Minister Zulfikar Ali Bhutto (1928–79), who revered Lal Shahbaz as his patron saint. During his premiership, the devotional hymn about Qalandar was elevated to an informal national anthem and sung at the public rallies he addressed.

The Sufi saint's grave with its silver canopy sits inside a large square chamber with a marble floor. Copies of the Quran are stacked in a row of folding wooden stands on one side, with smouldering joss sticks and rows of small earthen oil lamps – integral parts of Hindu temples – providing light and a fragrant smell. The inscription on the tomb reads: 'I am Haideri [referring to Haider, a second name for Imam Ali, held in high esteem by Shias], Qalandar, and *mast* [intoxicated with inspiration], I am a servant of [Imam] Ali Murtaza, I am leader of all saints, because I am a follower of the lane of "Allah's Lion" [a description of Ali Murtaza].'

The three-day annual celebration of Lal Shahbaz's death anniversary is a national event, full of prayers, music, dancing, and physical and spiritual intoxication as well as self-flagellation. It draws up to half a million devotees and wandering dervishes – both Sunni and Shia – from all over Pakistan. They choke Sehwan's narrow, unpaved streets bordered by stalls selling glass bangles as well as garlands of roses, marigolds and jasmine. Drawn by the incessant beating of large drums at the shrine, they rush towards its golden entrance with gifts of garlands, embroidered shrouds, or green sheets inscribed with Quranic verses in silver and golden thread. Unsure of gaining entrance to the inner sanctum, they touch the doorpost, pray and mumble their wishes, and rub their palms over their foreheads.

The leading spiritual ritual is *dhamal*, a devotional trance dance – a frenzied and ecstatic swirling of the head and body combined with skipping from foot to foot – performed to the rhythmic beat of a huge barrel-shaped drum placed in the courtyard. Around a small band of drum-beaters and a raucous chanter – shouting: '*Sakhi Shahbaz Qalandar duma dum mast*!' (Guardian Shahbaz Qalandar, forever intoxicated [by him]) – assemble a swirling sea of men with kohl-rimmed eyes and brightly coloured garments.[6] On the other side, behind a rope barrier, stand women and children, who watch wide-eyed. Designed to help the devotee attain union with the Divine, dhamal is less constrained in rules and movement than the dance of the whirling dervishes in Konya, Turkey. Here, in a carnival atmosphere engendered by the addition of gongs, cymbals, and horns, mendicants in long robes, beads, bracelets, and coloured headbands whirl faster and faster in a hypnotic trance as the air grows hot and wet with the dancers' sweat and blends with the scent of rose petals and acrid smell of hashish, which aids a mystic along the path to enlightenment.

As the sun sets and the air cools, the number of pilgrims and devotees dancing the dhamal outside the precincts of the shrine increases. A throng of half-naked boys and young men arrive to recite a funereal dirge to Imam Hussein, the Great Martyr, relating the tragic tale of the Battle of Karbala in 681 when, heavily outnumbered, Hussein was killed and decapitated. They lift their arms in unison, and then, in military fashion, let their hands slap hard against their chests to exorcize the guilt they feel for having let down Imam Hussein in his hour of need – a variation of the practice of some Catholics who on Good Friday beat themselves until their bodies bleed in the belief that such self-inflicted punishment will cleanse their sins.

The continuing mass appeal of Lal Shahbaz Qalandar shows that the attacks on the Sufi saints by the likes of the Al Qaida and Taliban, and the orthodox, puritanical ulema of the Salafiya and

Wahhabi movements have failed to dislodge Sufism from the hearts and minds of Pakistani Muslims. As it is, the country's prime minister, Sayyid Yusuf Raza Gilani, is a Sufi pir, as is its former foreign minister, Shah Mahmoud Qureshi. As descendants of Sufi saints, they are the custodians of their spiritual legacies. Paying one's respects at the shrine of a holy Islamic personage is an integral part of the religious life of a typical Pakistani Muslim. The popularity of shrine-visiting and Sufism in Pakistan can be judged by the fact that there are 534 shrines in Punjab and seventy-eight in Sindh. Many of these contain the remains of Sufi saints.[7]

As for Pakistan's politicians, irrespective of their party affiliation, they invariably visit the stunning mausoleum of Abul Hassan Ali bin Hujwiri (990–1077), popularly known as Data Ganj Bakhsh or Data Sahib, in Lahore for his blessings. Benazir Bhutto, leader of the Pakistan People's Party, who twice served as prime minister, was a devotee of Data Ganj Bakhsh as well as Lal Shahbaz Qalandar. On his return from a seven-year exile in Saudi Arabia to Lahore, his birthplace, the first port of call of Muhammad Nawaz Sharif – leader of the Pakistan Muslim League (N) who also served as prime minister twice – was Data Ganj Bakhsh. Unlike Benazir Bhutto, an adversary of General Muhammad Zia ul Haq, Nawaz Sharif was a protégé of the Islamist military dictator.

Born in the Afghan town of Ghazni, Ali bin Hujwiri died in Lahore as a Sufi saint and scholar. He played a major role in spreading Islam in the northern region of the Indian subcontinent and is revered as the spiritual protector of Lahore. Surrounded by stalls selling food and flowers, his spacious mausoleum, with its series of arched columns and two minarets flanking a tiled dome, stands out in the crowded city. The ill-clad beggars appeal to the charitable mood in which the pilgrims approach the shrine. On festival days the lit-up mausoleum pulsates with life, with the visiting mendicants dancing to the qawwalis played by the musicians.

On the evening of Thursday, 1 July 2010, two suicide bombers blew themselves up inside the mausoleum, killing forty-four, engulfing the site in a huge cloud of smoke, and leaving the white marble floor splattered with blood, body parts, and devotees' personal belongings. This monstrous act was condemned universally, including by ultra-orthodox Sunni groups. Responding quickly to the outcry, the jihadist Tehrik-e Taliban Pakistan denied responsibility. Earlier, in March 2010, a cultural centre in Lahore, Peeru's Café, was also bombed during its annual Sufi festival.

Because of its impact on literature, particularly poetry and music, Sufism is part of South Asian culture. Shah Abdul Latif Bhitai (1689–1752), the pre-eminent poet of the Sindhi language, was a Sufi saint. He summed up the Sufi way thus:

> Master the lesson thoroughly
> that law does teach man,
> Then contemplate and meditate
> till 'truth' comes near you –
> Vision of the Ultimate Reality will be
> the reward of seekers true.

His poetry enchanted me as a pupil in my secondary school in Sindh. Almost all of my classmates were Hindu like me. And at our school a high premium was placed on reciting Bhitai's poems faultlessly. One of his more popular stanzas was:

> Sufi is not limited by religious bounds,
> He discloses not the battle he wages in his thought,
> Aids and assists those who against him fought.

Born into a household of mystics in southern Sindh, Bhitai traversed the land in the company of Hindu yogis. Later he established his retreat at a sand mound called Bhit near Hala, his birthplace. This is where he is entombed. His large mausoleum consists of a white dome, flanked by four minarets, sitting atop a steeped structure embellished with blue glazed tiles, while the front courtyard is pierced by a series of blue-tiled arches between elegant columns. It is so striking that the Pakistani government had it printed on a postage stamp in 1987.

As is the practice at all Sufi shrines in South Asia, every Thursday evening devotees assemble to pay homage to the saint. In Bhitai's case, they gather in the forecourt of his mausoleum and, sitting cross-legged, hear the musicians sing his lyrics, which remain popular to this day. The assembly is exclusively male. Yet it is not uncommon to see a group of Hindu women in bright frocks and pantaloons and muslin *hijabs* (head scarves) arrive, unannounced – from the surrounding arid desert in the middle of a musical performance, and walk slowly to the inner sanctum to pay their respects to Bhitai, with the seated Muslim men instantly shifting their weights to let them pass.

It was the presence of women at the shrine of Rahman Baba (aka Abdul Rahman Mohmand, 1653–1711), on the outskirts of Peshawar, the capital of the Pushtu-speaking North-West Frontier Province – renamed in 2010 as Khyber Pakhtunkhwa[8] – that angered TTP leaders. Rahman Baba, a turbaned mystic with a snow-white beard and kindly expression, was a renowned Sufi saint and one of the most popular poets of the Pushtu language. His mausoleum was the site where musicians assembled to recite his verses of love and tolerance. A stanza of one of his poems encapsulated his philosophy:

> Sow flowers,
> So your surroundings become a garden.
> Don't sow thorns;
> for they will prick your feet.
> We are all one body.
> Whoever tortures another, wounds himself.

TTP leaders demanded that women be banned from the shrine since their presence led to the mixing of unrelated men and women, which is prohibited in orthodox Islam. When their demand was ignored, their militants blew up the site on 5 March 2009 – to the horror of most Pakistani Muslims. As if this were not enough, the next day, the shrine of Bahadur Baba, another Sufi shaikh, in the nearby Nowshera district was hit by a rocket.

The bombings of the Sufi shrines were condemned by government officials and mainstream Islamic parties and gave rise to some street protests. But that did not lead to any steps being taken to overcome an inherent weakness of the Sufi movement. There is no single sacred day in a year to commemorate the universally accepted founder of Sufi Islam as there is in Shia Islam, Imam Ali being the founder. Shias commemorate the death of Imam Ali's son, Imam Hussein, in 681 and thereby demonstrate their unified identity in public. Each of the scores of Sufi saints has a different death anniversary which his devotees celebrate with much fanfare. In addition, the absence of a centralized, coordinating body of Sufis is a major handicap in mobilizing followers. In normal times the decentralized structure of the Sufi network is an asset and contributes to the movement's popularity. But the present situation in Pakistan is far from normal.

To the despair of many enlightened Pakistanis, the attacks on leading Sufi holy places have failed to goad moderate Islamic scholars and leaders of the mainstream political parties to forge a common front to counter jihadist violence. That required, inter alia, explaining to the tens of millions of followers of Sufism at public rallies and through the media the dangers of being cowed by the terrorism of the jihadist minority. An educational drive needed to be coupled with such practical steps as providing armed guards at Sufi shrines.

Like other destructive acts of jihadists, the demolition or damaging of Sufi shrines had started in Afghanistan during the Soviet military involvement in that country.

SUFISM IN AFGHANISTAN

When the Afghan Taliban ruled most of Afghanistan from 1996 to 2001, they strongly disapproved of Sufism and Sufi shrines and banned women from visiting them.

Among such places was the Mosque of Shah-e Do Shamsher (Dari, 'King of Two Swords') sandwiched between a narrow street with an incessant flow of traffic and the Kabul River in the Old City of the Afghan capital. It is believed to be the site of an ancient Hindu temple of great renown. In a battle in 871, the invading Muslim Arab army defeated the Hindu ruler of the Shahi dynasty and captured Kabul. According to legend, the commander of the Muslim force continued to fight with a sword in each hand even after he had been decapitated. It is to his memory that the Mosque of the King of Two Swords was raised.

The mosque is an elegant stone building with an arched dome and two minarets. The many steps leading to it are occupied by beggars, cobblers, and vendors, some of them hawking SIM cards for mobile phones. The Sufi ceremony of zikr is conducted here after the dawn prayer on Wednesdays. It is an overwhelmingly male affair, with a few women in burqas huddling in a corner. Unlike at the Nizamuddin Auyila mausoleum in Delhi, where a single word describing God – 'Allahu' – often constitutes the zikr, here the ceremony consists of recitations from the Quran alternating with singing. This continues for a few hours until the devotees lose themselves in a trance – a state achieved through the dhamal dancing at Qalandar's shrine in Sehwan.

As a bastion of Buddhism, and then reformed Hinduism, Afghanistan had started turning to Islam on a large scale only from the ninth century. In the process it fostered several Sufi brotherhoods. The Chishti Order originated in western Afghanistan. Abul Hassan Ali bin Hujwiri and Qalandar were respectively natives of the Afghan towns of Ghazni and Marwand. At the same time, embracing Islam did not lead the Afghan tribes to discard entirely their pre-Islamic laws and values, which differed from the Sharia.

Thus Islam in Afghanistan emerged as a mixture of orthodoxy and Sufism. In cities and towns there were properly trained ulema. But in most of the 38,000 villages, where 85 per cent of Afghans lived, the locally appointed mullahs were often only semi-trained, having been educated by an *alim* (religious–legal scholar; plural ulema) at a local madrasa.

There were very few Islamic seminaries of repute in Afghanistan. For proper training in Sunni Islam, an aspiring alim had to go either to Al Azhar University in Cairo or the Dar al Ulum in Deoband, 60 miles (100 km) north of Delhi. Established in 1866, the Dar al Ulum specialized in the Hanafi legal system. While opposed to the cult of saints, the Hanafi school was tolerant of such orthodox Sufi orders as Naqshbandi. For the Shia, advanced theological education was gained in Mashhad in eastern Iran or in Najaf in Iraq. A typical village mullah in Afghanistan was an integral part of the rural elite by marriage or birth, often himself being a substantial landlord. Besides performing religious rites, he imparted elementary religious and other education to village children, and was also a folk healer.

A lot changed during the anti-Soviet jihad in the 1980s. The Afghan jihadists were in thrall to the Muslims from Saudi Arabia, the Land of the Prophet, and after an initial reluctance often abandoned their traditional Sufi practices for the Wahhabi or Salafi version of Islam.

But once the Soviets withdrew from Afghanistan in 1989, the pressure on Afghans to switch to orthodox, puritanical Islam eased. Even the attendance at the shrine of Timur Shah Durrani, who ruled Afghanistan from 1772 to 1793, returned to the levels of peaceful times. Timur Shah Durrani was not himself overly religious, but because his grave was capped by a blue dome – associated with Sufi saints – many Afghans came to revere him as a Sufi shaikh.

His mausoleum stands across the narrow street from the Mosque of the King of Two Swords on a high platform. After leaving my shoes at the threshold, I entered a narrow carpeted antechamber and finally the inner sanctum, a small rectangular enclosure. The walls were painted green and decorated with calligraphic verses from the Quran at the top. Lower down were flowery patterns and more prayers to God. A green light shone on the tomb which was enclosed in a ribbed glass case, open at the top to let devotees drop their presents of banknotes and other valuables over the grave. As elsewhere, the tomb was draped in green chadors. Prayer books lay next to the glass enclosure. Several pilgrims, mainly women, both veiled and unveiled, stood with cupped hands raised in prayer and supplication.

In stark contrast to the cacophony of the traffic, bleating of the sheep for sale at the nearby market, pollution, and dust outside the crypt, it was incredibly peaceful inside.

Peace and orderliness are not terms usually associated with the reign of Timur Shah Durrani, a prim-looking man with a finely trimmed beard and neatly sewn, tight-fitting turban. Though an ethnic Pushtun, he could not pacify the disaffected non-Durrani Pushtun tribes around Kandahar, so he moved the capital from Kandahar to Kabul in 1776. This enabled him to exercise greater control over the major non-Pushtun ethnic groups – Tajiks, Uzbeks, and Hazaras – inhabiting the northern, western, and central regions.

Whereas most of the land inhabited by ethnic Tajiks and Uzbeks fell under the control of the Russian tsar in the mid-nineteenth century, a large majority of Pushtuns found themselves ruled by British monarchs as part of their Indian Empire. When that imperial possession split into the independent states of India and Pakistan in 1947, Pakistan inherited two-thirds of the ethnic Pushtun population. That demographic fact has led to the entwining of the chronicles of Pakistan and Afghanistan. In a way, this could be viewed as a revival of the linkage that had been made by Zahiruddin Muhammad Babur, who, as the ruler of the Domain of Kabul from 1504 to 1525, had captured the northern region of the Indian subcontinent and laid the foundation of the Mughal Empire there.

2

AFGHANISTAN AND PAKISTAN

THE BEST VANTAGE point from which to view the western and southern sectors of Kabul, a city of hills, is the historic Babur Garden, popularly known as Bagh-e Babur, in the Chehlstun neighbourhood. Walled and terraced, it is home to the enclosed tomb of Emperor Zahiruddin Muhammad Babur. A man of middle size, stout, fleshy-faced with a scanty beard, Babur had been the ruler of the Domain of Kabul – containing modern eastern and southern Afghanistan – for twenty-one years before establishing the Mughal dynasty in northern India in 1526.

To approach his tomb, the visitor has to mount a terraced hill. During the Afghan civil war of 1992–96, when the contending parties used hilltops to fire mortars and artillery shells, the Babur Garden was reduced to a near-ruin. Since the overthrow of the Taliban in late 2001, however, it has been restored to its former glory. Its museum contains many large paintings of Babur planning and guiding the construction of well-laid gardens, his first such venture being in 1504 in Istalif. References to gardens and garden planning appear frequently in the diary he maintained from the age of eleven. The resulting *Babur Nama* is the earliest example of autobiographical writing by a ruler in world literature.

'There are many different tribes in the Kabul country,' he wrote in his journal in 1504.

> 'In its valleys and plains are [nomadic] Turks and Mughals and Arabs. In its town and many villages are Sarts [i.e., Persians]. Out in the districts and also in villages are the Pashay, Paraji, Tajik, Birki and Afghan tribes. In the western mountains are the Hazara and Nikudari tribes . . . To the south are the places of the Afghan tribes . . . Eleven or twelve languages are spoken in Kabul: Arabic, Persian, Turkish, Mughali, Hindi, Afghani, Pashay, Paraji, Gibri, Birki and Laghmani. It is not known if there is another domain with so many different tribes and such a diversity of languages.'[1]

Exactly five centuries later, Article 4 of the newly promulgated constitution read: 'The nation of Afghanistan is comprised of Puhstun, Tajik, Hazara, Uzbek, Turkmen, Baluch, Pashay, Nurstaini, Aymaq, Arab, Kyrgyz, Qizilbash, Gujar, Brahui, and other ethnic groups.'

The phrase 'so many different tribes' sums up the contemporary composition of Afghanistan, a landlocked country surrounded by Iran, Turkmenistan, Uzbekistan, Tajikistan, China, and Pakistan. Babur was conscious of ethnic identities, blaming, for example, the Mughals and the Uzbeks (speakers of the Uzbek language) for the devastation they had caused to Alma Ata, now in Kazakhstan.[2] Ethnic distinctions and rivalries continue. Indeed, they have been a primary factor in shaping the history of Afghanistan, as demarcated by Britain and tsarist Russia to become a buffer state between Russia, British India, and Iran. Other elements that have impacted on Afghanistan's chronicle are its inhabitants' adherence to Islam, their fiercely independent spirit stemming chiefly from living in isolated valleys and a weak central government. Clinging to medieval Islam, most Afghans resisted modernization well into the last quarter of the twentieth century.

AFGHANISTAN, A BUFFER STATE

A brief outline of the country's past shows how history keeps repeating itself, with a succession of episodes impacting on an ever-widening area in the region and beyond. Instances of long memories and never-ending feuds abound.

Following Babur's establishment of the Mughal Empire in the Indian subcontinent, it competed with the Safavid Empire of Persia for control of Afghanistan. In 1729, Nadir Shah Afshar, having expelled the Afghan tribes from Persia, went on to subdue Kandahar in southern Afghanistan. He was assassinated in 1747 by Abdali Afghans centred around Kandahar – a bastion of Pushtuns, which today is the foremost stronghold of the Taliban. They chose Ahmad Shah Abdali as their leader.

A bearded, fierce-looking man of medium height but regal bearing, Abdali (r. 1747–72) assumed the title of *Durr-e Durran* (Persian, 'Pearl of the Age'), which became bowdlerized into Durrani. He was a member of the Popalzai tribal confederation, a rival to the Barakzai to which his chief rival, Jamal Khan, belonged.

The rivalry between Popalzai and Barakzai continued until the civil war of 1818–26, when Dost Muhammad Khan Barakzai emerged as the victor. But this was not the end. Astonishingly, the see-sawing of fortunes has continued well into the twenty-first century. In 2002, Gul Agha Barakzai in Kandahar province elbowed out the members of the Popalzai tribal confederation from positions of power. In return, a few years later Ahmed Wali Karzai, a younger brother of President Hamid Karzai, a Popalzai leader, blatantly favoured the members of his own tribe at the expense of those of the Barakzai and other tribal confederations. Tribal loyalty remains a crucial socio-political factor in Afghanistan. Based on common descent, tribal identity stands above extended family and clan, and maintains its cohesiveness through blood solidarity.

Abdali seized parts of the decadent Safavid and Mughal Empires, and added bits of the Tajik territory in the north. But his son, Timur Shah Durrani, who ruled until 1793, proved unequal to the task of maintaining control over this far-flung territory. And his successors did no better. Dost Barakzai, the victor in the civil war, founded the Barakzai dynasty in 1826. A similar fate would befall Afghanistan after the 1992–96 civil war with the Taliban replacing the fractious regime of the Islamic Alliance of Afghan Mujahedin, (Afghan Mujahedin for short) and opening a new chapter in Afghan history.

Later, rivalry between imperial Britain and tsarist Russia led to wars between Afghanistan and British India during 1839–42 and 1878–80. In the First Anglo-Afghan War, the British encountered the most intense combat in the south-western region of Helmand. And, in a repeat of history, so have the United States-led forces of NATO in recent years. The British occupation of eastern Afghanistan, which followed the earlier conflict, was resisted by the Afghans in the same way that the Pushtuns are resisting foreign occupation now.

In the 1878–80 armed conflict, the deciding battle was fought at Maiwand in Kandahar province. On 27 July 1880, over 2,500 British troops commanded by General Gerald Burrows, operating out of Kandahar, faced the Afghan soldiers of Ayub Khan. Though the Afghans suffered heavy casualties, the end result was a rout of the British, with 950 dead. Since then, July has become the day of *jashan* (Dari, 'celebration') for Afghans. They celebrate it with the same ardour as Americans do 4 July. A central Kabul square is named after Maiwand, as is an important thoroughfare.

It is noteworthy that the arrival of the British troops in the neighbouring province of Helmand in 2006 was viewed by the locals as an attempt by Britain to avenge the defeat suffered in 1880, which had led to its expulsion from Afghanistan. London's only consolation then was that it managed to keep control of Afghanistan's foreign relations.

These wars proved double-edged. They engendered a strong sense of identity among Afghans while isolating their country politically and diplomatically. They also led traditional tribal and Islamic leaders to view all reform and modernization as Western innovations which had to be resisted. In an Afghan man's personal appearance, an index of his modernization is to be found in the way he treats his facial hair. A chest-long beard is an unmistakable sign of Islamic traditionalism whereas a clean-shaven face signifies irreligious innovation – with the intermediate states of facial hair, from a well-trimmed moustache to a clipped goatee beard, indicating an uneasy compromise between the two extremes.

ABDUR RAHMAN, THE STRONGMAN

It was against this background that Abdur Rahman assumed power in 1880. A short, portly man with a large head, penetrating eyes, and a beehive beard, he radiated resolution. It was during his reign that the generations-old rivalry between Britain and tsarist Russia, both intent on grabbing Central Asia, was finally resolved in 1895 by the creation of a wedge between tsarist Central Asia and the London-ruled Indian subcontinent by adding a narrow strip to north-eastern Afghanistan.

At home, starting with a firm control of the Kabul area, Abdur Rahman staged several campaigns to subdue the Pushtun tribes in the south and south-east. He then imposed control over the Uzbek and Turkmen (speakers of the Turkmen language) tribes in the north. When Persian-speaking Shia Hazaras, squeezed into the inhospitable Hazarajat mountains, rebelled in 1888, he rallied Pushtun, Uzbek, and Turkmen tribes under the banner of Sunni Islam, and subdued them in 1891. Nine decades later, history would repeat itself. The leaders of different ethnic groups and sectarian loyalties would coalesce to form the Afghan Mujahedin to fight the troops of the Soviet Union – wedded to scientific atheism – and their communist Afghan allies.

What distinguished Hazaras from all other ethnic groups were their Mongoloid features, with scanty facial hair for men, and the absence of the veil or burqa for women – the burqa being a shroud from head to toe with a lattice window at the eye level to see and breathe through. But, like the rest of the ethnic communities, they believed in the Quranic injunction of 'life for life, an eye for an eye'.[3] More than four decades later, a young Hazara would avenge Abdur Rahman's massacre of Hazaras by assassinating King Muhammad Nadir Shah: another example of the long memories and endless feuding that make Afghanistan exceptional.

To resolve the simmering rivalries between London and St Petersburg, the increasingly assertive Abdur Rahman signed an agreement with

British India to delineate the 1,610-mile (2,576 km)-long Afghan-Indian border in 1893. Since the British signatory was Henry Mortimer Durand, foreign secretary of British India, the demarcation became known as the Durand Line. By acquiring all the passes of the Suleiman Mountains, the British now controlled the strategic heights of this mountain range. In return, Afghanistan gained Kafiristan (Persian, 'Land of the Infidel'; later renamed Nuristan) north of the Khyber Pass.

But since the Durand Line split Waziristan, and thus the Waziri and Mehsud tribes, it sowed the seeds of instability in the border region. Realizing that Afghanistan had been treated unfairly, Abdur Rahman's successors would challenge the Durand Line – unsuccessfully. And, as the successor state to the western part of British India, independent Pakistan would inherit the problem, which remains unresolved to this day.

After the Durand Line came the Anglo-Russian Boundary Commission two years later. This separated British India from tsarist Central Asia by demarcating a 100-mile (160 km)-long and 10- to 40-mile (16 to 64 km)-wide corridor called Wakhan (*wa* meaning 'and', plus khan 'lord'), giving Afghanistan a 15-mile (24 km)-long common border with China. This enhanced Abdur Rahman's stature at home.

The following year he converted the inhabitants of Kafiristan, dotted with Christian missions, to Sunni Islam. Thus Afghanistan became 99 per cent Muslim: 85 to 90 per cent Hanafi Sunni, the rest – mostly ethnic Hazaras – Shia of the Jaafari school.

In embracing Islam, the Afghan tribes had not totally discarded their pre-Islamic laws and values. The Pushtun tribes, for instance, followed *Pushtunwali*, or *Nang-e Pushtun*, the 'Way of Pushtun'. Pushtunwali is both an ideology and a corpus of common law with its own institutions and sanctions. Some of the major features of Pushtunwali are: to avenge blood; to defend to the last any property entrusted to the Pushtun; to be hospitable and provide for the safety of the persons and property of guests; to pardon an offence (other than murder) on the intercession of a woman of the offender's lineage, a *sayyid* (a male descendants of Prophet Muhammad), or a mullah; to punish all adulterers with death; to refrain from killing a man who has entered a mosque or the shrine of a holy man; to fight to the death for a person who has taken refuge with a Pushtun, no matter what his lineage. Therein lies the explanation as to why Osama bin Laden and his followers felt safe for many years within the folds of the Pushtun tribes in the tribal belt of Pakistan.

According to Pushtunwali, a ruler derives his power from the tribal *jirga* (Pushtu, 'assembly'). Without disputing this traditional view, Abdur Rahman asserted that only 'divine guidance' could ensure that the people would choose a true and legitimate ruler. So he saw himself championing the cause of Islam and liberating the Afghan soil from the domination of infidel and foreign forces, thus becoming both the emir, commander-ruler, and imam, religious leader. Towards the end of the twentieth century, Mullah Muhammad Omar, the leader of the Taliban, would cast himself in a similar mould.

After adopting the honorific of *Zia al Millet wa Din* (Arabic, 'Light of Nation and Faith') in 1896, Abdur Rahman published a treatise on jihad. In it he argued that the demands of jihad overrode those of family, clan or tribe. A century later, Osama bin Laden would echo similar thoughts, citing the same Quranic verses as Abdur Rahman. The pertinent verses are: 2:109, 2:190, 2:194; 5:13; 6:106; 9:5; 15:94; 16:125; 22:39–40; 29:46; 42:15; and 50:39. Among these, 9:5 in the chapter titled 'Repentance' – known as the 'Verse of the Sword' – is particularly important. It reads:

> Then, when sacred months are over
> slay the idolaters wherever you find them
> and take them, and confine them, and lie in wait
> for them at every place of ambush. But if they
> repent and perform the prayer, and pay the alms, then let them go their way;
> God is all-forgiving, all-compassionate.

Many argue that this verse relates to the ending of a truce with unbelievers that Prophet Muhammad had agreed, and that it should not be read in isolation. In any case, whereas Abdur Rahman's writing had a limited audience, that of bin Laden ended up impacting globally.

As a concession to the Pushtun tradition, Abdur Rahman appointed a *Loya Jirga* (Pushtu, 'Grand Assembly') consisting of aristocrats from the royal family, village notables, landlords, and ulema, but treated it as an advisory body only. He secured the loyalty of mullahs by turning them into state employees.

SOCIAL CONSERVATISM TRUMPS TOP-DOWN REFORM

Such a concentration of power was bound to generate countervailing demands. These arose during the reign of his successor, Habibullah Khan (r. 1901–19). But when liberal secularists called for a constitutional monarchy, he executed some of their leaders and jailed many more.

A powerfully built man with a neatly trimmed moustache and beard, sensuous mouth, and intense gaze, Habibullah Khan favoured the idea of the Triple Alliance of the Ottoman Empire, Iran, and Afghanistan as a barrier against Russia's expansion into the Middle East. But during World War I he failed to side with Ottoman Turkey against Britain, which controlled Afghanistan's external affairs. This led to his assassination during a hunting trip to Jalalabad in 1919, and the accession of his son Amanullah to the throne.

Breaking with tradition, Amanullah Khan shaved, retaining only a clipped moustache, to reveal a chubby face and sad expression. He was fond of wearing well-cut Western suits. Violating the Durand Line, he attacked British India along its Afghan border in 1919 to recover the Pushtun land he felt Britain had annexed wrongly, and gain control of Afghanistan's external relations. His military offensive failed, and the Durand Line stayed. But he secured the right to conduct Afghanistan's foreign affairs according to the Treaty of

Rawalpindi signed on 19 August 1919. With that, 19 August became the nation's Independence Day.

Amanullah offered the nation a written constitution in 1923. In it he declared Islam to be the official religion of Afghanistan. But when he then opened government schools to train future administrators and professionals, banned child marriage, and transferred the ulema's power to pass judgement in family affairs to the state, he faced stiff opposition from the religious establishment. The subsequent disaffection escalated into a tribal rebellion in the eastern province of Khost in 1924. Amanullah crushed it. But his hiring of German and Russian pilots for the campaign incensed traditionalists, who resented the intrusion of infidels into the internal affairs of Muslims. A similar sentiment would emerge in Afghanistan during the 1980s and again in the first decade of the twenty-first century when Afghans witnessed the presence of tens of thousands of 'infidel' troops, first from the Soviet Union and then the West, in their midst.

Feeling confident that his rule was secure, Amanullah undertook a nine-month-long tour (from October 1927 to July 1928) of India, the Middle East, and Europe. At receptions in Europe his wife, Soraya Tarzi, a doe-eyed beauty, appeared unveiled in a Western dress. Photographs of her 'un-Islamic' appearances circulated in Kabul and beyond. This sowed the seeds of Amanullah's deposition – an event that has been embedded in the minds of Afghan elites ever since. The prime example is provided today by no less than Afghanistan's president. Notwithstanding the fact that his wife, Zeenat Quraishi, is a trained obstetrician, Hamid Karzai has never allowed her to accompany him in his public appearances. 'My husband doesn't like it,' she is reported to have said. 'I cannot go out without his permission.'[4]

The special Loya Jirga that Amanullah Khan convened on his return to Kabul went along with his proposal for a representative government based on votes for all, and military conscription for men. But it opposed modern education for girls and age limits for marriage. When he tried to implement legal and financial reform, the ulema argued that the Sharia, having been derived from the Word of Allah – that is, the Quran – needed no elaboration.

Disregarding the opposition, Amanullah issued decrees outlawing polygamy among civil servants and permitting women to discard the veil. In October 1928, a hundred women, led by Queen Soraya, appeared unveiled at an official function in Kabul. His decree that all Afghan men residing in or visiting Kabul must wear Western dress complete with a European hat was to be enforced from March 1929 onward. Clerics regarded the insistence on the European hat blasphemous. Since it interfered with the Islamic way of praying, which requires the believer to touch the ground with his forehead. The ulema's attitude was summed up by a telling quip: 'When reforms come in, Islam goes out.'

When Fazl Muhammad Mujaddidi, a leading cleric, began collecting signatures against the reforms, Amanullah ordered his arrest. Violent rioting broke out in Kabul. In November 1928, the Pushtun tribes in the east revolted. Amanullah dispatched royal forces to quell the uprising, only to see them defect to the other side. Disaffection within the ranks stemmed from his secular reformist actions as much as from his employment of European military advisers. Amanullah's major weakness was that he lacked a properly trained, disciplined, and loyal army. (In today's Afghanistan nothing illustrates President Karzai's impotence more starkly than the feeble domestic military.) It would not be until 1953 that the situation would change when, led by Muhammad Daoud Khan (1973–78), the army would become the primary power centre.

To quell the rebellions in Laghman and Jalalabad, Amanullah dispatched most of his soldiers to the north and east, leaving Kabul vulnerable. This enabled Habibullah Kalakani, a former Tajik soldier who had rallied support in the Shomali plain in the north – a stronghold of Islamists – to besiege the capital in early January 1929.

Kalakani had the support of the ulema, who in turn had popular opinion on their side. Pressured by him, Amanullah agreed to close girls' schools, withdraw permission for women to discard the veil, and cancel the Western dress order for men. Furthermore, he promised to abide by the Sharia as interpreted by orthodox ulema, and rule in consultation with a council of fifty religious and tribal leaders. But he failed to hold on to the throne. On 14 January 1929, aided by the defectors from the royal troops, Kalakani captured Kabul and pledged to establish the rule of the Sharia. Amanullah fled south.

Kalakani handed over the task of running state courts and schools to the ulema, but failed to consolidate his own authority in the face of growing political anarchy and a severe economic crisis. Also, his Tajik ethnicity proved to be a liability. Resenting the rise of a Tajik as the ruler, Pushtuns resorted to calling him *Bacha-e Saqqao* (Pushtu, 'Son of a Water-Carrier') since his gardener father had once served as a water-carrier in the army. In contrast, the minority Tajiks regarded him as a legitimate king.[5] His rule proved short-lived. In October, he was overthrown and executed by Muhammad Nadir Khan – a third cousin of Amanullah – with the aid of Fazl Umar Mujaddidi in Kabul and Sher Agha Naguib, a religious leader in Jalalabad.

Obligated to religious luminaries for his position, King Nadir Shah – a bespectacled man with a walrus moustache, heavily clipped beard and an expression of permanent surprise – established the Jamaat-e Ulema (Persian, 'Group of the Ulema') and ordered that all civil and criminal laws should be based entirely on the Sharia. The Jamaat ruled that women were not entitled to vote. The king consulted the ulema on all important social, educational and political issues.

The constitution that he promulgated in 1931 described the Islam of the Hanafi school as the official religion and required that the king be a Hanafi Muslim. Other articles institutionalized the powers he had conferred on the ulema and Sharia courts, and confirmed the right of the ulema to educate Muslim children. The constitution specified a consultative council based on votes for all males. The first parliament assembled in 1931, but Nadir Shah did not live to see the second parliament three years later. He was assassinated in November 1933 by Abdul Khaliq, a teenage Hazara, to avenge the massacre of Hazaras by Abdur Rahman.[6]

MUHAMMAD ZAHIR SHAH, THE LAST KING

What runs through this chronicle of independent Afghanistan is the attachment that its people and rulers have shown towards Islam, a socio-political fact that has not altered to this day.

Amanullah's nineteen-year-old son, Muhammad Zahir Shah (r. 1933–73), now succeeded Nadir Shah. Power was initially exercised in his name by his three uncles, with one of them becoming prime minister for thirteen years, followed by another, Shah Mahmoud. A portly man of medium height, sporting the de rigueur moustache and wearing horn-rimmed glasses, Zahir Shah looked more like a professor than a king.

The events of World War II, in which Afghanistan remained neutral, made the palace realize the pressing need for rapid reform and modernization in order to preserve the country's independence and tackle rising socio-economic problems.

In the post-war era, Prime Minister Shah Mahmoud allowed comparative freedom to voters in consultative council elections, the results of which had been predetermined by the palace in the past. Of the 120 members of the Seventh Council (1949–52), forty or so were considered liberal. The emerging nationalist reformers challenged the religious traditionalists. The resulting conflict weakened both camps and, unwittingly, prepared the ground for the palace to enter the political fray with its own active player: the military.

In September 1953, Muhammad Daoud Khan, commander of the Central Forces in Kabul and a cousin of the king, staged a coup against Mahmoud with a nod from the palace, and himself became prime minister. A bald man with a barely noticeable moustache below his bulbous nose, Daoud Khan had a commanding presence. To modernize the military, he relied heavily on the Soviet Union, which had signed a Treaty of Neutrality and Non-Aggression with Afghanistan in 1925. Kabul's subsequent neutrality in World War II had left its cordial relations with Moscow intact.

The emergence of an independent Pakistan in August 1947 revived an old dispute. A Loya Jirga in Kabul refused to accept the Durand Line, arguing that since Pakistan was a new state the border had yet to be defined. Afghanistan laid claim to Pakistan's autonomous Federally Administered Tribal Agencies (FATA). In 1949, when the Pushtun tribes on the Pakistani side declared the formation of Pashtunistan, Kabul recognized it. This led to border clashes. Pakistan cut off fuel supplies. This cooled Kabul's ardour for Pashtunistan.

As Pakistan drifted towards Washington, formalizing its military links with America with a Mutual Security Pact in 1954, Kabul tilted towards Moscow. To avoid upsetting Pakistan, the United States refused to sell arms to Afghanistan. Daoud Khan started attaching Soviet advisers to the Afghan military academies and sending Afghan military officers, pilots, and tank drivers for training in the Soviet Central Asian republics. At the same time he successfully solicited funds and experts from the US and other Western nations for development projects. Between 1956 and 1968, Washington's aid to Kabul amounted to $250 million and Moscow's to $550 million.[7] To underscore its importance to America's policy of containing the Soviet Union, Pakistan highlighted the Kremlin's inroads into Afghanistan.

The autocratic Daoud Khan centralized state authority through the military and implemented socio-economic reform through decrees rather than democratic debate and consensus. After turning the Jamaat-e Ulema into a toothless organization, he began replacing orthodox ulema in the justice and education ministries with fresh graduates from Kabul University's Faculty of Theology.

In 1957, Kabul Radio introduced female singers and announcers. At the Independence Day celebrations on 19 August 1959, the wives and daughters of senior government officials appeared unveiled on the review stand. The ulema protested, Daoud Khan replied that if they could find indisputable injunction for the burqa in the Sharia, he would impose it. They could not.

The appropriate verse in the Quran states:

> And say to the believing women, that they cast down their eyes and guard their private parts . . . and let them cast their veils over their bosoms, and not reveal their adornment save to their husbands, or their fathers, or their husbands' fathers, or their sons, or their sisters' sons, or their women . . . or their children who have not yet attained knowledge of women's private parts.[8]

This could not be interpreted to mean that women should don the burqa.

Unbowed, the ulema started calling Daoud Khan an anti-Islamic leader, who was letting atheistic communists and Western Christians undermine the Islamic way of life. They were particularly agitated about the presence of Soviet advisers, apprehensive that they steer Afghans away from Islam as they had done the Muslim inhabitants of the Soviet Central Asia.

In response, the government arrested fifty clerical leaders for treason and heresy. The severity of the charges shook them. By promising to cease their defiance, the clerics won their release. Thus ended the protest against the unveiling of women. This was in marked contrast to what had happened under Amanullah in 1929. The key difference between then and now was that Daoud Khan commanded a loyal, well-disciplined, modern army.

In the final analysis, though, the military was loyal to the monarch. This reassured Zahir Shah, who had been overshadowed first by his uncles and then by Daoud Khan. He now decided to assert his authority. In October 1964, he promulgated a liberal constitution, which supposedly ushered in constitutional monarchy. In fact, it would prove to be the last chapter in the long history of monarchy in Afghanistan.

The new constitution restated that Islam was the sacred religion of Afghanistan and that the king had to be a Hanafi Muslim. Article 64 ruled out any law 'repugnant to the basic principles of the sacred religion of Islam'. There was provision for a fully elected *Wolesi Jirga* (Pushtu, 'People's Assembly') and a partly elected *Meshrano Jirga* (Pushtu, 'Nobles' Assembly'). The first Wolesi Jirga consisted of three main groups: clerics led by the Mujaddidi family, nationalist centrists who looked to the king to pursue progressive policies, and Marxists. A press law passed by the parliament led to the founding of many new publications.

By now, the traditional ulema had been supplanted in important administrative and religious posts by the graduates of Kabul University's Faculty of Theology, which was headed by Professor Ghulam Muhammad Niyazi. His ideology was moulded by the writings of Sayyid Muhammad Qutb (1906–66), an Egyptian Islamic fundamentalist. Soon the Persian translations of the works of Qutb became available – as did those of the Pakistani ideologue Abul Ala Maududi (1903–79), written in Urdu. They presented Islam as a modern ideology, not an obscurantist faith associated with traditional ulema and village mullahs.

Across the border, by the early 1960s the security services of Pakistan, ruled by General Muhammad Ayub Khan, were encouraging local Islamist groups to find ideological allies in Afghanistan. They would play a key role in the formation of the Jamiat-e Islami (Persian, 'Islamic Society') in Afghanistan with the active aid of Pakistan's Jamaat-e Islami (Urdu, 'Islamic Group').[9]

In Afghanistan, secondary education had expanded so rapidly by then that only a minority of applicants to Kabul University gained entry. Those who did became critical of the teaching facilities and complained bitterly. Soon their protest became politicized, turning the university into a hotbed of Marxists and Islamists. The latter opposed the autocracy and corruption of the palace as much as they did the rising tide of Marxism. Dissent also grew in secondary schools and colleges, with students and unemployed graduates blaming the royal court for their problems and backing radical solutions.

The palace decided to focus on the Marxists, since leftist students had taken to allying with industrial workers and their periodic strikes. This spurred the ulema and their followers to harass moderate Marxists and target their magazine *Parcham* (Persian, 'Banner'). Then Islamists began attacking the monarchical regime's steady drift towards secularization and the growing presence of female students in secondary schools and universities. They argued that the introduction of non-traditional education in schools and colleges was eroding morality among the young and undermining traditional social values. What reinforced their viewpoint was the presence of thousands of young Western men and women and their licentious behaviour in Kabul, which was on the hippie trail from Europe to India.[10]

In 1972, the Kabul-based press reported a famine in the provinces due to a two-year drought which claimed nearly 100,000 lives. Islamists demonstrated against foodgrain hoarders and demanded limits on personal wealth, holding the palace responsible for the prevailing sense of drift, decadence, and turmoil in society.

On 17 July 1973, while King Zahir Shah was in Italy for medical treatment, Daoud Khan seized power in the name of returning Afghanistan to Islamic values. He abolished the monarchy and set up a republic, with himself as executive president.

MONARCHY OVERTURNED, VILLAGE LIFE UNPERTURBED

In republics, the stress is on the public. In the case of Afghanistan, this meant villagers since they accounted for seven out of eight Afghans. Historically, as inhabitants of small, isolated valleys, their lives had remained unaffected by events in the capital. No wonder the latest coup meant little to them.

One striking feature of Afghan villages is the way that, except the open-door mosque and the assorted goods in shops and makeshift tea stalls, everything is shielded from view by high, blank walls enclosing mud-brick or stone-walled houses, flat-roofed, with a courtyard containing a small vegetable plot and cattle. Here, an extended family consisting of two or more generations lives under the tutelage of the oldest man, the patriarch. By virtue of his age, he is a member of the village shura, presided by the head man, or *malik*, an appointee of the shura. The patriarch's word at home goes uncontested. A typical peasant house is furnished with cheap rugs, a folding wooden stand for a Quran (even when nobody is literate enough to read it), and family photos. The headman's residence stands out because it has a large, carpeted room for meetings, and walls decorated with prayer rugs and clocks.

When two adult Afghans meet, they greet each other in an elaborate fashion. '*Salaam Aleikum* (Arabic, "Peace be upon you"),' says one. '*Waleikum Salaam*,' responds the other. Then: 'How are you?' 'Is your soul healthy?' 'Is your household doing well?' 'May your family prosper.' 'Is your body strong?' 'May you be not tired?' All with appropriate responses. And finally: 'May you live long!'

For their livelihood, most households are dependent on agriculture, which, except for cash crops like opium poppies, has not progressed beyond subsistence farming. Just as social values of family honour, pride, and respect for other family members have remained constant for centuries, so too have farming techniques. A wooden plough pulled by an ox, driven by a peasant, is the primary tool. A split tree trunk, drawn by bullocks, is used to level the soil after it has been ploughed and seeded. Along with a plough and split trunk, spades, shovels and sickles complete the armoury of tools used for agriculture.

Under King Zahir Shah, with only one-eighth of the country's 158 million acres being arable, there was much pressure on agricultural land, whose ownership was highly skewed. Of the twenty million acres of arable land, only two-thirds was irrigated by rainfall or molten snow supplied to fields through irrigation channels. The top 2.2 per cent of the landowners, holding 30 acres or more each, owned 42 per cent of the nation's agricultural land.

Afghanistan's soil and weather are conducive to the growing of fruit and vegetables, which are therefore an integral part of the rural cuisine, centred around a flat bread called nan. Afghans' respect for flat bread is legendary. It must not be thrown on the ground and, if it falls by chance, it must be retrieved and placed on a high ledge for birds to eat. It must not be placed upside down as that would bring bad luck, so goes a widely held belief. Before dinner, the main meal of the day, is served, the traditional carpet or rug in the living room is covered with a colourful cloth for the whole family, except the main cook, to sit down on and wash their hands with water from a copper basin carried by a youngster before starting to eat.

Like the nation's cuisine, Afghan clothing has not changed. Indeed, it was from Afghanistan that the dress of baggy trousers (salwar), and long shirt (kameez) for men, was exported to the adjoining regions of Pakistan and northern India. In the case of Pushtuns, along with the salwar kameez goes a skull cap over which a turban is wound. Tajiks wear a round hat called a *pakol*, or a fez cap of karakul wool, as well as a coat called a *chapan*. To stress that he is president of both Pushtuns and Tajiks, President Karzai complements his salwar kameez with a karakul hat and a chapan. Irrespective of their ethnicity, Afghan women wear a long loose shirt or high-bodice dress with a swirling skirt over their baggy trousers, and a wide shawl drawn over their heads.

There is no role for women as workers outside the home except at harvest time when they pitch in (mostly in non-Pushtun areas). In their spare time some women engage in embroidery or carpet weaving. Colourful carpets provide a welcome contrast to the gray and sandy colours of the mountains and arid zones of Afghanistan. The carpets' rhythmic compositions reflect the flora and fauna of the area – bushes, flowers, vegetation, irrigated fields, and animals – while excluding representations of humans, which are forbidden by the Quran.

Outside the home, the villager is subject to three centres of power: political-administrative, economic, and religious. Political-administrative authority rests with the shura and the malik; economic power with the *khan* (large landowner) and the *mirab* (controller of water supplies) where irrigation facilities exist. Then there is the mullah, who acts as prayer leader, judge, and religious teacher. The mosque is the most important public place, serving both religious and social purposes, with the mullah accorded much respect and showered with donations in cash and kind. In the final analysis, though, it is the economic power that counts most. And given the highly uneven ownership of land, this rests with the large landlords. Tenant farmers pay such high rents in kind to the landlord that they are left with little or no cash for seed and so need to borrow from a moneylender – who is often a large landlord.

President Daoud Khan was aware of the inequalities of this centuries-old socio-economic set-up. So, to win popularity in the countryside, he announced land ceilings of 20 and 40 hectares respectively for irrigated and unirrigated land. But, in the absence of an effective administrative apparatus, his decree remained largely unimplemented.

URBAN POLITICS

To enlarge his support in urban areas, Daoud Khan secured the cooperation of the leftist Parchami (Persian; derivative of *Parcham*, 'Banner') group. This had split with its radical rival, the Khalqi (derivative of *Khalq*, 'Masses') faction, in 1966 – a year after the formal founding of the (Marxist) People's Democratic Party of Afghanistan (PDPA). Parchamis, led by Babrak Karmal, regarded Daoud's republic as an improvement on the deposed monarchy, whereas Khalqis, headed by Nur Muhammad Taraki, did not.

With Parchami Marxists co-opted, and the nationalist centrists crippled by the execution of their leader, Muhammad Hashim Maiwandwal, the only party hindering Daoud Khan's path to total power was that of the Islamists. The president therefore ratcheted up the pressure on it. In June 1974, his government arrested two hundred Islamists in Kabul as they gathered to discuss a blueprint for an Islamic republic where the Sharia would be applied in its totality.

The three top Islamist leaders pursued different tactics, Gulbuddin Hikmatyar fled to the Pakistani city of Peshawar. Niyazi and Burhanuddin Rabbani, a Tajik, made one more attempt to persuade Daoud Khan to break with the Parchamis. They failed. Rabbani then escaped to Peshawar, where he became a 'guest' of the Pakistani

Foreign Office's Afghan Cell, established after the anti-royalist coup in Kabul. Professor Niyazi ended up in jail.

Henceforth, Afghani and Pakistani politics became inextricably linked.

AFGHANISTAN AND PAKISTAN ENTWINED

In Peshawar, Rabbani proposed a long-term strategy of infiltrating the Afghan military and seizing power through a coup in Kabul. But Hikmatyar was for an immediate armed uprising, a plan that suited Pakistan's prime minister, Zulfikar Ali Bhutto. The Pakistani leader wanted to strike at Daoud Khan, whose army was training over twelve thousand Pushtun and Baluch volunteers in Afghanistan to harass the Pakistani army.[11] So he provided arms and training to Hikmatyar's followers.

July 1975 was chosen as the date for a national uprising in Afghanistan. But very little happened except in the north-east, which gave Daoud Khan a pretext to tighten his grip on power. He banned all privately owned publications, formed the National Revolutionary Party, and secularized commercial and civil laws, thus blatantly contradicting his claim of seizing power to revive Islam.

In 1976, the split between Rabbani and Hikmatyar became final. Lacking a classical religious education, Hikmatyar failed to win the support of the ulema. He formed the Hizb-e Islami (Persian, 'Islamic Party'), which believed inter alia, that the piety of a believer should be judged primarily on his political actions and only secondarily on his religious behaviour and expertise. Rabbani, a graduate of the famed Al Azhar University in Cairo and a literary critic, was respected by orthodox ulema as well as leaders of the Sufi orders. Wearing the de rigueur barely trimmed beard and a silk turban, he had an avuncular look. The ideology of his party, the Jamiat-e Islami of Afghanistan, was based on the writings of Maududi, who had founded the Jamaat-e Islami first in India and then in the newly created Pakistan.

What made Maududi attractive to pious young Afghans – caught in the web of Western cultural influences and Soviet military and commercial links – was his argument that Islam stood apart from both Western and socialist ways of life. He offered a democratic interpretation of the government under Prophet Muhammad and the First Four (Rightly Guided) Caliphs – Abu Bakr, Omar, Uthman and Ali. He prescribed that the leader of today's Islamic state – heading the legislative, judicial, and executive organs – shall be elected by the faithful, as should the shura. Its members should judge whether or not the leader was following Islamic policies. Maududi had no objection to candidates contesting elections on party tickets, but insisted that after getting elected they should owe allegiance only to the Islamic state, and vote on issues according to their individual judgement. But in social and family affairs he stuck to tradition. He favoured sexual segregation and the veil for women. Arguing that since the objective of the Sharia is to curb indecency and obscenity, 'nothing can be more unreasonable than to close all the minor ways to indecency but to fling the main gate [i.e., the face] wide open.'[12]

While sharing his ideology, Rabbani disagreed with Maududi's strategy of establishing a party of those who were imbued with an Islamic ideology. Intent on making the Jamiat-e Islami a mass organization, he adapted it to the existing tribal institutions.

In a different context, Daoud Khan showed much flexibility. After crushing the rebellion in the north-east, he set aside the Pushtunistan issue. He purged the Parchamis from his administration. Then he started persecuting them as well as the Khalqis. Thus pressured, the two Marxist groups merged in July 1977 to re-establish the PDPA, with Taraki as its leader. A moustached man with sharp features and a far-away gaze, he had a doctorate in economics from Harvard University and a master's degree from Columbia University.

Meanwhile, politics were in turmoil in Pakistan. Following a disputed general election in March, which returned Bhutto's Pakistan People's Party (PPP) with a large majority and led to widespread and bloody protest, General Muhammad Zia ul Haq, chief of the army staff, overthrew Bhutto on 5 July and imposed martial law.

A man of medium height, Zia ul Haq was notable for his fixed stare, well-trimmed moustache, and thinning hair parted in the middle. His obsequious manner made him appear humble and unthreatening, which had encouraged Bhutto to promote him to the highest military rank in October 1976. Born in 1924 in Jullundur (now in Indian Punjab and spelled Jalandhar), Zia ul Haq grew up in the household of his intensely religious father, Akbar Ali, a maulvi. He recalled later that, whereas his fellow officers in the army spent their leisure time drinking, gambling, dancing, and listening to music, he prayed. Now, on assuming supreme power as chief martial law administrator, he called himself 'a soldier of Allah,' and added, 'I consider the introduction of [an] Islamic system as an essential prerequisite for the country.'[13]

Zia ul Haq started monopolizing power once the Supreme Court had invoked the 'doctrine of necessity' in October to legitimize the coup. The court also allowed him to suspend the 1973 constitution. He then promulgated a provisional constitution which authorized him to amend the 1973 document at will. Thus armed with absolute authority, he set out to Islamize the Pakistani state and society. He did so partly because he believed in it, partly because he wanted to engender a popularity for his military regime which it had lacked, and partly to use Islam to forge national unity and transcend acute ethnic differences. As a result, Islamabad's ties with the Afghan Islamist leaders strengthened.

By contrast, in Afghanistan, following the confession of the assassin of the planning minister, Ahmad Ali Khurram, in December 1977, the government arrested fifty-four Islamists, accusing them of plotting to assassinate Daoud Khan and his cabinet.

With the coffers of the hydrocarbon-rich Iran overflowing with cash following the quadrupling of oil prices in 1973–74, the pro-Washington Muhammad Reza Shah decided to influence policies in Kabul. Given the parlous economic state of Afghanistan, where foreign grants and loans accounted for more than 60 per cent of the 1977–78 budget, Daoud Khan welcomed the shah's offer of aid. In return, encouraged by Iran's intelligence agency, his security agents resorted to murdering leading Marxist figures. PDPA leaders did not know how to react to this bloody tactic. However, the assassination of Mir Akbar Khyber, a respected trade union leader and a former editor of *Parcham*, on 17 April 1978, altered the situation abruptly. The PDPA mounted a massive anti-government demonstration in Kabul.

Daoud Khan ordered the jailing of all PDPA leaders. But Taraki escaped arrest. Advised by Hafizullah Amin, a fellow Khalqi leader, he activated the Marxist network in the military that had been built up over the past two decades. The result was a coup by leftist military officers on 27 April 1978 *against the advice of the Kremlin* – an event officially called the Saur (April) Revolution. Daoud Khan was killed in the fighting at the presidential palace, and his official titles of president and prime minister both went to Taraki. Karmal and Amin became deputy prime ministers.

The coup was the culmination of a dual process: the Afghan Marxists' recruitment of military commanders; and the Afghan government's policy, initiated by Daoud Khan in the mid-1950s, of sending its officers to the Soviet Union for further training. Since the Afghan officers were trained at military academies in the Central Asian republics, they felt racially and culturally at home. At the same time they could not avoid comparing the economic, social and educational progress of the predominantly Muslim inhabitants of Soviet Central Asia with the backwardness of Afghans. As a result, they became pro-Soviet and ripe for recruitment into the military network of the Afghan Marxists.

RIPPLES OF THE MARXIST COUP

The Marxist coup in Afghanistan alarmed the US administration of President Jimmy Carter, which now hastened to resume the development aid to Islamabad that it had earlier stopped.[14] In Pakistan, eager to counter the PPP's influence, Zia ul Haq had Bhutto arrested and charged with the murder of Ahmad Reza Kasuri, a former PPP leader, three years earlier – a step that would culminate in the hanging of Bhutto. At the same time Zia ul Haq pursued Bhutto's project of building an atom bomb with greater vigour. To present himself as a civilian leader, he gave up the title of chief martial law administrator in September 1978 and instead called himself president. It was in this capacity that he received his Afghan counterpart, Taraki, in Islamabad. He advised his guest to be fearful of Allah and recognize obligations towards Him. Taraki replied, 'God is *aadil* (just). We don't have to fear God. To serve the people is to serve God.'[15]

While Pakistan under Zia ul Haq grew closer to Washington, the Afghan government reinforced its ties with Moscow by signing a Treaty of Friendship and Cooperation in December 1978. This specified close military, political, and economic links between the two neighbours. Article 4 stated that the signatories 'shall consult with each other and take, by agreement, appropriate measures to ensure the security, independence and territorial integrity of the two countries.'[16] This provision would later be invoked by the Afghan government to invite Soviet troops.

Once in power, the PDPA's unity proved fragile. Whereas the Khalqis led by Taraki and Amin wanted rapid changes, the moderate Parchami wing of Karmal advocated a gradualist approach.

In retrospect, this split within the ruling political party would turn out to be the beginning of a civil war – active at certain times, passive at others – which ravaged the country and led to the arrival of tens of thousands of foreign troops from near and far and whose last chapter has yet to be written.

Conscious of national history and popular culture, PDPA leaders reiterated their faith in Islam. All their public utterances began with the invocation '*Bismillah al Rahman al Rahim*' (Arabic, 'In the name of Allah, the Merciful, the Compassionate'). So too did all official statements, and radio and television broadcasts. PDPA luminaries assured the public that the aim of the socio-economic reform package they offered was in line with Islam. Nonetheless, there was opposition to it from various quarters, all of whom linked their stance to Islam.

The PDPA's overambitious reforms included eradicating illiteracy, cancelling all pre-1973 mortgages and loans, decreeing equal rights for women, outlawing child marriage, and implementing land redistribution. Though long overdue, this was once again revolution from the top. In its haste, the new regime failed to create a groundswell of grass-roots support for its measures. It thus failed to resolve the key problem. Lacking political consciousness, the potential beneficiaries of the leftist reform – the vast majority of rural Afghans – accepted their abject poverty and exploitation as part of the divine order. PDPA leaders should have encouraged its urban cadres to return to their home villages and organize local committees to demand social and economic changes at the expense of the traditional religious elite – with the central government stepping in later to meet popular demands. That process would have taken upward of five years to implement but the subsequent reforms would have held.

The immediate 'jihad' against illiteracy – 75 per cent among males and 95 per cent among females – went well in urban areas, but not in rural. The opposition in villages to the mixing of the sexes, particularly in adult education, was very strong. Due to the paucity of female instructors, the task of teaching adult women fell on male teachers from towns, considered by the rural folk to be hotbeds of licentiousness. The expulsion of mullahs from the educational system swelled the ranks of anti-government clerics and led to periodic murders of secular teachers by Islamists. The literacy campaign in villages peaked in early 1979 and then declined sharply.

A decree issued in July 1978 abolished all pre-1973 mortgages and debts, and drastically reduced the excessive interest rates (often 100 per cent a year) on later loans, thus potentially benefitting four out of five peasant families. But many mullahs, often related to landlord-moneylenders, ruled that cancellation of debts amounted to stealing and was un-Islamic. In reply, the pro-regime minority among clerics cited the Quranic verse against *riba* (usury).[17] The authorities started dismissing or arresting rebellious mullahs.

By September, the hardline Khalqis had emerged as the dominant force within the PDPA – with the moderate Karmal being dispatched as ambassador to Czechoslovakia. The pace of radical reform and secularization quickened. By challenging all the traditional centres of power at once, the Khalqis dug their own political grave.

In October, the government replaced the national tricolour – black, red and green – with a red flag, flagrantly similar to those of the Soviet Central Asian republics. The disappearance of the Islamic green from the flag made many conclude that the state had taken the path of atheism. This view was reinforced when the invocation of Allah at the beginning of broadcasts or official statements was dropped by the state-run media and political leaders. These steps undid all that had been achieved by months of propaganda insisting that the new regime wanted to uphold Islam. They also virtually neutralized the impact of the decree on marriage and family relations. Women were granted equal rights, forced marriage was banned, and minimum ages for marriage were prescribed: sixteen for females and eighteen for males. The decree fixed the bridal price at $7, the going rate then being $1,000. This provision was meant to help poor prospective bridegrooms, but was extremely hard to enforce in villages.

In November came the overdue land reform. Forty per cent of the peasants, being landless, were hired for about 100 days a year. Another 40 per cent possessed only 1.5–6 acres each. One-tenth of the remaining 20 per cent possessed more than 40 per cent of the total arable land. The decree divided land into three categories, and fixed ceilings of 30 acres for perennially irrigated land and 300 acres for dry land. To implement the law, the government set up land committees composed mainly of urban-based PDPA members. From January 1979 onward, these committees – backed by radicalized, well-paid policemen – began visiting villages to give title deeds to the landless. Trying to break the centuries-old power structure in rural Afghanistan was a bold, but very risky, venture.

Predictably, rich landlords protested while their religious allies, local mullahs, issued verdicts that taking somebody's land was tantamount to robbery, and that those receiving such property would be transgressing the Sharia. This, and the fear of violent reprisals from the landlords after the departure of the land committees and the urban-based police, discouraged many landless villagers from accepting the title deeds. By March 1979, the government claimed to have distributed 512,000 acres to 104,000 families.[18]

The aggregate effect of these decrees was to polarize society, with opposition to the reforms becoming more vociferous and gaining more supporters. Such Islamic leaders as Muhammad Ibrahim Mujaddidi condemned the measures as un-Islamic and preached against the government. After some hesitation, in January 1979 the authorities sealed his offices and arrested all adult male members of his family. They executed some religious figures, but did not make this public. However, word of mouth spread. Many Islamic and Sufi leaders fled to join the Peshawar-based Islamist groups.

Resistance against the Marxist regime hardened during the winter of 1978–79, with the seasonally inaccessible Nuristan falling into the hands of the (Islamist) Nuristan Front. In the Hazarajat highlands, the Revolutionary Council of the Islamic Union of Afghanistan took charge.

By then Pakistan had moved in the opposite direction to that being followed by the Afghan government. Official letters began with the 'Bismillah . . .'. Flogging of criminals became widespread. Content on state-run radio and TV changed radically. On 1 Muharram 1399 (2 December 1978), the government announced that Islamic punishments of theft (cutting off of hands), drinking (seventy-four lashes) and adultery (death by stoning) would be enforced from Prophet Muhammad's birthday the following year.

Pakistan's lurch towards Islamization did not bother the Carter administration. Indeed, traumatized by the Islamic revolution in Iran which toppled the pro-American shah in February 1979, it further tightened its links with Zia ul Haq's regime.

The Iranian drama impacted on Afghanistan as well. In March, some of the several dozen Afghan Islamists, returning to Herat from Iran, established contact with pro-Islamic officers in the local garrison. Others mobilized the faithful in the surrounding villages on the issue of male teachers educating women. On 16 March, a Friday (the weekly congregational prayer day), after murdering male educators, the rebellious villagers converged on Herat. They were joined by disaffected townsmen and defectors from the local garrison led by Captain Ismail Khan. He disobeyed the central government's orders to fire on the protestors. The insurgents attacked PDPA cadres and military officers as well as their Soviet military advisers and their families, killing 350 Soviet citizens. They took over Herat.

Unnerved, Taraki appealed to the Kremlin for military support. A few days later, when the rebels saw a column of armoured cars approaching from the direction of Kandahar waving a green flag and a copy of the Quran, they welcomed it as a boost to their uprising. But once the newcomers had entered Herat and received air cover, they attacked the rebels and recaptured the city, thanks to the three hundred tanks that now arrived from the neighbouring Soviet Turkmenistan. (This was the only occasion when the Kremlin responded positively to Taraki's twenty earlier requests for military assistance, the difference this time being the killing of Soviet citizens by the insurgents.) The five-day insurrection caused some five thousand deaths, including several hundred loyalist troops and PDPA functionaries.[19] Ismail Khan and his partisans fled to Iran. Kabul blamed Islamic Tehran for the insurgency.

To meet the rising danger of counter-revolution, a government of 'national deliverance' was formed on 1 April 1979, with Amin as the prime minister. Like Taraki, he had a master's degree from Columbia University. A tight-lipped, clean-shaven, well-coiffured man with swaggering self-confidence, he was staunchly nationalist and an unbending hardliner. He began purging the government of the Parchamis, much to the chagrin of Taraki, who had moderated his stance in office.

A power struggle thus ensued at a time when, having recovered from the shock of the shah's downfall, the Carter administration had devised a new policy for the region. The loss of Washington's listening posts in Iran led the US president to approach Zia ul Haq. He obliged with alacrity. Assisted by Pakistan's Inter-Services Intelligence (ISI) directorate, the Central Intelligence Agency (CIA) upgraded the ISI's electronic interception facilities and began receiving the data.

The US administration decided to impede the consolidation of the pro-Moscow regime in hitherto (nominally) neutral Afghanistan. On 3 July 1979, Carter signed a Presidential Finding authorizing covert assistance to the anti-Marxist Afghan insurgents. He did so nearly six months *before* the arrival of Soviet troops in Afghanistan.[20] The CIA began channelling money secretly to the Afghan rebels. This was later confirmed by General Fazle Haq, governor of Khyber Pakhtunkhwa from 1978 to 1985, in an interview with Christina Lamb, a British journalist and author.[21]

Washington's growing dependence on him emboldened Zia ul Haq to curtail the democratic rights of Pakistanis. After banning 'political activity' in March 1978, he outlawed 'all political parties' and then postponed the promised general election in November 1979. Zia ul Haq's primary aim was to weaken and then eliminate the PPP as a political force. Therefore, he let Islamist parties such as the Jamaat-e Islami function. Indeed, he went on to appoint its members to the judiciary, civil service, and educational institutions, and encouraged its activists to join the jihad in Afghanistan.

In Kabul, Premier Amin took over the defence ministry – and counter-insurgency operations. In mid-September 1979, there was a shoot-out at the presidential palace between his guards and Taraki's – a prelude to further violence, which ended with the official announcement on 6 October that Taraki had died after a 'serious illness'. In reality, he had been suffocated with a pillow by assassins working for Amin.

STRONGMAN AMIN FORCES MOSCOW'S HAND

As president, Amin began talking of following a 'more balanced' foreign policy which would take into account the interests of both Pakistan and America. This led Soviet leader Leonid Brezhnev to re-appraise the Afghan leader. Brezhnev believed that Amin's expected policy shift was a ruse to pave the way for the US to avenge the shah's downfall by intervening in Afghanistan. The reports of KGB (*Komitet Gosudarstevenoy Bezopasnosti*, or Committee for State Security) operatives in Kabul that Amin had had secret meetings with an agent of the CIA fuelled the Kremlin's suspicions. Zia ul Haq would later reveal that Amin often appealed to him 'frantically' for help.[22]

The Kremlin urged Amin to allay public hostility towards the regime. To retain Moscow's indispensable economic and military aid, he freed several thousand political prisoners, reintroduced the invocation of Allah in official statements and broadcasts, and ordered repairs of mosques at state expense. He promised 'profound respect for and widescale support to Islam'.[23]

Proclaiming an amnesty to a quarter of a million refugees, he invited them to return. This was a futile gesture. Anti-government sentiment was running high among the refugees in Pakistan where the Hizb-e Islami was active. It had also started assassinating PDPA leaders in Kabul.

Amin called on the Soviets to help him fight the rebels in the Paktia province bordering Pakistan. The joint Afghan-Soviet campaign was successful. Marshal Ivan Pavlovsky, commander of the Soviet ground forces, toured Afghanistan to prepare overall plans for countering insurgency. This was the start of a process that would culminate in the arrival of tens of thousands of Soviet troops. From late October 1979 onward, Soviet Central Asian contingents – ethnically indistinguishable from Afghans – began taking over guard duties from Afghan soldiers to allow the latter to fight the rebels while elite *Spetznaz* (Russian, 'Special Purpose') troops guarded Soviet positions in Kabul.

At the meeting of the Politburo of the Communist Party of the Soviet Union on 10 December, four of the attending members (out of twelve) – Brezhnev, KGB chief Yuri Andropov, Foreign Minister Andrei Gromyko and Defence Minister Dmitry Ustinov – decided to dispatch a large number of troops to Afghanistan. Marshal Nikolai Ogarkov, the chief of the Soviet defence staff, and his deputy, Marshal Sergey Akhromeyev, were skeptical. During their meeting with Ustinov, they referred to the nineteenth-century experiences of the British and tsarist armies there, and urged caution. Ustinov told them to 'shut up and obey orders', according to the Politburo minutes released in 2009. Dissatisfied, Ogarkov met Brezhnev, warning him that large-scale military intervention 'could mire us in unfamiliar, difficult conditions and would align the entire Islamic East against us'. Brezhnev's trademark bushy eyebrows bristled with impatience. 'Focus on military matters; leave the policy making to us and to the party,' he bellowed.[24]

What Brezhnev and Ustinov failed to tell Ogarkov was that the Politburo had only a limited aim to stabilize the situation in Afghanistan and pull out after about six months, according to the released archives. 'We thought it would be over quickly,' said Lt General Ruslan Aushev, who served in Afghanistan for almost five years in the 1980s. 'The opposite happened. The civil war intensified.'[25]

In mid-December 1979, two Soviet battalions arrived at Bagram air base, 32 miles (50 km) north of Kabul, which came increasingly under the Kremlin's control. Next, more Soviet troops landed at Bagram on 22 December, raising their total to 8,000. Finally, more soldiers poured in on the night of 25–26 December overland from Uzbekistan at Termez, bolstering the aggregate Soviet militia strength to 50,000 soldiers compared to an Afghan force of 80,000 troops. The elite Spetznaz troops, dressed in Afghan uniforms, seized military installations in Kabul, attacked the presidential palace, killed Amin, and took over the state broadcasting station. Karmal, who had been in exile in Moscow for a year, returned to lead the new regime.

To legitimize the Soviet military intervention, in his broadcast on Kabul Radio on 27 December, President Karmal requested 'political, moral, and economic assistance including military aid' from the Soviet Union in accordance with the December 1978 treaty.

Washington had little time for such sophistry. 'The Soviet invasion of Afghanistan is the greatest threat to peace since the Second World War,' President Carter reportedly said. 'It is a sharp escalation in the aggressive history of the Soviet Union.'[26]

It brought about a dramatic reversal in America's policy towards Pakistan's nuclear ambitions. In his classified memo to Carter, titled 'Reflections on Soviet Intervention in Afghanistan', national security adviser Zbigniew Brzezinski wrote: 'It will require a review of our policy toward Pakistan, more guarantees to it, more arms aid, and, alas, a decision that our security policy toward Pakistan cannot be dictated by our non-proliferation policy.' He added: 'It is essential that Afghanistan's resistance continues.'[27]

Thus the two superpowers faced each other directly in Afghanistan, with the United States using Pakistan as its proxy, and the Soviet Embassy in Kabul emerging as the most important place of power in Afghanistan.

3

THE AFGHAN TRAP

DAR UL AMAN, the name of a four-mile (6 km)-long avenue in Kabul, beginning at the Kabul River flowing through the city, is symbolic. It means an abode of safety – neutral territory that lies between Dar al Islam (Arabic, 'House of Acceptance or Peace') and Dar al Harb (Arabic, 'House of War'). Such indeed was the official position of Afghanistan in international affairs for many decades. It remained neutral in World Wars I and II, and also during the first thirty-odd years of the Cold War.

The avenue acquired its name from its westward destination, Dar ul Aman, or the House of (King) Amanullah – a sprawling three-storey palace on a hill constructed in 1923. Amanullah also had a short railway track built, and purchased an engine and coaches so that he could journey to the centre of the capital and, equally importantly, familiarize his subjects with a modern mode of travel. His plan failed. Islamic and tribal leaders considered railways a Western innovation which had to be shunned.

The king also had a success of sorts. He linked the palace with Kabul by a wide avenue lined with tall, white-stemmed poplars. In front of these majestic trees ran streams between grass margins, and behind them shady footpaths. Those streams would later turn into open, deep channels to carry sewage while all the poplars would disappear.

Open or partly covered channels carrying pitch black sewage are an abiding feature of today's Kabul. The stink from these drains permeates the air of the more recent upscale neighourhoods as much as it mixes with the fragrance of fresh mint, coriander, garlic and cardamom in the centuries-old vegetable market in the old city.

Today, a drive along the avenue from downtown Kabul rewards newcomers with a view of the elegant two-storeyed Kabul Museum, rebuilt from the smashed shell it was reduced to during the 1992–96 civil war. What remains to be renovated as yet is the palace, shattered during the savage strife, and presently guarded by NATO troops. Past these historic buildings appear high concrete walls behind which stand multistorey concrete buildings with small windows – an architecture that makes no concession to the local style. This is the Russian Embassy.

The present complex is a reincarnation of the former diplomatic mission of the Soviet Union, which became a centre of exceptional activity after 1980. Following its ransacking during the subsequent civil strife, it was turned into a refuge for thousands of internally displaced Afghans for almost a decade. Russia, the successor to the Soviet Union, started in situ renovations in 2003. Four years later, like the proverbial Phoenix, the embassy emerged with spacious, carpeted rooms ornamented with freshly quarried marble and shining chandeliers. However, it needed to stand out in a way no other Russian mission abroad did. Such was the decision of the Kremlin. As a result, the vast compound of the reborn embassy contains a simple, yet dignified war memorial to the 13,500 Soviet troops who perished in Afghanistan in the 1980s.

Since the dissolution of the Soviet Union in 1991, there has been much soul-searching among former Russian decision makers regarding the role played by the Kremlin in Afghanistan, with the balance of opinion conceding the mistakes made by the Soviet leadership. By contrast, the chief policy maker in the Carter administration, Zbigniew Brzezinski, has remained obstinately unrepentant about his role. As for the Afghan Marxist leaders, Nur Muhammad Taraki and

Hafizullah Amin were killed in 1979, followed by Muhammad Najibullah in 1992. By then Babrak Karmal was a minor figure in poor health, leading an obscure existence in Hairatan next to Termez in Uzbekistan. He remained loyal to the Kremlin until he died of cancer in 1996 in Moscow.

KABUL SOFTENS, WASHINGTON HARDENS

On assuming power in Kabul after Christmas 1979, Babrak Karmal ordered the release of all political prisoners, and proclaimed the abolition of 'all anti-democratic, anti-human regulations, and all arrests, arbitrary persecutions, house searches and inquisitions', respect for 'the sacred principles of Islam', protection for family life, and the observance of 'legal and lawful private ownership'.[1] Relegating the use of the red flag to the People's Democratic Party of Afghanistan (PDPA), he restored the national tricolour. His attempt to undo the damage done by Amin's excesses had the Kremlin's staunch backing.

On the other hand, Moscow's flagrant military intervention led thousands of nationalist-minded professional men to leave their urban homes to join the resistance in the countryside or enroll with the anti-Marxist parties, religious and secular, based in Pakistan and Iran. There were six Afghan (Sunni) Islamic parties in Pakistan. The chief incentive for them to maintain their individual identity was Islamabad's decision to channel charity to Afghan refugees through them rather than through its own bureaucracy. Refugees were required to register with one of the six parties, all but one of which were based in Peshawar, to get free rations.

Three of the parties were hardline Islamist: the Hizb-e Islami (led by Gulbuddin Hikmatyar), the Jamiat-e Islami (headed by Rabbani) and the breakaway Hizb-e Islami Khalis (led by Maulavi Muhammad Yunus Khalis, an unsmiling, heavily bearded cleric). The rest were traditional Islamic parties, ready to restore King Zahir Shah as the constitutional monarch under certain conditions. They drew their support from village mullahs, tribal chiefs, landlords, and Sufi shaikhs.

The National Islamic Front of Afghanistan (NIFA) was under Sayyid Ahmad Gailani, the only Islamic leader with a patchy beard; and the National Liberation Front of Afghanistan (NLFA) led by the spectacled, white-turbaned Sibghatullah Mujaddidi, sporting a wispy salt-and-pepper beard. Then there was the Islamic Revolutionary Movement (IRM), the only group based in Quetta, Baluchistan, headed by Maulavi Muhammad Nabi Muhammadi with a hooked nose and a beehive black beard fringed by white next to his cheeks.

Besides the religious groups there were also nationalist, secular factions such as Musavat, led by Bahauddin Majrooh, an academic; and Afghan Millat of Abdul Haq Ahadi. They were ignored by Zia ul Haq. Indeed, later, Pakistan's Inter-Services Intelligence (ISI) directorate and its cohorts in the Hizb-e Islami harassed and even killed their leaders.

At the Carter White House, an intense debate raged between hardliners and moderates. The hawkish Brzezinski prevailed over the dovish Secretary of State Cyrus Vance. A lawyer by training, who preferred negotiation to conflict, Vance advocated a measured response to Moscow. Had he won the debate, the US would have pressed the three traditionalist Afghan Islamic groups to ally with the nationalist, secular factions to forge an anti-Marxist, anti-Moscow coalition, and marginalized the radical Islamist parties. By so doing, Washington would have aborted a process that culminated twenty-one years later in 9/11 directed by the Afghanistan-based Osama bin Laden. As it was, Vance was so marginalized by President Carter that he was not even informed of the clandestine plan – devised by Brzezinski and implemented, unsuccessfully, in April 1980, to rescue the American diplomats taken hostage in Tehran – that he resigned in protest.

Meanwhile, reflecting Brzezinski's hawkish stance, Carter declared in his State of the Union address to the US Congress on 24 January 1980: 'An attempt by any outside force to gain control of the Persian Gulf region will be regarded as an assault on the vital interests of the United States. It will be repelled by use of any means necessary, including military force.'[2] Brzezinski argued that since the Pakistani province of Baluchistan abutted Iran, the whole of Pakistan should be considered part of the Persian Gulf region.

Eighteen years later, when the Taliban ruled most of Afghanistan, Brzezinski was interviewed by a journalist from the Paris-based *Le Nouvel Observateur*. 'And neither do you regret having supported the Islamic fundamentalism, having given arms and advice to future terrorists?,' asked the interviewer. Brzezinski replied, 'Regret what?' and added, 'That secret operation [Cyclone] was an excellent idea. It had the effect of drawing the Russians into the Afghan trap and you want me to regret it? What is most important to the history of the world? The Taliban or the collapse of the Soviets? Some stirred-up Muslims or the liberation of Central Europe and the end of the Cold War?'[3] His argument was deeply flawed. The collapse of the Soviet bloc and then of the Soviet Union resulted from the chronic economic stagnation and mismanagement from the mid-1970s onwards, made worse by excessive expenditure on armaments, which the sclerotic leadership of the ailing Leonid Brezhnev, surrounded by fawning aides, could not overcome. The malaise proved incurable by the time Mikhail Gorbachev became the supreme leader in March 1985. The orderly withdrawal of Soviet troops from Afghanistan, agreed in principle in May 1986, played a very minor role, at most, in the collapse of the Soviet Union.

Afghanistan would soon turn into the hottest front in the Cold War between Moscow and Washington that had started in 1946. CIA-supplied weapons would be used to kill Soviet troops in Afghanistan, an intervention so provocative that the Carter administration decided to work through a proxy – Pakistan's ISI – so as to be able to exercise 'plausible deniability'. Initially, as part of its clandestine Operation Cyclone, the CIA equipped the Afghan jihadists with Soviet-made arms drawn partly from its own stores built up during previous regional conflicts and partly by procuring them from Egypt, a one-time ally of Moscow.

At the White House, Brzezinski reasoned that it was not enough to expel the Soviets from Afghanistan. This was a great opportunity to export a composite ideology of nationalism and Islam to the five Muslim-majority Central Asian Soviet republics with the aim of destroying the communist system there. Indeed, a Polish-American of aristocratic background, he was as much opposed to communism as he was to Russians per se.

He emerged as the architect of the Washington-Islamabad-Riyadh alliance whereby the US, the overall coordinator, became the sole supplier of arms to be channelled exclusively through Pakistan, the staging post for Afghan guerrillas. In this scheme, the ISI acquired a key role.

THE RISE AND RISE OF THE ISI

The ISI had come a long way from its modest beginnings in 1948 when Pakistan's deputy chief of army staff, Major General R. Cawthorne, hived it off during the 1947–48 Indo-Pakistan War, from the Military Intelligence, and turned into an independent agency. General Muhammad Ayub Khan, the chief of army staff, used it to keep increasingly querulous politicians under surveillance.

Its authority grew when Ayub Khan seized power in 1958, becoming in effect the military's political arm. As a result of its intelligence failures in the Indo-Pakistan War in September 1965, Ayub Khan reorganized it. His successor, General Agha Muhammad Yahya Khan (r. 1969–71) expanded it and assigned it the task of gathering political intelligence in East Pakistan. The next ruler, Zulfikar Ali Bhutto (r. 1971–77), set up a special 'Election Cell' within the ISI, and deployed it to harass his political adversaries. It became the primary source of smear campaigns against Opposition politicians and journalists.

Accepting the advice of ISI chief Lt General Ghulam Jilani Khan, Bhutto promoted Zia ul Haq to chief of army staff. Later, Jilani Khan went on to help Zia ul Haq to mount an anti-Bhutto coup. In 1979, Zia ul Haq replaced Jilani Khan with General Akhtar Abdul Rahman Khan, who was also chairman of the joint chiefs of staff.

The ISI operated from a drab, unmarked red-brick building behind high stone walls on Khiyaban-e Suhrawardy in Islamabad. It had about a hundred military officers who maintained an internal and external intelligence network of thousands of agents and freelance spies.

With its new, ambitious assignment in Afghanistan and a vastly increased budget, the ISI would now expand its staff and agents, engaging Pakistanis fluent in Persian and Pushtu as well as thousands of Afghans with promises of money and domicile for their families in Pakistan. That would push the total number of ISI employees, full- and part-time, to almost 100,000 by early 1988.

Its long and deep involvement in the Afghan Islamist resistance brought its officers into close contact with radical Islamists. It was thus that a section of Pakistan's officer corps became infected with this extremist ideology. This development, running parallel to Islamabad's successful efforts to produce an atom bomb, would create the possibility of Islamist officers cooperating with militants intent on acquiring weapons of mass destruction – a frightful scenario that would come to haunt the White House.

THE ISLAMIZATION AND NUCLEARIZATION OF PAKISTAN

Like the rest of the military, ISI officers and agents underwent religious education as mandated by Zia ul Haq. Equally compulsory for soldiers was prayer led by officers. Likewise, civilian bureaucrats were instructed to pray five times a day, and their religiosity was noted in confidential reports.

In June 1980 Zia ul Haq set up Sharia courts at the high court level in the provinces, and the appellate Sharia bench at the Supreme Court level. They were authorized to decide whether a particular law was Islamic or not. He introduced Islamic punishments for theft and adultery – chopping off hands of convicted thieves and death by stoning for adulterers. (In practice, these penalties could not be carried out due to the non-cooperation of surgeons; only the ones involving lashing were actually implemented.) Zia ul Haq specified a ten-year period for the Sharia to prevail in all spheres of life, to be endorsed in a referendum at the end of that period. These official measures were buttressed by the promotion of Islam through mosques and the media. A review of all textbooks was undertaken and any regarded as un-Islamic were removed.

Zia ul Haq showed similar zeal in advancing his country's nuclear arms programme to compete with India's plans, which in turn were dictated by China's testing of an atom bomb in October 1964. Pakistan's programme was being pursued at Kahuta near Tarbela Dam – a beauty spot in a hilly terrain once favoured by diplomats and other foreign residents of the capital – 18 miles (29 km) from Rawalpindi, which housed the general headquarters (GHQ) of the military. Within months of China exploding its first atomic bomb, India's technicians were found to be removing fuel rods from the plutonium processing plant at Trombay near Mumbai, designed and constructed entirely by Indian scientists and engineers. After the September 1965 Indo-Pakistan War, Bhutto, then a cabinet minister, said, 'If India builds the [atom] bomb, we will eat grass or leaves, even go hungry, but we will get one of our own. We have no alternative . . . an atom bomb for an atom bomb.'[4] During his visit to Beijing, he persuaded the leaders of China, a long-time political and military ally of Pakistan, to help his country to manufacture an atom bomb.

In May 1974, India tested a nuclear device at Pokhran in Rajasthan.[5] To discourage non-nuclear states from acquiring nuclear arms, US Senator Stuart Symington's amendment in 1976 to the Foreign Assistance Act of 1961 specified ending aid to any country that imported uranium-enrichment technology. The following year, Senator John Glenn's amendment to the Foreign Assistance Act stipulated the termination of aid to any country that imported reprocessing technology. The US Congress passed the Non-proliferation Act in March 1978. It barred any country from receiving

American assistance if it tested a nuclear weapon, and imposed sanctions against any state that attempted to acquire unauthorized nuclear technology.

While acknowledging the construction of a uranium-enriching facility, Zia ul Haq said that it would be used solely for generating electricity, and declared that no Pakistani government could compromise on the nuclear issue in response to the American pressure. In his meeting with Cyrus Vance in October 1978, Pakistan's foreign minister Agha Shahi said, 'You don't have to be a nuclear weapons expert to understand the strategic importance of having one. The value lies in its possession, and not in its use.'[6]

That month the jailed Bhutto claimed that Pakistan was on the verge of attaining 'full nuclear capability' prior to his overthrow in July 1977. In 319-page document smuggled out of his cell, and published as a book, *If I Am Assassinated*, in 1979, (by Vikas Publishing House, Delhi), he took credit for developing Pakistan's nuclear energy programme and indicated that Pakistan only needed a reprocessing facility to attain nuclear weapons capability. 'My single most important achievement, which, I believe, will dominate the portrait of my public life, is an agreement which I arrived at after assiduous and tenacious endeavors, spanning 11 years of negotiations,' he wrote in *If I Am Assassinated*. 'The agreement of mine [with China] concluded in June, 1976, will perhaps be my greatest achievement and contribution to the survival of our people and our nation.'[7]

Soon after, the Carter administration obtained solid evidence of Pakistan's uranium-enrichment programme. It broached the subject with Islamabad. Dissatisfied with the response he received, Carter cut off economic and military assistance, except food aid, in April 1979. He reiterated that the assistance would be resumed only if he was able to certify that Pakistan would not develop or acquire nuclear arms or assist other nations to do so.

In June 1980, the BBC TV's documentary 'Project 706 – the Islamic Bomb' provided the fullest account so far of Pakistan's uranium-enrichment programme. The stalemate between Washington and Islamabad continued.

A FAUSTIAN DEAL

The situation changed sharply when the US presidency was won by the Republican Ronald Reagan. His description of the Soviet Union as the 'evil empire' would become his signature. While he lacked Carter's intelligence, he was a superb communicator, having spent many years as an actor in Hollywood. His persuasive manner would help him to overcome Congressional resistance to his policies. His first Secretary of State, Alexander Haig, described Pakistan's nuclear programme as 'a private matter'. All he wanted was that Pakistan would not actually detonate an atom bomb, thus emulating the example of Israel, which had refrained from testing its nuclear weapons, first acquired in 1966.

In May 1981, the Senate Foreign Relations Committee reversed its previous stance and sanctioned $3.2 billion of aid to Islamabad over the next six years, divided equally between civilian and military assistance. The White House argued that supplying Pakistan with modern US weaponry would *reduce* the chance of its pursuing the nuclear option. The Senate adopted the committee's bill seven months later.[8] In reality, Islamabad pushed ahead on both fronts, conventional and unconventional armament. It accelerated its nuclear weapons programme out of fear of an attack by Delhi in response to the active assistance it was giving to the Sikh separatists in the adjoining Indian Punjab against the Central government.

Reagan appointed William Casey as the new CIA director and accorded him the unprecedented status of a cabinet member. A bald, corpulent man with a rubbery face and oversize spectacles, Casey had started his working life with the CIA's predecessor organization, Office of Strategic Surveys, and established himself as an unconventional operator, callous and combative in equal measure. Now, though, a personal rapport quickly developed between him,

ISI director Abdul Rahman Khan and Prince Turki ibn Faisal, head of the Saudi intelligence agency known as Istikhabarat.[9] The Afghan insurgency picked up.

Had Casey opted for marginalizing radical Islamists by backing moderate Islamic nationalist parties along with nationalist, secular, anti-Marxist groups, the history of the region and the world would have been starkly different. Since the latter factions respected Afghan traditions in religion and governance by a king, they enjoyed far more popular support than did the anti-royalist fundamentalist groups, who were far too radical for the conservative, traditionalist majority among Afghans. A survey of Afghan refugees in Pakistan in 1986, sponsored by Prof. Bahauddin Majrooh, showed that nearly 75 per cent wanted King Zahir Shah back as the head of state.[10]

In Islamabad, Casey quickly earned the nickname of Cyclone – after the code name of the CIA's Afghanistan operation. He was given to delivering anti-communist perorations during his meetings with the ISI's Afghan Bureau officers headed by Brigadier Muhammad Yousaf. He had no qualms about hiring conmen and thugs as long as they were keen to kill Soviet soldiers and civilians. Once the ISI's top officers had proved their anti-Soviet credentials, Casey readily accepted Zia ul Haq's demand that US-supplied arms and money be distributed solely by Pakistan. As the US did not want to create a paper trail in order to deprive Moscow of evidence of its involvement in Afghan affairs, thus raising the spectre of a regional conflict escalating into an international one, all money dealings were in cash. This gave ample opportunities to the ISI to siphon off the foreign funds. It did so and funnelled the cash into Pakistan's expensive nuclear programme.

To increase financial support for the Afghan Mujahedin, Casey opened a clandestine bank account for the pro-Mujahedin governments. Saudi Arabia volunteered to match US aid, dollar for dollar. In addition, there were contributions by affluent Saudi citizens and charities as well as sums collected in mosques. By 1986, contributions soared to $240 million a year,[11] almost half the Afghan budget, including foreign aid. The Riyadh government became a leading recruiter of jihadists from all over the Muslim world.

In 1981, the militant Afghan parties had 75,000 active cadres, the three radical Islamist ones accounting for two-thirds of the total, with Hikmatyar's Hizb-e Islami being in the lead. It had a command structure stretching as far as Herat near the border with Iran, with a network of recruitment centres, training camps, medical facilities, warehouses and offices. In contrast the three traditional religious parties were even in strength.

Hikmatyar wanted to reform the religious establishment, eradicate the Sufi orders, and enforce the Sharia completely by eliminating the traditional Pushtunwali code. While he ran a tightly knit party, Rabbani opened the Jamiat-e Islami's membership to ordinary Afghans even if they did not subscribe to its ideology. But he was a Tajik, a group only half as large as Pushtuns, and therefore, his party was much smaller than Hikmatyar's.

Alone among the anti-Soviet leaders, Hikmatyar talked of carrying guerrilla raids beyond the Oxus River into Soviet Central Asia and rolling back communism from there. This plan appealed to Casey and the rest of the US administration, which chose to overlook the embarrassing fact that during his White House visit in 1985 Hikmatyar refused to shake hands with Reagan. Consequently, there was an upsurge in US military and financial assistance to the Afghan Mujahedin and a simultaneous hardening of Islamabad's stance on the nuclear issue. 'We have given no assurances of any kind to the United States with regard to our nuclear program,' said Pakistan's foreign minister Agha Shahi, in an interview with the London-based *Financial Times* in January 1982. 'Whether we explode a nuclear device will be a decision Pakistan will take knowing the consequences. We make a distinction between an explosion and weapons. We do not rule out the possibility of a detonation if it is necessary for our programme.'[12]

As 1982 unrolled, Pakistan received from China the complete design for a 25-kiloton nuclear bomb and sufficient weapons-grade uranium for two bombs. Beijing went on to provide Islamabad with the design of one of its warheads.[13] At the same time ties between Islamabad and Washington grew tighter. The year ended with Zia ul Haq having dinner with Reagan at the White House.

In 1983, China helped Pakistan with triggering devices needed to explode an atom bomb. These were either conventional charges or electronic trigging circuits. The Pakistani experts, led by Dr Abdul Qadeer Khan, started conducting cold tests in a tunnel in the Chagai Hills of Baluchistan to devise a perfect triggering device. Success came only at the end of more than a score of such tests. That was the final step in assembling an atom bomb, which they almost did by the end of the year.

In Washington a now-declassified US government assessment in 1983 concluded: 'There is unambiguous evidence that Pakistan is actively pursuing a nuclear weapons development programme. We believe the ultimate application of the enriched uranium produced at Kahuta is clearly nuclear weapons.'[14] Yet no action was taken against Pakistan. The Reagan White House had concluded that hurting Pakistan by imposing sanctions against it would aid Moscow. So, faced with the choice of expelling the Soviets from Afghanistan by all possible means, or stopping Islamabad from building a nuclear bomb, it opted for the former. It was so unwaveringly committed to this policy, that it deployed underhand tactics to quash irrefutable evidence that State Department officials would periodically furnish to show Islamabad inexorably racing to produce a nuclear weapon.

This Faustian deal between America and Pakistan would later raise the horrific prospect of a nuclear device falling into the hands of Islamist terrorists operating in the Pakistan-Afghanistan region – or AfPak, as the US administration would officially designate the region.

THE AFGHAN MUJAHEDIN FORGE AHEAD

For now, though, to the White House's satisfaction, the situation on the Afghan resistance front was going its way. The three moderate

Islamic factions formed a joint council. Then the three radical Islamist parties set up the Islamic Alliance of Afghanistan (Persian, *Ittihad-e Islami Afghanistan*) under the chairmanship of Abdul Rasul Sayyaf, a tall, heavily built academic with a chest-long beehive beard, who was an adherent of Wahhabi Islam. The coalescing of different groups facilitated the ISI's distribution of arms and ammunition to the Afghan resistance, which were arriving at the rate of several planeloads a week. Besides training an average of twenty thousand Afghan Mujahedin a year, the ISI created a network of four hundred commanders inside Afghanistan under its direct control to conduct its operations. This network would prove to be a vital asset when the ISI decided to boost the fledgling Taliban in the mid-1990s.

Bankrolled by the Saudi intelligence agency, Sayyaf won over some floating Afghan activists and transformed the Islamic Alliance of Afghanistan into his own party. His paymasters were pleased to note that in the Afghan refugee camps' madrasas, a traditional curriculum of philosophy, poetry and the learning of Persian had given way to one with marked Wahhabi characteristics of puritanical Islam and the learning of Arabic.

Fearing their exclusion from the United Nations-sponsored negotiations between Kabul, Moscow, Islamabad and Tehran to solve the Afghanistan crisis, all seven Islamic parties agreed to form the Islamic Alliance of Afghan Mujahedin – popularly known as the Afghan Mujahedin – in May 1983. Led by Sayyaf with Mujaddidi as his deputy, it began operating from Peshawar.

It was also in Peshawar that bin Laden, supported by Saudi Prince Turki, ran a centre for recruiting volunteers from the Arab world to join the anti-Soviet jihad. This scheme was later extended to the non-Arab Muslim world. According to Hamid Gul, a former ISI director, by the time the Afghan Mujahedin captured Kabul in 1992, an estimated 50,000 militants from twenty-eight countries had been trained by the ISI, nearly two-thirds of them from Arab states, with the Saudi kingdom being the leader.[15] A further 100,000 Muslims were directly influenced by those personally engaged in the anti-Soviet jihad.

At the first camp set up by bin Laden, the volunteers were trained by Pakistani and American officers. The military training was based on the manuals used by the Pentagon and the CIA, translated into Persian and, later, Arabic and Urdu. It involved learning the most effective ways to strangle and stab; handling explosives, fuses, timers, and remote-control devices; making booby traps; carrying out industrial and other forms of sabotage; and operating small arms as well as anti-tank and anti-aircraft missiles.

Nineteen eighty-four was *the* pivotal year. After receiving an atom bomb assembled in Kahuta in January, the Chinese detonated it successfully at their test site at Lop Nor in Xinjiang province in March.[16] This led to discreet jubilation among top officials in Islamabad and Kahuta. Having thus acquired parity with India in defence, Pakistani leaders felt confident to challenge India's claim to regional hegemony. Until this super-secret event came to light more than a decade later, what Pakistan's leader Zia ul Haq, a master in dissimulation, would admit was that his country had acquired a very modest uranium-enrichment capability for peaceful purposes.

During Casey's visit to Pakistan in February, Zia ul Haq demanded increased aid for the Afghan Mujahedin. Casey readily obliged. US financial assistance, which had been running at $60 million a year since 1981 shot up to $250 million. In 1985, it rose to $300 million a year. According to Milton Beardon of the CIA, by the time the Soviets left Afghanistan, the CIA had spent $6 billion and Saudi Arabia $4 billion.[17]

In late 1984, A.Q. Khan, heading the country's nuclear weapons programme, said he was ready for a hot test in Baluchistan but Zia ul Haq ruled it out. He did not wish to embarrass the Reagan administration which had been overly generous to his government and had repeatedly turned a blind eye to its nuclear arms programme. Zia ul Haq had another major reason to be cautious. In April 1984, the US Senate Foreign Affairs Committee had adopted a restrictive provision, proposed by Senator Larry Pressler and two others, regarding the continuation of economic assistance and military sales to Islamabad. The president needed to certify that Pakistan did not possess a nuclear explosive device, and that the new aid would significantly reduce the risk that it would possess such a weapon. It was not until August 1985 that the Pressler Amendment was attached to the Foreign Assistance Act covering the fiscal year 1985–86. In the House of Representatives, Congressman Stephen Solarz's amendment stipulated a ban on *all* military and economic aid to those non-nuclear nations that illegally procured or tried to procure nuclear-related materials from America.

But there was an overriding provision that applied to all such amendments. The president was authorized to waive them if he thought it was in the national interests to do so. Reagan did not use that option, though. Instead, while incontrovertible evidence from several sources piled up showing Pakistan's unflinching drive to produce an atom bomb, year after year the president certified to the contrary. He did so to keep the US military and economic aid flowing into Pakistan while its government boosted the destructive power of the Islamist insurgents in Afghanistan.

AFGHAN MARXISTS ON THE DEFENSIVE

Faced with a mounting onslaught by the Islamist guerrillas, the Marxist regime in Kabul did its utmost to align itself with the popular practices and rituals of Islam. President Karmal prayed in public regularly, and began his official statements with an invocation to Allah. His audience responded to his public speeches with intermittent cries of '*Allahu Akbar*' (Arabic, 'God is Great'). He set up Office of Islamic Teachings under his direct supervision. Radio and television reintroduced recitations of the Quran. They and the print media widely reported the activities of the Ministry of Religious Affairs and Trusts, which gave increased importance to the ulema, whose salaries rose sharply. In return, clerics became more willing to explain official policies and reforms to their congregations. The ministry initiated a widely publicized programme of building new mosques and madrasas, and began exchanging Islamic delegations with the Soviet Central Asian republics.

Radio broadcasts from these countries in Persian, Tajik, Uzbek and Turkmen languages stressed that Islam was safe in the Soviet system and that any danger to it came from America, Britain, China and Israel. This was partly the Kabul regime's response to anti-Soviet propaganda aired by the US-funded Radio Liberty/Radio Free Europe, directed at Central Asian Muslims to create and intensify Islamic consciousness and ethnic nationalism in the region to undermine the Moscow-directed Soviet system. The example of Radio Liberty/ Radio Free Europe was followed by Saudi Arabia, which combined religious propaganda with courses on the Quran and the Sharia – and later by Egypt, Qatar and Kuwait.

The Kabul government tried to block the cross-border movement of the guerrillas by offering money, weapons and promises of regional autonomy to the tribes along the Afghan-Pakistan frontier. Its intelligence service, Khad (Persian, *Khidmat-e Amniyat-e Dawlati*; 'State Security Service'), worked in cooperation with the KGB, ensconced in a large KGB enclave in Kabul. Due to the tension between the border tribes, who were steeped in tradition, and the leaders of the radical Islamist parties who lacked high status by traditional standards, the regime had some success. The members of the tribes, who professed loyalty to Kabul, began harassing the Afghan Mujahedin.

To expand its popular base, the Karmal government founded the National Fatherland Front in 1981, giving due consideration to the composition and characteristics of various ethnic groups, tribes and clans. The Front included the Jamaat-e Ulema and numerous tribal jirgas. Its major task was to publicize and explain official policies to the people. It claimed a membership of 100,000 affiliated to 400 local councils. By contrast, the PDPA had 90,000 full and candidate members. But the activities of both organizations were limited mainly to urban centres since large parts of the countryside had slipped out of Kabul's jurisdiction.

The official figures released in early 1983 showed the reach of the Islamist guerrillas. They had destroyed or damaged nearly half of the schools and hospitals (1,814 and 31, respectively), 111 basic health centres, three-quarters of communications lines, 800 heavy transport vehicles and 906 farmers' cooperatives.[18] Human casualties were mounting too. By early 1984, the number of dead or injured Afghan troops was put at 17,000 and guerrilla casualties at 30,000. The estimates of Soviet casualties at 13,500–30,000 included 6,000–8,000 fatalities.

The immediate future pointed to more violence. By now, the CIA was delivering more than 5,000 tonnes of arms and ammunition a month to the port city of Karachi from where they were transported by trucks to the ISI's massive arms depot at Ojhiri near Rawalpindi and a few smaller ones in Khyber Pakhtunkhwa province. In the process as much as 60 per cent of the weapons went astray with the ISI's connivance.[19] Pakistani army officers exchanged their old arms for new ones. They sold the remainder on the black market and channelled the cash into the country's expensive nuclear programme. The trade in illegal arms helped escalate inter-ethnic violence in Sindh province between native Sindhis and Muslim immigrants from India. Later, when pilfered weapons began appearing in the arms bazaars of the Afghan-Pakistan border towns, the Pentagon decided to dispatch an audit team to Pakistan. On the eve of its arrival in April 1988, the Ojhiri arms depot, containing 10,000 tonnes of munitions, went up in flames, with rockets, missiles and artillery shells raining down as far away as Islamabad and Rawalpindi, and more than a hundred people getting killed.[20]

In Afghanistan firm lines were drawn between the Afghan Mujahedin and the Marxist regime in the mid-1980s. Heavily dependent on 115,000 Soviet troops, backed by nearly 500,000 military and paramilitary forces of its own,[21] and generous military aid from Moscow, the Karmal government was determined to subdue the resistance in rural Afghanistan, while maintaining control over the cities and major towns, the circular national highway and airports.

It therefore deployed KGB-trained guerrilla units masquerading as anti-Soviet Mujahedin to mislead the opposition, draw out the real Mujahedin, and attack them. By 1983, nearly ninety such units were in the field, provoking clashes between different genuine Mujahedin groups, and occasionally 'surrendering' to the authorities in order to boost the morale of the Karmal camp.

It was against this backdrop that the UN-sponsored talks between various parties proceeded, centred around the timetable for the Soviet pullback, the cessation of foreign arms aid to the Afghan Mujahedin, and the return of the refugees. The Afghan parties wanted an immediate and unconditional Soviet withdrawal, whereas the Moscow–Kabul duo proposed a staged Soviet withdrawal over four years *after* the termination of foreign military assistance to the Mujahedin. Soon after Mikhail Gorbachev became Secretary General of the Communist Party of the Soviet Union in March 1985, the Kremlin slashed the period of Soviet withdrawal to eighteen months. When he realized that the Mujahedin would not deal with Karmal, Gorbachev worked behind the scenes to ease him out.

To lighten the burden on Pakistan's cash-strapped public exchequer to finance the nuclear programme, A.Q. Khan came up with a plan to establish a nuclear export programme and got the go-ahead from Zia ul Haq. The CIA obtained evidence to that effect. Yet, in November 1985, Reagan recycled his previous statement about Pakistan lacking an atom bomb or a plan to build one. This cleared the way for US aid to continue flowing into Islamabad.

In April 1986, on being promoted to deputy director of the CIA, Robert Gates found that Islamabad was siphoning off funds meant for the Afghan Mujahedin through the Bank of Credit and Commerce International and was spending that cash on its nuclear programme.[22] Yet three months later, the Reagan administration decided to increase its financial assistance to Pakistan to more than $4 billion. This pushed the total US military aid to Islamabad during 1980–87 to $7.2 billion.

While Washington was upping the ante, Moscow showed signs of de-escalating the conflict as a prelude to its withdrawal.

KARMAL OUT, NAJIBULLAH IN

In May 1986, Karmal resigned as the PDPA's Secretary General and gave way to Muhammad Najibullah,[23] the erstwhile head of Khad. A barrel-chested physician, he was nicknamed 'the ox' because of his strong constitution. By announcing shortly afterward that it would withdraw 6,000 Soviet troops in October, the Kremlin underlined its intent to settle the Afghanistan crisis.

This emboldened the US-Pakistan-Mujahedin alliance. Casey encountered little resistance among US lawmakers when he proposed supplying US-made shoulder-held Stinger anti-aircraft missiles to shoot down Soviet helicopter gunships *and* assigning Americans to train the guerrillas. This measure was designed to counter Kabul's air superiority, stemming from its extensive use of helicopter gunships. By so doing, Washington reversed its seven-year-old policy of not overtly introducing US personnel or arms into the Afghan conflict. It went on to purchase British-manufactured Blowpipe anti-aircraft missiles as well. It airlifted some 150 Stingers to Pakistan in late spring 1986, followed by 300 Blowpipes several months later. The Kremlin under Gorbachev was in no mood to protest.

The Afghan Mujahedin started firing the new missiles extensively in the autumn of 1986, downing sixty helicopters before the year's end. They found them to be more effective than the Soviet-designed SAM-7s (surface-to-air missiles), clandestinely procured from Egypt and China by the CIA, which they had used previously.

In October 1986, Reagan again certified that Pakistan lacked a nuclear weapon – a blatant fiction. According to Norm Wulf, the assistant director of the Arms Control and Disarmament Agency, the US National Security Agency (NSA) had been reading all the communications between A.Q. Khan's agents in Britain, Dubai, France, Germany, Switzerland and Turkey for years, and had obtained the floor plans for the Kahuta plant and its supply lists.[24]

To assist the Afghan government, Moscow began using elite units, Spetsnaz, instead of regular troops to shut off rebel supply lines from

Pakistan. Fifteen years later, Washington would follow into the Soviet footsteps by assigning the task of tackling the cross-border traffic to the CIA's Special Operations Force units.

Once Karmal had given up his presidency in favour of Najibullah in November 1986, Afghan and Soviet forces jointly seized Kama Dakka, a vital staging post for delivering Pakistani weapons to the Afghan Mujahedin. They also continued to exhort and bribe the border tribes to impede the passage of arms and guerrillas from Pakistan. But the overall situation did not improve.

The Soviet archives released by the Kremlin in 2009 show that, at the Communist Party's Politburo meeting on 13 November 1986, Marshal Sergey Akhromeyev, commander of the Soviet armed forces, said, 'There is barely an important piece of land in Afghanistan that has not been occupied by one of our soldiers at some time or another. Nevertheless, much of the territory remains in the hands of the terrorists. We control the provincial centers, but we cannot maintain political control over the territory we seize. To occupy towns and villages temporarily has little value in such a vast land, where the insurgents can just disappear into the hills.' He added: 'About 99 per cent of the battles and skirmishes that we fought in Afghanistan were won by our side. The problem is that the next morning there is the same situation as if there had been no battle. The terrorists are again in the villages where they – or we thought they – were destroyed a day or so before.' To this Gorbachev replied, 'After all this time we have not learnt how to wage war there [in Afghanistan].'[25] Two decades later, the American and other NATO troops would find history repeating itself.

In early March 1987, Hikmatyar, a favourite of bin Laden and Zia ul Haq, scored a striking achievement. After crossing the Oxus River, small units of his Hizb-e Islami fired rockets at a frontier guard post near Piyanj in Soviet Tajikistan. This act heralded a future Islamic State of Afghanistan's role as a springboard for exporting Islamic revolution to the Soviet Central Asian republics. Casey was overjoyed. He rushed to Pakistan secretly. Accompanied by Zia ul Haq, he crossed into Afghanistan and reviewed the Hizb-e Islami units.[26] Two months later he would die of brain cancer – satisfied in the knowledge that on any given day some seventy thousand Afghan Mujahedin guerrillas were undermining the leftist regime.

In 1987, there were bungled attempts by Pakistani agents to acquire American nuclear technology illegally. This and A.Q. Khan's statement in an interview that 'What the CIA has been saying about our possessing the bomb is correct' put the final seal on the development of a nuclear weapon by Pakistan.[27]

Despite the rising audacity of the Islamist insurgents, neither Kabul nor Moscow was prepared to cede the dominant position that the PDPA visualized for itself in any future coalition government. Surprisingly, despite the mayhem resulting from the Soviet occupation of Afghanistan, its industrial capacity rose by 50 per cent due to the opening of new factories and the development of its gas fields with the help of Soviet engineers and technicians.[28] During the nine years of its rule, the PDPA had spawned its own constituencies: the peasants who had secured land; the emancipated women who, inspired by the sight of Soviet Central Asian women working as helicopter pilots, doctors, engineers and translators, dreaded being relegated back to the home and the veil; and all those who had benefitted, materially and otherwise, from the literacy campaign.

On the opposite side, the traditional Islamic factions within Afghanistan, which had their heyday in the 1930s and 1940s, had merely maintained the networks that had existed before the April 1978 revolution.

In sum, the Marxist revolution, and the resources and facilities provided by both official and private sources in Pakistan, Iran, the Persian Gulf states, Egypt, and America had bolstered radical Islamism in a society that was ethnically heterogeneous and economically underdeveloped. Until the 1978 revolution, the state had made minimal inroads into the individual or social life of Afghans. In a sense the resistance by rural Afghans to the Kabul government was as much a rebellion against rapid socio-economic reform as it was against the central state itself. Village Afghans' distrust of Kabul has continued. While both the PDPA and the Islamist radicals were convinced that a strong central government would revolutionalize Afghan society, moored to centuries-old feudalism and tribalism, neither had a blueprint for creating such a state and funding its expanded role. In the event, therefore, each ended up depending on foreign powers.

The result of the multiparty parliamentary elections in April 1988 – held under the new constitution adopted in January, which declared Islam to be the state religion – showed the PDPA securing only 27 per cent of the seats and the National Front, an umbrella body, 28 per cent, with the rest going to such popular organizations as the Peasants' Justice Party, the Islamic Party, and the Workers' Revolutionary Party. Alluding to the election results, Najibullah urged a PDPA conference not to underestimate the role of Islam and the importance of the ulema, and reminded his audience that the objectives of the Afghan revolution should not be realized by military means.

His words were timely. Moscow was poised to undertake the first stage of its troop withdrawal on 15 May 1988 in accordance with one of the four agreements it had signed with Washington and Islamabad under the UN aegis in February. Another agreement required Pakistan to stop transporting military supplies into Afghanistan and close down training camps for Afghan rebels on its soil. In the event, to the chagrin of Kabul and Moscow, Islamabad openly breached this agreement. On top of that, the two superpowers exchanged secret letters that allowed them to continue military supplies to their allies. So peace proved elusive.

With the Soviet troops reduced by half to about sixty thousand by August 1988, the Najibullah government vacated many border posts and garrisons in order to consolidate strategic positions. It raised its budget for the Ministry of Religious Affairs and Trusts to such an extent that it amounted to three times the Foreign Ministry's.

The deaths of Zia ul Haq and General Akhtar Abdul Rahman

Khan, chairman of the joint chiefs of staff, in a mid-air explosion of their aircraft at Bahawalpur on 18 August made no difference to Pakistan's Afghan policy. General Hamid Gul, the ISI director since 1987, was even more committed to the Afghan Mujahedin than his predecessor, and was close to Hikmatyar. Following a general election, Benazir Bhutto, daughter of Zulfikar Ali Bhutto, and leader of the Pakistan People's Party, became the prime minister in December.

Even though Pakistan was found to have violated US export controls regarding nuclear-related material, Reagan once more waived an aid cut-off for Pakistan in 1988.[29]

As 15 February 1989, the final date for the Soviet withdrawal, approached, there were predictions that with the disappearance of the cement that held the Afghan Mujahedin together – the Soviet military presence – the coalition would disintegrate. But it did not. The chief reason was that the US, under the new administration of President George Bush Senior, pledged to supply weapons to the Afghan Mujahedin to the tune of $500 million a year (as acknowledged publicly), with Riyadh matching the US dollar for dollar. Any faction splitting from the Mujahedin would have lost its share of arms – and thus its followers in the field whose loyalty rested largely on a steady supply of cash and weapons. With more than two million registered Afghan refugees in Pakistani camps, they had a large enough pool to draw from. (In addition, there were more than one million Afghan refugees in Iran.) Yet their coexistence was uneasy, with personal and ethnic rivalries – especially between Pushtuns and Tajiks – resurfacing, now that their common foe was gone. Little wonder that they failed to form an interim government.

Meanwhile, the Kremlin handed over its vast military stores to the Afghans, and airlifted more arms and ammunition. It also promised to honour the December 1978 Afghan-Soviet Treaty of Friendship, which specified mutual consultations about 'the security, independence and territorial integrity of the two countries'. The post-1978 conflict had resulted in the deaths of 813,500 people, all but 13,500 being Afghan.

Sadly, for Afghanistan, the loss of Afghan lives would continue.

4

THE RISE AND RISE OF THE TALIBAN

A VAST, SPRAWLING capital, today's Kabul has very little in common with the charming city of three-quarters of a million people living on streets lined with poplars and pines who witnessed the Saur Revolution of April 1978. The guerrilla activities in the countryside during the 1980s led to an increased influx into Kabul from rural areas. By the time the Muhammad Najibullah government fell in 1992 – closing the leftist chapter in the country's chronicle – twice as many Afghans inhabited the capital than was the case fourteen years before.

What stands out about Kabul is the sight of barren, brown shale hills. There are about thirty of them. On their gravelly surface have mushroomed hundreds of thousands of hastily built houses which provide shelter to most of the city's 3.5 million residents, the vast majority of them newcomers. Almost invariably the hilltops are now crowned with towers servicing the twenty-two TV channels and several mobile-phone companies. It is tempting for a visitor to scale one of the hills, a task that requires not only a local guide but also extraordinary manual dexterity to manoeuvre the slippery slope turned muddy by an overnight shower. The reward is a panoramic view of the city – provided the trip is made early in the morning before the smog rises.

At the peak, a TV tower with supersize antennae, embedded in a solid foundation of concrete and guarded by a couple of armed soldiers equipped with an olive-green jeep, dwarfs the nondescript guard house. However, that breeze-block structure warms the heart of the visitor after his upward trek through slums, a deeply depressing experience.

The slum residents can bear the heat and dust, but find rain a nightmare. Porous roofs leak. A deluge of muddy garbage rushes down, flooding the already choked cesspits and street sewers. The one-bedroom houses on both sides of the unpaved streets are built – illegally – of mud bricks and wood, without a kitchen or a bathroom or provision for water supply. On most mornings a truck rumbles up the hill to sell water. Those who are too indigent to pay have a back-breaking option: rush downhill with empty eight-gallon plastic containers to the government's tap at the bottom, a source of free water. On average it takes half an hour to do a single trip. So, to store, say, 50 gallons of water requires three hours of hard labour. Such is the fate of four out of five Kabuli households.

Another feature of these hills that grabs the attention is the sight of rocks painted white or red. White is the symbol of safety and red of danger. If a path has been marked by rocks painted white, it is a sign that that section of the hill has been demined. Rocks painted red signify the opposite – this area of the hill has not yet been swept for mines. Such is the legacy of the 1992–96 civil war which turned Afghanistan into one of the three most mined nations on the planet.

Most of the capital's hilltops harboured fighters of the assorted battling groups, equipped with rockets, mortars, and tank shells.

Reflecting the demographic distribution of the major ethnic groups in Afghanistan, Kabul was largely Tajik in the north, Pushtun in the south, and Hazara in the west. So, during the civil war, the northern hills were controlled by Burhanuddin Rabbani's Jamiat-e Islami, and its supreme commander, Ahmad Shah Masoud, the southern hills by Gulbuddin Hikmatyar's Hizb-e Islami, and the western ones by the Hizb-e Wahdat (Persian, 'Party of Unity') of Hazaras.

The civil war erupted about three years after the pullout by the Soviet troops. On the eve of their departure, Najibullah declared a state of emergency and appointed a new twenty-two-member Supreme Council for the Defence of the Homeland. He recalled thousands of Afghans in Soviet schools and military academies, and raised 45,000 Special Guards to replace the departed Soviet troops.

In March 1989, his soldiers frustrated a bid by the Afghan Mujahedin Alliance's interim government to capture Jalalabad. The Mujahedin camp's morale fell, but not enough to cause a split between its moderate and hardline factions. In the debate between hawkish American 'bleeders', intent on humiliating Moscow, and pragmatic 'dealers', keen to sideline radical Islamists, the hardliners won. President George Bush Senior publicly sanctioned half a billion dollars of military aid to the Afghan Mujahedin Alliance for the next financial year.

FALL OF NAJIBULLAH

As spring gave way to summer, the simmering tensions between the Hizb-e Islami of Hikmatyar, a Pushtun, and the Jamiat-e Islami of Masoud, a Tajik, led to vicious killings. This angered and disappointed Osama bin Laden, whose pleas that all believers were equal in Islam, irrespective of colour, race, or ethnicity, fell on deaf ears. Pre-Islamic ethnic animosities trumped shared religion.

Following the assassination of his Palestinian mentor Abdullah Azzam, bin Laden decided to continue running Azzam's organization, the Maktab al Khidmat (Arabic, 'Bureau of Service'), under the title of Al Qaida (Arabic, 'The Base'). He aimed to create an international network of those who had participated in the anti-Soviet jihad. With the inter-ethnic violence among the Afghan Mujahedin showing no sign of declining, bin Laden returned to his native Saudi city of Jeddah in the spring of 1990.

Well supplied with arms, fuel, and food from the Soviet Union, Najibullah got the leaders of the People's Democratic Party of

Afghanistan to change the party's name to Watan (Persian, 'Homeland') in January 1990. He gave autonomy to Hazaras and Uzbeks, which won him the backing of the 10,000-strong Uzbek militia, led by General Abdul Rashid Dostum, who defected from the Mujahedin camp.

Noticing the erosion of support for his government, Najibullah offered to step down in favour of a broad-based coalition. But, urged by Washington and Islamabad, the Afghan Mujahedin Alliance continued to shun him. Indeed, his conciliatory move encouraged the Jamiat-e Islami and Hizb-e Islami to extend their areas of control. By the end of 1991, the Kabul government had lost jurisdiction over three-quarters of the countryside.

The annual cost to the Kremlin of backing the Kabul government was far less than the $250 million estimated by Western sources. A lot of the military goods were surplus supplies from the Soviet stores being closed in eastern Europe following the demolition of the Berlin Wall in November 1989.

However, the break-up of the Soviet Union on 31 December 1991 caused sharp policy shifts in Moscow, Islamabad, and Kabul. Russian president Boris Yeltsin stopped fuel supplies to Najibullah's army. Discarding discretion, Pakistan's Inter-Services Intelligence (ISI) blatantly manipulated the assembly of the Afghan Mujahedin delegates in Peshawar in January 1992 to elect an interim government with Sibghatullah Mujaddidi as the president and the pro-Riyadh Abdul Rasul Sayyaf as the executive prime minister.

A desperate Najibullah appealed to the presidents of the newly independent Central Asian republics for assistance. They supplied him with six million barrels of oil and 500,000 tonnes of wheat to survive the winter.[1] They did not want his government supplanted by Islamist radicals who, they feared, would destabilize their regimes. (The same feeling prevails in these capitals today.) However, deprived of the Soviet largess, Najibullah had difficulty maintaining the loyalty of some eighty thousand tribal militiamen, most of whom had abandoned the Afghan Mujahedin camp due to the generous grants of money, arms, and food from his government.

In his meetings with Najibullah in the first half of March 1992, the United Nations special envoy Benon Sevan informed him that there would be no UN aid for Afghanistan so long as he remained in office. On 18 March, Najibullah informed Sevan that he would hand over power to 'an interim government' of fifteen nominees of the UN, as a preamble to establishing a transitional, broad-based coalition. The next day he broadcast his decision. He did so without first consulting any of his fifty military generals or other leading civilian backers – a blunder that would cost him his life.

His broadcast confused and demoralized his supporters. To save their own lives, the commanders of garrisons and militias started striking deals with local Mujahedin units under the overall command of Masoud. These commanders included Dostum. The newly forged alliance seized Mazar-e Sharif after bitter street fighting and set up a military council at the end of March. From there the rebel forces advanced on the capital.

By the time Najibullah urged the assembled military leaders in Kabul on 12 April to stand by him, it was too late. The response was poor. On 15 April, when he tried to fly out to join his family in Delhi, he was barred by rebel militia controlling Kabul airport. He then put himself in the hands of the UN mission. It tried to get him out of Afghanistan but failed.

The fourteen-strong Mujahedin leadership, meeting in Peshawar on 15 April 1992, decided to confer the presidency of Afghanistan on Mujaddidi, the head of the interim government, for three months on a rotating basis. It established a Leadership Council of fifty-one members including chairman and deputy chairman, divided equally among the seven constituents of the Afghan Mujahedin Alliance. Afghanistan's vice-president, Rahim Hatif, negotiated the entry of the forces of Masoud and Dostum into the capital while ignoring the partisans of Hikmatyar.

President Mujaddidi's arrival in Kabul, now under the military control of Masoud and Dostum, marked the end of the fourteen-year conflict between Afghan Marxists and Islamists that had started in April 1978.

Once Moscow intervened militarily, in December 1979, the civil conflict escalated into a battle between the two global superpowers. Washington's increased commitment to Afghan Islamists was reflected in the financial aid it provided them: up from the publicly acknowledged \$20 million (a fraction of the actual figure) in 1980 to \$700 million in 1988, the last year of both Ronald Reagan's presidency and the Soviet military presence in Afghanistan. Besides the publicly declared figures, larger sums came from the US Defense Department's secret annual budget, which quadrupled to \$36 billion during the 1980s. The Afghan operation, involving the procurement of arms and ammunition for the Mujahedin, was an important item on the Pentagon's list.[2] Estimates of Soviet military aid to the Kabul regime varied from \$1 million to \$4 million a day for roughly ten years – \$3.5 to \$14 billion – plus economic aid comprising food and fuel. Part of this was offset by the Afghan natural gas that Moscow bought at a giveaway price.[3]

The estimated human losses of one million people – or 110,000 a year – comprised deaths caused directly and indirectly by the conflict. The direct category covered those killed either in combat between the warring camps or among the various constituents of each camp, or owing to acts of sabotage or widespread drug trafficking in Afghanistan and Pakistan. The indirect category largely comprised infants whose deaths could be linked to malnutrition or the breakdown of health services, and those blown up by the tens of thousands of mines scattered throughout the countryside.[4]

The withdrawal of Soviet troops from Afghanistan in early 1989 loosened Moscow's ties with that country, but did not end them. So Afghanistan's fate continued to be linked with the state of play in the Cold War which ended nearly two years later. Though the amalgam of Afghan nationalism and Islam adopted by the Mujahedin was a powerful force with which to confront the secular, leftist regime in Kabul, it proved inadequate to destroy it.

In the final analysis, it was the lure of American and Saudi money and weapons that held together the seven factions within the Afghan

Mujahedin Alliance. Thus Washington emerged as the crucial player in bringing about the victory of Islamists over Marxists in Afghanistan. This was an unpalatable fact for such extremist Muslim leaders as Hikmatyar and bin Laden, who persisted in their unsupported assertion that the Mujahedin had won their anti-Soviet jihad strictly on their own. Equally, Washington was loath to admit that it had achieved its Islamist victory in Afghanistan while vociferously condemning Islamism in neighbouring Iran, and that it had acted, willy-nilly, as a midwife – along with Pakistan and Saudi Arabia – to the latest Muslim fundamentalist state.

THE MUJAHEDIN IN KABUL: THE SECOND (HOT) CIVIL WAR

The new regime changed the country's name from the Democratic Republic of Afghanistan to the Islamic State of Afghanistan and declared the Sharia to be the sole source of Afghan law. But it lacked the capacity to implement this declaration since the country quickly became embroiled in a ferocious civil war that would last four years. The main players were Hikmatyar, Masoud, Dostum, and Karim Khalili, an ethnic Hazara. While Hikmatyar and Masoud remained implacable foes – until the emergence of the Taliban – Dostum and Khalili changed sides for opportunistic reasons.

Having enjoyed access to large quantities of weapons and money in their decade-long anti-leftist jihad, the non-Pushtun minorities felt confident to challenge the Pushtuns. With Tajik, Uzbek, and Hazara fighters controlling Kabul, and the defence ministry run by Masoud, the ethnic minorities had the wherewithal to frustrate the Pushtuns' attempt to become the sole ruling group.

In late July 1992, Mujaddidi stepped down as president; Burhanuddin Rabbani, a Tajik, succeeded him. It was the first time since 1929 – when Habibullah Kalakani became king – that a Tajik had assumed supreme power. Hikmatyar was incensed. He started stressing Pushtun nationalism more than radical Islamism. In early

August, his fighters, based in Charasayab, 20 miles (32 km) south of Kabul, rained shells and mortars on the capital, killing 2,500 people and making 500,000 homeless before a ceasefire came into effect a fortnight later.

When Rabbani's presidential tenure ended in late October, he managed to get an extension of three months by cajoling the Leadership Council. Hikmatyar unleashed another deadly round of shells and mortars on Kabul. Unbowed, Rabbani got a packed jirga (assembly) of elders in December to extend his tenure by a further two years. The subsequent fighting reduced the western and southern suburbs of the capital to rubble.

The sectarian fighting between the pro-Riyadh (Sunni) Islamic Alliance of Sayyaf and the pro-Tehran Wahadat fighters added another dimension to the ongoing conflict between the partisans of Hikmatyar and Masoud. Dostum remained neutral until the warring factions agreed a truce to replenish their ammunition in late December. He then attacked the Tajik fighters in central Kabul. Hikmatyar joined him. After a week-long non-stop bombing of Kabul in January 1993, intense fighting continued intermittently for two more months. Half of the city's residents lost their homes. When Rabbani refused to step down on 28 June 1994 in accordance with the agreement brokered by the Pakistani government, the civil war intensified. Rabbani's Tajik fighters routed Hikmatyar's partisans in south-eastern Kabul and snatched Kabul airport from Dostum's militia.

None of the regional countries or the UN had any success in ending the violence. The Afghan factions, originally fostered by foreign powers, had become autonomous. At the UN, Russia and the US were content to see Afghans continue their internecine violence since they visualized, correctly, that a stable Islamic Afghanistan would actively aid Islamist forces in Tajikistan and elsewhere in Central Asia and damage their own regional interests. Little wonder that after 1990 the UN Security Council did not debate the situation in Afghanistan for six years.

THE BIRTH OF THE TALIBAN

It was in this vacuum that many Pushtun mullahs in southern Afghanistan, unattached to the warring factions, held conclaves to end the violence. Their aim was shared by Pakistan, keen to purchase much-needed raw cotton from Turkmenistan and Uzbekistan for its textile mills. After several sessions they agreed a three-point programme: restoration of peace, disarming of civilians, and a total application of the Sharia. Long before this development, the term *Taliban* – plural of *Talib* (Arabic, 'knowledge-seeker'; 'student') – had been applied generically to those clerics who were experts on the Sharia and dispensed Islamic justice in the south.

In October 1994, about forty-five clerics and tribal leaders meeting in the white mosque in the village of Sangisar, the base of Mullah Muhammad Omar, decided to establish the Taliban movement with Mullah Omar as its emir, or commander-ruler. Every attendee swore on the Quran to stand by him and fight corruption and vice on earth. 'We took up arms to achieve the [real] aims of the Afghan jihad and save our people from further suffering at the hands of the so called Mujahedin,' Mullah Omar later explained.[5]

As a commander in the Quetta-based Islamic Revolutionary Movement, Mullah Omar, a Pushtun, had been trained by Brigadier Sultan Amir Tarar (aka Colonel Imam) of Pakistan's ISI.[6] A graduate of the Pakistan Military Academy, Tarar underwent training in guerrilla warfare at the US Special Forces School at Fort Bragg, North Carolina, and obtained the status of a Green Beret in 1976. During the anti-Soviet jihad he ran a network of CIA-funded training camps in FATA and Baluchistan. As a result of Mullah Omar's participation in the anti-Marxist jihad, he suffered injuries four times, including when a rocket exploded near him, blinding him in the right eye. Born in the Hotak tribe of the Ghilzai tribal confederation to a landless peasant in Nodeh, a village near Kandahar, he studied at a madrasa in the city. Following his father's death in the mid-1980s, he became the sole breadwinner. He settled in Sangisar in Kandahar province as the local mullah and opened a madrasa – an enterprise that did not deter him from engaging in guerrilla actions against the Marxist government. He was noted more for his piety than charisma. Later, he would be remembered for issuing handwritten orders on small pieces of paper, and maintaining a treasury in a tin trunk, filled with local currency, to be subsequently supplemented by another containing US dollar bills. Given his seclusion, and his strict ban on photography and representation of the human body, his appearance became a subject of speculation. During the first three years of the Taliban, he gave only two interviews, both to Rahimullah Yusufzai, a Pushtun Pakistani journalist freelancing for the British Broadcasting Corporation (BBC), in the former governor's residence in Kandahar. Those who saw him described him as a tall, bearded, one-eyed man with a fair complexion and a Grecian nose.

Soon after being elected Taliban leader, Mullah Omar, backed by the local Taliban contingent, delivered summary justice by hanging a commander of the nearby military camp from the barrel of a tank for raping two teenage girls and seizing the camp's arms and ammunition. Later, he intervened in a public fracas between two commanders in Kandahar over an attractive young boy whom they wanted as a homosexual partner – an act deserving capital punishment according to the Sharia – and freed the boy.

THE ISI ADOPTS THE TALIBAN

What gave the Taliban a crucial boost during its infancy was the offer of funds to Mullah Omar by Pakistani truckers whose business depended on unhindered use of the highway from Quetta to Herat in western Afghanistan. They wanted him to clear the highway currently blocked by nearly two hundred barriers erected by local warlords to collect tolls. Leading a force of two hundred Taliban fighters in the late autumn of 1994, Mullah Omar started at the border crossing of Spin Baldak, where Hikmatyar's Hizb-e Islami had its garrison. Aided by the Pakistani ISI, Omar overran the garrison and seized eighteen thousand Kalashnikovs, dozens of artillery guns, ammunition, and many military vehicles.

Then, as a dry run, the Pakistani government sent a convoy of thirty trucks carrying medicine as well as ISI operatives. When it reached the outskirts of Kandahar, a local warlord, Mansour Achakzai, stopped it. The ISI stepped in and neutralized the most important warlord in Kandahar with a hefty bribe. It then approached Mullah Omar, who agreed to help. As his heavily armed militia appeared on the horizon, Achakzai's men fled, assuming them to be Pakistani soldiers. This eased the way for the Taliban to capture the country's second largest city and its airport. The Taliban acquired half a dozen Soviet MiG-21 fighters and scores of tanks and armoured vehicles – not to mention an abundant store of small arms. They removed all roadblocks to Herat, and introduced their own one-toll system.

With Afghan madrasa students in Afghanistan and Pakistan joining in droves, the size of the Taliban's militia rose to twelve thousand. The Taliban became a serious player, politically and economically.

Mullah Omar disarmed civilians and irregular militias and imposed his fanatically puritanical version of the Sharia under the title of 'promoting virtue and preventing vice', derived from the Quranic verse:

> Let their be one community [*umma*] of you, calling to good,
> and bidding to honour, and forbidding dishonour;
> those are the successful ones (3:100).

He required women to wear a burqa, and men to don salwar kameez and turban, and to grow a beard. He banned nail polish, lipstick, and make-up for women. He closed all girls' schools and forbade women from working outside the home. His blanket ban on music and television resulted in the destruction of audio and video tapes as well as television sets. The reason for prohibiting music, singing, and dancing was that they were likely to arouse lust and lead to fornication, thus undermining marital fidelity and stable family structure, the foundations of a truly Islamic social order.

Mullah Omar also prohibited such leisure activities as chess, football, kite flying, and pigeon racing. The reason for banning kite flying and pigeon racing was that they were done from flat roofs, which enabled boys and men to look into the women's quarters of neighbouring houses. To prevent idolatry, he ordered the tearing up of all pictures and portraits, and prohibited photography. He outlawed gambling and the charging of interest on loans. He prescribed compulsory prayer, and banned all traffic during prayer times. These edicts were to be enforced by the Department of Propagating Virtue and Preventing Vice.

Over the next three months the Taliban captured province after province, often by bribing local warlords with funds supplied first by the Pakistani ISI and later by the Saudi intelligence agency run by Prince Turki. By opening up blocked roads, they helped lower food prices and gained popularity. By disarming all irregular militias, summarily punishing corrupt officials and warlords, and restoring law and order, the Taliban expanded their popular base among a people who had grown weary of incessant violence and graft. In February 1995, the Taliban captured Charasayab, the headquarters of Hikmatyar, forcing him to relocate to Sarobi to the east of Kabul. But their advance further north was stopped by the heavy air and artillery bombardment by Masoud's Tajik forces. The Taliban lost the momentum that had so far gained them a third of Afghanistan.

With the internecine war among the erstwhile Mujahedin factions entering its fourth year in 1996, Saudi Arabia felt frustrated. But after the Taliban seized Herat from the pro-Tehran general Ismail Khan, a Tajik, who belonged to Rabbani's Jamiat-e Islami, Prince Turki formed an alliance with Mullah Omar. This led Tehran to increase its assistance to Rabbani, and help him to form a ten-member anti-Taliban committee, which included not only Khalili but also Hikmatyar and Dostum.

While maintaining its siege of Kabul from the south, the Taliban consolidated their political-religious standing. After much deliberation in April 1996, an assembly of 1,200 Sunni clerics and tribal leaders from all over Afghanistan, except the north, meeting in Kandahar decided to accept Mullah Omar as the *Emir al Muminin* (Arabic, 'Commander of the Faithful'). They collectively swore their fealty to him by repeatedly shouting 'Emir al Muminin!' as Mullah Omar presented himself on the roof of a tall building, covered in the *Khirqa* (Arabic, literally, 'used cloth'; figuratively, 'cloak') of the Prophet Muhammad – brought to Kandahar in 1768. By covering himself in the Prophet's mantle, he assumed the right to lead not just all Afghans but all Muslims.[7]

To counter Iran's assistance, Islamabad increased its support for the Taliban. It had already repaired the power and transport infrastructure in the south. Besides maintaining its steady supply of food, fuel, and ammunition to the Taliban, it improved Kandahar's airport, furnished the Taliban with a telephone and wireless network, and provided military and intelligence personnel to direct its military activities. It also provided the Taliban with officers to act as their military planners. Riyadh too was generous with fuel and cash, as well as pickup trucks used extensively in fighting.[8]

Unknown to the world at large, Taliban leaders secretly discussed with the visiting Prince Turki the ISI plan to capture Kabul before winter. After seizing the surrounding areas of Kabul, two mobile columns of Taliban militia, packed into Toyota pickup trucks, converged on the capital from the east and the south as another column rushed north to cut off the Bagram military air base from the city. At nightfall on 26 September, the Taliban forces drove into Kabul a few hours after Masoud had ordered an evacuation, taking most of the artillery and tanks with him to the north. President Rabbani offered to take Najibullah with him to the north. But Najibullah rejected the gesture, seeing in it a betrayal of his Pushtun ethnicity. So, when push came to shove, the diehard Marxist fell back on his ethnicity, providing an outstanding example of ethnic identity trumping all others.

'Every building along the road to the Afghan capital [from Jalalabad] bears the scars of heavy fighting,' reported David Loyn from the road leading to the capital. 'Lorry containers are used as warehouses; shops and houses lie burst open by shell fire on the sand. It is like an archaeological site layered with the evidence of nearly two decades of war. Mounds of shell cases lie at the side of the road, but the tanks which fired them have gone.'[9] Unlike the previous takeover of Kabul by the Afghan Mujahedin, which was accompanied by plundering by the victorious soldiers, this time there was no looting or breakdown of law and order.

The lightning speed with which the Taliban captured Kabul dazed not just them and their domestic enemies but also the neighbouring states – except Pakistan. For an organization that had barely registered on the political radar of Afghanistan two years earlier, this was a dazzling achievement. Nobody could have guessed then that history would repeat itself in reverse five years hence, with the Taliban fleeing overnight from Kabul.

THE TALIBAN IN POWER

Around 1 a.m. on 27 September, a special Taliban unit broke into the UN compound in Kabul and seized Muhammad Najibullah and his brother Shahpur Ahmadzai. After castrating Najibullah and dragging him behind a jeep a few times around the nearby presidential palace, the Taliban militia shot him in the head. At first light they hung his blood-soaked corpse from a traffic control post just outside the palace in Ariana Square, the site of several public rallies he had addressed as president. They hung his murdered brother by his side. The Taliban passed death sentences on Dostum, Rabbani, and Masoud but not Hikmatyar, a fellow Pushtun, in yet another show of ethnic solidarity.

Operating from Kandahar, Mullah Omar appointed a six-man Shura Council, headed by Mullah Muhammad Rabbani. A Pushtun from the Uruzgan province, and no relative of President Rabbani, Mullah Rabbani became prime minister of the interim government.[10]

On 28 September, Radio Shariat (a variant of Sharia) – the

renamed Radio Kabul – broadcast the imposition of puritanical decrees that the Taliban had implemented elsewhere under their newly established Department of Propagating Virtue and Preventing Vice. Further decrees followed. Displaying photos of animals or humans was forbidden. All non-Muslims – that is, Hindus, Sikhs, and Jews – must wear something yellow, and indicate their abode by flying a yellow flag.[11] The ban on high heels for women was later accompanied by the edict 'Women are duty-bound to behave with dignity, to walk calmly and refrain from hitting their shoes on the ground, which makes noise.' These social injunctions were an amalgam of an extremist interpretation of the Hanbali school of Sunni Islam and Wahhabi practices. Most Sunni Afghans, however, belonged to the Hanafi school.

By disarming civilians and non-Taliban militias, the new regime brought peace and tranquility to Kabul, where some fifty thousand people had died in the 1992–96 civil conflict. This consideration weighed so heavily on most Afghans that many non-Taliban politicians, including Hamid Karzai, who had briefly served as deputy foreign minister in the Burhanuddin Rabbani government, backed the fanatical movement.

The Taliban's dramatic triumph alarmed Iran as well as Russia, the Central Asian republics, and India. In contrast, Pakistan was quietly jubilant for having installed its protégé in Kabul. This reaction was to be expected. But what was totally unexpected was Washington's reaction. Instead of raising alarm at the victory of the most diehard Islamic fundamentalist party, the US State Department spokesman said there was 'nothing objectionable' about the domestic policies pursued by the Taliban.[12]

Ironically, while the ruling Iranian clerics condemned especially the Taliban's ban on women's education, describing it as contrary to the Quranic verse that enjoins upon all believers – male and female – to acquire knowledge, the Clinton administration remained silent on the subject for several weeks while its envoy dispatched to Kabul conferred with the Taliban regime.

The Taliban were impervious to what Iran in particular, or the international community in general, thought of them. What mattered to them was how their policies were viewed by their most active constituency – young Afghan males, those who had grown up in refugee camps in Pakistan, where life was even more conservative than in Afghan villages, and who had flocked to fight for the ultra-orthodox movement.

Lacking a well-defined Afghan policy of its own in the post-Najibullah period, the White House allowed itself to be led by Pakistan. Islamabad reassured the Clinton administration, which was keen to curb the use of hard drugs in America, that the Taliban government would control firmly the growing of poppies, the source of heroin. With Turkey, Iran, and Pakistan enforcing strict drug control laws during 1972–80, war-torn Afghanistan had become a leading producer of opium. Its output increased fivefold to 500 tonnes during 1979–86, about a third of global production. The figure rose to 1,200 tonnes at the time of the Soviet withdrawal in 1989, and then peaked at 3,200 tonnes in 1994, amounting to over half of the world total.[13] By the mid-1990s, the opium/heroin trade had become such an integral part of the economies of Afghanistan and Pakistan that any hope of the Taliban curtailing it was fanciful.

Pakistan stressed the Taliban's anti-Russian disposition. That went down well in Washington, bent on countering Moscow's renewed attempts to regain influence in Afghanistan. Equally, the Taliban's anti-Iran stance pleased the US. In contrast, the Taliban's triumph alarmed the five Central Asian republics. Their leaders met in the Kazakh capital of Alma Ata on 4–5 October to review the development. The Uzbek president, Islam Karimov, urged his counterparts to strengthen Dostum's Northern Alliance government, which controlled six provinces. He provided it with military and economic aid.

In short, the emergence of the Taliban as the predominant force in Afghanistan divided the region into two camps: Pakistan and Saudi Arabia on one side; Iran, Central Asia, Russia, and India on the other. Today, while Pakistan's assistance to the reborn Taliban continues unabated, Saudi Arabia has made unsuccessful attempts to mediate between the Taliban and America. India, Central Asia, and Russia remain resolutely opposed to the Taliban, while Iran tries to juggle its position between backing Afghan president Hamid Karzai, stiffly opposing the US, and maintaining clandestine contacts with Taliban leaders.

Once the Taliban had consolidated its position in Kabul, Mullah Omar instructed Prime Minister Rabbani to talk to bin Laden who, after arriving in Jalalabad in May 1996, had moved to the Tora Bora cave complex near the Pakistani border. It was only after several meetings with Taliban envoys, during which he praised the Taliban's achievements and took an oath of allegiance to Mullah Omar, that bin Laden received the protection of the regime. The ISI played a crucial, covert role in bringing about this alliance.

Osama bin Laden took up residence at the airport near Kandahar. He and Mullah Omar became close friends. Engaging in night-long conversations, they came to share political and religious views, with Mullah Omar gradually turning against America and the West, and losing interest in gaining their recognition of his regime. By late 1997, pressure from the influential feminist lobby in Washington had precluded any prospect of US diplomatic recognition of the Taliban regime. Meanwhile, bin Laden had started to lend the services of his seasoned Afghan Arab fighters and his vehicles to the Taliban during their campaigns to extend their realm, and was generous in his cash contributions.

Having brought 70 per cent of the country under his jurisdiction by early 1997, Mullah Omar resolved to expel the anti-Taliban forces from the rest of Afghanistan. He overcame resistance from Mazar-e Sharif, the opposition's main base where President Rabbani had joined Dostum, by bribing commanders to defect. Rabbani fled to Tajikistan. This provided a rationale to Pakistan to recognize the Taliban regime formally on 26 May 1997. Saudi Arabia and the United Arab Emirates followed.

Installing a regime in Kabul administered by an Afghan organization fostered and strengthened by the ISI was the most outstanding foreign-policy achievement of Pakistan. For once, its politicians, generals, and religious leaders were unanimous in applauding the accomplishment.

At the same time, winning this trophy reminded them all of their failure in the neighbouring, Muslim-majority Kashmir. After half a century of assorted efforts – from repeated appeals to the international community to instigating and sustaining guerrilla warfare, their latest strategy, with the active cooperation of Al Qaida – nearly two-thirds of the state of Jammu and Kashmir remained outside the control of Pakistan. But then, those who delve deep into Kashmir's history discover that its overwhelmingly Muslim Kashmir Valley has inherited a substantial body of Hindu legends and holy sites.

5

TARGET KASHMIR

THE NAMES OF places, mountains, and caves as well as the locations of the revered shrines of Hindus and Muslims in Jammu and Kashmir – Kashmir for short – are enlightening. Composed of two Sanskrit words, Srinagar, the name of the summer capital of the state, means 'City of Abundance'. The town of Anantnag – literally, 'Endless Serpent' – is the place where Lord Shiva, journeying to the Amarnath Cave, discarded all his possessions, including the guardian snakes enveloping his body. Hari Parbhat, the Sanskrit name of a mountain, translates as 'Mountain of God'.

On the southern slope of Hari Parbhat stand the shrines of two eminent Muslim religious leaders, and on its western slope the Hindu temple of Parvati, the consort of Lord Shiva. Equally striking is the name of the 1,100-foot (350 m) high hill above Srinagar – Takht-e-Suleiman (Persian, 'Throne of Suleiman') – at whose peak stands the Shankaracharya Temple, dating back to 371 BC. Inside this temple is an inscription in Persian chiselled on the orders of Mughal emperor Shah Jahan (r. 1628–58). This is a graphical illustration of the mutual tolerance and respect shown by Muslim and Hindu luminaries towards their respective religions.

The Hazratbal (Kashmiri, 'Majestic Place') Mosque, containing a hair from Prophet Muhammad's beard, is pre-eminent among the

Muslim holy places in Srinagar. There is a legend attached to it. The hair, originating in Medina, the burial place of Muhammad, was brought to the southern Indian city of Bijapur in 1635 by Sayyid Abdullah, a descendant of the Prophet. Lacking sufficient resources to safeguard the relic, he sold it to a visiting Kashmiri businessman, Nouruddin Eshai. After Eshai's death, his daughter, Inayat Begum, set up the shrine for the holy relic.

Since antiquity, the Kashmir Valley's stunning scenic beauty and numerous caves have attracted those seeking enlightenment through contemplation and meditation. Its snow-capped mountains, streams of pure water, and caves became part of the Hindu mythology. One such cave, named Amarnath (Sanskrit, 'Immortal Lord'), revealed three ice stalagmites. In Hindu mythology, the largest one is attributed to Lord Shiva, the medium-sized to his consort Parvati, and the smallest to their son, Ganesha. It was in this cave, so goes the legend, that Lord Shiva explained to Parvati the sexual secret of life. Half a million Hindu devotees now visit the cave annually.

Myths such as this survived the arrival and rise of monotheistic Islam in the Kashmir Valley. The principal reason is that it was a Sufi thinker, Mir Sayyid Ali Hamadani (1314–84), who became the foremost proselytizer for Islam, turning the Valley into an overwhelmingly Muslim area. His liberal message of respecting other religions was reiterated by Zainuddin Shah as well as Nouruddin Rishi, who came under the influence of Lalleshwari, born a Brahmin, and established the Rishi Order of Sufism in the Valley.[1]

Nouruddin's influence remained undiminished until the late 1980s, when the recently triumphant jihadists in Afghanistan and Pakistan directed their fervent attention to the Indian-administered Kashmir, which includes the populous Valley.

THE ROCKY POLITICS OF INDIAN KASHMIR

Foremost among those who embarked on liberating Indian Kashmir from the Delhi government were Al Qaida, the Lashkar-e Taiba, a creature of Pakistan's Inter-Services Intelligence (ISI) directorate, and Jamaat-e Islami (JeI), the oldest Islamist party in Pakistan. Their timing was propitious.

The state assembly election of March 1987 was rigged massively in favour of the alliance of the local National Conference of Farooq Abdullah and the Indian National Congress – Congress party for short – forged at the behest of the Delhi government. The opposition Muslim United Front, an alliance led by the Jammu and Kashmir wing of the JeI, won only four of the forty-four seats it contested, with the leading figures opposing India's rule faring unexpectedly badly. The police expelled their agents from the premises before the vote count. 'The losing candidates were declared winners,' admitted Khem Lata Wukhloo, a Congress party leader, several years later. 'The electoral rigging shook the ordinary people's faith in the elections and the democratic process.'[2]

What drove the Central government to this extremity was the unpopularity of Farooq Abdullah. A prematurely bald, rubber-faced, rotund man, he trained as a doctor first in India and then in Britain, where he married Molly, a nurse. He returned briefly to Kashmir in 1976 to assist his father, Shaikh Muhammad Abdullah, in the election campaign. Shaikh Abdullah died six years later in office. With the memory of his demise still fresh in the public mind, the National Conference, now led by his son, won forty-six seats out of seventy-six in 1983.

But when Farooq Abdullah fell out with India's ruling Congress party and Prime Minister Indira Gandhi, his government was dismissed by Delhi in 1984. After an interregnum of two years, a fresh alliance was forged between his National Conference and the Congress party, and he was sworn in as the state's chief minister. Heading the cabinet after the 1987 poll, he served until 1990 when, against a backdrop of escalating separatist insurgency, his government was again dismissed and direct rule by Delhi imposed.

India blamed Pakistan for escalating armed Islamist insurgency. Islamabad denied the charge.

THE KASHMIR DISPUTE: IN THE SHADOW OF SHAIKH ABDULLAH

Since 1947, when British India was partitioned into independent Muslim-majority Pakistan and Hindu-majority India, the princely state of Jammu and Kashmir has been a bone of contention between the two neighbours. Established in 1901 within its present (legal) boundaries, Jammu and Kashmir enjoyed local autonomy under British rule. Its population was 77 per cent Muslim, but its ruler Hindu. In 1947, Maharaja Hari Singh Dogra was the monarch. With his princely state sharing common borders with both Pakistan and India, he could choose to join either. To pre-empt his options, the predominantly Muslim inhabitants of the Poonch–Mirpur region established an independent government and sought help from contiguous Pakistan to liberate the rest of the state.

On 21 October 1947, a 5,000-strong force of Afridi and Mehsud tribes from Tirah and Waziristan in Pakistan's Federally Administered Tribal Agencies (FATA) began marching towards Kashmir. It crossed the international boundary three days later and overpowered the local troops. Hari Singh fled from Srinagar to Jammu in the south. Treating this to be one of the traditional raids in FATA, the poorly disciplined tribal forces resorted to plundering and rape, thereby slowing their advance.[3]

On 25 October, the maharaja, in consultation with Shaikh Abdullah, leader of the secular National Conference, acceded to India, with the provision of ceding authority to Delhi only in defence, foreign affairs, finance, and communications. Later, Article 370 of the Indian constitution, promulgated in January 1950, would specify that the Indian parliament would need the state government's agreement to apply laws in other administrative areas of the territory. As a result, non-Kashmiri Indian citizens were not allowed to settle permanently in Kashmir or purchase immovable property there.

While accepting Hari Singh's Instrument of Accession on 27 October, India's Governor General, Lord Mountbatten, wrote: 'In consistence with their [the Defence Committee's] policy that in the case of any State where the issue of accession has been the subject of dispute, the question of accession should be decided in accordance with the wishes of the people of the State, it is my Government's wish that, as soon as law and order have been restored in Kashmir and its soil cleared of the invader, the question of the State's accession should be settled by a reference to the people.'[4]

India requisitioned all private planes to fly its soldiers to Srinagar post-haste. (It was not until around 1957, when the 2-mile [3.2 km]-long Banihal Tunnel was completed, that Kashmir was linked to the rest of the Republic of India by road.) The Indian troops succeeded in blocking the attacking tribals gathered near the city's airport. On 30 October, forty-two-year-old Shaikh Abdullah became head of the emergency government.

Due to the death of his father soon after his birth in a village near Srinagar, Muhammad Abdullah had grown up in poverty. Yet he managed to obtain a master's degree in science from Aligarh Muslim University in northern India. He was a gangling young man, 6 feet 4 inches (1.93 m) tall, oval-faced, with a sharp, straight nose and a middle-distance gaze. Back in Srinagar he was one of the founders of the Muslim Conference in 1932. After its demand for democratic rights for citizens was ignored by the autocratic maharaja, he came under the influence of the secular Jawaharlal Nehru – a descendant of Kashmiri Brahmins born in the northern Indian city of Allahabad and a future prime minister of India. During 1937–39, Shaikh Abdullah lobbied, successfully, to get the Muslim Conference to open its membership to all communities and to change its name to the National Conference.[5] The National Conference's demand for voting rights landed Shaikh Abdullah in jail in 1946. After his release in September 1947, he declared: 'We have a religion in common with [Muhammad Ali] Jinnah [of Pakistan] but a dream in common with Nehru.'[6] From then on, whether in office or prison, he would dominate the state's politics until his death.

Shaikh Abdullah's rise to power in October 1947 did not end the fighting. In January, India lodged a complaint with the United

Nations Security Council that Pakistan had armed and abetted its tribals from FATA to attack Kashmir, and that it should vacate the gains of its aggression. It did so under Chapter VI of the UN Charter (Pacific Settlement of Disputes), Article 35. Along with the preceding article, this authorizes the Security Council to investigate any dispute in order to determine if it was 'likely to endanger international peace and security'. Pakistan responded by filing a comprehensive counter-complaint.

Having listened to both sides, the Security Council passed resolution 47 on 21 April 1948. This stated that, to ensure the impartiality of the plebiscite on the state's future, Pakistan must withdraw all tribesmen and nationals who had entered the region to fight, and that India should leave only enough troops in place to maintain civil order. Since it was passed under Chapter VI, it was non-binding and lacked mandatory implementation.[7] Only resolutions passed under Chapter VII require mandatory implementation.

Ignoring the Security Council resolution, Pakistan introduced regular troops into Kashmir. The combat continued until January 1949, when a UN-brokered truce came into effect, leaving Pakistan with 37 per cent of the territory – later divided into the Northern Areas, renamed Giligit–Baltistan, and Azad Kashmir (Free Kashmir), with its capital at Muzaffarabad. To monitor the ceasefire line, the Security Council appointed the UN Military Observer Group in India and Pakistan.

Crucially, India retained control of the 85-mile (136 km)-long and 20-mile (32 km)-wide Kashmir Valley which lies between the Pir Panjal and Karakoram mountain ranges of the Himalayas. Guarded by snow-capped peaks, carpeted with verdant forests, fir and pine trees, and wild flowers of riotous colours in spring, and irrigated by the Jhelum River and its tributaries, it has been described by poets and others as 'Paradise on Earth'.

In 1951, Hari Singh Dogra abdicated in favour of his son, Karan Singh Dogra, while Shaikh Abdullah remained the state's chief executive. Article 370 in the secular Indian constitution accorded

Kashmir the right to have its own constitution. The state's popularly elected Constituent Assembly began drafting it. When the staunchly pro-Indian group in the assembly insisted on Delhi's right to impose Central rule in certain circumstances, open division surfaced. Tensions mounted when Shaikh Abdullah gave a speech suggesting the possibility of an independent Kashmir. Karan Singh ordered his arrest in August 1953 and kept him imprisoned for eleven years, with a brief break in 1958.

When Pakistan signed a Mutual Security Pact with Washington in 1954, the Kashmir issue got sucked into Cold War politics. The Soviet Union described Kashmir as 'an integral part' of India. In 1957, when the Kashmir issue was raised at the Security Council, Moscow vetoed the debate, describing it as India's internal problem.

Delhi offered a three-point rationale for refusing to hold a plebiscite. First, US military aid to Pakistan altered the situation. Second, if Kashmiri Muslims opted for Pakistan, that would trigger a Hindu backlash and jeopardize the lives of Indian Muslims. Third, the integration of Kashmir was essential to India's territorial integrity as a whole. Its secession would encourage other states to follow its example. Pakistanis as well as jihadists rejected such reasoning . . . They argued that it was puerile to say that India with its 160 million Muslims living outside Kashmir must retain Kashmir with its five million Muslims in order to maintain its secular image.

The Kashmiri constitution was promulgated in 1956. The elections held in 1957 and 1962, held under the premiership of Bakshi Ghulam Muhammad, were rigged. The successors to Shaikh Abdullah, handpicked by Delhi, lacked popularity. The Indian government shored them up by bribing local politicians and other public figures. In October 1964 Muhammad was replaced by Khwaja Shamsuddin.

Two months later, the disaffection that had been building up since Shaikh Abdullah's arrest ten years earlier took the form of huge demonstrations in the Kashmir Valley after the disappearance of the hair of the Prophet Muhammad's beard from Srinagar's Hazratbal shrine. Protest on such a vast scale shook Indian prime minister

Nehru. Though the missing relic was soon recovered, popular agitation did not subside even after Shamsuddin stepped down in favour of Ghulam Muhammad Sadiq in February 1964. Nehru tried to pacify the protest by releasing Shaikh Abdullah in April. At his behest, the Kashmiri leader travelled to Pakistan to arrange a meeting between President General Muhammad Ayub Khan and Nehru. But Nehru died soon after.

In November the Indian government extended to Kashmir the constitutional provision which allows it to impose presidential rule in a state. Shaikh Abdullah protested, demanded a plebiscite to decide the state's future, and formed the Plebiscite Front.

In March 1965, to ingratiate himself with Delhi, Sadiq had the legislative assembly amend the state constitution and alter the title of head of state from *sadar-i-riyasat* (Urdu, 'president of province') to governor, and prime minister to chief minister, thus removing the constitutional distinction between Jammu and Kashmir and other Indian states. At that time Shaikh Abdullah was on a foreign trip – primarily to perform the hajj pilgrimage in Mecca – during which he met Prime Minister Zhou Enlai of China – then hostile to India – in Cairo. On his return home in May, he was arrested. This led to massive demonstrations in the Kashmir Valley.

Pakistan saw a window of opportunity to alter the status quo.

THE INDIA–PAKISTAN WAR, 1965

Goaded by his hawkish generals, relying on the intelligence reports that Kashmiri Muslims would welcome Pakistani troops as liberators, and confident that Pakistan-trained and armed Kashmiri fighters called Mujahideen Companies would defend Pakistani positions along the ceasefire line, Ayub Khan mounted Operation Grand Slam on 1 September 1965. The goal was to capture India-held Kashmir. But due to their poor operational strategy, the Pakistani forces failed to seize the strategic road linking Jammu with the Kashmir Valley. India responded by staging a three-pronged attack along Pakistan's (undisputed) international boundary, forcing its military high command to ease the pressure on the Kashmir front.

Consequently, neither side penetrated more than 8 km (5 miles) into the enemy territory. The United States suspended military supplies to both sides, preventing the repairs of US-made military hardware. So Pakistan and India accepted the UN-brokered ceasefire on 24 September.

Delhi's political response to the Pakistani aggression was to integrate Kashmir further into the Indian Union – the official term for the Central government. National Conference leaders dissolved the organization and resurrected it as the state unit of the Congress party.

The 1967 state election was rigged. Following the invalidation of the nomination papers of the pro-independence or pro-Pakistani candidates, the Congress party won twenty-one of the fifty-four seats unopposed. Sadiq continued as the chief minister until his death in December 1971 when India and Pakistan were engaged in war in the eastern and western wings of Pakistan. That conflict resulted in the secession of Pakistan's eastern wing and the establishment of the sovereign state of Bangladesh. This disheartened the anti-India opposition in Kashmir. Despite this, the March 1972 poll was marred by manipulation at the behest of Delhi.

In their meeting in the Indian city of Shimla in July, Pakistan's president, Zulfikar Ali Bhutto, and India's prime minister, Indira Gandhi, agreed that the two countries should settle their differences by peaceful means through 'bilateral negotiations'. This ruled out any role for the UN in resolving the dispute. They also decided to call the ceasefire line in Jammu and Kashmir the Line of Control (LoC), thus letting Delhi take the view that 'actual control' was now synonymous with 'legal possession'.

Ruminating on the 1971 Bangladesh War, Shaikh Abdullah concluded that it was better to put an end to the politics of confrontation, which had the potential to cause further break-ups in Pakistan and India, and to pursue reconciliation. After his release from detention in late 1972, he negotiated a deal with Indira Gandhi in 1974. She reiterated that relations between the Central government and Kashmir would remain within the ambit of Article 370 of the constitution. In return, Shaikh Abdullah dropped his demand for a plebiscite and settled instead for genuine self-rule by a government elected in free and fair elections. Kashmir's Congress chief minister, Syed Mir Qasim resigned.

Shaikh Abdullah became the chief minister in February 1975 after disbanding the Plebiscite Front and reviving the National Conference. In a rare fair election in 1977, his National Conference won forty-seven of the seventy-six seats, with a voter turnout of 68 per cent – a welcome change.

Since Shaikh Abdullah had spent eighteen years in prison or under house arrest, his standing among Kashmiri Muslims was high. Yet he found it expedient to have the state legislature pass the draconian Jammu and Kashmir Public Safety Act in 1978. It authorized the government to detain people for up to two years without charge to prevent them from threatening the 'security of the state and the maintenance of public order'. During Shaikh Abdullah's second term in office, the Kashmir Valley experienced a boom in tourism, an important source of income for the inhabitants. He also had the state constitution altered to extend the state assembly's term from five to six years.

The succession of his son, Farooq, as the chief minister, following another free and fair poll in 1983, implied stability in the state. Yet a radical change was in the offing. A whole new generation had grown up since Shaikh Abdullah's arrest in 1953. Due to the great leap in literacy and higher education, the number of high-school and university graduates had multiplied, but the economy had not developed fast enough to provide them all with jobs. Of the 5,000 qualified engineers, 3,000 were jobless, forming 30 per cent of the 10,000 unemployed university graduates. And the number of jobless high-school graduates was four to five times the figure for their university counterparts.[8]

Little wonder that most young Kashmiri Muslims felt alienated from Indian rule. 'We [Kashmiri Muslims] did not relate to the symbols of Indian nationalism – the flag, the national anthem, the cricket team,' noted Basharat Peer, an Indian Kashmiri writer. 'We followed every cricket match India and Pakistan played but we never cheered for the Indian team.'[9]

At the behest of Delhi, Governor Jagmohan (aka Jagmohan Malhotra) encouraged defections from the National Conference. Within a year of his taking office in 1983, Farooq Abdullah's government fell. When its successor failed to stem communal rioting in the state, the governor dismissed the cabinet in March 1986. The instability in the state's governance was a symptom of a much deeper malaise: the failure of the authorities in Srinagar and Delhi to accommodate the aspirations of the generation of Kashmiri Muslims who had grown up after partition.

1987: A TURNING POINT

Nineteen eighty-seven proved to be a turning point not only for Indian Kashmir and India but also for Pakistan and Afghanistan. Once Soviet troops started withdrawing from Afghanistan in August, Pakistan's ISI decided to focus on expelling the Indian forces from Kashmir. This illustrated the interconnectedness of Afghanistan, Pakistan and India. When Islamabad was accused of backing terrorists in Kashmir, it argued that it was doing nothing more than offering 'moral and diplomatic' back-up to the indigenous movement of armed resistance in Kashmir.

The flagrant poll-rigging in March 1987, awarding an incredible sixty-three seats out of seventy-six to the National Conference–Congress party alliance, deeply disillusioned many. 'Kashmiri youths participated in the 1987 elections with great enthusiasm and seriousness and after due thought,' said Professor Abdul Ghani Bhat, a prominent oppositionist. 'But the poll results fired them with anger. They decided to fight violence with violence.'[10] The resulting tension adversely affected the annual flow of tourists from the rest of India, which in the preceding years had risen to almost a million – a remarkable figure for the Kashmir Valley, then home to fewer than four million people.

Among other things the egregious poll-rigging paved the way for the Jammu and Kashmir Liberation Front (JKLF) – founded by Amanullah Shah, an Indian Kashmiri expatriate, in the British city of Birmingham in 1977 – to open branches in the Valley. A nationalist, secular organization, it sought independence for the state from both India and Pakistan. Working closely with its offshoot in Muzaffarabad in Azad Kashmir, it resorted to armed struggle. Soon, Muzaffarabad would become the leading centre for coordinating the training of anti-India and pro-Pakistan militant groups.

With the loss in 1971 of its eastern wing, containing a substantial Hindu minority, the rest of Pakistan became more cohesive religiously. The usurpation of state power by Muhammad Zia ul Haq in 1977, followed by Pakistan's headlong involvement in fostering and intensifying anti-Soviet jihad in Afghanistan, impacted on Islamabad's policy on India-held Kashmir.

What had so far been viewed by the contesting parties as a territorial dispute was now placed in the wider ideological context of Islamism by Zia ul Haq. By so doing, he forged a link between the Kashmir dispute and his Islamization of Pakistan, and started using Islam as a powerful tool to extend Islamabad's influence beyond Pakistan's borders. In turn this prepared the ground for non-governmental bodies in Pakistan to wage jihad against India.

Zia ul Haq had a symbiotic relationship with the country's oldest Islamist party, the Jamaat-e Islami. In 1986, he allocated 3 square miles of land to the Markaz ud Daawa wal Irshad (Arabic, 'Centre for Islamic Call and Guidance'), founded a year earlier by three young acolytes of Osama bin Laden, including Hafiz Muhammad Saeed, at Muridke 20 miles (32 km) north-west of Lahore. Subsequently, funded by affluent Saudis, the Markaz would build a mosque, an educational complex, a farm, and a garments factory to make itself economically independent. It went on to sponsor an armed wing called the Lashkar-e Taiba (LeT).

The LeT arrogated to itself the role normally played by an Islamic state. It argued that, in the absence of such an entity, it would monitor standards of individual behaviour such as paying *zakat* (Islamic tax) and rally individual Muslims to conduct jihad wherever their co-religionists outside Pakistan were being oppressed. Actively backed by the ISI, it focused on Indian-administered Kashmir.[11]

The conditions seemed ripe. On the Indian Republic Day, 26 January 1989, Kashmiris went on a protest strike. The anti-India peaceful protest continued throughout the year, affecting one third of all working days. Between early 1988 and late 1989, many young Kashmiri Muslims crossed over to Pakistan-administered Kashmir and received military training by the armed wing of the Jamaat-e Islami of Jammu and Kashmir (JeI), popularly known as Hizb ul Mujahideen (Arabic, 'Party of Mujahedin'; HuM), as well as the LeT, and other organizations associated with the ISI, which also aided the JKLF. On their return home with arms and ammunition, they trained others clandestinely.

The resulting upsurge in insurgency caught the public imagination throughout India in late 1989. On 8 December, JKLF militants, directed by twenty-one-year-old Yasin Malik, abducted Dr Rubaiya Sayeed, a twenty-three-year-old intern at a women's hospital in Srinagar. Since she was a daughter of Indian home minister Mufti Muhammad Sayeed, a Kashmiri Muslim, her kidnap became the lead story in the Indian media. After highly publicized negotiations, the kidnappers freed her in exchange for five jailed JKLF leaders. On their release, they were greeted by celebrating crowds in Srinagar as heroes. This episode boosted the opposition's morale.

So also did the barbed criticism of the Indian authorities made by a highly respected lawyer. 'It is very likely that Pakistan has provided military training and arms to the militants in Kashmir,' wrote Vithal Mahadeo Tarkunde, an Indian Supreme Court attorney and a founder of the People's Union of Civil Liberties, in the March 1990 issue of the Delhi-based *Radical Humanist* magazine. 'But it is not responsible for the disaffection of the people of the Valley from the government of India. The cause of the Kashmir debacle is the initial denial of the right of self-determination and the subsequent anti-democratic policies pursued by the Indian government.'

Militants now went on the offensive. The number of bomb blasts and assassinations increased. So too did the intimidation of National Conference activists, carried out with the objective of forcing them into retirement and bringing about the collapse of the political process.

In January 1990, the Central government reappointed Jagmohan as governor after an interregnum of six months and imposed direct rule, which would continue for an unprecedented six years. Given Jagmohan's anti-Muslim bias, Delhi made a colossal mistake. On the night of his appointment – 19 January 1990 – the police carried out a house-to-house search in a neighbourhood of Srinagar suspected of being a militant stronghold, and arrested some three hundred men (releasing most of them later without charge). At daybreak, a large, spontaneous assembly of protestors built up. As they crossed the Gawakadal Bridge over the Jhelum River on their way to the administrative buildings, the Central Reserve Police Force (CRPF), opened fired. They killed up to fifty men, and an equal number died by drowning as they jumped into the water. This was to become the first of several massacres. A twenty-four-hour curfew was imposed in Srinagar and other cities in the Valley for a week.

The bloody episode inflamed popular sentiment. The slogan of *Azadi* (Freedom) rang through the Valley. Street walls were splashed with slogans such as 'War till victory' and 'Self-determination is our birthright.' Streets filled with protestors as soon as the curfew was lifted. 'With this [Gawakadal Bridge] incident, militancy entered a new phase,' noted Balraj Puri, a Kashmiri Hindu writer and political activist. 'It was no longer a fight between the militants and the security forces. It gradually assumed the form of a total insurgency of the entire population.'[12]

INDIAN KASHMIR: THE SIEGE WITHIN

The popular anti-India upsurge in the Kashmir Valley elated politicians and the public in Pakistan and Azad Kashmir. They celebrated a 'Solidarity Day' on 5 February.[13] Indian intelligence sources claimed that some ten thousand Kashmiri Muslims had gone to Pakistan for arms training, and that there were forty-six safe houses in Azad Kashmir where militants were given weapons and explosives training.

Indignant, Governor Jagmohan jailed all opposition leaders, making no distinction between those who favoured independence (a majority) and those who advocated accession to Pakistan (a minority). He dissolved the state legislature, the only avenue for debate except the mosque. With all international journalists barred from the Valley, the only reliable source of information which could not be censored was foreign radio news, particularly the BBC's World Service.

On 28 February, as protestors in Srinagar began marching to the Line of Control to submit a memorandum to the UN Military Observer Group, they faced live fire from the security forces. Forty-seven lay dead. That brought one million Kashmiris – an eye-popping figure – onto the streets of the capital. Which in turn led to the loss of further lives. A vengeful Jagmohan ordered the Central Reserve Police Force to shoot at sight.

The protest marches in Srinagar and elsewhere were often headed by men in white shrouds, signifying their readiness to become martyrs, as they sang pro-independence songs. Remarkably, protestors always marched to the Sufi mausoleums nearest to them while onlookers threw flower petals at them as they do at the shrines. By so doing, they showed there was no contradiction between being a tolerant, peaceful Sufi and agitating for the Muslim community's legitimate right to self-determination. Therefore, the later terrorist attacks on prominent Sufi shrines by Sunni jihadists in Pakistan would leave most Kashmiri Muslims indignant and puzzled.

Whether in cities or the countryside, people of different classes and trades came together. Referring to the march in his village of Seer Hamadan of five thousand inhabitants, Basharat Peer wrote:

> The contractor who carried whiskey in a petrol can and the upright lawyer who would wait for passers-by to greet him, the tailor who entertained the idle youth in his shop with tall stories while poking away on his sewing machine and the chemist who would fall asleep behind the counter, the old fox who bragged of his connections with Congress politicians in Delhi, and the unemployed youth who had appointed himself the English-language commentator for the village cricket team's matches, the Salafi revivalist who sold plastic shoes and the Communist basket weaver with a Stalin mustache, all marched together, their voices joining in a resounding cry for freedom.[14]

Delhi rushed army and paramilitary troops to the Valley. When his iron-fist strategy failed to quash the uprising, Jagmohan resigned in May. He was succeeded by Girish Chandra Saxena, a former head of India's foreign intelligence agency, called the Research and Analysis Wing (RAW).

By the summer of 1990, a pattern had become established: armed militants' assaults on specific targets, resulting in reprisals by the security forces, with arrests and cordon and search operations to flush out guerrillas and discover arms and ammunition, leading to strikes called by the militants.

The Indian parliament passed the Armed Forces (Jammu and Kashmir) Special Powers Act, 1990, in July. This authorized the state government to declare Jammu and Kashmir or any part of it a 'disturbed area', allowing the armed forces to shoot any person who was acting in contravention of 'any law' or was in possession of deadly weapons, to arrest without a warrant anyone suspected of having committed an offence, and to enter and search any premises to make such arrests. The act gave the armed forces legal immunity for their actions.[15] In essence, it provided the security forces with carte blanche to do what they wished without worrying about accountability.

Security personnel based themselves not only in cities but also in villages and towns. School buildings were their first choice for setting up their camps. So the anti-India guerrillas resorted to burning down school buildings not yet occupied by the armed forces. The mantra of the Indian security personnel was 'area control'. Having marked out the boundaries of their territory with coils of barbed wire and watchtowers, they protected it against attacks by erecting sandbag bunkers at all doors and windows, manned by dour, moustached soldiers in khaki cradling machine guns. The surrounding roads and streets were patrolled by soldiers in flak jackets and greenish bulletproof helmets and carrying automatic or semi-automatic machine guns.

The dictum of 'area control' required all approaching vehicles to halt 100 yards from the camp and disgorge their passengers, who had to raise their arms as they were shepherded to a bunker to be frisked and have their identity papers checked.

Often, small paramilitary units drove off in the mornings to nearby villages on search-and-arrest missions. Away from the military camps, soldiers at checkpoints, erected at 10- or 15-miles (16 or 24 km) intervals, monitored vehicular traffic. All passengers were required to alight, hold up their identity papers, undergo a body search, and then walk for ten minutes or so to reboard the same vehicle after it had been searched thoroughly while parked far away from the checkpoint.

Hidden by tall trees, foliage, or stalks of wheat or rice, Pakistan-trained guerrillas, equipped by ISI-linked organizations, ambushed military or paramilitary convoys. They also detonated roadside landmines. Their second priority was to create fear among their adversaries. They did so by assassinating pro-India Muslim activists and informers. In an attempt to make the Kashmir Valley 100 per cent Muslim, they killed hundreds of Kashmiri Hindus, often called pandits – a term that, strictly speaking, applies only to Brahmins. This caused an exodus of the Hindus, whose proportion in the population fell from 10 to 3 per cent.

Despite their overwhelming presence in urban and rural areas, the Indian security forces, aware of the intense hostility of the public, were often jittery and trigger-happy. Neither CRPF officers, taught to catch armed criminals, nor Border Security Force (BSF) soldiers, trained to patrol the borders and guard pickets and outposts, had the skills to counter urban terrorism or guerrilla attacks. So their instinct was to pull their triggers at the first sign of trouble, real or imagined.

Frightened by a tyre burst in the capital's densely populated neighbourhood of Chhota Bazaar in June 1991, a patrol of Central Reserve Police Force paramilitaries fired indiscriminately, killing fifty people, including shopkeepers, women, children, and old people. By then the Indian military and paramilitary personnel in the state totalled 150,000. The estimates of the armed militants ranged from 10,000 to 40,000.

The list of those who had been tortured, or had simply 'disappeared', or become victims of extrajudicial executions by the Indian security forces, was lengthening by the week. Torturing suspects became routine. Of the numerous prisons, the one nicknamed 'Papa-2' acquired an odious notoriety. Among its hundreds of inmates was 'Ansar', who described it as a place that 'scars you forever'. 'They took you out to the lawn outside the building,' he told his Kashmiri interviewer years later after getting an assurance that his real name would not be used. 'You were asked to remove all your clothes, even your underwear. They tied you to a long wooden ladder and placed it near a ditch filled with kerosene oil and red chilli powder. They raised the ladder like a seesaw and pushed your head into the ditch. It could go on for an hour, half an hour, depending on their mood.' Other times the torturers would attach the fully clothed suspect to a ladder, then tie his long pants near the ankles and insert mice. 'Or they burnt your arms and legs with cigarette butts and kerosene stoves used for welding,' Ansar continued. 'They burn your flesh till you speak.' He rolled up his right sleeve above the elbow to show an uneven dark-brown patch of flesh.[16]

After being taken to a tin shed glowing with powerful electric lights, 'Hussein' was forcibly undressed and tied to a chair. 'Then they tied copper wire to my arms and gave me electric shocks. I could not even scream. They had stuffed my mouth with a ball of cloth . . . They would suddenly stop, take the cloth off and ask questions. I fainted a few times. They brought me back to my senses and inserted a copper wire into my penis. Then they switched on the electricity.' Subjected to such barbaric treatment, most suspects broke down after two days. 'You cannot bear pain beyond a point. Everybody talks.'[17] It emerged later that the torturers resorted to such abominable acts with most boys and young men. 'We have had hundreds of cases here,' said Shahid, a doctor at the Sher-e-Kashmir Institute of Medical Sciences in Srinagar. 'Those electric shocks led to impotence in many, and many lost their kidneys.'[18] Some of those who talked were hired as part of the Concealed Apprehension Tactics to identify fellow militants.

The brutal ways of the Indian security forces in Kashmir were widely and prominently reported in Pakistan, ruled by a democratically elected government after Zia ul Haq's death in 1988. The switch from dictatorship to democracy made no difference to Islamabad's policy on Kashmir, however, implemented in essence by the ISI.

Indeed, the Afghan Mujahedin Alliance's victory over the leftist regime of Muhammad Najibullah in April 1992 lifted the morale of jihadists in the region. That is, the ripples of Afghan politics now extended to India, a thesis that underlines this analytical narrative.

The nationalist JKLF lost ground to such pro-Pakistan, Islamist groups as the Kashmir-based Hizb ul Mujahideen (HuM) and the Pakistan-based Harkat ul Mujahideen (Arabic, 'Movement of Mujahedin'), LeT, Jaish-e Muhammad (Urdu, 'Army of Muhammad'), and Harkat ul Ansar (Arabic, 'Movement of Helpers'), an extremist breakaway faction of the older Jamiat-e Ulema-e Islam (Urdu, 'Society of Islamic Ulema') of Pakistan. They increasingly resorted to assassinations, car bombings, and assaults on villages, causing many civilian casualties.

Reversing his predecessor's policy, Governor Saxena allowed diplomats and foreign journalists into the Valley. He freed opposition figures in April 1992. Their consultations to form an umbrella organization gathered momentum after the razing of the historic Babri Mosque in the north Indian city of Ayodhya in December, which inflamed Muslim feelings throughout the subcontinent. In February 1993 they announced the establishment of a confederation of twenty-six political, social, and religious organizations, called the All Parties Hurriyat Conference (APHC; *hurriyat* in Urdu means 'freedom'). They elected Mirwaiz (Urdu, 'Chief Preacher') Omar Farooq – the teenage son of Mirwaiz Maulavi Farooq, assassinated three years earlier, as their leader.[19]

The APHC's goal was to achieve the right to self-determination for the state's people according to UN Security Council resolution 47 of 1948. This was also Pakistan's aim. In any case, the formation of the APHC and its adoption of the UN resolution had come three years after US president George Bush Senior had dropped Washington's backing for a plebiscite and recommended that the dispute be settled through negotiations between India and Pakistan. His reference to the current situation as a 'dispute' meant that America did not recognize Kashmir as an integral part of India. (This continues to be Washington's stance.)

Taking advantage of the growing presence of international reporters from spring 1993, JKLF and HuM leaders, escorted by their bodyguards, began parading outside the Hazratbal Mosque, then being used not only as a hideout but also as an interrogation centre by the militants. This was a provocative act.

On succeeding Saxena as governor in March 1993, K.V. Krishna Rao, former army chief of staff with counter-insurgency experience in north-eastern India, set up a unified command for the Border Security Force, the Central Reserve Police Force, and the army to coordinate all military and paramilitary forces. He initiated the policy – commonly adopted by regimes facing insurgency – of infiltrating the militant factions with official intelligence agents, and using turncoat militants to lead the security forces in their counter-insurgency operations. Its implementation was assigned to RAW, which used the codename Operation Chanakya. (Chanakya Kautilya, the author of an ancient Indian treatise on statecraft which recommends political cunning, has been compared to Niccolò Machiavelli.) Some of the jailed guerrillas won their freedom by agreeing to carry out extrajudicial killings of their former colleagues – an assignment that the authorities would later give to the Kashmir police's Special Task Force and the Indian army's Rashtriya Rifles.[20] At the same time Rao tried to present a softer face for his administration by giving free access to the Valley's inhabitants to medical facilities and latest Bollywood movies.

The governor then decided to tackle the open defiance of the guerrilla leaders outside the Hazratbal Mosque. In October, he ordered the security forces to surround the area. That left about a hundred militants and some civilians ensconced inside the mosque. But instead of mounting a frontal attack on the holy site and setting the protesting Valley alight again, Rao conducted a month-long negotiation against the background of generally peaceful protest marches. In the end, the militants left the shrine unconditionally. But to prevent the guerrillas from occupying the mosque again, the authorities surrounded it with security forces posted in bunkers.

Responding to widespread criticism of its brutal violation of human rights at home and abroad, the Indian Parliament passed the Protection of Human Rights Act, 1993, and established the National Human Rights Commission. The critical omission was that the Act did *not* cover the security forces operating in such disturbed areas as Kashmir or the north-eastern region.

After Benazir Bhutto was elected prime minister of Pakistan in 1994, she refused to hold further talks with her Indian counterpart unless and until Delhi ended its flagrant human-rights violations in Kashmir. Unsurprisingly, there was no change in Islamabad's policy of active assistance to the freedom fighters in Indian Kashmir. Indeed, taking its cue from the founding of the APHC, Islamabad sponsored the formation of the United Jihad Council, consisting of eight jihadist organizations in Muzaffarabad, in the summer of 1994. This streamlined the ISI's distribution of arms, ammunition, telecom equipment, and propaganda literature. It also facilitated the coordination and pooling of resources of the constituent groups to share intelligence, choose targets in Indian Kashmir, and plan operations there. According to Bilal Lone, a senior APHC functionary, all the key personnel in the APHC, including himself, were on Pakistan's payroll. He made this statement in an Indian TV interview in December 2009, eighteen months after he had stopped taking Pakistani funds.[21]

THE CHARAR-E SHARIF EPISODE

Finding their mountainous hideouts unbearably cold and their paths to Pakistani Kashmir covered with deep snow, a group of seventy heavily armed insurgents took refuge inside the mausoleum of Nouruddin Rishi at Charar-e Sharif, 22 miles (35 km) west of Srinagar, in January 1995. Aligned with the HuM, they were led by Master Gul (aka Mast Gul), a former merchant from Pakistan's Khyber Pakhtunkhwa who had participated in the anti-Soviet jihad. Their presence went unnoticed by the intelligence agencies until early March, when, in a fracas with a Border Security Force unit, they killed two soldiers. The army responded by besieging the shrine and cordoning off the town. The militants fortified the mausoleum.

The fear of damaging one of the holiest sites in the Valley inhibited the military from staging an armed assault. The Indian government offered safe passage to the insurgents, but they did not trust its word. The stand-off continued for about two months with occasional exchanges of fire. The climax came on 8 May when the army started ramming its way through the town to the mausoleum complex. Encountering local resistance, it used force, killing many residents. The fighting that ensued at the holy site on 11 May resulted in the burning of the five-and-a-half-century-old shrine. The insurgents managed to break the military cordon and fled.[22]

Given the bloody mayhem in the town and around Charar-e Sharif, nobody could be certain who was responsible for the razing of the holy shrine. The Indians said the insurgents had set it alight to save their own lives. But the Kashmiris pointed out that the Indian troops had fired mortars at the mausoleum complex. What was certain was that 1,500 houses and shops had been reduced to ashes, and that more than forty civilians had been killed. (Later the Charar-e Sharif complex and the town would be rebuilt with funds from the Central and state governments.) When the grieving Kashmiri Muslims marched towards the burnt remains of the complex, afterward, they faced the bullets of the Indian soldiers.

To placate local feeling, the Indian authorities invited APHC leaders to Delhi for talks. But the aggrieved Kashmiris insisted that India should admit that Kashmir was a disputed territory. This was unacceptable to Delhi.

INDIA'S COUNTER-INSURGENCY STRATEGY

Having infiltrated the guerrilla factions, Governor Rao implemented the next phase in his counter-insurgency strategy: using cash to engineer splits in the militant groups and sponsoring fake resistance factions with jihadist titles to decimate the genuine organizations. For instance, a breakaway group of the Ikhwan ul Muslimeen (Arabic, 'Muslim Brethren'), calling itself Ikhwan ul Muslimoon popped up in 1994. Headed by Muhammad Yusuf, a former popular folk singer, it proved effective in reducing the HuM's operations by helping the security forces to eliminate armed HuM and JeI activists. Other examples were the Muslim Liberation Army, Al Ikhwan, and Al Barq. The Border Security Force-sponsored Kashmir Liberation Jihad Force, consisting of former resistance fighters, led the security forces' anti-militant operations in the capital.

At the same time the Kashmiri freedom movement began to lose its moral high ground because of the excesses committed by its members. Some had resorted to massacring Hindus and assassinating secular politicians; others had taken to smashing liquor shops and attacking cinemas, and forcing women to wear a veil. Many had targeted fellow Kashmiris suspected of collaborating with India. What bewildered and befuddled ordinary Kashmiri Muslims was the plethora of resistance factions, the divisions among their activists concerning their final goal, and Islamabad's shifting stance towards different groups.

This turn of events did not translate into creating pro-Delhi sentiment among Kashmiri Muslims, but the recruiting pool for jihadist groups began to shrink. A typical guerrilla lasted two years in the field, according to the Indian authorities. During that period he was either killed or captured, or he lost his zeal for violence. The routine use of torture at sixty-three detention centres in the Valley was yet another means of discouraging potential recruits.

Indian intelligence sources estimated that the number of militants in the Valley had fallen to 6,000 from a peak of 20,000–25,000.[23] Of these, 2,500 belonged to the HuM, whose political wing, the JeI, dominated the APHC. In November 1995, the BBC aired a documentary showing evidence of the JeI's support in Azad Kashmir camps, where fighters, openly expressing their intent to wage jihad in Indian Kashmir, were being trained. This was a violation of the 1972 Shimla Agreement between India and Pakistan.

Delhi declined to state the total strength of its security forces in Kashmir. Unofficial estimates by Indian and Pakistani experts varied widely, from 210,000 to 600,000. What India announced, with much fanfare, was the amount of weapons its security forces and Kashmiri police had seized between 1989 and 1995: 13,450 AK47 Kalashnikovs, 1,682 rockets, 750 rocket launchers, and 735 general-purpose machine guns. Due to improved intelligence, the authorities confiscated 590 stored bombs in 1995, almost twice the figure for 1994. As for fatalities, an unofficial estimate of 40,000 for 1988–95 was three times the official figure. The London-based Amnesty International cited 17,000 plus several thousand more deaths that were unaccounted for.[24] Of these, almost half were believed to be militants.

Given the comparative decline in violence, the Delhi government announced its intention to hold elections to the state legislature. But since the APHC was not prepared to participate in the poll and Farooq Abdullah's National Conference was lukewarm about the idea, the project was stillborn. Even the holding of the ballot for the parliamentary elections in May 1996 proved problematic, with the army brazenly pressuring citizens to vote.

Nationally, that general election ended the sixteen-year rule of the Congress party and ushered in a coalition government opposed by the defeated party. The newly installed administration undertook a thorough review of the Kashmir policy and concluded that the absence of a representative government – however skewed – for six years had been a destabilizing factor.

THE RETURN OF THE BALLOT

During his visit to Srinagar in August 1996, Prime Minister H.D. Deve Gowda announced a plan to lift the presidential rule and order an election for the state's legislative assembly. On the eve of the poll in September, he unveiled a hefty package of financial aid of Rs 3.52 billion ($100 million) to improve infrastructure and wrote off outstanding loans of up to Rs 50,000 ($1,400) per person – a flagrant example of electoral bribing.

Reversing his previous stance, Farooq Abdullah decided to contest the state elections. 'People like to see *azadi* [independence] but they don't see the consequences of that azadi,' he said. 'We are landlocked with powerful neighbors of China and Pakistan. If we get independence and India quits, I am sure Pakistan will march in overnight and take over.'[25] It was better to take the plunge and see how best to alter the situation rather than let the situation stagnate with no public involvement, he argued. In contrast, APHC leaders stuck to their stance of a boycott of the poll.

With contesting candidates facing dire threats from the militants, the authorities offered them bulletproof vehicles and security personnel, and arrested all APHC leaders. Very few people voted voluntarily in the Kashmir Valley; many others were pressed to go to the polling booths by the security forces, who warned citizens of 'consequences' if they failed to show indelible ink on their index fingers, used at the polling stations, in the evening. Unsurprisingly, the National Conference won fifty-nine of the eighty-seven available seats. Abdullah became the chief minister.

September 1996 also happened to be the month when the Taliban captured Kabul. That lifted the spirits of the Pakistani people and politicians as well as the pro-Islamabad groups in Indian Kashmir. This impacted directly on Kashmiri politics. The resulting rise in the influence of pro-Pakistan groups within the APHC led to the replacement of Mirwaiz Omar Farooq as leader by Syed Ali Shah Geelani in 1997. Born in Zoorimunz village in north Kashmir, the latter's views were formed by the Islamist writings of Abu Ala Maududi. A slim bespectacled man with a narrow face and neatly trimmed white beard, he always appeared in public in a large furry cap. An unflinching opponent of India's occupation of Kashmir, he was the leader of the JeI in Kashmir. Reiterating the Kashmiri people's right to self-determination, he favoured accession to Pakistan, a view that had led to him being arrested and detained on numerous occasions.

In Kabul, the Taliban regime fell in line with the ISI's programme of aiding Kashmiri freedom fighters by handing over the Al Badr training camp near Khost to Harkat ul Ansar, a militant Kashmiri group. Typical of those who trained there was 'Ghulam', a Kashmiri Muslim. He had signed a two-year contract for 400,000 Pakistani rupees ($8,400) and had undergone three months' training in a camp in Afghanistan.[26] Tellingly, all those killed in the American air strikes on Afghanistan in August 1998 were Kashmiris or Pakistanis.

After the coalition government, headed by the Hindu nationalist Bhartiya Janata Party (BJP), with its leader Atal Bihari Vajpayee as the prime minister, assumed office in Delhi in April 1998, India hardened its stance on Kashmir and Pakistan. The following month it tested five atom bombs; and Islamabad reciprocated by detonating six.

Guerrilla activities in the Valley escalated. The Vajpayee government responded by dispatching additional security forces to Kashmir, pushing the total most likely to 400,000 military and paramilitary troops, 80,000 of whom were deployed along the Line of Control. Counter-insurgency operations mounted. So too did the consequent fatalities – from 2,200 in 1998 to a peak of 4,500 in 2001, with militants' deaths rising from 880 to 2,700.[27]

While using an iron fist in Kashmir the Vajpayee government softened its stance towards Pakistan after it had acquired parity with India in the manufacturing of atom bombs. When the long-suspended bus service between Delhi and Lahore was resumed in February 1999, Vajpayee became its first passenger. In Lahore he was greeted by his Pakistani counterpart, Muhammad Nawaz Sharif. The two leaders agreed to resolve all outstanding issues, including Kashmir, peacefully.

Little did Nawaz Sharif realize then that his topmost general, Aziz Khan, was secretly planning a military move in the Kargil region to change the status quo in Kashmir.

KARGIL BATTLE LEADS TO PAKISTANI COUP

The sole highway linking Srinagar with Leh, the regional capital of Ladakh, passes through the Kargil region close to the 460-mile (740 km) long Line of Control. Here jagged peaks soar to 16,500 feet (5,000 m), and average winter temperatures drop to an incredible –60°C. Such harsh conditions led India and Pakistan to reach an understanding in the mid-1970s to leave their pickets unmanned in the Kargil area from mid-September to mid-April. In early spring 1999, however, Pakistan violated this informal agreement. Under cover of heavy artillery and mortar fire, it airlifted 600 Kashmiri militants, commanded by Pakistani officers, into the Kargil region. Trained in high-altitude fighting, they were equipped with shoulder-held Stinger anti-aircraft missiles. The operation was masterminded by General Aziz Khan, chief of the general staff. He was also the chief of the Sudhan clan, dominant in the Poonch district of Pakistani-held Kashmir. During and after the anti-Soviet jihad, he had supervised the establishment of the training camps for the radical Harkat ul Ansar (renamed Harkat al Mujahedin after being listed as a terrorist organization by Washington in 1997). The infiltrators occupied 130 unmanned Indian outposts along the 85-mile (136 km) front, and positioned themselves to threaten the Srinagar–Leh highway.

It was only in early May that the Indians realized what had happened and protested. Islamabad maintained that local Kashmiri freedom fighters were responsible. Later that month, India launched air strikes as part of its Operation Vijay. But aerial bombing amidst jagged peaks was only partly effective.

APHC leaders tried to use the Kargil campaign to draw global attention to the Kashmir dispute but failed. Indeed, the communiqué issued by the G8 (group of eight industrialized nations) summit at Cologne on 20 June 1999 declared: 'We regard any military action to change the status quo [in Kashmir] as irresponsible. We therefore call for an immediate end to these actions [and] restoration of the Line of Control.'[28]

But the fighting continued. Tensions between Delhi and Islamabad rose sharply. While India declared that it would not be the first to use nuclear weapons, Pakistan's information minister, Mushahid Hussain, appearing on the BBC World's HARDtalk programme on 23 June, refused to give the same guarantee, describing the idea of a nuclear war as 'too far-fetched'.[29] Almost three years later, Bruce Riedel, a former senior director at the National Security Council and special assistant to US president Bill Clinton on South Asia, revealed in a policy paper at the University of Pennsylvania that US intelligence had information that General Pervez Musharraf, Pakistan's army chief of staff, was preparing a nuclear arsenal for possible use in a wider war with India, most likely without the knowledge of Nawaz Sharif.[30]

Alarmed by the prospect of a nuclear holocaust in the Indian subcontinent, Clinton invited Vajpayee and Sharif to Washington for talks. Mentioning previous commitments, Vajpayee declined, aware that a tripartite meeting in the US on this subject would compromise the long-held Indian position that Kashmir was a bilateral, not an international, issue. After their three-hour meeting at the White House on 4 July, American Independence Day, Sharif and Clinton issued a joint statement that steps would be taken to restore the UN-specified Line of Control, thus facilitating a ceasefire. There was, of course, no mention of the secret deal that was also struck then. In it, Clinton agreed to ease US economic sanctions against Islamabad, imposed in the wake of Pakistan's nuclear tests in May–June 1998, and recommend to the International Monetary Fund (IMF) not to withhold its next loan to Pakistan. In return, Sharif promised to call off the Kargil campaign and actively cooperate with Washington in apprehending Osama bin Laden. On his return home, Sharif justified his decision by arguing that the Kargil offensive had drawn the attention of the international community to the Kashmir dispute.

But his announcement of Pakistan's withdrawal of support for the Kargil campaign angered the armed forces high command and paved the way for his downfall. On 12 October 1999, General Musharraf overthrew Sharif's government. The reason given by Musharraf's spokesman for this dramatic move was that Sharif was about to promote the undeserving General Ziauddin Butt, his personal favourite, to the status of army chief of staff. This explanation was unconvincing. Musharraf declared himself Pakistan's chief executive, leaving the incumbent, Rafiq Taroor, in place as president. In the fifty-two-year history of Pakistan, this was the fourth military coup.

Two factors had triggered the coup: Pakistan's involvement in the Muslim separatist insurgency in Indian-administered Kashmir and the fate of bin Laden. 'Sharif brought disgrace to the Pakistani army by bowing down before the U.S. administration for an abrupt pullout from Kargil,' one military officer told the Islamabad-based *News* within hours of the coup. 'In the aftermath of the Kargil crisis we went through almost a revolt in the army as the rank and file thought that the government had betrayed them.'[31]

Earlier, bin Laden had emerged as the chief suspect behind the bombings of the American embassies in Kenya and Tanzania in August 1998. Capturing or killing him thus became a top priority of the Clinton White House. As part of his bargain with Clinton, Sharif had dispatched General Butt, then ISI director, to Washington in early October 1999 to coordinate the next move to seize bin Laden.

With the aerial attacks on the World Trade Center and the Pentagon on 11 September 2001, bin Laden became the most wanted fugitive in the world.

President George W. Bush's subsequent declaration of a global war on terror was welcomed in New Delhi. After the explosion of a massive car bomb outside the state legislature in Srinagar on 1 October, killing thirty-eight people, the Indian government issued a draconian Prevention of Terrorism Ordinance. This empowered the authorities to detain suspects for up to two years without charging them. Anti-terrorist rhetoric reached fever pitch two months later.

INDIA AND PAKISTAN ON BRINK OF WAR

On 13 December 2001, five gunmen carrying grenades, Kalashnikov rifles, and explosives went through the perimeter entrance gate to the mammoth, circular Parliament House in Delhi – built on a high platform with chambers for both houses of the federal legislature – in a white car with a red flashing beacon on the roof, typically used by parliamentarians. But when their car hit another in front of the entrance used by Upper House members, they rushed up the steps, firing and wounding an unarmed sentry who was guarding the huge carved door. Despite his injury, the sentry managed to close the door and raise the alarm on his walkie-talkie. Swiftly, the other eleven entrances to the building were shut tight. In the firefight that ensued on the steps of Parliament House, four of the assailants were shot dead while the fifth, carrying explosives, blew himself up; five policemen and sentries lost their lives, as did two civilians.

The terrorists had planned on entering the building and massacring many of the 800-odd Indian lawmakers inside, with their focus on the front benches of the Lower House occupied by cabinet ministers. It transpired later that, along with the car accident, the terrorists' plan had gone awry owing to a quintessentially Delhi experience: a sudden power cut. Electricity failure that morning deprived Muhammad Afzal (aka Afzal Guru) – a Kashmiri Muslim, arrested later as the suspected sixth co-conspirator – of the ability to execute his task: to sit at home watching all television news and inform the terrorist team by mobile phone of the arrival of cabinet ministers, including Vajpayee, at the parliament building.

Therefore, Afzal did not know that the Lower House had adjourned five minutes after opening (due to a noisy protest by the opposition over a defence ministry scam of paying excessive sums for soldiers' coffins) and that Vajpayee had therefore decided to stay at his official residence. When Afzal informed the terrorists' leader in the car of his failure to access the news, the latter, got angry, and went ahead with the assault, nonetheless.

The official statement by Delhi described the event as 'an attack on not just the symbol, but the seat, of Indian democracy and on the sovereignty of the Indian people'. The American embassy called it 'an outrageous act of terrorism' and 'a brutal assault on the heart of Indian democracy'. The episode transformed all Kashmiri Muslims living in the rest of India into potential terrorists. Delhi blamed the Pakistan-based LeT and JeM for the audacious attack, accussing the LeT's Hafiz Muhammad Saeed of masterminding the operation. It called on Musharraf to outlaw the two organizations and freeze their assets. Pakistan condemned the attack. But, claiming that it had never allowed its soil to be used for terrorism, it rejected the Indian demands. By contrast, Washington went on to ban the two groups which, according to later Pakistani briefings to American reporters, had been responsible for 70 per cent of the recent attacks in Indian Kashmir.[32]

Delhi's strategy was directed at both Islamabad and Washington, well aware that, as the aggrieved party, it held the high moral ground.

While the Bush administration, committed to eradicating terrorism worldwide, had no option but to go along with India, it could not afford to get too rough on Musharraf. After all, he had played a pivotal role in the overthrow of the Taliban regime in Afghanistan, and his continued cooperation was essential to destroy the remnants of the Taliban and Al Qaida. All the same, the Bush White House could not deflect the argument offered by Delhi. India equated Pakistan's support for the LeT and the JeM with its earlier backing for the Taliban, with the ISI's Kashmir and Afghan cells being the respective primary engines behind these jihadist organizations. It reasoned that Islamabad pointed out the contradiction between waging war on terrorism on its western frontier (Afghanistan) while supporting it on its eastern border (Kashmir).

Delhi demanded that Islamabad hand over twenty terrorists living in its territory, six of them Pakistani citizens. The list included Muhammad Ibrahim Azhar, one of the hijackers of an Indian Airlines plane two years earlier, whose brother Masoud had founded the JeM in March 2000. In the absence of an extradition treaty between the two countries, Islamabad refused to comply, calling on India to pass on the evidence it had against the Pakistani nationals.

Protesting at Islamabad's delaying tactics, India reduced its diplomatic staff in Pakistan and unilaterally suspended rail and bus links between the two countries. In late December, as part of Operation Parakram, the Vajpayee government put its military on high alert, with the soldiers along the international border with Pakistan and the Line of Control in Kashmir sheltering in trenches. The two neighbours moved missiles closer to each other's border, while exchanging mortar and artillery fire along the Kashmir front. By early January 2002, India had mobilized some 500,000 troops and three armoured divisions on the Pakistani border, concentrated along the Line of Control in Kashmir. Pakistan deployed around 120,000 troops in that region. This was the largest build-up on the subcontinent since the 1971 war.

Pressured by Washington to defuse the mounting crisis, Musharraf delivered an hour-long TV address to his nation on, 12 January 2002. 'Pakistan rejects and condemns terrorism in all its forms and manifestations,' he declared. 'Pakistan will not allow its territory to be used for any terrorist activity anywhere in the world . . . No organization will be allowed to indulge in terrorism in the name of Kashmir.' He then added that Pakistan would not surrender its claim to Kashmir: 'Kashmir is in our blood. No Pakistani can afford to sever links with Kashmir . . . We will continue to extend our moral, political and diplomatic support to Kashmiris.'[33] He banned five extremist organizations, including the LeT and JeM.

While maintaining his backing for self-determination for Kashmiris – the principle that, when applied to the Muslims in British India, had resulted in the creation of Pakistan – Musharraf disengaged the issue from the pan-Islamist movement, as was done first by Zia ul Haq and then by bin Laden.

Delhi responded positively to Musharraf's address. It noted approvingly his closure of 390 offices of the banned organizations and the detention of about 1,500 of their activists under the Maintenance of Public Order Ordinance, which allowed the police to detain suspects for thirty days without charge. Yet it took many weeks of active diplomacy by the US to persuade the two neighbours to pull back from the brink of war.

However, the resulting thaw vanished on 12 May. On that day, three armed Kashmiri militants in Indian army fatigues boarded a bus destined for Jammu. Just before reaching the army camp at Kala Chak, they stopped the vehicle, sprayed it with gunfire and left seven passengers dead. They then entered the camp and killed thirty more people by lobbing hand grenades and firing their automatic weapons before getting killed by the Indian soldiers. This daring attack on a military facility riled the Indian government.

Tensions built up again. Islamabad expected an offensive by Delhi by the end of the month. On 25 May, President George W. Bush publicly called on Musharraf to stop the infiltration into Indian Kashmir. After securing an assurance on that count from the Pakistani leader, the White House pressured India. Washington and London advised around sixty thousand Americans and twenty thousand Britons, including many thousands of business executives, to leave India. That shook Delhi. It scuttled its planned commando raid across the Line of Control in Kashmir to overrun the extremists' training camps, an operation likely to escalate to a full-scale war. Yet it was not until December 2002 that the Vajpayee government decided to lower the 'high alert' state of its armed forces.

It transpired later that India's dropping the idea of cross-border raiding of the extremists' training camps did not return the Indo-Pakistan relations to the pre-crisis level. The BJP-led government instructed its military planners to refine the idea for future use. The military high command would announce its new strategy of blitzkrieg, called 'Cold Start', in April 2004 – a month before the BJP's defeat in the general election. The Cold Start doctrine required the formation of eight division-size Integrated Battle Groups, each including infantry, artillery, armour, and air support, and able to operate independently on the battlefield. In the case of terrorist attacks from or by a Pakistan-based group, these would rapidly penetrate Pakistan at unexpected points and advance no more than 30 miles (48 km) beyond the border, disrupting the command and control networks of the opposing military while staying away from the locations likely to trigger a nuclear retaliation. The overall aim was to launch a conventional strike swiftly but to inflict only limited damage in order to deny Pakistan justification for a nuclear response.[34]

Although the threat of war in the spring of 2002 passed, tensions did not subside. This was so because of the admission by US Secretary of State Colin Powell that Washington lacked evidence 'whether infiltration has stopped on a permanent basis or not'.[35]

Nonetheless, the Indian authorities began preparations for the state elections in Kashmir, with the National Conference contesting them under the leadership of Omar Abdullah, the inexperienced son of Farooq. As before, the secessionists were opposed to the exercise. During the two months of electioneering, over eight hundred militants, civilians, and security personnel were killed.

THE TWILIGHT PHASE

Despite the allegations of vote-rigging and a low turnout of 43 per cent, the election, held in September–October, produced an astonishing result. The National Conference was reduced to twenty-eight seats, followed by the Congress party with twenty. The newly launched People's Democratic Party (PDP) of Mufti Muhammad Sayeed – calling on Delhi to have 'an unconditional dialogue' with Kashmiris to resolve the long-running crisis – won sixteen seats, and the People's Democratic Forum (PDF) – an opponent of the National Conference – seven. A coalition of the Congress and the PDP, backed by the PDF, formed the government. The new chief minister, Sayeed, was to step down after three years to make way for a Congress leader.

In Pakistan, having consolidated his power by appointing himself president, Musharraf could afford to moderate his country's traditional stance on Kashmir. In December 2003, he offered a step-by-step approach to tackling the seemingly intractable issue: Let the two disputants accept the ground rule that Kashmir is the primary bone of contention; next each side should set out its case, and the two should then discard whatever is unacceptable to either of them, and thus devise a common platform acceptable to both; finally, that agreement should be put to referendum on both sides of the Line of Control. Predictably, the president was criticized in Pakistan for abandoning the demand for a plebiscite. When that happened, Musharraf backtracked, explaining that a plebiscite remained one of the options.

Musharraf's moderation had occurred against the backdrop of a split in the APHC, with the majority of its constituents favouring talks with the Delhi government, and the leader of the minority faction, Geelani, leaving the umbrella body to set up the Tehrik-e Hurriyat (Urdu, 'Movement of Freedom'). With the Congress-led coalition, headed by Manmohan Singh, a member of the Sikh minority, returning to power in Delhi in May 2004, there was a further easing of tensions in Kashmir. In October, the Singh government allowed a group of Pakistani journalists to visit Indian Kashmir. To their astonishment, they found themselves free to interview anybody they wished. Next June, an APHC delegation was permitted to travel to the Pakistani-administered Kashmir. And three months later the Indian prime minister met APHC leaders in Delhi.

On 8 October 2005, a 7.6 Richter scale earthquake, with its epicentre near Muzaffarabad, wreaked havoc in the region, killing 79,000 people, including at least three thousand in the Indian Kashmir, and rendering two million homeless. Following an appeal by the Azad Kashmir government for cooperation with India to improve relief, Musharraf agreed to open the Line of Control temporarily. India reciprocated.

Three weeks later, three bombs killed fifty-nine people in Delhi. Claiming responsibility, a militant Kashmiri group described the explosions as a rebuff to India's claim that its military and paramilitary crackdown and the recent thaw with Pakistan caused by the earthquake had finished off the extremists. Despite this, in February 2006, the Indian government withdrew five thousand troops from Kashmir, promising further pullouts.

The return to normalcy was jolted when the Indian authorities concluded an agreement in May 2008 with the state government, then headed by Congress party leader Ghulam Nabi Azad, to transfer 99 acres of forest land to the Shri Amarnathji Shrine Board in the Baltal area to build temporary shelters and facilities for the Hindu pilgrims on their way to the holy cave of Amarnath. The state government made the plan public in June. Most Kashmiri Muslims viewed it as the thin end of the wedge, leading to non-Kashmiris owning land and immovable property in Kashmir, a right denied under the Indian constitution. APHC leaders' call for protest was so successful that one rally in Srinagar drew half a million people. Most government offices and schools closed, as did many businesses.

The government reversed the order on 1 July. Some Hindu

organizations in Jammu imposed a road blockade on the Kashmir Valley which hurt the Kashmir Valley's economy. These protests turned violent and caused seven deaths. The PDP withdrew its support for Azad, and his government fell on 11 July. Finally, with the active intervention of Governor Narinder Nath Vohra, a compromise was reached on 31 August. This allowed the Shri Amarnath Shrine Board to make 'temporary' use of the 99 acres during the six-week period of pilgrimage. The episode demonstrated the fault lines not only between religions but also between Kashmir's regions.

During the LeT-orchestrated siege of Mumbai's leading hotels in November, the terrorists made repeated references to the plight of the Kashmiri Muslims – thus highlighting that the Kashmir issue continued to resonate with many Pakistanis.

The Mumbai attacks occurred in the midst of Kashmiri elections, held between 17 November and 7 December. The APHC's call for a boycott went largely unheeded: the turnout of 61 per cent was normal. A coalition of the National Conference (twenty-eight seats) and the Congress party (seventeen seats), led by Omar Abdullah, formed the new government. 'People voted for roads, electricity, water and other local issues,' remarked one APHC leader. 'They did not vote for the resolution of the Kashmir issue.' Another APHC leader, Mirwaiz Omar Farooq, acknowledged: 'Rural people have genuine problems like water and electricity and Hurriyat [APHC] is not in a position to address them.'[36]

In March 2009, Omar Abdullah claimed that the number of militants in the state was down to 800, only a third of them being Kashmiris. That encouraged the Central government to withdraw a further 30,000 troops.

On the other hand, a twenty-hour gun battle between LeT fighters and the Indian security forces, following an attack on a police station in Srinagar in January 2010, offered a fresh reminder that the Valley was far from stable or secure.

The street protest triggered by the killing of a teenage student by security forces in mid-June mushroomed into wide-ranging strikes, resulting in curfews and more killings by police and paramilitaries. When a parliamentary delegation, headed by the home minister, Palaniappan Chidambaram, arrived from Delhi in September to talk to local leaders, its motorcade drove along empty streets and past shuttered shops, with police officers armed with machine guns posted every few hundred yards. Reflecting the views of the majority of secessionists, Geelani spelt out his preconditions for talks: declare Kashmir an international dispute, withdraw troops from civilian areas, end human-rights violations, repeal the Armed Forces (Jammu and Kashmir) Special Powers Act, and release all political prisoners. Since these conditions were unacceptable to the authorities in Delhi, the stalemate continued.

This time around, however, the Indians agreed that the popular protest was indigenous and that Pakistan's ISI was not involved. But that did not mean the jihadist organizations in Pakistan had abandoned their mission of liberating Kashmir from the yoke of Hindu India.

Indeed, it was this idea that had driven Muhammad Ajmal Amir Kasab, the sole surviving terrorist in the Mumbai attacks, to join the LeT. Another terrorist had yelled angrily at his captives in the Taj Mahal Hotel, 'Did you know that a Zionist general [Avi Mizrahi] visited Kashmir two months ago?' To express its wrath, the LeT had included the Nariman House (aka Chabad House), run as a Jewish outreach centre near the landmark hotel, on its list of targets.

6

INDIA, ISRAEL AND AMERICA

COMMENTING ON THE November 2008 terrorist incidents in Mumbai, some analysts claimed that the assault on Nariman House and the Leopold Café, popular with Western tourists, were the primary targets, and that other sites had been added merely to burnish the overall impact. That seemed unlikely. Though a synagogue was housed inside the sleek, five-storeyed Nariman House, there were seven others that Mumbai had hosted since 1796. Its main attraction to the terrorists' sponsor, the Lashkar-e Taiba (LeT), was that it was the principal point of passage for hundreds of young Israelis pouring into the city on thrice-weekly flights from Tel Aviv. Most of them, having endured a strict regime during their compulsory draft, were intent on doing in freewheeling India what was forbidden in the Israeli army: growing long hair, wearing sandals instead of polished shoes, and smoking hashish.

This Jewish outreach centre was run by a young Orthodox couple. Bearded Rabbi Gavriel Holtzberg, with expressive eyes behind his spectacles, was seldom seen in public without the black hat of the Orthodox or ultra-Orthodox. Born in Israel, he grew up in Brooklyn, New York. His pleasant-looking, raven-haired, oval-faced wife, Rivka, was a native of Israel. Along with four others at Nariman House, they would die at the hands of the jihadist terrorists.

Their arrival in Mumbai in 2003 was exceptional for several reasons. Unlike the settled Jewry in India, they were Ashkenazi Jews, European in origin. Their settling represented a move that contrasted sharply with the outflow of about twenty thousand Indian Jews from India to Israel during the first quarter-century of Israel's existence. Equally odd was the young couple's affiliation with a subsect within Orthodox Judaism. So far, the Jewish community in India had consisted of Cochin Jews, who had arrived as traders and settled in the southern region of Cochin two-and-a-half millennia ago; Bene Israelis with a history in India stretching back 2,100 years; and Baghdadis, the generic term used to describe the Jews from Iraq and Iran who arrived in the mid-eighteenth century. Later that century, Orthodox Judaism split into four subsects named after places in Poland or Russia, with the qualifying 'Chabad', being the Hebrew acronym for *Chochmah*, *Binah* and *Daasa* ('Wisdom', 'Understanding', and 'Knowledge'). The Lubavitch branch took its name from Lyubavichi, a Russian town. The Brooklyn-based Menach Mendel Schneeroson, the son-in-law of Yosef Schnnersohn, the sixth leader of this leading subsect, transformed the movement into a powerful force within Judaism during World War II.

With the establishment of Israel in May 1948, the Chabad-Lubavich established a strong presence in the Jewish Quarter of the Old City in Jerusalem.

INDIA'S SIDELINING OF ISRAEL

India, which had achieved independence in August 1947, did not recognize Israel. Averse to dividing a country on the basis of religion, India's prime minister, Jawaharlal Nehru, instructed the Indian representative at the United Nations General Assembly to vote against partitioning Palestine to resolve the conflict between the Jews and the Arabs in November 1947.[1] In May 1949, India opposed the admission of Israel to the UN, arguing that it could not recognize an Israel which had been achieved through 'the force of arms and not through negotiations'.

When India's recognition of Israel finally came in September 1950, it did not lead to the establishment of diplomatic ties. It was not until two years later that India upgraded the consular agent in Mumbai to an honorary consul to deal with trade, shipping, and passports and visas. Nehru refused to open an Indian consulate in Tel Aviv, however. One of the chief reasons for his reluctance was the Kashmir dispute. Delhi's ties with Israel would have armed Pakistan with an additional diplomatic tool to direct against India. Due to Israel's collusion with Britain and France in invading Egypt in 1956, any prospect of India establishing diplomatic relations with Israel disappeared.

DELHI–WASHINGTON RELATIONS

It took another war – between Delhi and Beijing – to bring about a softening of Nehru's stance on Israel. And that only happened because of the intervention of the United States.

A study of a country's foreign and domestic policies often shows a symbiotic relationship between the two. Such is the case with India after independence. Its non-alignment with either of the global power blocs, led respectively by Washington and Moscow, was a reflection of its domestic paradigm: planned economic growth within a Western democratic political system. Little wonder that Delhi looked forward to having cordial relations with the US whose president, Franklin D. Roosevelt, had pressured Britain to grant independence to its Indian colony. His successor, Harry Truman, accorded Nehru a warm reception in Washington in October 1949.

By contrast, Delhi's relations with Moscow remained strictly formal so long as Joseph Stalin was the supreme leader because of his policy of friendship only with avowedly socialist countries. It was only after Stalin's death in March 1953 that there was a thaw in relations between the Soviet Union and recently independent non-communist states like India. A trade pact between the two countries followed later that year.

Whereas the convening of the conference of the twenty-seven independent Afro-Asian nations in Bandung, Indonesia – in which Nehru played a pivotal role – was welcomed by Moscow, it caused unease in Washington. Though unhappy at the increasing warmth between Delhi and Moscow, Washington continued to give India economic aid, including foodgrains under Public Law 480 of 1950. That legislation allowed the US administration to sell agricultural commodities at a discount and accept the bulk of payments in the recipient country's currency. In the case of India, Washington reimbursed 80 per cent of the amount in grants and loans for India's development projects, using the remainder to maintain its embassy and consulates in India. The US wished to see India win the economic race against communist China and demonstrate the superiority of Western-style democracy over communism to other Afro-Asian nations. On the eve of Nehru's visit to Washington in November 1961, President John F. Kennedy said, 'Chinese Communists have been moving ahead the last 10 years. India has been making some progress, but if India does not succeed with her 450 million people, if she can't make freedom work, then people around the world are going to determine, particularly in the underdeveloped world, that the only way they can develop their resources is through the Communist system.'[2] By 1963, India owed America $2.32 billion, more than half of the total Indian money in circulation.[3] Unable to match Washington's economic aid to Delhi, Moscow decided to back India on the sensitive and emotional issue of Kashmir. It vetoed a discussion on the subject at the United Nations Security Council in 1957 and won immense goodwill among Indian intellectuals.

Communist China emerged as the chief villain for both America *and* the Soviet Union when it refused to subscribe to the concept of 'peaceful coexistence' between socialism and capitalism – as agreed by US President Dwight Eisenhower and Soviet leader Nikita Khrushchev at their meeting at Camp David, Maryland, in October 1959. Two months later, Eisenhower received a rousing reception on the streets of Delhi against the background of escalating tensions between India and China.

In 1960, the Soviet Union and communist China parted company. The Kremlin favoured India in its border disputes with China and started supplying Delhi with military hardware, including heavy transport planes and helicopters.

THE INDIA–CHINA WAR: A GAME-CHANGER

Large-scale hostilities between India and China flared up in October 1962. Within a month the Chinese overran Indian border posts and marched into the north-eastern province of Assam, and consolidated their position in the eastern Aksai Chin sector of Jammu and Kashmir, covering 15.5 per cent of the state's territory, which they had first penetrated in 1954.

Nehru panicked. 'Late that night [20 November 1962] Nehru made an urgent, open appeal for the intervention of the United States with bomber and fighter squadrons to go into action against the Chinese,' stated Neville Maxwell, a British journalist and author. 'This appeal was detailed, even specifying the number of squadrons required – fifteen.'[4] In response, an American aircraft carrier was dispatched from the Pacific towards Indian waters. But the crisis passed within twenty-four hours of Nehru making his appeal. The Chinese declared a unilateral ceasefire and began withdrawing immediately. The US aircraft carrier turned back before reaching the Bay of Bengal.

Nehru had also appealed to several other leaders for assistance. And, encouraged by Kennedy, he had approached Israeli prime minister David Ben-Gurion for small arms. Israel dispatched 81mm and 120mm mortars and some pack howitzer artillery pieces. This represented a diplomatic success for Washington. Since the Arab-Israeli truce of January 1949, it had been urging the independent nations in Asia and Africa to recognize Israel.

However, the 1962 Sino-Indian armed conflict had far wider implications. After the truce, Delhi received a squadron of large transport planes from the Pentagon. Special American and British military missions laid the ground for United States–United Kingdom military assistance worth $120 million over the next three years. In a similar vein, retired Israeli general and intelligence officer David Shaltiel visited Delhi clandestinely in 1963, and signed a secret agreement on the exchange of military intelligence – focused on their common foes, Pakistan and China – and the mutual supply of military hardware.[5] These contacts were kept supersecret because they clashed with India's public stance of cordial relations with the Egypt of Gamal Abdel Nasser, who shared Nehru's desire for the decolonization of Asia and Africa, and also followed a non-aligned foreign policy.

With the outbreak of war between India and Pakistan over Kashmir in September 1965, Washington stopped supplying arms and spares to both sides. This helped to shorten the fighting. On the other hand, it drove India to accelerate its development of an indigenous military industry – an enterprise in which the Kremlin came to play a leading role when Western arms manufacturers refused to give licences for the assembly or production of their wares in India. Under the circumstances, there was no chance of Delhi–Tel Aviv ties progressing beyond clandestine dealings.

As tensions built up between Egypt and Israel in late May 1967, the Indian government of Indira Gandhi, the daughter of Nehru, took a strong pro-Cairo stance in public. Yet during the subsequent Arab-Israeli War, it returned Israel's earlier favours by sending spares for the Israeli Mystère fighter aircraft and AMX 13 tanks.[6] After the conflict, Gandhi called for an Israeli withdrawal from the occupied Arab territories, and the exercise of Palestinians' right to self-determination.

The next year, Gandhi established a foreign intelligence agency, initially as a wing of the main Intelligence Bureau, with the innocuous title of the Research and Analysis Wing (RAW), but reporting directly to the prime minister's secretariat. Its activities were to be concealed not only from the public but also parliament. As a countermeasure to the growing intelligence and military links between

Pakistan and China, Gandhi instructed RAW's head, Rameshwar Nath Kao, to cultivate links with Israel's foreign intelligence agency, Mossad (Hebrew, 'Institute'), which also reported directly to the prime minister.[7] This duplicitous behaviour would become standard practice in Delhi for a quarter-century. But then the intelligence world as a whole is murky, and nothing there is as it seems. Shielded from the scrutiny of voters and parliament, spy agencies cooperate with one another, exchanging sensitive information, even when their respective governments display mutual hostility in public.

By signing a Treaty of Friendship and Cooperation with the Soviet Union in August 1971, Indira Gandhi ensured Kremlin backing for her plan to 'liberate' the eastern wing of Pakistan from the central authority based in Islamabad in West Pakistan. Though Pakistan was an integral part of the Washington-led power bloc, Israel, being suspicious of any strong Muslim nation, whether Arab or non-Arab, saw an advantage in a weakening Pakistan. In the December 1971 Indo-Pakistan War, therefore, it shipped small arms and ammunition to India.[8]

With the quadrupling of oil prices in 1973–74, the importance of the sparsely populated oil-rich Gulf States rose sharply. For their booming development projects and construction industry, they began importing manual and skilled workers from India on a large scale. This provided an economic basis for Delhi to continue its pro-Arab and pro-Palestinian stance. In November 1975, India was among the seventy-two nations at the United Nations General Assembly that voted for a resolution describing Zionism as 'a form of racism and racial discrimination'.[9]

In the international arena, both Moscow and Washington continued to bolster India as a counter-force to China, which became a nuclear power in 1964. The launching of an unmanned Indian satellite from a Soviet cosmodrome at Baikonur with a Moscow-supplied launcher rocket and Washington-supplied space-grade components in April 1975 was a vivid example of the ongoing convergence of US and Soviet policies on India.

INDIAN-AMERICAN-ISRAELI TIES TIGHTEN

A great bonus for Israel – as well as America – came in January 1977. In that month, Morarji Desai, heading a coalition of anti-Congress factions called the Janata Party, became India's new prime minister. He caught the public imagination in the West by revealing that he drank his urine twice a day for 'health reasons'. What very few knew then that this conservative, right-wing politician – sacked as deputy prime minister by Indira Gandhi in 1969 – had signed up as a CIA 'asset' for $20,000 a year. When his cover was blown in 1983 by Seymour M. Hersh, an American prize-winning investigative journalist, in his book *The Price of Power: Kissinger in the Nixon White House*, he denied the charge. He went on to sue Hersh in the US for defamation, but lost the case.[10]

Desai's premiership opened up unprecedented opportunities for Israel in India because the CIA had been working clandestinely to secure recognition of Israel in the Arab world and beyond since its founding. In August 1977, Israeli foreign minister Moshe Dayan, wearing his trademark black eyepatch, made a secret visit to India to meet Desai and his foreign minister, Atal Bihari Vajpayee. Dayan failed to get the Israeli consulate upgraded to a consulate general and moved to Delhi because that would have aroused the curiosity of the media and opposition politicians. But the two Indian leaders decided to formalize covert relations with Israel and put RAW–Mossad cooperation on a firm footing.

In July 1979, Desai was succeeded by Charan Singh, a former chief minister of Uttar Pradesh, the most populous Indian state. Soon after the Kremlin's military intervention in Afghanistan on Christmas Day 1979, his government called for the withdrawal of Soviet troops from Afghanistan while expressing its apprehension about Washington's renewed military commitment to Pakistan – fearing that the newly acquired US weapons could be used against India rather than to secure the Pakistan–Afghanistan border.[11]

In the general election of January 1980, Indira Gandhi was returned to power. During her meetings with Soviet leaders in the Kremlin later that year and in 1982, she privately advised a Soviet pullout from Afghanistan. Her counsel was ignored. By then India's defence industry was tied up with its Soviet counterpart so closely that she lacked any cards to play in her dealings with the Kremlin.

As a result of India's testing of a 'nuclear device' in 1974 during Gandhi's previous premiership, Pakistan had accelerated its programme to build an atom bomb – dubbed the 'Islamic Bomb' by Zulfikar Ali Bhutto – a prospect that disturbed Israel as much as it did India.

In late 1982, following Israeli defence minister Ariel Sharon's offer to attack Pakistan's Kahuta nuclear facility in conjunction with India, military officers from Delhi travelled to Tel Aviv clandestinely in February 1983 to purchase electronic equipment to neutralize Kahuta's air defences.[12] These moves did not remain secret for long from Pakistan's Inter-Services Intelligence (ISI) directorate. Following an ISI approach to RAW, a critical meeting took place in a Vienna hotel in the autumn. Munir Ahmad Khan, chairman of the Pakistan Atomic Energy Commission, warned Raja Ramanna, director of the Bhabha Atomic Research Centre at Trombay and the father of India's atom bomb, that if India, whether in conjunction with Israel or alone, attacked Kahuta, Pakistan would hit the Trombay facility, with horrific consequences for the millions of Mumbai residents nearby.[13]

RAW had taken to dispatching its officers to Israel for specialist training and purchasing Israeli electronic intelligence equipment. Following Indira Gandhi's assassination in October 1984, it secured the services of a senior officer in Israel's domestic intelligence agency, Shin Beth, (Hebrew, acronym of *Sherut Betakhon*, 'Security Service'), to tighten up the Indian prime minister's security. For all the expertise that Shin Beth purportedly passed on to the Indians, it failed to prevent the assassination of its own prime minister, Yitzhak Rabin, in November 1995.

Rajiv Gandhi, who succeded his mother as prime minister, had to deal with the ongoing Soviet military involvement in Afghanistan as well as Pakistan's nuclear weapons programme. Following in the footsteps of his predecessor, he refrained from criticizing the Kremlin in his address to the UN General Assembly in October 1985. The next month, India abstained for the sixth time in a vote on the General Assembly resolution calling for the withdrawal of Soviet forces from Afghanistan. Because of this, the Reagan administration placed India in the Soviet column, arguing that its purported non-aligned policy was in reality tilted towards Moscow and against Washington. This overarching view became the conventional wisdom in the West. It also took hold in the minds of most Pakistanis and all anti-Soviet jihadists.

The murky issue of the clandestine nuclear weapons programmes of India and Pakistan continued to dog their leaders, with periodic reports of Delhi preparing to hit Pakistan's facility at Kahuta. To end the speculation, Rajiv Gandhi and Muhammad Zia ul Haq came to an informal understanding in December 1985 not to attack each other's nuclear sites.

Two months earlier, during his visit to the United Nations, Gandhi had met Israeli prime minister Shimon Peres. This was a remarkable event, coming as it did after more than three years of strained relations. In June 1982, the Indian government had expelled the Israeli consul, Yossef Hassin, after he had characterized India's pro-Arab policy as 'purely venal' in an interview with the Mumbai-based *Sunday Observer*, downgraded the mission head to vice consul, and refused to accredit a diplomat Israel wanted to dispatch to India.

However, this public spat had no impact on the strengthening of links between RAW and Mossad. In the early 1980s, Israel equipped RAW's two Boeing 707s belonging to its Aviation Research Centre for aerial reconnaissance with specialist equipment to gather signals intelligence.

Following the well-established pattern of what happened to Indian prime ministers during their visits to the US, Rajiv Gandhi found himself pressured by America's influential Jewish and pro-Israeli organizations to normalize relations with Israel. Lacking the cunning of his mother or the intellectual convictions of his maternal grandfather, Nehru, he began to ease up on Israel. In 1987, he allowed Tel Aviv to head its mission in Mumbai by a consul. In June 1988, he agreed to meet Morris Abrams, president of the Conference of Major Jewish Organizations, to discuss India's diplomatic relations with Israel. He thus set a precedent that would lead, inter alia, to the powerful American Israel Public Affairs Committee (AIPAC) guiding Indian immigrants in the US on how to establish lobbies and make them effective.

When in 1987, it became common knowledge that Pakistan was within 'a turn of a screwdriver' of assembling an atom bomb, the possibility of India collaborating with Israel to strike the Kahuta facility cropped up again in the media in all three countries. In July 1988, there was a secret meeting in Paris between Indian and Israeli officials.[14] Israel could not accomplish an attack on Kahuta on its own. And the Indian government had to weigh the military and political consequences of undertaking such an aggressive move with Israel. It realized that its own strategic military and economic sites were vulnerable to conventional Pakistani air strikes. Therefore, it decided to refrain from taking action.

The net outcome of this near-crisis was that the governments of Rajiv Gandhi and the newly elected Benazir Bhutto in Pakistan signed a written agreement not to attack each other's nuclear facilities, effective from 1 January 1993.[15] But that still left intact the covert Indian–Israeli cooperation on missile technology undertaken after their refusal to join the informal 1987 missile regime initiated by the G8.[16]

JIHADISTS TRAIN THEIR GUNS ON INDIA

The growing links between India and Israel made headline news in the mainstream Pakistani media, particularly when the stories, originating with the ISI, were given an alarmist spin. They were highlighted by the Islamist parties and jihadists based in Pakistan and Afghanistan and their publications. The latter nursed a grudge against India for giving a wide berth to the Kremlin in Afghanistan despite its bloody involvement there.

In Pakistan, the Markaz ud Dawa wal Irshad, led by Hafiz Muhammad Saeed – a bespectacled, former academic with a tapering, hennaed beard, and a veteran of the anti-Soviet jihad in Afghanistan – paid particular attention to the Indian–Israeli links. As an institution, it set itself apart from most Muslim organizations engaged in preaching Islam by motivating believers to devote themselves to jihad. According to Saeed, the overall aim of jihad should be to eliminate evil and ignorance and make Islam dominant throughout the globe. The primary targets of his jihad were Hindus, the most blatant polytheists, and Jews, described in the Quran as enemies, whose State of Israel had been aiding the Indian security forces against Kashmiri Muslims. Following the Soviet withdrawal from Afghanistan in 1989, assisted by the ISI, the Markaz ud Dawa wal Irshad's armed wing, the Lashkar-e Taiba (LeT), intensified the jihad against India's armed forces in Kashmir.

Another jihadist organization that took a keen interest in the Indian–Israeli links was the Harkat ul Jihad Islami (Arabic, 'Movement for Islamic Jihad'; HuJI), founded in 1984 by Fazlur Rahman Khalil and Qari Saifullah Akhtar, both of whom participated in the anti-Moscow jihad. The difference between the Markaz and the HuJI was that, whereas the former followed the Wahhabi ideology,[17] the latter was influenced by the Taliban's version of Islam as enforced in Afghanistan. A breakaway faction of the HuJI would later mutate into the Harkat Mujahedin and become an important player in the insurgency in Indian Kashmir.

AFTER THE SOVIET DISSOLUTION

Nineteen ninety-one was a memorable year not only for the Soviet Union but also for India. Following the Kuwait crisis, caused by

Iraq's invasion of the country in August 1990, the remittances of the hundreds of thousand of Indians working in the Gulf region fell sharply and India's oil bill more than doubled. Its trade deficit rocketed while its foreign debt remained unbearably high at $70 billion. In mid-1991, the government of Pamulaparti Venkata Narasimha Rao, who had succeeded Rajiv Gandhi after the latter's assassination in May, found the country's foreign reserves down to less than $1 billion, barely enough to pay for a month's imports. Only by selling 200 tonnes of its gold stock in London to buy foreign currencies, using special aid by Japan and Germany, and drawing on the IMF's special facilities in June, did Delhi manage to avoid defaulting on its debt payments. The IMF's assistance came only after India agreed to devalue its currency by 22 per cent and accelerate economic reforms. Delhi unveiled a liberalized industrial policy, reducing tariffs, curtailing the role of the public sector, abolishing industrial licensing, and allowing private companies into banking, insurance, telecom, and air travel. This endeared it to Washington several months *before* the break-up of the Soviet Union on 31 December.

A fortnight earlier, India had displayed its moderation towards Israel in public. At the United Nations General Assembly, it voted in favour of revoking the 1975 resolution describing Zionism as a form of racism and racial discrimination. In October at the Middle East peace conference in Madrid, under the co-chairmanship of America and the Soviet Union, Israel and the Arab states sat down to sort out their relations.

On the eve of Rao's trip to New York in late January 1992 to attend the UN Security Council summit,[18] India established full diplomatic relations with Israel. During that year, three delegations of Israeli arms manufacturers visited Delhi. Before according Israel its much-coveted recognition status, Rao had sought and secured clearance from Yasser Arafat, chairman of the Palestine Liberation Organization (PLO), by inviting him to Delhi for consultations. After these talks, Arafat said that India was free to pursue any policy that was in its national interest.

Israeli officials privately attributed India's move to a broader strategy to improve relations with the winner of the Cold War. Many saw in this development – rightly, as it would turn out – the emergence of an Indian-Israeli-American triad.

In short, after the dissolution of the Soviet Union it became incumbent on the Indian government to cultivate cordial relations with the sole superpower. And the pressing need to counter the escalating insurgency in the Kashmir Valley led it to forge strong links with Israel, which had ample experience in countering armed Palestinian resistance since the founding of the PLO in 1964.

'India and Israel can provide a joint democratic counterbalance to the kind of forces that breed fundamentalism,' declared Yehuda Haim, Israel's first ambassador to Delhi.[19] Not wanting to be left out, during his visit to India in May 1993, Israeli foreign minister Shimon Peres suggested 'demographic changes' in Kashmir to resolve the dispute, implying a transfer of Kashmiri Muslims from the Valley[20] – a proposal that exposed his anti-Muslim bias. It riled Indian Muslims and inflamed Pakistanis.

There was a mushrooming of exchanges of visits by military delegations between India and Israel, with the total reaching fifty before the end of the decade. Most of the 150 Israeli defence companies, with combined annual revenues of $3.5 billion, wanted a piece of the Indian pie. They found that the problems encountered by the Indians in producing their own light combat aircraft (to replace aging Soviet-made MiGs) and the Arjun main battle tank were similar to those they had faced when designing the Lavi fighter in the 1980s and the Merkava tank later. Active Israeli assistance followed. Also as a result of this collaboration, the Indians would later learn how to upgrade their Agni missile along the lines of Israel's Barak missile.[21]

Furthermore, Israel's military delegations reportedly offered India technologies relating to a cruise missile, an unmanned reconnaissance aircraft, and a multipurpose unmanned aerial vehicle (UAV). The reasons for such wide-ranging cooperation were as much political as economic. There was immense pressure on Israeli arms producers to achieve economies of scale by increasing exports and generating cash for expensive research and development programmes to stay ahead of their foreign competitors. This made Israel, a country of a mere seven million, the fifth largest international arms supplier after America, Russia, Britain, and France.

Another area where Israelis excelled was in electronics and avionics. This enabled their military technicians to upgrade old systems in tanks and fighter aircraft, and improve the accuracy of missiles. The Israeli military had captured Soviet-made weapons during their wars with the Arabs; consequently, their technicians knew how to upgrade them. In 1996, Israel Aircraft Industries started upgrading the Indian air force's Soviet-era MiG-21 ground-attack aircraft.

During that year, India purchased a sophisticated Air Combat Manoeuvring Instrumentation system from Israel, which was installed at the Jamnagar air base, 150 miles (240 km) from the Pakistani border. Israel Aircraft Industries agreed to build two Dvora MK-2 patrol boats in India while Soltam Systems announced that it would supply tens of millions of dollars' worth of 155mm self-propelled guns to the Indian army. Tadiran Communications, an Israeli company specializing in military communications, started providing hundreds of millions of dollars' worth of equipment to India's armed forces.

The possibility of Israeli military intervention in the subcontinent arose soon after India's Defence Research and Development Organization carried out five nuclear-bomb tests on 11 and 13 May 1998. As Pakistan prepared to test its atom bombs on 28 May, its military spotted a US-made F16 in the airspace. It was aware that Israel used two-seater F16s, equipped with advanced reconnaissance equipment, which at 45,000 feet (14,000 m) could take pictures of objects many miles away. Fearing that this was part of an Indian–Israeli plan to launch a pre-emptive strike at its test site in the Chagai Hills of Baluchistan, it alerted both the US and the United Nations. They in turn immediately contacted the Israeli government, which assured them that it had no such plan.[22] Pakistan was not reassured. Its president, Rafiq Taroor, suspended the constitution and declared a state of emergency due to 'external threats'. Soon the government announced a 50 per cent cut in all expenditure except development projects.[23] The situation was touch-and-go. On 27 May, Indian intelligence had picked up a coded message to Pakistan's high commissioner in Delhi from Islamabad that it had 'credible info' that India was all set to mount a predawn attack on its nuclear installations.[24]

There was much bluffing by both sides about the number and explosive yields of tests. Experts at the Incorporated Research Institutions for Seismology – a consortium of ninety research universities operating a global network of one hundred seismic monitoring stations – endorsed a study of these tests by Terry Wallace of Arizona University, published in *Seismological Research Letters*. This said that two of the five tests announced by India may never have taken place; and only two of the six tests announced by Pakistan actually involved 'real nuclear explosions', one of them being a tactical weapon with a low explosive yield.[25]

Nonetheless, invoking the 1994 Nuclear Proliferation Prevention Act, the Clinton administration blocked all aid, banned loans by American banks and exports of products with military uses such as computers, and curbed military technology exports to India and Pakistan. This had the unintended effect of strengthening India–Israel links.

Meanwhile political relations between India and Israel had been on a similar track. When, for instance, Lal Krishna Advani, president of the Hindu nationalist Bhartiya Janata Party (BJP), visited Israel in 1995 – when his party was in opposition – he was received warmly by the country's top politicians.

THE TRIAD'S SECURITY–MILITARY COLLABORATION

Israel Aerospace Industries signed a $2.5 billion deal to develop an anti-aircraft system and missiles for India – the biggest defence contract in Israel's history at the time. To replace obsolete Soviet systems, it started developing the Barak-8-8 missile for the Indian navy and air force, which was capable of protecting sea vessels and ground facilities from aircraft and cruise missiles.

In January 1997 came the state visit of Israeli president Ezer Weizman. As a pilot in Britain's Royal Air Force who had been posted in Bangalore during World War II, he showed a keen interest in upgrading military cooperation between the two countries. Israel offered its Combative Manoeuvring Instrumentation System to the Indian air force. Two months later, the Indian army chief of staff, General Ved Prakash Malik, undertook a four-day trip to Israel. During a visit to the Israeli–Lebanese frontier, he saw the hi-tech anti-infiltration systems and 'innovative tactics' that Israel had deployed to make its border secure.[26]

Once the BJP-led coalition assumed office in Delhi in April 1998, India–Israel relations thrived as never before. Besides their common agenda in countering cross-border terrorism in Indian Kashmir and in Israel, there was an ideological convergence between the two governments. The compulsory draft for all Israeli Jews, male and female; the discipline of a militarized society such as Israel; and the iron hand with which the Jewish state acted against Palestinian terrorists appealed greatly to Hindu nationalists. Underlying all those factors was a shared prejudice against Muslims. Since its founding in 1980, the BJP had been a vocal critic of what it perceived to be the Congress party's pro-Arab and pro-Palestinian stance abroad and pro-Muslim policy at home.

Little wonder, then, that the BJP-led government allowed the use of Indian territory to Israel, short of space, for military tests. In 2000, Israel tested an anti-missile missile by firing it at an Israeli-made cruise missile off India's eastern shore, most likely near Balasore in the Bay of Bengal.[27] By then the two countries were involved in twenty-two joint research projects in information technology, biotechnology, and water technology.

Washington's sanctions against India in the wake of Delhi's nuclear tests left the private sectors in the two nations unaffected. Following India's economic liberalization package in 1991, US-based multinational corporations had rushed to set up business in India either on their own or in partnership with local companies. On the other hand, information and communication technology (ICT) firms in India were able to mint money when a scare spread in America and elsewhere in the West that most computers with an inbuilt time notation going up only to 1999 would crash at midnight on 31 December 1999. At a fraction of the fee charged by US-based companies for immunization against 'the millennium bug' – Y2K – the Indian firms offered to do the job. They were overwhelmed with orders, and worked round the clock until zero hour at the entry into the twenty-first century.

The dramatic Y2K opening paved the way for Indian ICT companies to expand their businesses in America. What aided India-based firms further was the drastic decline in global telecom charges. Staffed by educated, English-speaking employees, these companies' payroll represented a mere fraction of the salaries paid in developed economies. These factors converged once widespread use of the Internet enabled people from all over the globe to compete, and trade, in real time. Another innovation that helped economic expansion in India, deficient in landline telephones, was the cellphone.

It was against this backdrop that President Clinton spent five days in India in March 2000. He signed agreements on science, technology, and commerce. He spoke of institutionalizing the India–US dialogue up to the highest level and of continuing talks on the nuclear issue. In contrast, he spent only five hours in Pakistan, where he gave his listeners a lecture on do's and don'ts. By then, Pakistan had emerged as the foster parent of the Taliban in Afghanistan, a regime that had allowed its soil to be used for terrorist attacks on the US embassies in East Africa and in India-held Kashmir.

In contrast, India had allowed Israeli experts on terrorism to visit the Kashmir Valley. During his first overseas trip – to Israel, in June 2000 – as India's home minister, Advani said, 'Defeating the designs of our neighbour [Pakistan] who has unleashed cross-border terrorism, illegal infiltration and border management are concerns that have brought me to Israel.'[28] This was a clear, unambiguous declaration of Delhi and Tel Aviv sharing a common agenda.

Significantly, Advani's large delegation included RAW chief A.S. Dulat, Intelligence Bureau head Shyamal Dutta, and Border Security Force director-general E.N. Rammohan. Advani met not only the directors of Mossad and Shin Beth – Ephraim Halevi and Avi Dichter, respectively – but also, surprisingly for an interior minister, Israel's prime minister, Ehud Barak, as well as its foreign minister, Shimon Peres. His field trips to witness the techniques and equipment used by Israel to stop cross-border infiltration took him to the country's borders with Lebanon, Egypt (in the Negev Desert), and Syria (in the occupied Golan Heights). This prepared the ground for the sale of Israel's surveillance equipment, including thermal sensors and night-vision devices, to India, for use mainly in Kashmir. Later a team of senior Israeli counterterrorism officials toured Indian Kashmir and other areas of endemic anti-government violence. According to the British-based *Jane's Terrorism and Security Monitor*, in August 2001, Israel had posted 'several teams' in the Kashmir Valley to train Indian counter-insurgency personnel. [29]

THE JIHADISTS' RESPONSE

Pakistani politicians, whether secular or religious, noted these developments with growing alarm. In the eyes of Islamist leaders, an alliance of Hindus and Jews was emerging as an enemy of Pakistan and Islam. The LeT was foremost in its denunciation of the new foe. Its founding charter had argued that jihad was the sole path to be followed to restore the past power of Islam – to retake Spain, where Muslims had ruled for eight centuries, and reinstall Muslim rule in India. It stated that the ultimate aim of its campaign to liberate Kashmir was to liberate all of India.[30]

The LeT, led by Saeed, called its select foot soldiers *fidayeen*

(Arabic, 'self-sacrificers') and gave them audacious assignments which generated dramatic news. Between November 1999 and December 2000, it staged fifteen attacks on security forces in Indian Kashmir, killing fifty Indian armed personnel at a loss of twenty-four fidayeen. On 22 December 2000, two armed LeT fidayeen scaled the lower walls of the sprawling Red Fort in Delhi, part of which contained a military barracks and a high-security interrogation cell, and engaged in a firefight with the troops. Whereas the government announced that the terrorists were killed for the loss of three Indian soldiers, an LeT spokesman claimed that they had escaped safely to 'an undisclosed location'.

This daredevil attack was highly symbolic. The Red Fort, built by Mughal emperor Shah Jahan in 1638 on the bank of the Yamuna River, is a popular symbol of power in India. It is the site where the prime minister raises the national flag every 15 August, Independence Day, and delivers a nationally televised speech to a mammoth crowd. The sensational episode gave substance to Saeed's view that the liberation struggle in Kashmir was 'the gateway to the liberation of Indian Muslims'. 'The [Red Fort] action indicates that we have extended the jihad to India,' he said.[31]

The LeT kept up its attention-grabbing operations in Indian Kashmir. In January 2001, for instance, six of its fidayeen, wearing Indian army fatigues and driving an official vehicle, managed to get past the heavily barricaded gates of Srinagar airport. When later challenged, they engaged in a firefight, killing several Indian security personnel before they were shot dead.

Such events led to increased cooperation between Delhi and Tel Aviv even before the Al Qaida-directed attacks on targets in New York and Metropolitan Washington on 11 September 2001. As it happened, on that day India's national security adviser, Brajesh Mishra, was conducting a 'joint security strategy dialogue' with his Israeli counterpart, Major General Uzi Dayan, in Delhi.

9/11 SEALS INDIA-ISRAEL-AMERICA BOND

Soon after announcing his global war on terror, US president George W. Bush lifted the sanctions against Pakistan and India, thus returning Washington's relations with these neighbours to their pre-nuclear-testing level. That cleared the way for Israel to sell to India almost the whole range of its hi-tech defence products, often based on technology licensed in the US, whose administration could veto sales to third parties. Following the attack on the Indian parliament in December 2001 and the subsequent launch of Operation Parakram by Delhi, Israel dispatched military hardware to India.

The number of jihadist attacks on targets in India rose. Among them were the crash of an express train, caused by the removal of tracks in the northern city of Jaunpur, in May, killing twelve people, and an assault on a Hindu temple in the western Indian city of Ahmedabad four months later, causing thirty fatalities.

Before taking up his job as head of RAW in April 2003, C.D. Sahay underwent intelligence training in Britain and Israel. This was a departure from the long-established tradition of training future RAW chiefs with Britain's Secret Intelligence Service, known by its acronym of MI6 (Military Intelligence 6), and/or America's CIA.[32]

Addressing a meeting of the American Jewish Committee in May 2003, Mishra said that India, America and Israel 'have some fundamental similarities. We are all democracies, sharing a common vision of pluralism, tolerance, and equal opportunity. Strong US-India and India-Israel relations have a natural logic.'[33] Sharing a vision was one thing, realizing it quite another – as Palestinians, and even Israeli Arabs, knew only too well, as well as the Muslims in Kashmir and elsewhere in India. But, then again, jihadist organizations never subscribed to the concepts of 'pluralism, tolerance, and equal opportunity'.

This was the background to the red-carpet reception accorded to Israeli prime minister Ariel Sharon during his visit to Delhi in 2003. It started – significantly enough – on the second anniversary of 9/11.

Given Sharon's reputation as a merciless enemy of the Palestinians, many European governments refrained from inviting him as a state guest. No wonder that his Indian trip aroused the most widespread controversy and protest the republic had ever witnessed concerning a foreign leader's trip. Thousands of supporters of leftist parties and Muslim groups demonstrated, describing him as 'a terrorist and a war criminal'. During Sharon's trip, Israeli minister of science and technology, Eliezer Sandberg signed a memorandum of understanding with the Indian Space Research Organization.

Unsurprisingly, that month in his tape, aired by the Al Jazeera and Al Arabiya satellite TV channels, Al Qaida's number two, Ayman Zawahiri, strongly condemned the Hindu–Jewish alliance.

In January 2004, towards the end of its tenure, the BJP-led government signed a deal for three Phalcon (phased array L-band conformal) radar systems, designed and manufactured by a subsidiary of Israel Aerospace Industries, for $1.1 billion. Since Phalcon contained US-designed or made parts, the State Department had to clear the transaction. It did so even though it knew that India proposed to mount these radar and surveillance systems not on US-made Boeings but on Russian-supplied IL-76 aircraft.

Four months later, the BJP-led coalition in Delhi gave way to one headed by the Congress party, with Manmohan Singh as prime minister. It continued the previous government's policy towards Tel Aviv. The alliance with Israel had become such an important part of the national security mantra that neither of the major political parties could consider opting out of it. Actually, the situation was a rerun of what had happened to Delhi–Moscow relations when right-winger Morarji Desai became Indian prime minister in 1977. Though he and his foreign minister, Vajpayee, wanted to loosen Delhi's ties with the Soviet Union, they found their room for manoeuvre very limited due to the close integration of India's military industry with its Soviet counterpart. In 2005, therefore, the Indian government placed an order for fifty Heron Drones (spy UAVs) from Israel Aircraft Industries, with the prospect of joint production in the coming years. Trade in the civilian sector maintained its upward trend, rising from $384 million in 1996 to $2.4 billion in 2007.[34]

During his visit to the US in September 2004, Manmohan Singh met leaders of the American Jewish community and praised the contributions they had made to improving Indo-American relations as well as Indo-Israeli friendship.

Since the 1990s, the American Israel Public Affairs Committee, the American Jewish Committee, the Jewish Institute on National Security Affairs, and the American Jewish Congress had been cultivating close ties with the Indian diaspora in the US and the up-and-coming Indian lobby in Washington. Highly educated and affluent, the Jews and Indians in America were attached to their democratic homelands. The US–India Political Action Committee, founded a year after 9/11, made no secret of emulating the American Jewish groups. Hence, it and the American Israel Public Affairs Committee took to supporting, jointly, pro-India and pro-Israel candidates in US elections. They lobbied together, successfully, to secure the Bush administration's approval of Israel's sale of the Phalcon radar systems to India.

But, much to the satisfaction of Pakistan, the efforts of these lobbies, and the Indian Embassy in Washington, failed to block at Congressional level the sale of US arms to Islamabad, sanctioned by the Bush administration. This was welcomed by Pakistani officials and politicians of all hues, including jihadists. By the same token, officials and politicians in Pakistan were downcast to learn of the signing of a ten-year 'New Framework for the US–India Defence Relationship' agreement between Delhi and Washington in 2005 to identify common strategic goals and outline the means to achieve them. Then followed a bilateral 'Defence Procurement and Production Group' to supervise defence trade and prospects for co-production and technology collaboration.[35]

Further disappointment in Pakistani circles followed when the US House of Representatives passed the 'Henry J. Hyde United States-India Peaceful Atomic Energy Cooperation Act of 2006'. This allowed

American and Indian companies to participate in each other's civil nuclear-energy industries, even though Delhi had not signed the nuclear Non-Proliferation Treaty. These developments provided an unmistakable sign of the India-America-Israel triad firming up.

Subsequently, the number of jihadist terrorist assaults on Indian targets rose. The overall aim of those perpetrating them was to cause maximum casualties and/or inflame Hindu–Muslim relations. They therefore focused on crowded places such as markets, railway coaches, and Hindu temples. In July 2005, in a highly symbolic act, six LeT fidayeen tried to storm the site of the demolished Babri Mosque in Ayodhya – the putative site for the ancient Rama Temple to be rebuilt – ringed by security personnel. They failed and were killed. Later that month a bomb explosion on an express train left thirteen dead. And a series of bomb blasts in the markets of Delhi in October claimed nearly three score lives.

Between then and November 2007, bombings by jihadist organizations in Varanasi, Mumbai, and Delhi, targeting a temple, commuter trains, and bazaars, left more than three hundred people dead. But these vicious attacks did not lead to a deterioration in Hindu–Muslim relations. Nor did they impact on Indian–Israeli links.

In January 2008, Israel chose India's PSLV launch vehicle instead of its own home-made rocket, to launch its latest spy satellite, TecSAR, chiefly because it was the cheaper option. By then, Israel-made Tavor assault rifles, costing $6,500 apiece, capable of firing 750–900 rounds per minute, were in use in the Kashmir Valley. Press reports there referred to four battalions (totalling two thousand soldiers) being dispatched to Israel for special counter-insurgency training. Also, India had deployed seven Special Forces battalions in Kashmir, trained to conduct specialized tasks behind enemy lines and fight insurgents.[36]

In August, it was reported that India had become the single largest importer of Israel's military equipment, constituting almost half of Israel's defence exports and about 30 per cent of India's imports. On

10 November, Indian military officials visited Israel to discuss joint weapons development projects, additional sales of Israeli equipment to the Indian military, and counterterrorism strategies.

These reports formed the backdrop to the sensational terrorist attacks on targets in Mumbai on 26 November 2008, known in India as 26/11. Many experts viewed this episode as a riposte to the thriving India–Israel partnership. But instead of loosening its ties with Tel Aviv, the Indian government sought Israel's expertise to establish an elaborate intelligence network to counter terrorism, including making preparations for anti-terrorist raids inside Pakistan.

AFTER THE 26/11 MUMBAI ATTACKS

'We have a very special intense relationship with India,' announced the *Jerusalem Post* on 15 February 2009. 'It is now moving toward joint development of equipment. There are several projects in the pipeline.' In an interview with Indian journalists, Major General Udi Shani, head of Israel's Defence Export and Defence Cooperation Agency, said: 'There is now close cooperation [between the two countries] and the Indians respect Israeli systems and our experience in fighting terror.'[37]

Borrowing the technology of Israel's TecSAR, India manufactured its own spy satellite, RISAT-2, capable of taking high-resolution pictures at night and carrying out reconnaissance through dense clouds. It was launched in April 2009. A similar collaboration in missile technology would help India to produce its Prithvi and Agni missiles, emulating Israel's Jericho-I and Jericho-II missiles.

While these advanced weapons and surveillance systems were useful to Delhi in its external defence, they were of little help in pacifying the people in disaffected regions such as north-eastern India and Kashmir.

This became apparent when, after a lull of a year and a half, the Muslims in the Kashmir Valley once again resorted to street protest in the summer of 2010, with the authorities in Srinagar and Delhi falling back on their old tactic of applying ever-increasing force. What differentiated this phase of Kashmiri disaffection was that it was wholly indigenous, with no input from Pakistan. The security situation in Pakistan had become perilous, and the ISI had its hands full trying to fend off the challenge posed to the regime by the Pakistani Taliban. The state apparatus felt threatened everywhere, including in Azad Kashmir, which was used as the staging post for destabilizing Indian Kashmir.

7

LIBERATING INDIAN KASHMIR

NO DESCRIPTION OF Kashmir as 'paradise on earth' would be complete without a reference to the bow-shaped Valley of Neelum (aka Kishenganga), 100 miles (160 km) long and 50 miles (80 km) wide. The indigo-blue Neelum River flows down from a height of 8,000 feet (2,400 m) in a serpentine course through forests of majestic pine, fir, deodar, walnut, and strawberry trees, waterfalls, and flowering plants and medicinal herbs, to merge into the Jhelum near Muzaffarabad at an altitude of 2,000 feet (600 m).

Like other cities or major towns in Kashmir on both sides of the Line of Control, Muzaffarabad, the capital of Azad Kashmir, is home to the graves of Sufi saints. Of these, the shrine of Sakhi Saheli Sarkar stands out due to its majestic entrance gate, green dome, and verandahs with arched pillars of marble. It is the city's prime attraction for visitors. Despite the physical separation caused by the Line of Control, most Kashmiri Muslims on both sides of the divide continue to share a common attachment to Sufi thought and practices.[1] As a consequence, the inhabitants of Azad Kashmir have been less affected by the rise of radical Islamism than Punjabi or Pushtun Muslims. But they are a minuscule minority in Pakistan and operate on the fringes of its political life.

Cradled by lofty mountains, Muzaffarabad is prone to earthquakes.

The one that struck the region in October 2005, with Muzaffarabad at its epicentre, was so severe that it destroyed nearly half of the city's buildings. It damaged the Red Fort on the Neelum River, completed by the city's founder, Sultan Muzaffar Khan, in 1646.

This fort, as well as the one on the opposite bank of the river, was expanded by the descendants of Gulab Singh Dogra. It was he who secured possession of the State of Jammu and Kashmir in 1846 by paying the equivalent of $680,000 to the cash-strapped East India Company of Britain. The Dogra rulers used the forts as garrisons.

POST-INDEPENDENCE KASHMIR

After the partition of the Indian subcontinent in August 1947, the formation of the independent government of Azad Jammu and Kashmir (Azad Kashmir for short) by the Muslim Conference in the Poonch–Mirpur region led to the expulsion of the forces of Maharaja Hari Singh Dogra from the forts along the Neelum.

The appeal by Muslim Conference leader Muhammad Ibrahim Khan to the Dominion of Pakistan for help to liberate the rest of the state from the Hindu ruler was welcomed. Pakistan's all-powerful Governor General, Muhammad Ali Jinnah, had reserved the right to deal with the affairs of the semi-autonomous Federally Administered Tribal Agencies (FATA) along the Pakistan–Afghanistan border and Kashmir.

Jinnah noted with growing anxiety the events in Kashmir in October. When Indian soldiers, commanded by General Sir Robert Lockhart, flew into Kashmir, after Hari Singh had signed the instrument of accession with the Dominion of India, Jinnah ordered Pakistan's commander-in-chief, General Sir Frank Walter Messervy, to dispatch troops to Kashmir. The British general refused. He argued that the presence of the Indian forces in Kashmir was justified since the maharaja had acceded to India, and that introducing Pakistani troops into Kashmir would compel him to withdraw all British officers from the Pakistani military because British officers could not fight on opposing sides. So Jinnah, a lawyer by training, found his hands tied. Relations between him and Messervy became intolerably tense. Messervy took an early retirement in February 1948 and was succeeded by General Sir Douglas David Gracey.

After a lull in the fighting in Kashmir due to winter snows, the Indian side staged an offensive to recapture lost ground. This raised the possibility of the Indians advancing into Pakistan proper. Therefore Jinnah openly introduced Pakistani troops into the fight (started initially by the armed inhabitants of FATA) in April 1948 and established the Ministry of Kashmir Affairs. Though United Nations Security Council resolution 47 of April 1948 called for an immediate ceasefire, the truce came into effect only on 1 January 1949, with the assistance of the United Nations Commission for India and Pakistan (UNCIP). By then, Jinnah, the founder of Pakistan, was dead.

Following the truce, the Azad Kashmir government became the administrative authority for the territory west of the ceasefire line, including the Gilgit Agency – composed of Gilgit, Hunza and Nagar – and Baltistan. In 1949, Pakistan imposed direct rule on the Gilgit Agency and Baltistan after merging them, and named the new entity 'Northern Areas'. The following year the Pakistani government issued an ordinance, 'Rules of Business of the Azad Kashmir Government', which served as the basic law for the territory. The supreme head of this government functioned under the watchful eyes of the Ministry of Kashmir Affairs. Pakistan retained control of defence, foreign policy, and dealings with the United Nations, while the Azad Kashmir government continued to administer the territory and develop it economically.

In March 1950, UNCIP gave way to a UN representative charged with the task of bringing about demilitarization in both parts of Kashmir. The first such representative, Australian judge Owen Dixon, reported that since Delhi would never agree to demilitarization, two alternatives should be considered. One: Hold four regional plebiscites – in Jammu, the Kashmir Valley, Ladakh, and the Northern

Areas. Two: Partition the state, with some areas going to India, others to Pakistan, and hold a plebiscite only in the Kashmir Valley. Indian prime minister Jawaharlal Nehru showed interest in Dixon's proposals but his Pakistani counterpart, Liaquat Ali Khan, rejected them. He insisted on a plebiscite to decide the fate of all of Jammu and Kashmir, confident that its Muslim majority would opt for accession to Pakistan. This was the earliest of the missed opportunities to resolve a dispute by peaceful means which has since proved intractable.

A year later Liaquat Ali Khan was assassinated. Thus, within four years Pakistani lost its two pre-eminent founders, known respectively as the Quaid-i-Azam, 'Great Leader', and Quaid-i-Millat, 'Leader of the Nation'. Since none of the politicians who followed them in office had the charisma or popularity of Jinnah or Khan, the politics of the newly independent country began to unravel. However, all Pakistani politicians shared a common resolve to see that the predominantly Muslim population of Kashmir should exercise its right to self-determination through a plebiscite, certain of its outcome.

The other major impact that the Kashmir issue had on Pakistan's history was the induction of its military into a hot war with India within months of the founding of the new state. This conflict highlighted the vital importance of the armed forces to the polity – an overarching factor that has remained unchanged through the checkered history of Pakistan. Indeed, in thrall of their armed forces at the birth of Pakistan, most Pakistanis went along with military governance, followed by militarization under a nominal civilian authority, as happened during the rule of General Pervez Musharraf. Today, the military is the most trusted institution in the country, with a popularity rating six times higher than that of the civilian government.

KASHMIR'S VITAL IMPORTANCE TO PAKISTAN

The reason for Pakistani politicians' united stand on Kashmir was simple and profound. To see a Muslim-majority province integrated into Hindu-majority India undermined the very foundation on which Pakistan was based. The only way to safeguard the interests of Muslims, forming merely a quarter of the population of united India, was to carve out a portion of the subcontinent for them. They were more than a community; they constituted a nation on a par with the Hindu nation, argued Jinnah and his All-India Muslim League.

The post-independence behaviour of the predominantly Hindu Indian National Congress provided ample evidence to support Jinnah's scenario of the Muslims in independent, united India getting a raw deal. As the successor state to British India, independent India, ruled by Congress party leaders, stalled on implementing the division of 17.5 per cent of British India's assets to Pakistan. For several crucial months, it delayed the transfer of the cash balance of 750 million rupees – worth £1.5 billion today – to Pakistan. It also prevaricated in transferring Pakistan's share of 165,000 tonnes of defence equipment.[2] India's barely disguised intention was to thwart the founding of a viable Pakistan.

Though deplorable, such tactics were not surprising. Congress leaders accepted partition with the utmost reluctance, comparing it to the physical vivisection of Mother India. They nurtured ill will towards the new nation, born in the midst of savage inter-religious violence that claimed up to one million lives and led to the exchange of some fifteen million people across the newly created international borders. They wanted the new enterprise either to fail or falter.

Little wonder that following the fight over Kashmir a belief took hold among the Pakistani people and politicians that India represented an existential threat to their country. They came to define Pakistan as antithetical to India, the permanent 'other'. Under the circumstances, the armed forces emerged as the pre-eminent, overarching institution, with General Muhammad Ayub Khan, the commander-in-chief of Pakistan, becoming the defence minister in 1953. He broke the tradition of a civilian occupying that position. The following year he made the first move to extend the military into the civilian sector by forming the Fauji (Urdu, 'Army's') Foundation, an economic entity, charged with furthering the welfare of ex-servicemen.

After two wars focused on Kashmir and two major Kashmir-related eyeball-to-eyeball standoffs in 1999 and 2002 between India and Pakistan, the long-running dispute remains unresolved. As for the multi-ethnic, multi-religious India, with its 1.2 billion people and eighteen officially recognized languages, Kashmir, however troublesome, is just one of its twenty-eight states. The agenda of India's leaders is long and varied.

Not so with Pakistan. It comprises only four provinces, home to interrelated languages, with Punjab being predominant. Historically, Punjabis, foremost in Pakistan's officer corps and the top tier of the civil service, have been close to Kashmiri Muslims due to blood ties. The immigrants from independent India, forming a majority in Karachi, the country's most populous city, sense among Kashmiri Muslims their own yearning to live in an overwhelmingly Muslim country. Then there are Islamic preachers who visualize liberating Kashmiri Muslims from their Hindu oppressors as a religious duty.

These factors have led to Kashmir impacting on the national identity of Pakistanis and an ongoing debate about whether their country's inception was rooted, in essence, in Islamic ideology or in a pragmatic territorial carve-up. No matter which side of the argument is dominant at any given time, there has been no change in the policy of having an even bigger and better military in Pakistan.

In order to ensure ample supplies of modern weaponry, Pakistan's leaders turned to the United States. This led to Pakistan signing a defence agreement with the US in May 1954, and then joining the Washington-led South-East Asia Treaty Organization (SEATO) along with Thailand and the Philippines, to check communist expansion in the region. Nehru, an advocate of non-alignment in world affairs, strongly disapproved of Pakistan joining the US-led camp in the Cold War. He argued, rather unconvincingly, that Pakistan's move altered the context of the Kashmir dispute and released India from its obligation to hold a plebiscite in Kashmir.

PAKISTAN UNDER MILITARY DICTATORS

Further estrangement between the two neighbours occurred in 1958 when General Ayub Khan dismissed the civilian government of Pakistan, imposed martial law, and banned all political parties for three years. In contrast to India's adult franchise, introduced in 1950, he devised the 'basic democracy' model in Pakistan. He created eighty thousand constituencies, each of one thousand people, and gave them the option of voting for one of the pre-selected candidates to become a Basic Democrat. When, in early 1960, these Basic Democrats were asked, 'Do you have confidence in President Ayub Khan?', almost all them responded positively. Discarding his uniform, Ayub Khan began giving his military government a civilian façade, with officers of the armed forces being inducted into the civil service. By so doing, he integrated the army's plan to merge Pakistani identity with its defence against India with securing the right of self-determination for Kashmiri Muslims.

The Basic Democracy model was extended to Azad Kashmir. Due to its poverty and small taxation base, it depended on the federal government for its financial survival. Its administrative status remained in limbo. It was neither a province nor a federal territory of Pakistan. Like their counterparts in the Kashmir Valley, its inhabitants looked forward to the day when a plebiscite held under international auspices would settle their status.[3]

With that in mind, Ayub Khan sought and secured US president John F. Kennedy's promise of assistance in resolving the Kashmir issue during their meeting in Washington in July 1961. But when Kennedy met Nehru at the White House in November, he found the Indian leader inflexible on the issue.

Pakistan's despondency gave way to hope when massive demonstrations in the Kashmir Valley – following the disappearance of a hair of Prophet Muhammad's beard at the Hazratbal shrine in Srinagar in December 1963 – shook the Nehru government. The subsequent release of Shaikh Muhammad Abdullah from prison and his meeting with the Pakistani president in April 1964 raised hopes of a breakthrough. These died with Nehru's demise in May.

A year later, when Shaikh Abdullah once again found himself behind bars after his meeting in Cairo with Chinese premier Zhou Enlai, the Valley burst into mass protest. Ayub Khan saw a window of opportunity to solve the Kashmir crisis militarily. In early August, some thirty thousand irregular Kashmiri fighters in civilian clothes – belonging to the Mujahideen Companies, trained and commanded by Pakistan's officers – crossed the ceasefire line and took up positions at various points in Indian Kashmir. In a countermove, Indian soldiers entered Azad Kashmir on 15 August. By the end of the month, while the Pakistanis had progressed on three fronts, the Indians had seized the strategic Haji Pir Pass, 5 miles (8 km) into Azad Kashmir.

On 1 September, Pakistan mounted Operation Grand Slam to capture the strategic town of Akhnoor in Jammu and cut off the supply route from India to its troops in the Valley. Taken by surprise, India suffered heavy losses. Its military high command deployed warplanes to blunt the attack. In response the Pakistani planes targeted air bases not only in Kashmir but also in the Indian Punjab. India retaliated by unleashing its ground forces on the Pakistani Punjab on 6 September.

In his broadcast, Ayub Khan warned Pakistanis that 'Indian aggression in Kashmir was only a preparation for an attack on Pakistan.' After asserting that 'Indian rulers were never reconciled to the establishment of an independent Pakistan where the Muslims could build a homeland of their own,' he forecast that their defeat was imminent because 'the 100 million people of Pakistan whose hearts beat with the sound of "*La ilaha illallah, Muhammad ur rasul Allah*" ["There is no god but Allah, and Muhammad is the messenger of Allah"] will not rest till India's guns are silenced.'[4]

The Indian manoeuvre forced the Pakistanis to redirect their forces to the Punjab theatre and abandon their plan to capture Akhnoor. By the time a United Nations-sponsored ceasefire came into effect on 24 September, Pakistan had acquired 1,617 square miles (4,188 sq. km) of Indian territory and 210 square miles (544 km) of Kashmir, while India had gained 446 square miles (1,155 sq. km) of Pakistan and 740 square miles (1,917 sq. km) of Kashmir. During their subsequent meeting in the Soviet Central Asian city of Tashkent, chaired by Soviet prime minister Alexei Kosygin, in January 1966, Ayub Khan and Indian prime minister Lal Bahadur Shastri agreed to exchange captured territories.[5]

Ayub Khan's failure in Kashmir caused disaffection in his camp, with Zulfikar Ali Bhutto, whom he had mentored as the foreign minister from 1962 onward, parting company with him. A prematurely balding man with a sharp nose in a buttery face, Bhutto was charismatic and glib, with a penchant for catchy slogans. He established the Pakistan People's Party (PPP) in 1966. Significantly, its founding charter referred to 'jihad against India', and described the party's creed as 'Islam is our faith; Democracy is our policy; Socialism is our economy. All power to the People.' His slogan of 'Bread, clothing, and Shelter' (Urdu, *roti, kapra aur makan*) for all caught the popular imagination, as did his cries of 'Down with zamindars' and 'Equal rights for peasants'.

The emergence of the PPP coincided with growing disaffection in East Pakistan (consisting of East Bengal and the Sylhet district of Assam) with military rule and the domination of the country's western wing – containing 46 per cent of the national population – and the continued downgrading of the Bengali language at the expense of Urdu. Whereas the military consumed 60 per cent of the nation's budget, only 7 per cent of its ranks came from East Pakistan.

Opposition to the Ayub Khan government in the form of demonstrations and strikes escalated from the autumn of 1968 to the extent that in March 1969 Ayub Khan abrogated the 1962 constitution, re-imposed martial law, and resigned. He handed over power to the army chief of staff, General Agha Muhammad Yahya Khan, a stocky, bushy-browed Pushtun.

Yahya Khan expanded the ISI and assigned it the task of collecting internal political intelligence in East Pakistan. By then the ISI had an Indian rival, the Research and Analysis Wing (RAW), with its focus on China and Pakistan.

When Yahya Khan announced elections to the provincial and national assemblies in October 1970 on the unprecedented basis of adult franchise, he mandated that the national parliament should act as a constituent assembly and adopt a new constitution. RAW was active in East Pakistan. It devised ways to fund the Awami League of Shaikh Mujibur Rahman because the League wanted a federal constitution with the centre only dealing with defence and foreign affairs. Because of the hurricane and floods, the elections in the Eastern Wing were postponed for two months. Later RAW agents operating in the East Pakistani capital of Dacca (now Dhaka) would warn their handlers in Calcutta (now Kolkata) of an upcoming army crackdown on the Awami League in February 1971. They advised Mujibur Rahman to leave Dhaka, but to no avail. [6]

THE LOSS OF THE EASTERN WING AND ITS AFTERMATH

In December 1970, the Awami League won a stunning 288 of the 300 seats in the provincial parliament and 160 out of 162 allocated to East Pakistan in the National Assembly. By contrast, Bhutto's PPP secured eighty-eight seats in the National Assembly and majorities in the provincial assemblies of Punjab and Sindh.

In its assessment of Pakistan, RAW painted an alarmist picture of its military capabilities – which was duly reproduced in the Indian media – quantifying its troops and weaponry, and concluding that Islamabad had achieved 'a good state of military preparedness for any confrontation with India'. It judged 'the potential threat' of an attack on India 'quite real, particularly in view of the China-Pakistan collusion'. Besides, it added, the constitutional crisis in East Pakistan might encourage the generals to undertake a diversionary adventure, to begin, as in 1965, with 'an infiltration campaign in Jammu and Kashmir'.[7]

When Mujibur Rahman refused to budge on the question of federalism, Yahya Khan postponed the convening of the National Assembly. In March 1971, the Awami League's call for an indefinite general strike brought East Pakistan to a standstill. Following the arrest of Rahman, the soldiers of East Pakistani origin mutinied. Yahya Khan rushed troops from the western wing. General Tikka Khan, the military governor of East Pakistan, mounted Operation Searchlight to quell the popular uprising. The soldiers targeted Awami League activists and Hindus, forming about 14 per cent of East Pakistan's population of seventy million. This reign of terror led to a massive exodus of East Pakistanis. By early September, India hosted more than eight million refugees in numerous camps. They provided a rich source of volunteers to be trained as guerrillas, organized as a 20,000-strong Mukti Bahini (Bengali, 'Liberation Army') – an enterprise in which RAW cooperated with the Indian Army.

In its secret communications, the Indian government of Indira Gandhi began describing the events in East Pakistan as the 'struggle for Bangladesh'. On the other side, Yahya Khan's military government, which had accused the Awami League of close ties with Bengali Hindus, now referred to 'an Indo-Zionist plot [hatched] against Islamic Pakistan'.[8] This assessment contained a nugget of truth, as later revelations would show.

By late October 1971, shelling along the Indian–East Pakistani frontier had become more intense, affording the Mukti Bahini guerrillas opportunities to infiltrate the province. To break the stalemate and hoping to forestall the loss of East Pakistan, on 3 December Pakistan mounted its Operation Chengiz Khan. This involved bombing eleven Indian airfields on its eastern frontier and staging artillery attacks in Indian Kashmir. Delhi responded with massive air strikes, and moved its ground troops in Kashmir and Punjab. After recognizing the provisional government of the People's Republic of Bangladesh, the Indian Army advanced into East Pakistan on four fronts.

The war ended on 16 December when Lt General Amir Abdullah Khan Niazi, commander of the 90,000-strong Pakistani forces, surrendered to the joint forces of India and the Mukti Bahini. In the ground fighting on its western front, India gained 5,500 square miles (14,000 sq. km) of Pakistani territory in Kashmir, Punjab, and Sindh. According to a top Pakistani general, altogether about fifty thousand people were killed in East Pakistan in a chain of events that started with Islamabad's Operation Searchlight and ended with the emergence of Bangladesh.[9] By contrast, the figure given by Mujibur Rahman was three million.

The secession of its eastern wing was a disaster for Pakistan in more ways than one. It lost more than half of its population, as well as its main source of foreign currencies, earned by the export of jute from East Pakistan. More damagingly, the breakaway of East Pakistan undercut the seminal thesis of two nations inhabiting the Indian subcontinent, and upheld the view of Congress party leaders that the partition was a pragmatic resolution of its conflict with the All-India Muslim League rather than an ideological defeat. The secession proved that a common religion was not a strong enough glue to hold together two societies with different languages, cultures, and historical backgrounds. In the end, ethnic nationalism trumped religion – a bitter pill to swallow not only for West Pakistan's people and politicians, but also for those in Indian Kashmir who advocated accession to Pakistan.

After the 1971 war, a new dynamic emerged in erstwhile West Pakistan. The question of whether the right to autonomy exercised by Bengalis should be extended to other regional groups with distinct cultures became the prime subject of national debate.

At the same time the defeated leaders of West Pakistan, civilian and military, refused to forgive or forget the loss of the eastern wing. They attributed it primarily to the incessant, malignant designs of India, and secondarily to the drunken incompetence of the generals in East Pakistan, particularly the whiskey-swigging Yahya Khan. There was no overt soul-searching or critical analysis of the basic differences between the two wings – existing 1,150 miles (1,840 km) apart – which led to the final rupture.

The War Inquiry Commission, appointed by Yahya Khan in late December 1971 and headed by chief justice Hamdoor Rahman, submitted its report three years later. It was based on 300 testimonies and the examination of hundreds of classified army communications. It was considered so damaging to the reputation of the army that it was never released officially. It came to light only in 2002 when an Indian newspaper published it.[10]

Once the Shimla Agreement of July 1972 renamed the ceasefire line of December 1948 as the Line of Control, the government in Islamabad took a direct and open role in administering Azad Kashmir. This was tantamount to Pakistan absorbing Azad Kashmir.

By securing the release of about ninety thousand Pakistani prisoners of war as well as regaining control of the territory lost to India, as part of the Shimla Agreement, Bhutto did much to rehabilitate the military's reputation among the public at a critical time. Indeed, though Pakistan lost more than half of its population in 1971, Bhutto increased the size of the military from 370,000 to 502,000 by 1975.[11]

Bhutto was conscious of the inspiration that the secession of the Bengali-speaking eastern wing had provided, particularly to those speaking Baluchi, thereby energizing the movement for the autonomy of Baluchistan. He therefore assigned the task of crushing the Baluchi nationalists' armed struggle to the military. That raised the armed forces' status, and with it the clout of the army chief of staff.

It was as army chief that General Muhammad Zia ul Haq overthrew the democratic government of Bhutto in 1977. The later success of the anti-Soviet jihad in Afghanistan, which he backed staunchly, prepared the ground for Pakistan to avenge the defeat it had suffered at the hands of India in 1971, thereby underlining the linkage that exists in the politics of these nations of South Asia.

In the mid-1980s, officers of Pakistan's ISI directorate established contacts with the Jamaat-e Islami of Kashmir and the secular Jammu and Kashmir Liberation Front. In a clandestine meeting Zia ul Haq outlined a dual-track strategy on Kashmir.[12] Let us turn Kashmir into an ungovernable territory by escalating the cost to Delhi in men and money to an unsustainable degree, and internationalize the dispute by getting foreign jihadists, with experience in Afghanistan, involved in guerrilla and terrorist acts, he argued successfully. Thus, Kashmir became the linchpin between Afghanistan and Pakistan as well as between Pakistan and India, thereby creating the arch of crisis under study in this chronicle.

Kashmiris' loss of confidence in peaceful change – caused by the blatant rigging of the 1987 election – swelled the ranks of those in the secessionist movement who wanted to resort to armed resistance. That process was still in its infancy when Zia ul Haq was killed in an aircraft accident in 1988.

On becoming prime minister in late 1990, Muhammad Nawaz Sharif, who had made liberating Kashmir an important and emotional theme in his electoral campaign, backed Zia ul Haq's strategy. Evidence to that effect came from the US State Department. In its 1991 report on global terrorism, it referred to credible reports of Islamabad's support for Kashmiri militant groups, involving military training and supplies of arms and ammunition. By then, the ISI was actively assisting Pakistani and foreign militants, including veterans of the anti-Moscow jihad, to infiltrate Indian Kashmir. 'Thus, Kashmir's indigenous struggle for self-determination became linked with the global jihad of Islamists,' noted Husain Haqqani, who served as an adviser to Prime Ministers Nawaz Sharif and Benazir Bhutto.[13]

Continuing on that path raised the prospect of Pakistan being named as a state that sponsors terrorism. US law mandated strict sanctions against any such country, including restrictions on bilateral commerce and vetoing of financial assistance by the IMF and the World Bank. In a letter to Nawaz Sharif in May 1992, James Baker, the American Secretary of State, referred to reliable information he had received regarding the ISI and others continuing to provide material aid to terrorist groups, and pointed out the penalties specified in US law against any such country.

When Nawaz Sharif discussed this missive with his top officials, including Lt General Javed Nasir, ISI director, and General Asif Nawaz, the army chief of staff, Nasir remarked: 'These are empty threats . . . All we need to do is to buy more time and improve our diplomatic effort. The focus should be on Indian atrocities in Kashmir, not on our support for the Kashmiri resistance.'[14] General Nawaz proposed a compromise between Nasir's stance and terminating the secret support altogether: Alter the pattern of backing for Kashmiri freedom fighters. That is, help Kashmiri separatists through 'private channels' consisting of such organizations as the Jamaat-e Islami. The prime minister accepted the idea without telling his aides that he had earlier promised Washington that he would shut down training camps for Kashmiri separatists set up by private citizens and Islamist groups. In his response to Baker, he assured the US officials that any clandestine assistance by his government to anti-India militants would cease forthwith. Such duplicity would become the norm in Islamabad in the coming decades.

Once the threat of being listed as a terrorist state had passed, very little changed on the ground in Pakistan or Pakistan-held Kashmir. It was the same under the second premiership of Benazir Bhutto from October 1993 to November 1996. In a candid interview with the Delhi-based *Tehelka* magazine after her assassination in December 2007, Retired General Hamid Gul said, 'She was rather protective of the jihadis in the past. Benazir was never soft on the Kashmir issue, let me tell you that. I served as the ISI director-general under her [from 1987 to 1989]. The Taliban emerged during her second tenure in office and captured Kabul when she was the prime minister. Her interior minister [General Babar Naseerullah] used to patronize them openly.'[15]

As described earlier, the battle in the Kargil area of Indian Kashmir triggered a military coup by the army chief of staff, General Pervez Musharraf, in October 1999. This highlighted once more the importance of both Kashmir and the armed forces in Pakistan. After appropriating the presidency of the Islamic Republic of Pakistan, Musharraf retained his position as the army chief.

The assumption of supreme power by a general who had been a key player in the Kargil campaign alarmed the Bharatiya Janata Party-led government of Atal Bihari Vajpayee in Delhi. But the supreme office moderated Musharraf's stance on Kashmir. He realized that Pakistan's economy was too weak to continue bearing the high cost of its defence. In December 2000, he agreed to withdraw some of the Pakistani troops posted along the Line of Control whose presence had led to frequent exchanges of artillery fire. That prepared the way for a formal ceasefire between the two neighbours in June 2001. In return, Vajpayee invited Musharraf for talks without the precondition that Islamabad should first stop the infiltration of militants into Indian Kashmir.

However, their summit in Agra – home to the world-famous Taj Mahal – failed. Objecting to the final communiqué referring to Kashmir as the prime source of tensions between the two neighbours, Vajpayee insisted on raising the issue of cross-border terrorism. That in turn was unacceptable to Musharraf. In his televised press conference with Indian journalists on 16 July 2001, he remarked, 'I will keep on saying that the main issue confronting our two countries is Kashmir, whether anyone likes it or not.'[16] Given Musharraf's active involvement in intensifying the insurgency in the Indian Kashmir, these words carried weight.

9/11 AND AFTER

Following the 9/11 attacks, Musharraf consulted leaders of all political hues and social groups on the stance Pakistan should take regarding the Taliban in Afghanistan. He encountered resistance from senior clerics to the idea of cutting ties with the Taliban and lining up with the Pentagon in its War on Terror. In response, he assured them and other Islamist leaders that this turnaround would yield a payback from Washington: it would overlook an ISI-sponsored boost in insurgency in Indian Kashmir and force Delhi to come to the negotiating table.

Nothing of the sort happened. The Americans were aghast to find that most of the literature about guerrilla training that they seized at fifty sites in post-Taliban Afghanistan pertained to the training of jihadists for liberating Kashmir conducted under the supervision of Musharraf as the director general of military operations.[17]

So, later, it did not surprise American and non-American analysts to note that, of the 3000-odd Pakistani militants arrested after Musharraf's much-acclaimed denunciation of 'terrorism in the name of Kashmir' in his 12 January 2002 TV address, none was charged. By March, they were all released, and the banned extremist organizations had resurfaced under different names. Little wonder that going by the figures for violent deaths caused by insurgency and counter-insurgency in Kashmir, 2003 was the bloodiest year, with a record 2,600 fatalities.

In Pakistan, it was only after surviving two failed assassination attempts in December 2003 that Musharraf resolved to tackle jihadist terrorism. Among other things, this experience made him amenable to talking to Vajpayee on the margins of the South Asian Association for Regional Cooperation in Islamabad in January 2004. Here Musharraf reiterated that he would bar the use of Pakistani territory for terrorist activities, a reprise of what he had said two years earlier. In return, Vajpayee agreed to talks on settling the Kashmir dispute. The two leaders declared confidently that the resumption of dialogue would lead to a 'peaceful settlement' of all bilateral issues, including Kashmir. But such a settlement did not mean discarding Pakistan's traditional demand for self-determination for Kashmiris. Addressing newspaper editors in February 2004, Musharraf said, 'Pakistan has two vital national interests: being a nuclear state and the Kashmir cause.'[18] At the same time he convinced the military high command that only by pursuing a peace process with India could Pakistan achieve political stability and badly needed economic development by attracting foreign investment.

The installing of the Congress party-led coalition in Delhi, headed by Manmohan Singh, improved the chances of ending the Kashmir deadlock. When Musharraf and Singh met at the UN in September 2004, unknown to the rest of the world, they agreed to give a push to the secret talks that had been initiated between their respective national security advisers – Tariq Aziz and Jyotindra Nath Dixit. Aziz and Dixit's successor, Satinder Lambah, India's former high commissioner in Pakistan, would continue meeting secretly in hotels in Dubai, London, and Bangkok almost every other month for more than two years as they tried to hammer out a detailed proposal.

Soon Singh declared that any deal to resolve the Kashmir dispute would be acceptable so long as it was not based on religious division or the altering of India's boundaries. Remarkably, the first condition reflected the view of Congress party leaders before independence, which was also a guiding principle for the Indian government in its drive to curb the violent movement of Sikhs for an independent Khalistan.

On 25 October 2004, in an informal address at a breaking-the-fast dinner during Ramadan, Musharraf invited debate on alternatives to a plebiscite in Kashmir. He argued that since Jammu and Kashmir consisted of seven regions with different languages and sects, some could remain with India or Pakistan and the rest could be autonomous, placed under a UN trusteeship or a condominium, or be divided between the two countries. When a barrage of protest followed, he explained that his statement was *not* a substitute for the official Pakistani position about holding a plebiscite.[19]

But Musharraf's public retraction did not derail Tariq Aziz's clandestine talks with Singh's special envoy. These negotiations inched forward to the point that Musharraf felt it was time to test public opinion. In an interview with the Delhi-based NDTV in early December 2006, he outlined a four-point plan: Pakistan would give up its claim to Indian-administered Kashmir if people from both regions had freedom of movement across open borders; neither part of Kashmir could become independent, but both would have a measure of autonomy; there should be a phased withdrawal of troops from both sides of the Line of Control; and a 'joint mechanism', consisting of representatives from India, Pakistan and Kashmir, should be formed to supervise the issues affecting people on both sides, such as water rights.[20] In his autobiography, *In the Line of Fire*, published nearly two years later, Musharraf would describe his Kashmir plan as 'purely personal', which needed to be sold to the public by all the involved parties to gain popular acceptance.

The jihadists and other Islamists in Pakistan were livid at this betrayal of the Kashmiri Muslims. Little did Musharraf realize that his pragmatic approach would drive the Lashkar-e Taiba (LeT) leadership to plan an attack on India that was so outrageous that it would stop any movement towards a compromise on Kashmir in its tracks.

THE MAKING OF THE MUMBAI ATTACKS

Over the past couple of years, LeT leaders had noticed a growing number of their activists defecting to smaller, more radical groups. They therefore felt the need to bolster the LeT's fiery image by implementing a gigantic operation. They realized that in their ranks they had one Pakistani-American whose dedication to the cause was equalled by the training he had received at LeT camps. This was Daood Sayed Gilani, born in 1950 in the US to a Pakistani diplomat and an American socialite from Philadelphia.

After his education at an elite a military school near Islamabad, Gilani went to live with his divorced mother in Philadelphia to help her run a bar. He carried two passports, one American and the other Pakistani. His drug-smuggling activities took him to Pakistan and led to his arrest, first in 1987 and then in 1998, when he became an undercover agent for the US Drug Enforcement Administration (DEA). Soon after 9/11, the DEA sent him to Pakistan, even though it had been informed of his pro-Islamist views. In December 2001, attracted by the LeT's banner advertisement at a mosque in Lahore where he prayed, he joined the organization. Between 2002 and 2005, he underwent training in small arms and counter-surveillance at camps run by the LeT, a supposedly banned organization. He was anxious to participate actively in jihad and awaited a move by LeT leaders. When that failed to materialize, he set out for the Pakistan-Afghan border on his own and crossed into the tribal territory without an official permit. Here, he was arrested by an ISI officer. Once Gilani had established his LeT bona fides, that officer handed him over to 'Major Iqbal' of the ISI in Lahore. Major Iqbal became his minder. Taking his advice, Gilani changed his name to David Coleman Headley in 2006 during a stay in the US. Through one of his LeT trainers, Abdur Rahman Hashim (aka Pasha), a retired officer of the 6th Baluch Regiment, Headley established contact with Ilyas Kashmiri, who was linked to Al Qaida. The ISI gave him $25,000 to open a US visa facilitation office in Mumbai as a front for his clandestine activities. After scouting for targets in the city, he handed over computer memory sticks to the LeT and ISI. He went through the computerized images with Zaki ur Rahmn Lakhvi, the LeT's military operations chief. In 2007, Headley made six trips to Mumbai, two of them with his Moroccan wife, Faiza Outalah, where they stayed at the Taj Mahal Hotel. In September, his LeT minder instructed him to focus on that hotel. The following April, Headley hired boats to scout landing sites and passed on the global positioning system (GPS) coordinates to the LeT high command. 'Major Iqbal', working as the LeT's planner, supervised the making of a model of the Taj Mahal Hotel and arranged the communications system for the attack. Between June and August 2008, the LeT high command upgraded the operation from an assault on the Taj Mahal Hotel, with the two or three attackers escaping, to a mission involving several targets, with the operatives' role changed to that of suicide bombers. Appropriate indoctrination of ten terrorists followed. Their first foray by boat from Karachi failed. At their next attempt they barely escaped capture by the Indian Coast Guard. It was their third attempt that succeeded. After hijacking an Indian fishing trawler, they abandoned their own vessel and, guided by the GPS coordinates, landed safely in Mumbai.

This account of events emerged after Headley was arrested in Chicago in October 2009. To avoid capital punishment, he opted for a plea bargain, making a full confession and agreeing to cooperate with the authorities. In June 2010, he spent thirty-four hours talking to Indian investigators in the presence of US Federal Bureau of Investigations (FBI) agents. Four months later, the authorities released their 109-page report to the press.

Headley revealed that those who had broken away from the LeT from 2005 onward had defected either to radical organizations committed to waging global jihad – that is, Al Qaida – or engage in jihad specifically against the pro-Western regimes in Afghanistan and Pakistan as would the Pakistani Taliban. By contrast, the LeT wanted its activists to fight 'only for Kashmir and against India'. As for the ISI, it was under pressure from the top to stop the integration of Kashmir-based groups with the jihad-based factions and 'to shift the theater of violence from the domestic soil of Pakistan to India'. That is how the aims of the LeT and the ISI converged, and how they came together to bring off something truly dramatic against India and for Kashmiri Muslims.[21]

MUSHARRAF'S FALL

Concerning the Kashmir issue, what mattered in the final analysis at the official level in Pakistan was the opinion of the top generals, including the ISI's director general, until October 2007, Lt General Ashfaq Parvez Kayani. Since Musharraf continued to be the army chief of staff, it was hard for his subordinate generals to disagree with him even in private. So, when the secret document prepared by the national security advisers of Pakistan and India was finessed in early 2007, Musharraf presented it formally for review to his twelve corps commanders, including his deputy, and the foreign minister.[22]

Though deeply interested in devising a peaceful solution to the long-running Kashmir dispute, the Indian interlocutors had to ponder three major unknowns. Did Musharraf have the generals on board on this vitally important issue, which had played a critical role in raising the prestige and budget of the military since the birth of Pakistan? What was the likelihood of Musharraf being overthrown by his military high command, as had happened to General Ayub Khan? And what were the chances of the post-Musharraf regime, military or civilian, abiding by the provisional deal Musharraf struck with Delhi?

The answers to these questions came on two dates. On 28 November 2007, Musharraf was compelled to resign as army chief on constitutional grounds before being sworn in for a second term as civilian president. Then, on 18 August 2008, he resigned as president when he was faced with the prospect of impeachment by a parliament dominated by two anti-Musharraf parties in the aftermath of the general election in February. As stipulated by the constitution, the Speaker of the Senate, Muhammad Mian Soomro, became the acting president.

Musharraf's public standing nosedived as the domestic challenges escalated. In March 2007, his suspension of the chief justice, Iftikhar Muhammad Chaudhry, sparked street protests in which the opposition parties of Benazir Bhutto (the PPP) and Nawaz Sharif (the Pakistan Muslim League [N]), participated jointly. The military's storming of the Red Mosque complex, a bastion of jihadists in Islamabad, in July created a violent backlash by Islamist terrorists.

His imposition of a state of emergency on 3 November, soon after winning the majority of the votes of the provincial and national legislators in a controversial presidential poll, was an act of desperation. The poor performance of his Pakistan Muslim League (Q) in the general election in February 2008 showed the continued waning of his popularity. With the PPP's Yusuf Raza Gilani becoming prime minister, he had a powerful political adversary to contend with. His exit from power in August was received with relief by the public at large.

THE POST-MUSHARRAF PERIOD

Among those who celebrated Musharraf's fall were the pro-jihad radical groups, including the LeT. They addressed a mammoth rally in Muzaffarabad, a city where nothing of significance happens without the support of the Pakistani army and the ISI. This was a clear signal to Srinagar, Delhi, and the rest of the world that the Kashmir dispute remained unresolved.

More importantly, there was an increase in the infiltrations into Indian Kashmir by Pakistani jihadists and ceasefire violations by Pakistan's army. The Indians provided evidence of this to Gilani's national security adviser, Retired Major General Mahmud Ali Durrani, when he travelled to Delhi in October 2008. The next month, the LeT-orchestrated attacks in Mumbai put Islamabad on the defensive. Yet Gilani dismissed Durrani in January for issuing statements he considered too solicitous of Delhi.

On the surface, once Asif Ali Zardari, husband of the assassinated Benazir Bhutto, was elected president by the provincial and federal lawmakers in September 2008, a civilian democratic system was fully in place. In reality, though, real power still lay with the military.

Zardari has neither the intelligence nor the charisma of his wife, nor the political cunning of Nawaz Sharif. With his receding hairline, this square-jawed, dull-looking man, sporting a salt-and-pepper moustache, appears more like a character actor in a Pakistani movie than a leader charged with navigating a crisis-ridden republic through rough waters. Notorious for his corruption, and reputed to be one of the wealthiest men in Pakistan, his abiding characteristic remains insatiable avarice. His approval ratings fluctuate around 20 per cent.

In August 2010, while millions of Pakistanis were made homeless by the worst floods in eight decades, Zardari was filmed boarding a helicopter in Paris after his meeting with President Nicolas Sarkozy to visit his sixteenth-century château in northern France. In contrast, General Ashfaq Parvez Kayani, army chief since October 2007, was shown touring the flooded areas and consoling the hapless sufferers.

His popularity rating soared to 61 per cent. Little wonder that in its quarterly report to Congress in October 2010, the Obama White House pointed out that Zardari was 'out of touch' with his own populace.[23]

It is widely known that in Pakistan it is the military that decides any foreign policy that impinges on national security. Kashmir and India as a whole remain at the core of Pakistan's national security. Kayani has repeatedly made this clear to the policy makers in Washington. 'While the army does not want to escalate tension or lead to war with India it does not want to let go this [Kashmir] issue as that would reduce its significance and alter its image of the nation's guardian particularly when there is no indication that India is willing to resolve the issue by agreeing to any minor or major territorial changes,' writes Ayesha Siddiqa in her book *Military Inc. Inside Pakistan's Military Economy*.[24]

It is worth noting that Kayani is the last of the Pakistani military commanders to have undergone advanced military training in the United States. As a result he has a broader perspective on the events outside Pakistan than those officers who graduated after him and did not rise up the hierarchical ladder as he did. All such officers, imbued with the Islamist ideology during Zia ul Haq's rule, have an understanding of the outside world that is limited by their religious perspective. This bodes ill for the Kashmir impasse.

Though moderate in his views about India, Zardari cannot stand up to Kayani. When, for instance, he tried to transfer the ISI from the military to the interior ministry in May 2009, Kayani rejected the order. Within hours, Zardari backtracked. He should have known better than to try. Only when he follows the advice given to him by aides cleverer and more far-sighted than himself, he does well. For example, he made an astute move by extending Kayani's term in office, due to end in November 2010, by three years to be coterminus with the end of his presidency.

Earlier, he had shown political deftness by visiting the mausoleum of Muhammad Ali Jinnah in Karachi within two days of assuming the presidency on 9 September 2008 to pray and pay his respects to the republic's founder. But then, left briefly to his own devices, he demonstrated an astonishing lack of presence of mind. Instead of signing the visitors' book in Urdu, he scribbled, 'May God [which appeared as "Good"] give us the strut (sic) to save Pakistan,' – thus inadvertently displaying his semi-literacy in English. Under his initials appeared the date '11/9/2008', and then 'Asif Ali Zardari, President, Islamic Republic of Pakistan'.[25]

8

ZIA UL HAQ: THE ISLAMIST DICTATOR

IN THE HEART of the bustling, noisy, sprawling port city of Karachi lies a grand park occupying 185 acres, which is incredibly quiet except for the chirping of sparrows and cawing of crows. It is the site of the burial place and mausoleum of Muhammad Ali Jinnah. Since its unveiling in June 1970, it has become an outstanding landmark in his place of birth. A series of fountains lead to a 13-foot (4 m)-high platform. On it rises a simple, elegant, striking edifice in marble, with arched openings in the middle of each of its four 230-foot (75 m)-long sides, topped by a dome with small windows, rising 130 feet (43 m) above the platform. At night the illuminated mausoleum becomes a captivating sight.

It is a fitting monument to a towering personality, without whose tireless single-mindedness, combined with an equal measure of shrewdness and sharpness of intellect, Pakistan would not have come into existence. The country's leaders miss no opportunity to praise Jinnah's genius, in the process emphasizing why he richly deserves the honorific of Quaid-i-Azam. Besides the mausoleum, Karachi hosts the Jinnah Museum. The city's prime thoroughfare, connecting the port to the highway that runs northward through the province of Sindh, originally called Bunder (Urdu, 'Port'), now carries the name of Jinnah. So too does the international airport of Karachi.

It was from that site that Benazir Bhutto, on her return home on 18 October 2007 from an eight-year exile, was leading a procession of a quarter of a million admirers to the mausoleum of Jinnah when two bombs exploded near her open-top truck, killing around 140 people. They offered a grim reminder of the escalating violence afflicting Pakistan, a country that was born in the midst of much bloodshed six decades earlier.

A FRAGILE DEMOCRACY

It was not until 1956 that Pakistanis acquired their own constitution. Among other things, this turned the Dominion of Pakistan, with the British sovereign as its ultimate authority, into the Islamic Republic of Pakistan. But the second constitution, promulgated six years later by General Muhammad Ayub Khan and specifying an indirectly elected president, removed 'Islamic' from the country's name.

Yet when Ayub Khan was opposed by Fatima Jinnah, the sister of Muhammad Ali, in the 1965 presidential poll, his interior minister managed to obtain a fatwa, or religious decree, that a woman could not be the head of a Muslim state. This reduced the chances of Fatima Jinnah's success. She lost.

This flip-flop was a reflection of the equivocal attitude Muhammad Ali Jinnah displayed towards Islam during the decade before his demise on 11 September 1948. As a London-trained barrister who practised in the metropolis and owned a house in the upscale neighbourhood of Hampstead during 1930–34, he was to be seen imbibing whiskey and eating a ham sandwich in the company of his lawyer friends. On his return to Bombay (now Mumbai) in 1935, he became leader of the All-India Muslim League. Adopting his thesis that the subcontinent's Muslims were a nation apart from the Hindu nation, the Muslim League insisted on being the *exclusive* representative of the Muslim minority. This helped Jinnah to engender unity among his constituents who were otherwise divided by race, culture, and language.

In electoral politics, the cry of 'Islam in danger' in a Hindu-majority subcontinent, uttered vociferously by the ulema, paid rich dividends. But when, before and after the announcement of the partition by the British government in June 1947, religious passions rose to the point of mass killings of Hindus and Sikhs on one side and Muslims on the other, Jinnah was genuinely shocked. He realized too that a third of the subcontinent's 100 million Muslims would be left behind in Hindu-dominated independent India.

So he changed his tune. 'You are free, free to go to your temples; you are free to go to your mosques or any other place of worship in this state of Pakistan,' he said to the members of Pakistan's Constituent Assembly a few days before the establishment of Pakistan on 14 August 1947, with its capital in Karachi.

> You may belong to any religion or caste or creed; that has nothing to do with the business of the state . . . We are starting with this fundamental principle that we are all citizens and equal citizens of one state . . . Now I think we should keep that in front of us as our ideal, and you will find that in [the] course of time, Hindus will cease to be Hindus and Muslims will cease to be Muslims, not in the religious sense, because that is the personal faith of each individual, but in the political sense as citizens of the state.[1]

Extracts from Jinnah's speech were then widely disseminated in the hope that they would dampen the bloodthirsty frenzy that had gripped Hindus and Muslims alike in Punjab, Khyber Pakhtunkhwa, and Bengal.

But though calm returned to the subcontinent, the armed conflict between the two neighbours in Kashmir brought the communal question to the fore. So Jinnah did another about-turn. Addressing the Sindh Bar Association in Karachi in January 1948, he declared that Pakistan's constitution would be based on the Sharia, 'to make Pakistan a truly great Islamic state'.[2]

In March 1949, at the behest of prime minister Liaquat Ali Khan, the Constituent Assembly adopted the Objectives Resolution, which specified democracy, freedom, equality, and social justice 'as enunciated by Islam'. These Objectives reiterated the supremacy of 'divine over popular sovereignty', and required the state to 'enable' Muslims 'to order their lives in accord with the teaching and requirements of Islam as set out in the Holy Quran and Sunna'.[3] The preamble to the 1956 constitution read: 'Sovereignty over the entire universe belongs to God Almighty alone, and the authority which He has delegated to the State of Pakistan through its people for being exercised within the limits prescribed by Him is a sacred trust.' The constitution barred a non-Muslim from becoming head of state.

Pakistani politicians discovered that emphasizing Islam helped enormously in giving the fledgling state a sharply divergent image from that of secular India, which had an identity dating back to antiquity. It was a military leader, General Ayub Khan, who accelerated the process. To strengthen the state per se, he put the administration of all places of Muslim worship into the hands of the Ministry of Religious Trusts in 1959. Well aware of the popularity of Sufism, particularly in West Pakistan,[4] he treated Sufi shrines on a par with conventional mosques.

Ayub Khan tightened the state's grip on education and resorted to 'guiding' the media. As a consequence of the merging of the study of history, geography and citizenship into social studies at the primary and secondary levels of education, an officially sponsored historical narrative of Pakistan emerged. Its starting point was the arrival of Muhammad ibn Qasim from Arabia in modern Sindh and southern Punjab in 710. 'The history of Islam was presented, not [as] a history of religion or civilization, [but] as a prelude to Pakistan's creation,' noted Husain Haqqani, a former adviser to two Pakistani prime ministers. 'Muslim conquerors were glorified, and Hindu-Muslim relations were painted as intrinsically hostile, and the ability of Pakistanis to manage democracy was questioned.'[5]

Crucially, Jinnah's statement about Pakistan becoming a state of all religions was excised from his official biographies. He was presented as favouring an Islamic state with strict laws and codes of conduct. Paying particular attention to the armed forces, Ayub Khan ensured that the Islamic chaplains, called maulavis, in the army were of a higher quality than the ones serving civilians.

Before deciding to hold elections for the National Assembly (to be charged with drafting a new constitution) in late 1970, General Agha Muhammad Yahya Khan issued a Legal Framework Order on 30 March. This spelled out the basic principles of the proposed constitution. A later election law then prescribed a fundamental role for Islam in the constitution. Nothing came of it, however, because of the totally unexpected result of the elections, which led to a crisis. To suppress the popular uprising in East Pakistan, Yahya Khan co-opted such radical Islamist parties as the Jamaat-e Islami (JeI). He thus set a precedent that would be emulated by the later rulers of Pakistan, civilian and military.

POST-1971 PAKISTAN

In West Pakistan, at both popular and official levels, the defeat in the eastern wing was attributed to the un-Islamic behaviour of the generals under Yahya Khan, infamous for their drinking and fornication. The loss of East Pakistan and, with it, a substantial Hindu minority reduced the non-Muslim Pakistani population of Hindus and Christians to a mere 4 per cent.

Released of its pull towards the east, post-1971 Pakistan began looking westward to the Persian Gulf region, including Saudi Arabia, the birthplace of Islam. The dramatic growth in prosperity of the Gulf monarchies due to the quadrupling of oil prices in 1973–74 created an unprecedented demand for the Muslim workers of Pakistan. That in turn strengthened religious sentiment in their native land.

Zulfikar Ali Bhutto, a populist at heart, noted this rising tide of Islamic feelings. He was aware too of the left-wing policies sweeping through the Third World. So he coined the seductive concept of 'Islamic socialism'. The country's third constitution, drafted under the supervision of Bhutto, a trained lawyer, and promulgated in August 1973, renamed the country the 'Islamic Republic of Pakistan', reintroduced the parliamentary system, and for the first time declared Islam the official religion of the state. The next year, to placate the ulema, the Bhutto government rejected the plea of the Ahmadi minority that they were Muslim, and declared them non-Muslim.[6] As for the 'socialism' part of his slogan, Bhutto nationalized all banks and insurance companies and seventy other industrial enterprises, including some medium-sized factories, thus breaking the power of the top twenty-two families who dominated Pakistan's non-farm economy.

A leader of Napoleonic ambitions, Bhutto turned nationalization into a personal tool by extending it to all wheat-milling, rice-husking, and cotton-ginning units in 1976 in order to enfeeble his opponents. His autocratic manner alienated many left-wingers and others who had joined his Pakistan People's Party (PPP) in droves at its birth.

On the eve of the general elections in March 1977, all opposition factions and disempowered interest groups coalesced to form the nine-party Pakistan National Alliance (PNA), covering both religious and secular elements, to challenge the PPP. This caused consternation in the PPP camp. It led to vote-rigging, carried out by the all-powerful district commissioners in rural areas to an undetermined extent. When electoral officials declared the PPP to have won 155 of the 200 seats – 76 per cent of the total, up from 58 per cent in the previous general election in 1970 – with the PNA getting only 36 seats, Bhutto's adversaries contested the outcome. Massive protest demonstrations led by the Islamic parties followed. Bhutto responded with a declaration of martial law and firings by army troops to disperse the protesters.

When these measures proved ineffective, he made concessions to the religious camp, announcing that the Sharia would be enforced within six months. He banned alcohol and gambling, and closed nightclubs. He declared Friday, the holy day in Islam, the weekly rest day.

Bhutto's compromises failed to satisfy the opposition, and provided General Muhammad Zia ul Haq with a rationale to stage Operation

Fair Play on 5 July 1977, and overthrow the civilian government. The term 'fair play' implied that the army chief had intervened to end the street violence as a prelude to holding a free and fair poll.

But, on assuming power, Zia ul Haq said that he admired 'the spirit of Islam' that had inspired the PNA's street protest. Calling himself 'a soldier of Allah', he added: 'I consider the introduction of [an] Islamic system as an essential prerequisite for the country.'[7] Soon all government communications began with the Islamic invocation 'In the Name of Allah, the Merciful, the Compassionate'.

Zia ul Haq called himself the 'chief martial law administrator'. By issuing a provisional constitutional order that 'temporarily' transferred power to himself, Zia ul Haq bypassed the legal requirement of having to approach the National Assembly for legitimacy. In late July, he announced a fresh poll within three months and promised to hand over power thereafter to the elected representatives. But two-and-a-half weeks before the polling date, he postponed the elections. Once Fazl Ilahi Chaudhry's five-year tenure as president ended in September 1978, Zia ul Haq appointed himself to the office. By then the Supreme Court had invoked the 'doctrine of necessity' to legitimize his coup and allow him to hold the 1973 constitution in abeyance. Zia ul Haq promulgated a provisional constitution which authorized him to amend the five-year-old basic law.

Politically, he set out to eradicate the PPP. He attacked Bhutto's seductive slogan of 'bread, clothes, and home' for all. 'It is not for the employers to provide *roti, kapra aur makan*,' he said. 'It was for God Almighty who is the provider of livelihood to His people. Trust in God and He will bestow upon you an abundance of good things in life.'[8] As the unchallenged leader of Pakistan, Zia ul Haq upgraded the status of Islam from 'official' to 'state' religion. He undertook a wholesale Islamization of the government and the governed, which previous administrations, civilian and military, had only advanced haphazardly and often as a tactical move to fend off an incipient crisis or an immediate popular challenge.

ISLAMIZATION AT FULL STEAM

While in his teens, Zia ul Haq associated himself with the Tablighi Jamaat (Urdu, 'Society for Spreading Faith'; TJ) an Islamic missionary movement aiming to bring about the spiritual reformation of Muslims.[9] After his university education in Delhi, he was commissioned in the British Indian army in 1943. He joined the Pakistani army four years later. During 1962–64, he trained at the US Army Command and General Staff College, Fort Leavenworth, Kansas. 'Drinking, gambling, dancing and music were the way the officers spent their free time,' he recalled years later. 'I said prayers, instead. Initially, I was treated with some amusement – sometimes with contempt – but my seniors and my peers decided to leave me alone after some time.'[10] Aware of his Islamist views, Prime Minister Bhutto instructed him to 'Islamize the army' after promoting him to army chief of staff in March 1976.

Now, as the supreme authority in Islamabad, Zia ul Haq's plans extended beyond the military. Taking a panoramic view, he said, 'Education, agriculture, industrialization, there are 101 important issues [in Pakistan] but the fundamental issue is that this country must have the spirit of Islam.'[11] Actually, he did tackle education at its core – in school textbooks – as was done by the first military dictator, General Ayub Khan, with his introduction of compulsory social studies. During Khan's rule and after, these books had been thoroughly revised at the expense of historical fact. After examining six textbooks on social studies, the eminent Pakistani historian Khurshid Kamal Aziz – author of the much-acclaimed volume *The Murder of History* – concluded that they were so 'replete with historic errors' that teaching them amounted to teaching 'prescribed myths'. A few examples illustrate his point: 'The Hindus wanted to control the government of India after independence. The British sided with the Hindus but the Muslims did not accept this decision;' the outcome of the 1965 war with India was a Pakistani victory – India sued for peace because it was 'frightened of the Pakistani army and the people of Pakistan'; and the separation of East Pakistan was due to 'collaboration between Pakistan's internal and external enemies and the Indian aggression'.[12]

Under Zia ul Haq's direction, social studies gradually gave way to Pakistan Studies – a compulsory subject for students from the upper grades of secondary school to the first year at university. Furthermore, all Muslim students were required to take courses in Islamiyat, a term used to cover a study of Islamic tenets and memorization of key Quranic verses. 'In general, the curriculum is a composite of patriotic discourses, justification of the Two-Nation Theory, hagiographies of Muslim heroes, and endemic in the polemics about the superiority of Islamic principles over Hinduism,' wrote Yvette Rosser, an American author and specialist on South Asia. 'The rubric in these textbooks must be learned by rote in order for students to pass the required exam.'[13]

Special committees were appointed to bring existing textbooks in line with Zia ul Haq's views. In 1983, a directive of the University Grants Commission required all textbook authors to stress that the key to the founding of Pakistan lay with its people's shared experience of a common religion – Islam – which stood apart from any geographical, linguistic, or racial element; to popularize the ideology of Pakistan with catchy phrases; and to motivate readers to help achieve the final aim of Pakistan as a 'totally Islamized State'. The result was a collection of radically altered or entirely new textbooks packed with internal contradictions and dogmatic perorations. Overall, they also had an anti-democratic thrust – reflecting Zia ul Haq's perception that democracy and Islam were mutually exclusive.[14]

Zia ul Haq argued that believers should obey the divine law as revealed to Prophet Muhammad and recorded in the Quran, and that they did not have the right to legislate independently. But implementing the divine law, which was often lacking in detail, required a formalized system for consultation among believers, and that could only be achieved by some form of election. But sticking to his basic anti democratic belief, Zia ul Haq banned political activity and ordered party-less elections to be held in mid-November 1979. Once again, he reneged on his word.

THE CRUCIAL ROLE OF MADRASAS

Zia ul Haq also introduced religious education in the armed forces and ordered commanders to ensure that prayers were offered by the troops led by their unit officers. Later, he would extend this directive to all civil servants, making it compulsory for them to pray five times a day. In another unprecedented move, he opened up the civil service to the graduates of madrasas. His government declared that the diploma awarded by a madrasa – called the higher *sanad* (Arabic, 'chain of narratives') – was equivalent to a university degree, which entitled its holder to compete for civil-service posts. Since they offered lifelong tenure, ample chances for bribe-taking, and great potential for upward social mobility, these jobs were highly prized.

Once religious groups took to rallying Pakistanis to support the anti-Soviet jihad in Afghanistan from 1980, Zia ul Haq started giving them state support. He encouraged them to open madrasas and provided them with free land for the purpose. Cash funding from oil-rich Gulf states, particularly Saudi Arabia, and Islamic charities followed.

The religious managements of madrasas patronized different sects and subsects within Islam. Among the Sunni Muslims of the Hanafi school, there were Deobandi and Barelvi branches. Since Ahmad Barelvi (1786–1831) harnessed the leading Sufi orders within the framework of a reformed interpretation of the Sharia, his school was more popular than that of the orthodox Deobandis. The Deobandi school, originating in the Dar ul Uloom madrasa in the northern Indian town of Deoband, stressed the external aspects of the Sharia over its inner meanings as favoured by most Sufi saints. They believed in applying strictly the injunction of 'enjoining good and forbidding evil [Arabic, *amr bil maruf wa nahiy anil munkar*]' derived from a Quranic verse, and maintained separate madrasas. The Deobandi seminaries were affiliated to the Jamiat Ulema-e Islam (Urdu, 'Society of Scholars of Islam').

In 1947, there were 181 madrasas in West Pakistan – antiquated institutions with poorly educated clerics as teachers. A quarter of a century later, their number stood at 893. Of these, 40 per cent were Deobandi, and 30 per cent Barelvi. After eleven years of Islamization by Zia ul Haq, the madrasa total then ballooned to 2,801– with the Deobandis accounting for 64 per cent of the total, and the Barelvis only 25 per cent.[15] Situated mostly in Punjab, Khyber Pakhtunkhwa, and the megalopolis of Karachi, these modern madrasas were staffed by properly qualified and highly motivated clerics. Registered as charitable organizations, they were tax-exempt.

All Sunni madrasas followed the course of twenty subjects adopted by the Deoband seminary in 1867. Consisting of 'transmitted sciences' (that is, the ones passed on by previous generations) and 'rational sciences', this included the life of Prophet Muhammad, the sayings and deeds of the Prophet, memorizing the Quran, exegesis of the Quran, the Sharia, jurisprudence, Arabic literature, polemics, logic, grammar and mathematics. The primary function of the non-religious subjects was to enable the student to comprehend fully the religious literature. For poor parents, forming a majority in Pakistan, madrasas were the only realistic option for their sons' education. They provided students with free textbooks, board and lodging, as well as a modest stipend, but deprived them of extracurricular activities and access to radio and TV.

The upsurge in madrasa enrolment was also a result of the stagnant economy and failing state-school system. With the inflow of Saudi funds in these institutions, the curriculum began to combine Deobandi ideology with Wahhabism as reflected in the education imparted to students in Saudi Arabia. Wahhabi Islam divided the world into believers and unbelievers, and enjoined the former to convert the latter to the true faith. This intolerance towards non-Muslims is encapsulated in the line that Muslim pupils in radical madrasas chant at the morning assembly: 'When people deny our faith, ask them to convert and if they don't, destroy them utterly.'[16]

In the coming years and decades – with the number of madrasas rising above ten thousand in the mid-1990s – these seminaries would provide an unending supply of recruits for the jihadist organizations in Pakistan, Afghanistan and Indian Kashmir. Their students unsurprisingly harboured radical views. When asked, in 2003, whether Pakistan should take Kashmir from India in a war, 59 per cent of madrasa students said yes, whereas 58 per cent of those in state schools said no.[17]

The Zia ul Haq government attached clerics of the Deobandi school to military units and allowed the JeI to spread its propaganda within the armed forces provided it refrained from recruiting serving personnel as members. Soldiers were encouraged to attend Tablighi Jamaat (TJ) meetings. Established in 1926 in the north Indian town of Mewat, the socially ultra-conservative TJ shunned Western influences and called on Muslims to live their lives according to the true faith. Since it had no political ambitions, Zia ul Haq attended the movement's annual assembly at Raiwind on the outskirts of Lahore, and permitted it to function among armed personnel.

At the same time, Zia ul Haq maintained contacts with Islamic scholars of all sects and schools, and included Sufi shaikhs in any discussions he held on Islam. He was well aware of the hold that Sufi philosophy and practices had on the masses as well as on public figures. Indeed, it was during his rule that the first phase of the expansion and modernization of the Sufi shrine of Data Ganj Bakhsh in Lahore was completed, in 1978. And it was his protégé Muhammad Nawaz Sharif who, as the country's prime minister, would order the second phase of expansion twenty-one years later.

However, Zia ul Haq's relentless Islamization drive, backed by the ulema, changed the street scene in Pakistan's cities and towns. There was a noticeable rise in women wearing headscarves or even burqas, men growing beards and donning prayer caps, and a dramatic fall in the number of girls and young women riding bicycles.

THE SHARIA TRUMPS ALL

On the first day of the Islamic year of 1399 (2 December 1978), Zia ul Haq declared that the Sharia – Islamic law – on theft, drinking, and adultery would be enforced from the birthday of Prophet Muhammad, 10 February 1979. As such, flogging for lesser crimes became commonplace, but the respective Sharia punishments of amputation of the right hand and death by stoning for theft and adultery could not be carried out due to the non-cooperation of surgeons and others.

Zia ul Haq specified a period of ten years for the Sharia to cover all aspects of life, with his proposal to be put to a referendum in June 1990. It was easy to predict the result. He had already started to argue that since his government was following Islamic principles, those opposing it could face the charge of engaging in anti-Islamic activity.

The establishment of Sharia courts at the high-court level in the provinces and the appellate Sharia bench at the Supreme Court followed. They were authorized to decide whether or not a particular law was Islamic. According to the newly promulgated Law of Evidence, non-Muslims were not allowed to give evidence against Muslims in Sharia courts. Outside these courts, a non-Muslim's evidence had half as much standing as a Muslim's. This led to increased litigation by Muslims against non-Muslims.

More seriously, Zia ul Haq's regime created a special category of crime to which non-Muslims were far more susceptible than Muslims. It did so by issuing ordinances between 1980 and 1986, which amended the Pakistan Penal Code (PPC) and the Criminal Procedure Code. Section 2 of the Criminal Law (Amendment) Act (Act III of 1986) consolidated and capped these ordinances. Showing disrespect to the Quran carried a punishment of life imprisonment, and disrespect to Prophet Muhammad became a capital offence. Collectively, these amendments to Article 295 of the PPC were termed the Blasphemy Law, popularly known as the *Namoos-e Risalat*

(Urdu, 'Dignity of Prophethood') Act. The law would be misused by hardline clerics to persecute Christians and liberal Muslims.

Over the years, half of the accused turned out to be Christians, who were only 3 per cent of the population. Noting this blatant bias, General Pervez Musharraf, who seized power in 1999, decided to act. In April 2000, he proposed that a preliminary investigation should be conducted by the local police before a suspect was charged. This minor procedural amendment was enough to rile Islamists, who used it to attack his government. Their massive ongoing street protest in Karachi, involving hundreds of gun-toting militants, paralysed the commercial–industrial capital for several days in May. More ominously, Musharraf found his military corps commanders divided on the issue, with some openly sympathizing with the Islamist demonstrations and strikes. The general backed down.[18] A decade later, the case of a Christian woman, Aasia Bibi, sentenced to death for disrespecting Prophet Muhammad, and the subsequent assassination of Punjab's governor, Salman Taseer, would divide the nation from top to bottom and reveal the degree to which Zia ul Haq's Islamization mission had succeeded.

Zia ul Haq's enforcement of the external expressions of Islam led to the imposition of social controls and the remoulding of social norms. It meant compulsory segregation of the sexes in public places and an insistence on 'modest dress' for women. The government ordered the blanket closure of eateries between sunrise and sunset during the fasting month of Ramadan. There was also a dramatic rise in Islamic content on the state-run radio and television channels.

By appointing JeI activists to the judiciary, civil service, and educational institutions, Zia ul Haq consolidated his hold over civil society. His Zakat and Ushr Ordinance of June 1980 introduced compulsory collection of religiously enjoined taxes to be given to charity. Zakat amounts to 2.5 per cent of accumulated assets and savings; *ushr* is a land tax amounting to 10 per cent of its produce. Zakat was to be deducted from all bank accounts annually on the eve of the holy month of Ramadan. Ushr was to be collected by local clerics working with the district commissioner.

Shias protested. They argued that as believers they were required to pay one-fifth of their trading profits to a grand ayatollah of their choice. Even though they represented a minority – estimated to be 15 to 20 per cent of the total population – their leaders vociferously broadcast some important officially obscured facts: The family of Muhammad Ali Jinnah belonged to the Ismaili Khoja branch of Shia Islam, and his surviving sister, Fatima Jinnah, along with prime minister Liaquat Ali Khan, had petitioned the Karachi High Court to execute the deceased's will according to Shia inheritance law. Moreover, before the public funeral prayers led by a Deobandi cleric, there was a private funeral prayer inside Jinnah's official residence in Karachi offered according to Shia rituals. Finally, a later claim that Jinnah had converted to Sunni Islam had been rejected in court in 1976.[19]

Shias now mounted a nationwide protest which culminated in tens of thousands of them descending on Islamabad by bus and other means of transport, and besieging the federal government's secretariat. In response, Zia ul Haq backed down and exempted the sect from zakat. That restored peace, although the episode would later be perceived as the starting point of sectarian tensions that would turn bloody in the coming decade.

The central zakat organization distributed its cash through local committees composed of clerics, and this procedure enhanced clerical power and prestige. Ninety-five per cent of funds went towards facilities for religious education. As collectors of ushr in the countryside, the status of clerics changed as they worked closely with the district commissioner and local authorities. Islamabad's decision to allocate zakat cash to madrasas led to their rapid growth. In a typical district of Punjab, they now constitute a quarter of government schools.

As someone who attributed the traditional, skewed land ownership to the will of Allah, before the land reforms were implemented during Zulfikar Ali Bhutto's rule, Zia ul Haq was disappointed when the federal Sharia court declared in December 1980 that the reforms of 1972 and 1977 were in line with Islamic tenets. Its ruling was challenged and the matter placed before the Sharia appellate bench, to which Zia ul Haq appointed two new pro-landlord clerics. However, the judicial wheels turned at a snail's pace. It would not be until 1990 (two years after the military dictator's death) that the appellate bench finally reversed the federal Sharia court's verdict. Meanwhile, feudal lords had resorted to evicting their tenants and openly increasing their holdings way beyond the legal limits. The military government turned a blind eye to this wholesale violation of the law since it had dismissed the land reform legislation as Bhutto's way of rewarding his supporters and punishing his adversaries. After 1990, the pattern of landownership basically reverted to that prevailing during the period prior to the land reforms, with feudal lords openly referring to the thousands of agricultural labourers working for them on subsistence wages paid in cash or kind.

Zia ul Haq also upgraded the status and importance of the Council of Islamic Ideology. Established originally in 1962 as the Islamic Advisory Council, it was redesignated by the 1973 constitution as the Council of Islamic Ideology to offer legal advice on Islamic issues to the government and parliament. At the behest of Zia ul Haq, it issued fifteen reports between 1981 and 1984.[20] In its last report in 1984, it declared family planning un-Islamic.

THE ISLAMIZATION OF THE MILITARY

As a military man to his fingertips, Zia ul Haq's Islamization mission covered the armed forces comprehensively. He introduced Islamic teachings at the Pakistan Military Academy at Kakul, a suburb of Abbottabad in Khyber Pakhtunkhwa. Islamic philosophy and training were added to the course at the Command and Staff College in Quetta. He also established a directorate of Religious Instruction to educate the officer corps.

In 1980, *The Quranic Concept of War* by Brigadier S.K. Malik, published locally a year earlier, became a compulsory textbook for all officers at the Command and Staff College. Combing the Quran, Malik analysed the several battles that Prophet Muhammad had fought and won. From that material he distilled what he called 'the military-strategy principles of Islam'. As a senior military commander, well versed in modern warfare tactics and military philosophy, he did a professional job in explaining the Prophet's strategy in fighting. This so impressed Zia ul Haq that he penned a foreword to the book. Commending the volume to 'both soldier and civilian', he wrote:

> *Jihad Fi Sabil Allah* [Arabic, 'effort in the pathway of Allah'] is not the exclusive domain of the professional soldier, nor is it restricted to the application of military force alone . . . This book brings out with simplicity, clarity and precision the Quranic philosophy on the application of military force, within the context of the totality that is jihad. The professional soldier in a Muslim army, pursuing the goals of a Muslim state, CANNOT become 'professional' if in all his activities he does not take on 'the color of Allah'. The non-military citizen of a Muslim state must, likewise, be aware of the kind of soldier that his country must produce and the ONLY pattern of war that his country's armed forces may wage.[21]

Under Zia ul Haq's watch, professionalism in the armed forces was equated with religious piety and display of Islamic beliefs and practices. Those officers who failed to fall into line with the rising Islamization of the military and stuck to their secular ways, inherited from the days of British rule, were marginalized.

Out of Zia ul Haq's efforts emerged a nexus between the military and the mosque which had an impact not only at home but also in the region. For he sketched out a grand vision for Pakistan in the world of Muslims, the umma. He was keenly aware of Pakistan as the second most populous Muslim country after Indonesia; its strategic position – straddling Central, West and South Asia; and the strength of its military as the sixth largest army on the planet. He visualized it as the emergent first among equals in the Islamic world as it inspired and encouraged Islamist movements from Afghanistan to Turkey and the Muslim-majority states of Soviet Central Asia. Later, his vision would be adopted by the Pakistani Taliban, perceiving Pakistan as the core of a revived Islamic caliphate. Viewed thus, Zia ul Haq, a political darling of the United States, emerges as the forerunner of the demonic bin Laden.

THE DOWNSIDE

There was a downside to this zealous drive by Zia ul Haq. At the macro level it impacted negatively on relations between the major sects of Islam; at the micro level it caused a spurt in the country's murder rate.

In 1980, Zia ul Haq promulgated an Islamic law, rooted in the Sharia, that permited criminals to settle their crimes with victims privately. A decade later this provision was widened to allow criminals to reach an agreement with victims' families outside the purview of the courts. In the case of murder or other serious crimes, the traumatized family of the victim was encouraged to bypass state prosecution, and instead deal directly with the defendant's family and settle for 'blood money' or some other form of compensation. As a result, during the next twenty years, in the Punjabi city of Multan, for instance, only 3 per cent of the murder cases ended in conviction.[22] Overall, the justice system became dangerously distorted.

This was one of the main factors that caused an upsurge in the inter-sectarian killings and blighted many Pakistani cities, with an average of seventy-four murders being committed every day in the mid-1990s. Seen historically, however, the blame for this baneful development lay chiefly with sectarian madrasas where, invariably, the superiority of one particular sect over all others was overemphasized.

Another factor was the Islamic revolution in Shia-majority Iran in 1979, which emboldened the Shia minority in neighbouring Pakistan. Its successful protest against the compulsory collection of zakat by the government was led by Allama Mufti Jafar Hussein and resulted in the formation of the Tehrik-e-Nifaz-e-Fiqah-e-Jafaria (Urdu, 'Movement for Enforcement of Jafaria Jurisprudence'; TNJF) named after their sixth imam, Jafar al Sadiq. The Zia ul Haq government, whose penal code was derived from the Hanafi school of Sunni Islam, viewed it as a conspiracy hatched in Tehran to export its revolution and tried to create a division in the TNJF. It succeeded.

After the split, the majority section renamed itself Tehrik-e-Jafaria Pakistan.

In turn, that led to the emergence of the Sipah-e Sahaba Pakistan (Urdu, 'Soldiers of the Friends of the Prophet'; SSP) in 1985. This was led by Haq Nawaz Jhangvi, a Deobandi cleric from the district of Jhang in Punjab, where feudal lords were often Shia and bazaar merchants Sunni. It had close ties with the ISI directorate, which saw it as a bulwark against the export of Shia revolution in Iran. The SSP also received funds from the anti-Tehran Saudi intelligence agency, Istikhabarat.

The SSP's overarching aim was to restore the caliphate, a goal shared with Al Qaida. Claiming that Shias were non-Muslim, it aspired to make Sunni Islam the state religion of Pakistan. Its cadres were drawn from the Deobandi and Ahle Hadith madrasas. It soon established branches as well as a student wing and a welfare trust. In the mid-1990s, when sectarian violence reached a peak, it would claim a membership of 300,000 and several branches abroad.[23]

With Saudi Arabia and Kuwait pouring money into hardline Sunni organizations in Pakistan to counter the perceived Shia threat at home to their ruling families, Pakistan became the battlefield for a proxy war between Tehran and Riyadh. In 1986, Lahore was racked by severe anti-Shia riots. The SSP viewed attacks on Shias as part of the 'internal jihad', the external jihad being against the West, especially the United States. When Jhangvi was assassinated in 1990, the SSP's five to six thousand well-trained militants unleashed a reign of terror. Among their victims was Iran's consul general in Lahore.

Zia ul Haq's government put the blame for the inter-sectarian violence on India's intelligence agency, the Research and Analysis Wing (RAW), which it claimed was determined to destabilize Pakistan by all means. Since the 1971 Bangladesh War, blaming RAW for major domestic problems had become standard practice in Islamabad. Privately, however, the Zia administration saw RAW as trying to get even with it for giving refuge and weapons training to Sikh separatists agitating for an independent state of their own, to be called Khalistan (Urdu, 'Land of Khalsa Sikhs'), adjoining Pakistan.

The 1980s was an eventful decade for India as well. In 1981, a meeting of Sikhs in New York, chaired by Gurbachan Singh Tohra, president of the [Indian] Shiromoni Gurdwara Prabadhak Committee, passed a resolution declaring Sikhs a separate nation. This was the start of a movement for a sovereign Khalistan which, among other things, went on to claim the life of Indian prime minister Indira Gandhi in 1984. It was not until the late 1980s that the movement finally ran out of steam.

In Pakistan's domestic social sphere, the 1984 declaration of the Council of Islamic Ideology that family planning was un-Islamic merely sanctified the situation that already existed on the ground. Many studies have shown that family planning is related to literacy and income, with poor, illiterate couples having more children than those who are literate and have higher incomes. Given the poverty afflicting a large majority of Pakistanis, it is not surprising that the country's population rocketed from thirty-four million in 1951 to 103 million in 1986 – trebling in just a third of a century.

Taking pride in Pakistan's swelling population, Zia ul Haq remained oblivious to the fact that a nation of illiterates and semi-literates was more a liability than an asset. He was equally oblivious to the fact that due to the resistance of feudal lords, whom he favoured, illiteracy remained high in rural areas. Feudal lords wanted their surfs to be illiterate and to have large families to provide an ample labour force prepared to work for subsistence wages.

Nonetheless, on the eve of the diamond jubilee of the two neighbours' independence in August 2007, Pakistan lost its title of the world's second most populous Muslim country to India, which had an estimated 150 million Muslim citizens. This led many Hindu nationalists to rail against Muslims for having large families, and thus steadily increasing their proportion in the national population.[24]

However, that numerical growth had not resulted in any noticeable improvement in Muslims' status in India. Socially and economically, they remained at the bottom of the pyramid. They had much to complain about.

9

INDIAN MUSLIMS AMIDST HINDU REVIVALISM

AS THE YOUTHFUL taxi driver sped merrily along the potholed embankment of the Ganga Canal, on our way to the village of Sisola, I gripped the back seat tightly next to my companion, Mujtaba Khalid – a slim, bespectacled, PhD student at a prestigious university in Delhi. In the midst of our low-key conversation his voice rose suddenly. 'It was in this canal that the Meerut police dumped the bodies of forty-five Muslim youths in 1982,' he said, his index finger pointing at the waterway. Why? 'They were killed in the police firings on the Muslim demonstrators in Meerut. A gory fact the police chief wanted to hide.'

Meerut is a city in the state of Uttar Pradesh, about 6 miles (10 km) away from that canal. 'There was no arrest or a charge sheet issued against a single policeman,' he continued in his agitated voice. What led to the shootings? 'There was a riot in the Hashimpura Muslim neighbourhood of Meerut. And when policemen arrived, somebody threw a hand grenade at them.'[1]

The taxi left the embankment for a narrow tarred road cutting through green fields of sugar cane, mustard seed, with its spicy, aromatic smell, and gently swaying stalks of wheat, and leading towards Sisola. A settlement of five thousand people, the village is wholly Muslim, with a well-maintained mosque. A year earlier, Sisola's paths were paved with baked bricks and cement, with open drains on both sides. Because the channels are not cleared regularly, uncollected, simmering junk spills over and rots, creating a haven for flies and mosquitoes.

Young doe-eyed girls in colourful frocks of orange, red, purple, blue, and green, with an occasional flash of silver-thread embroidery, stopped playing hopscotch to stare at the visitors, shepherded by their local host, Salahuddin. Dressed in a beige bush shirt with matching pants of thick cotton cloth, the thirty-seven-year-old landlord and father of four, ready with a toothy smile, looked prosperous. Muslim women, wearing salwar kameez or cotton sari, were indistinguishable from their Hindu counterparts. Some of them sat on strong cots, charpoys, in front of their homes, braiding their long black hair or catching lice. Nearby, cows and water buffaloes chewed the cud, and discharged their malodorous excrement, providing a feast for flies and other insects. Being a typical South Asian rural settlement, Sisola offered no chance for a male stranger to talk to any woman, independently, even when (like me) he was fluent in Hindi and Urdu.

As the owner of nearly 17 acres of land and a tractor – an asset held by only 2 per cent of Muslim farmers – Salahuddin was affluent by the standards of rural India. 'Five years ago I added an extension to my house of baked bricks and cement. In my house I have a washing machine and a large metal silo to store food grains. Also a fridge. But there is electricity only for twelve hours a day. It alternates every two weeks, from 8 a.m. to 8 p.m., or 8 p.m. to 8 a.m. So we have to remove all the stuff from our fridge when the power is off.'

We were introduced to Salahuddin's guest from a nearby village: Sidaqat Ali. A dark, slim man of medium height with hennaed beard, dressed in a white shirt, tight pantaloons, and round cloth cap, he exuded neatness. 'Economically, life is better than before,' he said. 'More conveniences, roads, mobile phones, tarred roads, fertilizer, water for drinking and irrigation.' He too possessed enough land to lead a comfortable life. Yet he lamented the way Muslims in general were marginalized in the civil service and police. 'While dealing with government offices, I find that only 1 to 2 per cent of the officials are Muslim,' he said. 'And they are careful not to be seen favouring other Muslims. If you want to get anything done, your best approach is to give a bribe. A Hindu bureaucrat will easily accept a bribe from a Muslim. But a Muslim bureaucrat will worry that people would say that he was favouring his community.'

At the tiny barber's shop, scantily furnished, Abdul Hashim arrived carrying his semi-naked baby boy – his circumcised penis exposed to the elements – for a haircut. Fair-skinned, unshaven, oval-faced, with black eyes and a rich moustache, wearing grey pants and a dirty, white vest, the twenty-five-year-old was a day labourer. 'When there is a cricket match between India and Pakistan, we all support India,' he declared. This unprompted statement was highly significant. Whether they admit it in public or not, most Muslims in India take more interest in what Pakistan and Pakistanis do than any other community. In an off-the-cuff remark, Mujtaba Khalid had said, 'We [Indian Muslims] feel distressed when bombs explode in Pakistan and find that country going downhill.'

In his everyday existence, however, someone like Hashim had more practical situations to deal with. 'If there is a dispute between two people, and the police get involved, they ask the names of the disputants,' he said. 'Once a man says, "Ahmad or Qasim or Hassan", the policeman's baton comes down on him.' The small crowd that had assembled around us nodded in agreement.

Whereas the Muslims in this village and elsewhere in the state spoke with suppressed anger about the overt anti-Muslim discrimination by the police and government bureaucrats, the older ones tried to channel their anger into cynical remarks. Their disaffection was rooted in facts. Even though Muslims constituted 18 per cent of the state's population, their share in the police force was widely put at 'no more than 2 per cent'.

The subject came up again at the modest shop of seventy-five-year-old Khurshid Ali. Sporting a long, white beard, with a clean-shaven upper lip, he had opened a general store two years earlier, selling odd things, including sweets and notebooks. 'If things go wrong and the police get involved, they favour Hindus,' he noted.

Similar behaviour by politicians had not – yet – led to disenchantment with voting or the democratic system per se. 'I vote in elections,' was a universal response of the male interviewees. 'There are four major parties in Uttar Pradesh – the Congress, the Bharatiya Janata Party, the Bahujan Samaj Party of Chief Minister Mayawati, and the Samajwadi Party of Mulayam Singh Yadav,' said Ali. 'There is only one, Yadav's Samajwadi Party, that looks after Muslim interests. But in the last general election for the parliament it did badly. All its Muslim candidates lost.'

If a citizen has a grievance against a policeman or civil servant, his or her first preference is to approach the locally elected lawmaker. Often the legislator is inaccessible. 'If so, why not lodge a complaint in writing?' I asked. 'Whom to complain to?' Ali responded instantly. 'If you try to do that, the official will want a bribe to accept a complaint. As for the local member of the legislative assembly, before the election, candidates come with folded hands, saying, "I will do this and that for you." But when one of them gets elected he refuses to see you.'

How were relations with Hindus in the surrounding area and elsewhere? 'Overall relations with the Hindus are normal,' Salahuddin said. 'It is only when there is tension in nearby cities, or some hot-headed politician gives hateful speeches against Muslims, particularly during election time, that the situation changes for the worse.'

In general, common electoral rolls used in Indian polls are problematic for minorities. Even when a candidate of a minority religion or race is contesting an election on the ticket of a party that is open to all, his/her religious affiliation or racial background matters greatly to voters. For historical reasons, the situation of Indian Muslims is particularly tricky.

THE POPULAR VOTE AND THE MUSLIM MINORITY

Once the decision to partition the Indian subcontinent was announced in June 1947, communal violence of major proportions broke out in the eastern and western parts of Punjab, with Hindus and Sikhs in one camp and Muslims in the other. This emptied West Punjab as well as other provinces of West Pakistan of almost all their Hindus and Sikhs, and India's East Punjab of almost all its Muslims. But that still left some forty million Muslims scattered over independent India.

The Muslims in post-partition India faced a dilemma, which is described by Imtiaz Ahmad, an Indian social scientist, thus:

> The Indian Muslim had to learn to regard his brothers-in-faith in Karachi or Lahore, whom he had supported in the demand for Pakistan, as foreigners. He had to learn to view his Hindu neighbours, with whom he has never had much social intercourse, as fellow-citizens. And, he had to reconcile himself to the fact that political power [now] lay in Hindu hands . . . These were difficult emotional adjustments in themselves . . . [On top of that] the vast majority of Hindus blamed the Indian Muslims for the division of the sub-continent and doubted their political loyalty to the country.[2]

In other words, following the establishment of Pakistan, Muslims in India felt more threatened about their political status and cultural identity than they had in pre-partition India.

The situation worsened for Muslims as Hindus – realizing that they had at last become masters of their homeland after seven centuries of subjugation by foreign Muslim tribes, followed by the Christian British – began to reassert their identity. They did so while ostensibly recreating an 'Indian' personality, with the two notions of 'Hindu' and 'Indian' getting inextricably mixed up. There was the inevitable rewriting and rehashing of history, now to be taught to tens of millions of young Indians. Almost invariably, the resistance offered by the indigenous Hindus to the invading or trading non-Hindu foreigners was glorified. Hindi, the official language, was 'purified' – that is, words of Persian origin were replaced by those of Sanskrit. Slowly, the distinction between being Indian and being Hindu was reduced while officially both the government and the ruling Congress party reiterated their commitment to secularism – a term popularized by Jawaharlal Nehru and echoed by the lower echelons of his party and administration.

'Indians regard the River Ganges as sacred,' stated the new *Basic Hindi Reader*, prescribed for use in all government-supported schools and edited by the director of education of Uttar Pradesh. 'It is said that emerging from the feet of Lord Vishnu, the Ganges came to the thick hair of Lord Shiva and from there to the Himalayas . . . The Ganges is believed to wash away all sins.'[3] This is a Hindu myth. It offends the religious susceptibilities of Muslims who, unlike the pantheistic, idol-worshiping Hindus, are monotheistic and do not believe in gods and goddesses. This basic fact seemed to have escaped the minds of the education authorities of the 'secular' government of Uttar Pradesh, where Muslims were one-sixth of the population. 'With few exceptions, non-communal Hindus are ignorant, and therefore indifferent, to the militant communalism within their own midst,' wrote M.R.A. Baig, a former Indian Muslim diplomat. 'It is the apathy of secular Hindus that is the Muslims' despair.'[4]

In the political sphere, Muslims' sense of insecurity was aggravated by the continuing frosty-to-hostile relations between India and Pakistan, with the latter considering the Kashmir problem unsolved. The outbreak of war between the two neighbours in September 1965 intensified the traditional ill will against Muslims, with many Hindus suspecting them of being saboteurs, or spies for Pakistan.

Astonishingly, Indian prime minister Lal Bahadur Shastri, who succeeded the arch-secularist Nehru, invited Madhavrao Sadashiv Golwalkar, the supreme leader of the Rashtriya Swayamsevak Sangh (Sanskrit, 'National Volunteer Association'; RSS), the leading Hindu chauvinist organization, to a national security conclave in Delhi in 1965. By so doing, he removed the pariah status that the RSS had acquired after one of its members, Nathuram Godse, acting on his own, had assassinated the much-revered Mahatma Mohandas Gandhi in January 1948.

The RSS was formed by Keshava Baliram Hedgewar, a physician in the central Indian city of Nagpur, in 1925, soon after he came under the influence of Vinayak Damodar Savarkar, a militant Hindu leader. Arguing that the Hindus in the Indian subcontinent constituted a nation, Savarkar defined a Hindu as a person who loved the land that stretches from the Indus River to the 'seas in the east', and considered it both fatherland *and* holy land. To be a Muslim or a Christian, he stated, meant having a religion that draws its cultural resources from outside this holy land, and caused a division of loyalties and a weakening of the Hindu nation. He articulated his thesis in a book titled *Hindutva: Who is a Hindu?*[5] It behoved the militant Hindu to undertake the task of minimizing, and then eliminating, this division, and rejuvenating the Hindu nation, he concluded. In practical terms, this meant having Muslims and Christians adopt Hindu names and participate in such Hindu festivals as Holi, the festival of colour, and Diwali, the festival of light.

Hedgewar set out to realize Savarkar's vision by forming a volunteer corps modelled on the Italian Fascist Party. Its members wore a uniform, met daily, drilled and played games together, and attended political discussions and indoctrination sessions. Each year, at a grand ceremony, a recruit made a voluntary donation in cash to the leader of his branch.

Before and during World War II, RSS members openly admired Adolf Hitler. This was not surprising. In his book *We, or, Our Nationhood Defined,* published in 1939, their bespectacled, long-haired, bearded leader, Golwalkar, wrote: 'To keep up the purity of the Race and its culture, Germany shocked the world by her purging the country of the Semitic races – the Jews. Race pride at its highest has been manifested here. Germany has also shown how well nigh impossible it is for races and cultures, having differences going to the root, to be assimilated into one united whole, a good lesson for us in Hindustan [India] to learn and profit by.'[6] Turning to his homeland,

Golwalkar decalred: 'In Hindustan, land of the Hindus, lives and should live the Hindu Nation. All others are traitors and enemies to the National Cause, or, to take a charitable view, idiots . . . The foreign races in Hindustan . . . may stay in the country, wholly subordinated to the Hindu Nation, claiming nothing, deserving no privileges, far less any preferential treatment – not even citizen's rights.'[7]

Golwalkar's use of the terms 'Hindustan' and 'Hindu' undermined his basic argument. Hindustan is a Persian word, meaning 'Land of Hindus', the word Hindu being the Persian version of Sindhu, the Sanskrit name of the Indus River. Unluckily for Golwalkar, Persian did not originate in India. Actually, all those living beyond the banks of the Indus were called Hindus by the invaders and infiltrators from Afghanistan and Central Asia. So the term Hindu did not signal religious affiliation; it was a geographical appellation.

With the movement for Pakistan gaining ground among Muslims, the strength of the RSS increased – until the assassination of Mahatma Gandhi. The Indian government banned the organization and jailed Golwalkar, and many of his followers. However, once he had agreed to have his organization adopt a written constitution (which it had lacked) in March 1949, he and his jailed followers were released, and the ban on the RSS lifted four months later.[8] A little over a year later, the RSS re-established nearly five thousand branches, with an estimated 600,000 members and active sympathizers.[9]

Basking in the glow of attending the prime minister's national security conclave in 1965, Golwalkar presided over the founding conference of the Vishwa Hindu Parishad (Sanskrit, 'World Hindu Council'; VHP) in 1966 at the time of the Hindu festival of the Maha Kumbh at the confluence of the Ganges and Yamuna Rivers in Allahabad. 'The world has been divided into Christian, Islam[ic] and Communist [spheres],' said S.S. Apte, a founder of the VHP. 'All of them view Hindu society as very fine rich food on which to feast and fatten themselves. It is necessary in this age of conflict to think of and organize the Hindu world to save it from the evils of all the three.'[10]

This implausible piece of logic was a precursor to the formation of the Hindu Rashtriya Swayamsevak Sangh (Sanskrit, 'Hindu National Volunteer Association'; HSS), the overseas arm of the RSS.

As an ostensibly cultural organization, the VHP was not exposed to the compulsions of electoral politics which the RSS's political arm, established earlier, could not ignore. The founding of the HSS would set the scene for the RSS to spawn many other organizations which would collectively be known as the Sangh Parivar (Sanskrit, 'Family of Associations'). The HSS began to proliferate. Within a decade, a branch of the HSS would be founded by expatriate militant Hindus in Britain as a not-for-profit charity, followed by branches in the United States and Canada. These associations, along with Sewa International, another member of the Sangh Parivar, would allegedly turn into a rich source of funding for the RSS as well as the VHP and Bajrang Dal (Hindi, 'Army of Bajrang' – one of the names of the monkey-god who was loyal to Lord Rama), an organization of zealous Hindu youths.

In 1967, the Bharatiya Jan Sangh (Hindi, 'Indian People's Union'; BJS), the political arm of the RSS, won thirty-five seats in the directly elected Lower House of parliament, called the Lok Sabha (Hindi, 'People's Assembly'), a big jump from the three seats it had won after its birth in 1951. Significantly, the growth in the BJS's popularity ran parallel to the rise in the number of communal riots. At 462, the annual count for the period 1968–70 was more than six times the figure for 1954–59. And they became bloodier. Whereas the fatalities in 1954–62 were thirty-four, the figure was 301 for 1967 alone.[11] The total for 1969 was well into four figures since more than a thousand Muslims were killed in Ahmedabad, the capital of Gujarat, alone.

Earlier Ahmedabad had been the site of a massive rally where Golwalkar demanded that the Republic of India be declared a Hindu Rashtra – Nation – which would exclude all those whose religion did not originate in India, namely, Muslims and Christians. When, following the arson attack on the Al Aqsa Mosque in Jerusalem – the third holiest shrine in Islam – in July 1969, the Indian Muslims held protest marches, the BJS leader, Balraj Madhok, taunted them at a public rally in Ahmedabad for protesting about a mosque that was 'thousands of miles away'. That set the scene for a riot in which Muslims suffered badly.

'Among the Hindus, there was a feeling of jubilation over their "victory over Muslims",' noted Ghanshyam Shah, a Gujarati Hindu academic. 'For the first time,' a social worker and Congress party member said, 'Hindus were able to teach a lesson to Muslims. These attitudes are reflected [even] among the educated and prosperous sections [of Hindus] . . . They thought of various propositions: either Muslims should become Hindu, or go to Pakistan, or some other Islamic country. Not all Hindus had turned communalist, although there was no doubt that a vast majority had.'[12] Thirty-three years later, Ahmedabad would once again loom large as the site of a pogrom against Muslims, with the BJS's successor, the Bharatiya Janata Party (Hindi, 'Indian People's Party'; BJP), wielding power in Gujarat.

The BJS and RSS routinely criticized the ruling Congress party for appeasing Muslims in order to secure their votes. But the evidence contradicted such claims. Though in the mid-1960s Muslims formed 11.2 per cent of the national population, their share in public services 'of any significance' was about 3 per cent.[13] Only 5.3 per cent of Indian Administrative Service officers and 3.6 per cent of Indian Police Service officers were Muslim. And less than 1 per cent of the civil servants of the Central government were Muslim. In parliament, Muslims accounted for 5.5 per cent of the total, and the figure for the state assemblies was often lower.[14]

THE POST-BANGLADESH PERIOD

The break-up of Pakistan in 1971 benefitted India and Indians in several ways. With the demise of the two-nation theory, the popular Hindu suspicion of Muslims in their midst declined, while the return of Indira Gandhi as prime minister with a two-thirds majority in parliament reassured Muslims. But the dramatic hike in oil prices in 1973–74 caused inflation and popular disaffection. In 1975 Indira Gandhi was disqualified as a member of parliament (MP) due to electoral malpractices, leading to a declaration of a state of emergency by her government to forestall her removal from power. Opposition figures including BJS luminaries such as Atal Bihari Vajpayee and Lal Krishna Advani were arrested. Their brief incarceration gave them a popular appeal they had previously lacked. And their inclusion in the cabinet of Prime Minister Morarji Desai, as leader of the Janata Party, an anti-Congress coalition which won the 1977 parliamentary poll, enhanced their standing further.

Following the fall of the Desai government and the Janata Party's break-up in 1980, the BJS transformed itself into the BJP, with its membership open to all Indians. This concession came seven years after the death of Golwalkar, who, during his thirty-three years of unquestioned stewardship, had implanted his ideology of intolerant Hindu ultra-nationalism deep into the RSS. Spawning many popular organizations over the decades, its subsequent supreme leaders held firm to Golwalkar's creed.

From the early 1980s onward, President Zia ul Haq's drive for Islamization in Pakistan enhanced the chances of creating a countermovement of Hindu revivalism in India. What aided this process further was the terrorism perpetrated by Sikh militants – partly assisted by Islamabad – to achieve their aim of an independent, sovereign Khalistan next to Pakistan. The leaders of the BJP, which had secured only two seats in the parliamentary election of 1984, decided to grab the fresh opportunity presented by these circumstances. They replaced the moderate Vajpayee with Advani as the party's president in 1986. Born in Karachi before partition, the hardliner Advani joined the RSS at the age of fifteen. He set out to transform the placid, inclusive, Hindu civilization into an aggressive religious nation.

Advani derided secularism as the brainchild of Nehru and a cover for the Congress party's 'appeasement' of Muslims. The only example to back up his claim was the Muslim Personal Law – a legacy of British rule, when all major religious communities were subject to their respective faiths' edicts – whereby a Muslim could have four wives whereas a Hindu, under the Hindu Personal Law, could have only one. Simultaneously, the BJP alarmed Hindus by claiming that, due to the lack of family planning among Muslims, their population was rising so much faster than that of Hindus that by 2050 India would become a Muslim-majority country and unite with Pakistan. To convey this message simply and graphically, the VHP distributed millions of leaflets depicting a Hindu couple with three children next to a Muslim man with four wives and numerous children with the slogan: 'You five; Ours twenty-five'. These tactics caught the popular imagination of Hindus – at a price paid by Muslims. 'The [Hindu] militant attack by the Sangh Parivar on Nehruvian secularism and the VHP campaign against the myth of [a] multiplying population of Muslims not only weakened Indian secularism but made Muslims feel politically suffocated,' wrote Asghar Ali Engineer, an eminent Indian Muslim intellectual.[15]

THE BABRI MOSQUE CONTROVERSY

To capture the attention of the Hindu masses and keep it, the VHP focused on the Babri Mosque, built by Emperor Babur in 1528 in Ayodhya, a town of fifty thousand people in Uttar Pradesh, claiming that it had been constructed on the birthplace of Lord Rama, which was marked by a Hindu temple called Rama Janam Bhoomi (Hindi, 'birth place'). Hindus regard Rama, the legendary king of Ayodhya, as an incarnation of Lord Vishnu in the pantheon of the ancient Aryan tribes who settled in the Indian subcontinent.

An imposing monument built on top of a hill, the Babri Mosque had a large central dome flanked by two smaller ones. It was surrounded by high walls which enclosed a large courtyard containing a drinking-water well. At the entrance the Persian inscriptions on two stone tablets named the builder as Mir Baqi, who implemented Babur's orders.

The simmering argument about the origins of this structure took a dramatic turn on the night of 22–23 December 1949. A group of local Hindu zealots infiltrated the mosque while police guards were asleep and furtively installed idols of Rama and his wife Sita under the central dome. Idol worship is forbidden in Islam, and mosques do not display graven images. This sacrilege of their place of worship shocked local Muslims. Prime Minister Nehru intervened. He instructed the state's chief minister to restore the status quo ante. But when the order reached the local magistrate he surmised that removing the holy idols would lead to widespread rioting by Hindus. Both Muslims and Hindus filed civil suits. With that, the matter became sub judice. The state authorities declared the property 'disputed' and locked the gates.

In 1961, the Uttar Pradesh Sunni Central Waqf [Arabic, 'religious trust'] Board approached the court to restore Muslims' right to pray at the mosque. In 1964, several pending suits were amalgamated into one. It would be another thirty-six years before the Allahabad High Court would deliver its verdict!

From 1984, the issue became toxic, causing national repercussions. A series of developments brought about this change. Having organized its young followers under the banner of the Bajrang Dal, the VHP focused on constructing a new temple at the contested site. Then the case of a divorced Muslim woman named Shah Bano led to a nationwide debate centred on religion. The Supreme Court's verdict in 1985 that she was entitled to alimony from her former husband clashed with the Muslim Personal Law, which exempted ex-husbands from any material obligation towards divorced wives. Muslim leaders of all sects and political hues viewed the judgment as a further blow to Muslim identity in India and mounted a robust campaign to get the verdict nullified. This worsened the already fraught Hindu–Muslim relations. Faced with an almost unanimous stance by the Muslim community against the court judgment, the government of

Rajiv Gandhi gave in. Supported by three-quarters of all Lok Sabha members, it passed the Muslim Women (Protection of Rights on Divorce) Act, 1986, nullifying the Supreme Court's judgment and upholding the Muslim Personal Law.

Having insisted all along that the personal lives of Hindus must be governed by their religious edicts, the RSS and BJP now demanded that civil law should apply to *all* Indian citizens irrespective of faiths. They ratcheted up their traditional criticism of the ruling Congress party that it appeased Muslims to secure their vote in elections.

In order to 'balance' the adoption of the Muslim Women (Protection of Rights on Divorce) Act, the Gandhi administration decided to remove the locks on the Babri Mosque. The district court ordered its gates to be opened to let Hindus worship inside. This led aggrieved Muslims to form the Babri Masjid Action Committee.

Moreover, around the time of the removal of the seal on the mosque, the state-run television company, Doordarshan, enjoying a monopoly, sanctioned the airing of the Hindu epic *Ramayan*, in seventy-eight episodes on Sunday mornings. The serial, starting on 25 January 1987 and ending on 31 July 1988, intensified religious feelings among Hindus, forming 83 per cent of the population. Then followed the ninety-four-episode serialization of the other Hindu epic *Mahabharat*, shown every Sunday morning from 2 October 1988 onward. These TV presentations of Hindu epics engendered a shared symbolic lexicon around which the RSS, the VHP, and the BJP mobilized strong Hindu identification.

When the VHP succeeded in getting permission to perform a foundation-laying ceremony next to the Babri Mosque on the eve of the general election in November 1989, communal tensions escalated. This benefitted the BJP enormously. Its representation in parliament soared from four to eighty-nine seats.

Intoxicated by this dramatic upsurge in the BJP's popularity, Advani, one of the most media-savvy politicians, unleashed the second phase of his strategy to capture power in Delhi. Dressed in traditional Hindu attire – a dhoti and a long shirt – he boarded a chariot, called a *rath* in Sanskrit, decorated with saffron-coloured pennants (saffron being the colour of Hinduism), and undertook a 6,250-mile (10,000 km) religious journey, or *yatra*, from 25 September 1990 to 30 October 1991.

This started from the Somnath Temple near the port city of Veraval in Gujarat. In the Middle Ages, Veraval was the major seaport for Muslim pilgrims voyaging Mecca. In 1026, Sultan Mahmoud of Ghazni (in Afghanistan) attacked Somnath, then the site of a massive fortified temple of Lord Shiva, and captured it. That battle left fifty thousand people dead. Entering the inner sanctum of the temple, he broke the large stone phallus at its centre, to discourage worship of idols as enjoined by Islam. His booty was put at twenty million dirham (the Islamic currency then in circulation) worth gold, silver, and precious stones. The temple was rebuilt and ransacked several times in the succeeding centuries; its final reconstruction occurred soon after Indian independence in 1947.

By choosing the Somnath Temple, Advani exploited the past to resurrect the image of Muslims as invading marauders and to widen the BJP's popular base among Hindus by fanning hatred of Muslims. His plan was to highlight how the Somnath Temple had been resurrected repeatedly, and that it was time to restore the Rama Janam Bhoomi Temple at its original site. The downside was that his strategy increased Indian Muslims' feeling of insecurity and fear – particularly when the BJP-VHP-Bajrang Dal triad prepared a list of three hundred historical mosques, which they claimed were built where temples had stood before. Muslims lost their faith in Articles 25–30 of the Indian constitution which accord special religious and cultural rights to minorities.

The media glare on Advani's extraordinary journey yielded the BJP rich dividends in the general election held in May–June 1991. The party's representation in parliament rose to 120, making it the second largest group. The government of the Congress party, led by P.V. Narasimha Rao, was short of a majority. Dependent on the votes of small groups for its survival, it lacked resolve. That made the BJP and the VHP more audacious to demolish the Babri Mosque.

These developments boded ill for Muslims, who were highly sceptical of the 'evidence' that the VHP and the BJP furnished to prove that a temple dedicated to Lord Rama had existed on the disputed site. They had a particularly negative impact in Kashmir, where the separatist insurgency was gathering steam.

In 1991, leading Indian historians, including Ram Sharan Sharma, the founding chairman of the Indian Council of Historical Research, and Dwijendra Narayan Jha published a book titled *Historians' Report to the Nation*. In it they debunked the claims of the BJP and the VHP.[16] 'Ayodhya seems to have emerged as a place of religious pilgrimage [only after] medieval times,' wrote Ram Sharan Sharma in his booklet *Communal History and Rama's Ayodhya*. 'Although chapter 85 of the [ancient] *Vishnu Smriti* lists as many as 52 places of pilgrimage, including towns, lakes, rivers, mountains, etc., it does not include Ayodhya in this list.' If Ayodhya had been home to a Rama temple, it would have qualified as a holy place. Sharma also noted that Hindi poet Tulsi Das, who composed the *Ramcharitmanas* in 1574 during his residence in Ayodhya, did not mention it as a place of pilgrimage. So there was apparently no significant Hindu temple at the site of the Babri Mosque.[17] But neither the BJP nor the VHP was in a mood to pay attention to facts or logic.

On the Muslim side, several groups came together under the umbrella of the All-India Babri Masjid Movement Coordination Committee, which was committed to furthering its argument through peaceful means. Among its leading constituents was the Jamaat-e Islami Hind (Urdu, 'Islamic Society of India'; JIH). Originating as the Jamaat-e Islami in 1941, it acquired a new name after partition in 1947. Its revised constitution of 1956 committed it to secularism and democracy as enshrined in the Indian Republic's constitution. It focused on the social, cultural, and religious spheres of the Muslim community. It also set up a Students' Islamic Organization. When this began to weaken, JIH leaders encouraged the formation of the

Students' Islamic Movement of India (SIMI) at Aligarh Muslim University in Uttar Pradesh in 1977. It aimed to 'liberate' India from the corrupting influence of Western materialism and to persuade the Muslim community to live according to the Islamic code of conduct. However, when its young leaders began giving the new body a communal orientation, the parent JIH distanced itself from it.

Against the backdrop of the BJP-VHP-RSS campaign to demolish the Babri Mosque, SIMI became more radical. Its activists did not shy away from confronting Hindu militants on the street.

Before official permission was granted to hold a rally in front of the Babri Mosque on 6 December 1992, the organizers assured the Supreme Court that the mosque would not be damaged. Yet, on that day, nearly 200,000 Hindu militants led by the VHP and Bajrang Dal, surreptitiously in cahoots with BJP leaders, stormed the barricades erected around the mosque. Armed with pickaxes, ropes, and sledgehammers, they demolished the structure within four hours. The Central government's later decision to block off the site and heavily increase security around it was a classic example of shutting the stable door after the horse had bolted.

The government soon appointed a commission of inquiry led by a former high court judge, M.S. Liberhan. It would finally submit its report seventeen years later – in June 2009 – to Prime Minister Manmohan Singh. He would then keep it under wraps until a local newspaper published it on 23 November, thus forcing his government's hand.

The wanton destruction of a Muslim place of worship sent shock waves through India, Pakistan, and Bangladesh, which had a combined Muslim population of 400 million. The incident helped radicalize thousands of young Muslims in India. One of them was Riyaz Bhatkal (aka Riyaz Shahbandri) from the port town of Bhatkal in the southern state of Karnataka. He witnessed a succession of communal riots in his home town in the wake of the Babri Mosque's destruction. Lasting intermittently for nine months, these left seventeen people dead; hundreds of homes and shops were destroyed by arson. Bhatkal also witnessed skirmishes between Bajrang Dal activists and Islamists. Later, he would help found the home-grown Indian Mujahedin terrorist organization.

THE ENDLESS CYCLE OF COMMUNAL VIOLENCE AND COUNTER-VIOLENCE

On a wider scale, videorecordings of the mosque's demolition would provide the jihadist organizations in Pakistan and India with highly charged material with which to motivate their cadres to avenge the destruction with acts of terrorism. Indeed, the cycle of violence and counter-violence stemming from this event has yet to run its full course.

Indian Muslims felt stunned and enraged in equal measure. When they marched in protest they were often assaulted by bigoted Hindus, which led to reprisal assaults on Hindus in Pakistan and Bangladesh. Inter-religious riots erupted in several major Indian cities, including Mumbai, Delhi, Ahmedabad, and Hyderabad, killing more than two thousand people. Rioting was particularly intense in Mumbai and occurred in two phases. The initial Muslim backlash immediately after the mosque's destruction in December 1992 led to a counter-response by militant Hindus, led by a local group, Shiv Sena, from 6 to 20 January 1993. The death toll of nine hundred, two-thirds of them Muslim, was accompanied by widespread arson and destruction of property, which included not just slums but also tenement houses and apartments. The damage attributed to the riots was a staggering $3.6 billion. At the same time they left an ugly blot on India's secular image.

Moreover, these riots turned out to be only an opening salvo. On 12 March 1993, lethal bomb blasts in Mumbai, the financial capital of India, killed 257 people, most of them Hindus. Within two hours, thirteen bombs exploded, the first being a car bomb in the basement of the eighteen-storey Bombay Stock Exchange, killing fifty people. Other targets included hotels (where explosives were left inside suitcases by terrorist guests), banks, offices, a shopping complex, the head office of the militant Hindu organization – Shiv Sena – and a double-decker bus carrying more than a hundred passengers.

This military-style operation was attributed to Dawood Ibrahim, head of a Mumbai-based criminal syndicate, D-Company which traded in drugs, small arms and gold, and had its own intelligence apparatus. In the mid-1980s, Ibrahim moved to Dubai but maintained tight control of his network through his trusted deputy Chhota Rajan, a Hindu. Following the December 1992–January 1993 Hindu–Muslim riots in Mumbai, they split. Ibrahim made his services available to Pakistan's Inter-Services Intelligence (ISI), then directed by Lt General Javed Nasir, whose chest-long beard made him stand out as a committed Islamist among his unbearded colleagues. Nasir had expanded the list of Islam's enemies to include the Hindu leadership of India and the Zionists. He now supplied the explosive RDX to Ibrahim, who planned and funded bomb blasts in Mumbai.[18] According to the Mumbai-based Hussain Zaidi, author of *Black Friday: The True Story of the Bombay Bomb Blasts* (2003), Ibrahim facilitated the smuggling of RDX supplied by the ISI at the Sasool (aka Sassoon) Dock in Mumbai by bribing the coast guard and the police.

Hundreds of arrests followed all over India. The Central government set up a special court under the Terrorist and Disruptive Activities (Prevention) Act, 1985, to deal with the cases. Yet it was not until 2006 that a hundred of the 129 accused were finally found guilty and convicted. Many of them, including Ibrahim, were tried in absentia.

The relentless efforts of the BJP and its associated organizations to bolster their popularity by stoking anti-Muslim feelings bore fruit in the general election of 1998. Winning 179 seats out of 542, the BJP emerged as the largest group in parliament. But to achieve a majority, it had to cobble together a coalition of seventeen parties. In the process it had to smooth out some of its rough edges.

The BJP's assumption of power gave a fillip to the fortunes of the

RSS. Within two years, the number of RSS branches soared to sixty thousand and its volunteer corps to more than four million. In 2003, it claimed 4.5 million volunteers and nearly a hundred affiliate bodies. Its sympathizers were to be found in various government departments.[19]

On assuming office, the BJP-led government wasted little time in altering school and college textbooks to reflect RSS perceptions of history of the Indian subcontinent. Its actions led to protest. In 2001, referring to the report of the National Steering Committee on Textbook Evaluation – appointed a few years earlier by the National Council of Educational Research and Training – history professors Mridula Mukherjee and Aditya Mukherjee at Jawaharlal Nehru University's Centre for Historical Studies noted that 'the main purpose which these [altered or new] books would serve is to gradually transform the young children into bigoted morons in the garb of instilling in them patriotism.'[20]

Meanwhile, in Pakistan, despite the early retirement of Nasir in response to US pressure, the idea of the ISI and Pakistani jihadist organizations recruiting young Indian Muslims had taken root. SIMI seems to have figured prominently in their plans. As it was, during the 1990s SIMI came under the influence of those Muslims from Uttar Pradesh who had been working in Saudi Arabia, the bastion of fundamentalist Wahhabi Islam, which made them receptive to working closely with militant Pakistani groups.

The daring attack by Lashkar-e Taiba (LeT) militants on the Red Fort in Delhi in December 2000 unveiled a new chapter in terrorism in South Asia. Soon after 9/11, the Indian government banned SIMI, declaring it a terrorist organization.

THE GUJARAT POGROM AND ITS AFTERMATH

Following the audacious but unsuccessful assault on the parliament in Delhi in December 2001, the BJP-led Central government replaced the Terrorist and Disruptive Activities (Prevention) Act, 1985, with the Prevention of Terrorist Activities Act. The new law allowed the authorities to detain suspects for up to 180 days without charge, to withhold the identities of witnesses, and to treat a confession made in police custody as an admission of guilt.

In late February 2002, a railway coach carrying Hindu devotees and their families back from pilgrimage to Ayodhya caught fire just after leaving the railroad station of Godhra in north Gujarat, incinerating fifty-eight people, including thirty-five women and children. The immediate blame for the killings was pinned on the Muslims because of an earlier altercation between Muslim tea vendors and the Hindu travellers at the railroad station. (The investigative commissions set up by the railways ministry, the state administration, and the Delhi government reached different conclusions – from the incident being an accident to it representing a pre-planned conspiracy by the Muslims in Godhra. The Gujarat High Court ruled seven years later that there had been no conspiracy.)

The fire triggered widespread violence in Gujarat, then ruled by the BJP's chief minister, Narendra Modi – with the Muslims in Ahmedabad bearing the brunt of it. After the initial intense bloodletting, arson, and destruction of Muslim shops, intermittent violence continued for more than two months. Altogether, between 790 and 2,000 Muslims lost their lives, as did 254 Hindus, with a further 223 reported missing.[21] More than 500 mosques and prayer halls were damaged, while seventeen temples suffered the same fate. Nearly 61,000 Muslims were made homeless; the figure for Hindus was 10,000.

'Mothers were skewered on swords as their children watched,' reported Celia W. Dugger in the *New York Times*. 'Young women were stripped and raped in broad daylight, then doused with kerosene and set on fire. A pregnant woman's belly was slit open, her fetus raised skyward on the tip of a sword and then tossed onto one of the fires that blazed across the city.' Widespread allegations that the BJP and the World Hindu Council [i.e. Vishva Hindu Parishad, VHP] were complicit were denied by them. (A sting operation by the

Delhi-based *Tehelka* magazine five years later would reveal how the pogrom had been planned and implemented, and how Modi, other senior BJP figures, and assorted police officers had been personally involved.[22] 'But official statistics provided in June by the Police Department . . . show that the state of Gujarat, governed solely by the Bharatiya Janata Party, failed to take elementary steps to halt the horrific momentum of violence,' continued Dugger. The day after the train attack, police officers here in Ahmedabad did not arrest a single person from among the tens of thousands who rampaged through Muslim enclaves, raping and looting as well as burning alive 124 Muslims.'[23] Unlike in 1969, the grisly events in Ahmedabad were captured on video. These horrific images would be used by jihadist organizations in India and Pakistan to motivate their recruits to get even with the evil, polytheist Hindus.

On top of this came an on-camera interview in 2007 with Babu Bajrangi. In it, the bald, flabby-faced, middle-aged leader of the Gujarat branch of the Bajrang Dal would boast:

> We didn't spare a single Muslim shop, we set everything or. fire, we set them on fire and killed them . . . We believe in setting them on fire because these bastards don't want to be cremated, they're afraid of it . . . I have just . . . one last wish . . . Let me be sentenced to death . . . I don't care if I'm hanged . . . Give me two days before my hanging and I will go and have a field day in Juhapura [a Muslim-dominated area], where seven or eight lakh [700,000 to 800,000] of these people stay . . . I will finish them off . . . At least 25,000 to 50,000 should die.[24]

The Gujarat massacre resulted in leading jihadist organizations in Pakistan and the ISI redoubling their efforts and mounting reprisal attacks on targets in India. In September 2002, two militants of the Pakistan-based Jaish-e-Muhammad raided the Akshardham temple complex in Ahmedabad and killed thirty. A year later, two bomb blasts in Mumbai left a further fifty people dead. On 13 March 2003, a day after the tenth anniversary of the massive blasts in Mumbai, a bomb exploded in a first-class coach of a commuter train, killing ten people. This would prove to be a forerunner of a far bloodier assault three years later.

The replacement of the BJP-led government in Delhi by the Congress party-led coalition, headed by Manmohan Singh, a Sikh, in May 2004 made a difference to the Muslims and secular Hindus. The new administration reversed the alterations made to the textbooks by its predecessor and appointed a commission, headed by Rajinder Sachar, former chief justice of the Delhi High Court, to investigate the status of Muslims in India. It also repealed the draconian Prevention of Terrorist Activities Act, under which all but one of the 287 Indians detained without charge were Muslim.

But that made no difference to the agenda of the jihadist organizations. After the failed attempt by LeT fidayeen to storm the Babri Mosque site in early July 2005, a bomb detonated on a commuter train killed thirteen at Jaunpur in Uttar Pradesh later that month.

On 29 October 2005, on the eve of the Hindu festival of Diwali, three bomb blasts in the markets of Delhi left another sixty-one dead. The incident received massive publicity. Though the Pakistan-based Islamic Revolutionary Front claimed responsibility, prosecutors pointed out that Tariq Ahmad Dar, the operation's mastermind, called his LeT minders in Pakistan after the attacks to report the success of his mission.

A bomb explosion in a temple dedicated to Hanuman, a disciple of Lord Rama, in the revered Hindu city of Varanasi on 7 March 2006, a Tuesday, the Hindu holy day, left twenty-eight dead. Six more bombs were defused in other areas of Varanasi. While the spokesman of an obscure organization called Lashkar-e Qahab claimed responsibility and attributed the attack to the Delhi government's 'catch and kill' campaign in Kashmir, Indian officials blamed the LeT, but later charged Muhammad Waliullah, a leader of the Harkat ul Jihad Islami (HuJI), as the mastermind of the operation.

After every terrorist onslaught, Muslim leaders condemned the operation strongly, pointing out that it was un-Islamic to kill innocent civilians. Despite this, police rounded up hundreds of Muslims in raids. That in turn aggravated feelings of persecution in the community. Matching the death toll of 190 caused by bombs placed on commuter trains in Madrid on 11 March 2003, seven bombs exploded within eleven minutes in Mumbai during the evening rush hour of 11 July 2006. The bombs, containing RDX and ammonium nitrate, were left in first-class coaches. While the police blamed the LeT and SIMI, both denied responsibility.

MUSLIM DEPRIVATION QUANTIFIED

Based on interviews in fifteen states where Muslims are concentrated, and accessing all pertinent sources of information, the Sachar Commission submitted a report to parliament in November 2006. It painted a picture of Muslim exclusion, alienation, and impoverishment.

Since under 4 per cent of Muslims graduate from high school, they are caught in a vicious cycle of poverty and lack of education.[25] Impoverished parents press their young children into work, so the dropout rate of Muslim pupils at school is far higher than that of non-Muslims. Whereas Muslims form nearly 14 per cent of the national population, their share of government jobs is under 5 per cent; in the Central security agencies such as the Border Security Force and Central Reserve Police Force, it is 3.2 per cent. In urban centres with populations of between 50,000 and 200,000, their per capita expenditure is less than that of untouchable Hindus, called Dalits. In villages, under 3 per cent of Muslims are able to get subsidized loans for agriculture, and only one in fifty Muslim farmers owns a tractor.

Contrary to the myth spread by Hindu militants that the Muslims are breeding like rabbits, there is a substantial demand in the Muslim community for contraceptives, with over twenty million couples already using them. Muslim population growth has slowed. Politically, the Muslim community finds itself in an invidious position. On the one hand, it is vilified for being unpatriotic; on the other, it is described as benefitting from a policy of appeasement by the government.

The Sachar Commission's report recommended that all Central government schemes should allocate 15 per cent of funds to Muslim welfare and development; an Equal Opportunities Commission should be established to examine the grievances of *all* deprived groups and have the authority to implement its rulings; and those Muslims who in their socio-economic status approximate untouchable Hindus and other backward castes should be offered the same benefits as are available to their counterparts among Hindus.[26] Muslim leaders as well as secular Hindus welcomed the report and awaited the implementation of its main recommendations. Nothing happened.

Terrorist acts resumed, although most of the sixty-eight passengers killed on the Delhi–Lahore train on 18 February 2007 were Pakistanis, with the remainder being Indian civilians and soldiers guarding the train. The intent of the perpetrators seems to have been to sour relations between India and Pakistan – an abiding aim of jihadists on both sides of the Indo-Pakistan border.

The almost simultaneous bombing at the court houses in the Uttar Pradesh cities of Varanasi, Faizabad, and Lucknow on 23 November which claimed fifteen lives unveiled a new development. The terrorists sent emails to the media, citing an 'atrocity' against Muslims that was being avenged. Calling the blasts 'Islamic raids', the sender – identifying himself as 'Al Arabi Guru al-Hindi' – rationalized them as revenge against the lawyers who had allegedly assaulted two Jaish-e-Muhammad terrorist suspects and refused to defend Waliullah, the HuJI leader.

This was the signal for the appearance of the Indian Mujahedin (IM), a new player on the jihadist scene, possessing a sophistication not shown before by any such organization.

THE INDIAN MUJAHEDIN

In May 2008, the IM claimed responsibility for a string of nine bomb explosions in the markets of Jaipur, the walled capital city of Rajasthan, which killed sixty-one people. In an email titled 'The Rise of Jihad, Revenge of Gujarat', it referred to the Babri Mosque destruction, the 1992–93 Mumbai riots, the 2002 pogrom of Muslims in Gujarat, and other acts of anti-Muslim violence.

Far more symbolic was its detonation of sixteen synchronized bomb blasts on 26 July in Ahmedabad, which killed thirty-eight people. Five minutes before the explosions, in another email, signed by 'Al Arabi Guru al-Hindi', to the media, the IM sent a PDF of fourteen pages. This contained several verses from the Quran along with an English translation.

> 'Here we are back – the Mujahedin of India – the terrorists to the disbelievers – the radicals of Islam – after our triumphant and successful assault at Jaipur [13 May 2008], once again calling [those] who disbelieve in Allah and His Messenger Muhammad to accept Islam and bear witness that there is none to be worshipped except Allah, and that Muhammad is the Messenger of Allah. Accept Islam and save yourselves.
>
> O Hindus! O disbelieving faithless Indians! Haven't you still realized that the falsehood of your 33 crore [330 million] dirty mud idols and the blasphemy of your deaf, dumb, mute idols are not at all going to save your necks, Insha Allah [God willing], from being slaughtered?
>
> We call you, O Hindus, O enemies of Allah, to take an honest stance with yourselves lest another attack of Ibn Qasim [the Arab conqueror of Sindh in 708] sends shivers down your spines, lest another [Afghan] Ghori shakes your foundations, and lest another [Afghan] Ghaznavi massacres you, proving your blood to be the cheapest of all mankind! Have you forgotten your history full of subjugation, humiliation, and insult? Or do you want us to repeat it again? . . .
>
> Wait only for five minutes from now! . . . [S]uffer the results of fighting the Muslims and the Mujahideen . . . Await . . . to feel the fear of death.[27]

The document represented a call to Muslims to expand the sway of Islam in India by conducting a jihad against the infidels and to set up 'God's government' according to the Word of God, meaning the Quran.[28]

The political purpose behind this provocative rhetoric was to goad the likes of the RSS, the VHP, and the Bajrang Dal to perpetrate violence against Muslims, which in turn would radicalize the younger Muslim generation and swell the ranks of jihadist organizations such as the IM. At the very least, propagating such ideas was expected to impair Hindu–Muslim relations. This dovetailed with the agenda of the LeT and HuJI, active in Pakistan and Indian Kashmir, who also had a vested interest in seeing that relations between Islamabad and Delhi remained tense to hostile.

The IM's email also contained a demand addressed to the police in Hyderabad to free 'the imprisoned Muslim youth' immediately. No numbers were mentioned. But a fortnight after the Mumbai attacks, the local police revealed that forty 'potential recruits' for jihadist organizations had left the city under 'extremist guidance', and that 'many other young men' could not be traced.[29] Moreover, the IM's demand for the release of the jailed SIMI leaders showed the link between SIMI radicals and the IM.

It was not until the late 2000s that police interrogation of the leading Indian jihadists established that the IM began operating informally between 2003 (after the Gujarat pogrom) and November 2007, when it declared its existence to the media in emails.

Its Pakistani sponsors – the LeT and HuJI – wanted the new group to be exclusively Indian. So means had to be found to fund it domestically. This led to co-opting young Muslims with expertise in extortion, ransom, and bank robbery. Such criminal gangs existed in Mumbai and Kolkata. It was thus that Amir Raza Khan, a native of Kolkata, became one of the founders of the IM. As a mobster, he was involved in the kidnapping of a rich businessman. The killing of his bank-robber brother, Asif Raza, by police in 2002 radicalized him politically. Unable to withstand subsequent police pressure, he fled to neighbouring Bangladesh, and from there to Pakistan. After receiving basic weapons and explosives training, he then moved to Dubai. From 2003, he reportedly started receiving young Indian Muslim recruits, who used Dubai as a stopover on their way to Pakistan for terrorist training at the ISI-run camps in the desolate, mountainous areas of Baluchistan. On their return to India, they then awaited orders from their minders to strike.

The politically motivated element in the IM leadership was represented by Riyaz Bhatkal, who was born as Riyaz Shahbandri in 1976. His father, Ismail, left his coastal home town of Bhatkal in 1979 to open a leather-tanning factory in Mumbai. He earned enough money to send Riyaz to an engineering college, where he obtained a degree in civil engineering. At twenty-six, Riyaz married Nasuha Ismail, the daughter of an electronics store owner in Bhatkal's Dubai Market. He now came under the influence of his elder brother Iqbal, a cleric, and his brother-in-law, Shafiq Ahmad, who would later become head of SIMI's Mumbai branch. At SIMI's office, he befriended Abdul Subhan Qureshi, an expert software engineer and hacker and a future co-founder of the IM. Bhatkal allegedly used Amir Raza Khan's cash to finance the training of several terror operatives in Pakistan. He had earlier appeared on the police's radar as a suspect in an extortion-related attempt to murder a businessman, Deepak Farsanwalla.[30]

Later, the IM attracted Muslims with professional qualifications, particularly in information technology. They came to play pivotal roles in generating funds for the organization and in planning attacks. The sources of the emails sent by the IM between 13 May 2008 and 23 September 2008 varied widely. They included a cyber café in the Uttar Pradesh city of Ghaziabad, the WiFi network of a university college in central Mumbai, and the WiFi network of a power company in the Mumbai suburb of Chembur.

The last (September 2008) email pertained to the five bombs detonated within half an hour in three markets, a cinema, and a park in Delhi, with a death toll of thirty. The attack created immense pressure on Delhi police to produce results. In an 'encounter' with the occupants of an apartment in a four-storey building in the Muslim neighbourhood of Jamia Nagar on 19 September, the Special Cell of the Delhi police claimed to have killed two 'armed' terrorists, sixteen-year-old Muhammad Sajid and twenty-three-year-old Muhammad Atif Ameen (aka Bashir), with Inspector Mohan Chand Sharma losing his life in the firefight. Astonishingly, Sharma was not wearing a flak jacket, despite the fact that he was supposedly leading an assault on terrorists who were expected to be armed. As it turned out, the suspects were unarmed and that Sharma was killed accidentally by friendly fire. The police arrested Muhammad Saif, a native of Azamgarh district in eastern Uttar Pradesh.

THE COUNTRYWIDE POLICE OFFENSIVE

The death of a police inspector spurred on police forces throughout India to apprehend suspected terrorists. On 24 September, the Mumbai police arrested Sadiq Israr Shaikh, an electronics engineer and a prime suspect in the bombings in Mumbai in July 2006. He would be one of the twenty-one men subsequently named by the Mumbai Crime Branch and charged with conspiracy, damaging a place of worship, collecting arms, and waging war against India. Most of the other accused also turned out to be well-qualified professionals and had a shared birthplace in Azamgarh district.

As a result, police and intelligence agencies were given carte blanche to arrest suspected terrorists in this district (population, 4.6 million), where Muslims formed a slim majority. Uttar Pradesh's Anti-Terrorism Squad in plainclothes resorted to entering villages and intimidating, and even beating up, Muslims at will. Such behaviour only increased the alienation of the Muslims.

After the nationwide police crackdown, the following IM leaders reportedly fled to Pakistan or Bangladesh: Riyaz Bhatkal and his brother Iqbal, Muhammad Khalid, Shahzad Ahmed and Ariz Khan. Equally importantly, the police action against IM activists led LeT leaders to postpone their military-style assault on targets in Mumbai – originally scheduled for 27 September, during the holy month of Ramadan – for two months to let the vigilance in India subside.

Meanwhile, the detained Saif explained to interrogators the functions of the IM's four departments. Two – named after Sultan Mahmoud of Ghazni (aka Muhammad of Ghazni) and Shihabuddin Ghori, the Afghan Muslim conquerors of the northern Indian subcontinent in the eleventh century – were 'brigades' assigned respectively to northern and southern India. Another 'brigade', bearing the name of Abu Mussab Zarqawi – a Jordanian terrorist leader 'martyred' in Iraq in 2006 – was charged with the task of organizing suicide bombings. The remaining department, called the Media Wing, based in Pune, sent out emails and handled the print media before and after an 'operation'.[31] It was run by Asghar Peerbhoy, who worked for Yahoo.com prior to his arrest in October 2008.

The failure of the sensational attacks in Mumbai on 26 November 2008 to trigger a Hindu backlash against local Muslims disappointed the IM's rump leadership in India as well as its founders – believed to be living in Karachi under the ISI's protection as part of the so-called 'Karachi Project', as well as in Dubai. The fact that forty-three of the 138 Indians killed by the terrorists in Mumbai were local Muslims helped assuage anti-Muslim feeling in India.

Little of significance happened in India in 2009 because the intensification of the armed conflict between the Pakistani state and a coalition of jihadist factions called Tehrik-e Taliban Pakistan (TTP) kept the ISI as well as the LeT and HuJI fully occupied at home.

It was not until February 2010 that there was another significant attack. A bomb blast at an eatery frequented by westerners in Pune – the German Bakery near the Jewish Chabad House – killed seventeen people. The claims for the explosion by two previously unknown groups were dismissed, as was the accusation against the LeT which, by now, was the officially acknowledged perpetrator of the Mumbai assaults. That left the IM as the prime suspect, most likely acting on its own. Such a conclusion chimed with the previously established fact that, after the crackdown in Azamgarh in 2008, IM leaders had spread their net more widely. IM sleeper cells, consisting of three to five members, were believed to exist in Ahmedabad, Mumbai, Pune, and Hyderabad. The decision to activate sleeper agents lay with the political leadership, which closely monitored developments in India, Kashmir, Pakistan, and Afghanistan. Undoubtedly, it had noted the contents of the Liberhan Commission's report, leaked in November 2009. The commission held sixty-eight people responsible for the destruction of the Babri Mosque seventeen years earlier. They included BJP stalwarts like Advani and Vajpayee as well as the BJP chief minister of Uttar Pradesh, Kalyan Singh, a Hindu. While distancing themselves in public from the campaign to build the Rama Temple on the land occupied by the Babri Mosque, these leaders had conspired to demolish it, with the task assigned primarily to the RSS. Calling Advani, Vajpayee, and Kalyan Singh 'pseudo-moderates', the report said: 'They have violated the trust of the people . . . There can be no greater betrayal or crime in a democracy and this Commission has no hesitation in condemning these pseudo-moderates for their sins of omission.'[32]

Yet the Congress-led government of Manmohan Singh initiated no action against any of the named culprits. What puzzled and angered IM leaders and their sponsors was the failure of Indian Muslim leaders to demand action against the accused.

During the summer of 2010, the purely indigenous Muslim protest in Kashmir buoyed the spirits of IM luminaries. On the other hand, they were most likely disappointed that the decision by the Allahabad High Court in September to divide up the Babri Mosque land, giving only a third to local Muslims, did not engender anger among India's Muslims. After much deliberation, the Uttar Pradesh Sunni Central Waqf Board decided to take the case to the Supreme Court. By so doing, it chose to staying within the law of the land. This, in turn diminished the prospect of young, disaffected Muslims taking to the barricades to see the wrongs to their community righted.

Likewise, in Pakistan, while the heightened violence perpetrated by the TTP during 2009 went down well with the upper echelons of the IM, the continued economic weakness of that Muslim country, damaged further by the unprecedented floods of summer 2010, dampened their spirits.

However, for them the bottom line was that the Islamist institutions spawned and nourished by Zia ul Haq in the 1980s had grown strong roots and moulded a whole new generation committed to turning Pakistan into a Sharia state.

10

PAKISTAN'S JIHADISTS

ONE OF THE main thoroughfares out of the bustling metropolis of Lahore, the capital of Punjab, is the Grand Trunk Road. This historic highway, linking Sonargaon in Bangladesh and Landi Kotal on the Khyber Pass, completed by the British rulers, is as much 'a river of life' today as it was when it appeared in Rudyard Kipling's picaresque novel *Kim* in 1901.

On both sides of the thoroughfare lies fertile land of lush green paddy fields or covered with undulating stalks of sugar cane and millet, irrigated mostly by canals fed by the waters of one of the five rivers that have given the region its name, Punjab (Urdu, 'Five Waters'). The unfailing sign of a village along this route, or any other in the province, is the ubiquitous tea stall, with film music blaring at full volume. Customers drink the overboiled tea with milk and lumps of sugar out of small glasses or chipped cups and saucers.

Some 50 miles (80 km) along this highway appears Muridke (population 35,000), a town of low, red-brick buildings among which the multistorey Punjab Bank stands out. Another notable feature of the town is the frequency with which slogans appear on the walls. They invariably urge the reader to fight to 'Free Kashmir'.

The source of these militant calls lies on the outskirts of the settlement – a vast complex delineated by a meshed fence and hidden by tall trees. It is the Markaz-e Taiba (Urdu, 'Centre of the Righteous') compound set up by the Jamaat-ud Dawa (Arabic, 'Society of the Islamic Call') Pakistan, ideologically affiliated with the Ahl-e Hadith of the Wahhabi sub-sect within Sunni Islam.

A lane off the Grand Trunk Road leads through a small cluster of peasants' houses to a barrier guarded by armed men who allow through only those who have been cleared by the management of the Markaz-e Taiba. The inner entrance is marked by two large sky-blue panels on both sides of the opening bearing the Islamic invocation 'In the Name of Allah, the Merciful, the Compassionate' at the top, followed by a Quranic verse and a bottom line that reads: 'Jamaat-ud Dawa Pakistan.'

Beyond the entrance lies a 191-acre compound. At the centre of its built-up part, interspersed with manicured lawns, stands a vast mosque. Its loudspeakers are powerful enough to let the Friday prayer sermons be heard far and wide – not to mention the accompanying slogans for the liberation of Kashmir. The mosque is surrounded by a small shopping centre, a high school for boys, a secondary school for girls, and two tuition-free Ahl-e Hadith madrasas, one each for girls and boys. Pupils are all taught English, Arabic, and computers. Most of the 900-odd male and female students live in dormitories. Besides the educational institutions, the developed section contains a hospital, a guest house, a swimming pool, a turnip farm, and a fish-breeding pond. The overall aim of the vast complex is to create and sustain a self-sufficient community of believers, untainted by the corrupting influences that lie beyond the fence. The vast undeveloped part of the land is large enough to provide ample space for clandestine target practice and other elements of arms training.[1]

Foreign visitors are greeted by Abdullah Muntazir, the head of the information department. To counter the accusation that the Jamaat-ud Dawa is a terrorist body, he points out the improbability of such an organization existing so near the Grand Trunk Road, and stresses that the complex, run by an Islamic charity, is purely educational and residential.

In the wake of the 26 November 2008 bombing attacks in Mumbai, when the chances of an Indian air strike on the Markaz-e Taiba rose sharply, the management let Harinder Baweja, a reporter of the Delhi-based magazine *Tehelka*, visit the premises, with Abdullah Muntazir as her guide.

> HB: Do you support the LeT [Lashkar-e Taiba]?
>
> AM: We used to.
>
> HB: You used to?
>
> AM: Yes, we were like-minded but the group was banned after Indian propaganda following the attack on its Parliament [in December 2001], which was done by the Jaish-e Muhammad and not the LeT. We used to provide logistical help to the Lashkar, collect funds for them and look after their publicity.
>
> HB: Did you also provide them with arms?
>
> AM: They must have bought weapons with the money we gave them. They were obviously not using the money to buy flowers for the Indian Army.
>
> HB: The Lashkar has claimed responsibility for the attack on the Red Fort in Delhi and the airport in Srinagar.
>
> AM: We do not consider Kashmir to be a part of India. It is a part of Pakistan. Those who attack the security forces are not terrorists, they are freedom fighters.
>
> HB: Did you sanitize this place before bringing me in?
>
> AM: This is an educational complex and the Jamaat-ud Dawa is a charitable organization. There are very few people here because of the Eid [festival] break.
>
> HB: Does the ISI [Inter-Services Intelligence] support you?
>
> AM just laughs.[2]

The Markaz-e Taiba evolved out of the Markaz ud Dawat wal Irshad (MDwI), formed by a group of senior clerics at the behest of General

Muhammad Zia ul Haq in late 1985. It was later given prime land near Muridke. While preaching Islam and guiding the faithful to lead their lives according to the Sharia, the Markaz stressed that believers could not be legislators because Allah had laid down the law in the Quran. Describing democracy as a flawed Western concept of governance, it shirked electoral politics. Its core message was that Islam was *not* a private faith for Muslims and that religion and politics were inseparable.

In 1987, the MDwI set up its armed wing, the Lashkar-e Taiba, under the leadership of Muhammad Hafiz Saeed to participate in the anti-Soviet jihad in Afghanistan. Its recruits fought alongside the Afghan partisans of Abdul Rasul Sayyaf, a pro-Saudi adherent of Wahhabi Islam. The LeT and its parent body tried to advance the Wahhabi variant of Islam through their madrasas. That in turn led many affluent Wahhabi citizens of Saudi Arabia to provide most of the funds to develop the government-donated land near Muridke into a hub of educational and commercial activity. Following the Soviet withdrawal from Afghanistan in February 1989, the LeT and other jihadist organizations, in collusion with the ISI, decided to intensify the separatist movement in Indian Kashmir, a policy initiated by Zia ul Haq in 1987. The restoration of democracy after his death in the following year left Pakistan's stance on Indian Kashmir unaltered.

DEMOCRATIC INTERLUDE, 1988–99

The only foreign-policy change the government of Benazir Bhutto, leader of the Pakistan People's Party (PPP), made was to stop ISI backing for Sikh separatists in India. The ISI then went on to prop up the pro-Pakistan Hizb-ul Mujahideen at the expense of the long-established secular Jammu and Kashmir Liberation Front.

Unlike her father Zulfikar Ali Bhutto, who had served as a cabinet minister for several years before becoming the country's elected chief executive in 1972, Benazir Bhutto lacked administrative experience.

To make matters worse, her husband, Asif Ali Zardari, appointed minister for investments, soon earned the nickname of 'Mr 10 per cent' – that being the percentage he allegedly charged on government contracts, with the kickbacks channelled to him through his father.

Under their watch, corruption, graft, and embezzlement became rampant. The state-owned development finance institutions and nationalized commercial banks approved huge loans without collateral for dubious or non-existent projects. In 1989, loans by the National Development Finance Corporation rose by 242 per cent and those by the Pakistan Industrial Credit and Investment Corporation by 310 per cent. Alarmed by this upsurge in lending, the World Bank stopped disbursements to Pakistan's credit institutions.[3] A fair proportion of the funds provided by foreign aid ended up enriching officials rather than those in need. With only 20 per cent of its budget revenue allocated to development projects, the federal government failed to provide matching sums to carry out the plans as sanctioned by the World Bank. Consequently, according to a World Bank official in Islamabad, unspent foreign aid had accumulated to the tune of $2–$4 billion.[4]

At the same time the old practice of the military high command deciding the huge budget of the armed forces, with no input or oversight by the prime minister or parliament, continued. The ISI directorate still enjoyed the wide latitude it had acquired under Zia ul Haq to sponsor and fund jihadist factions while fine-tuning its own strategies. Benazir Bhutto was powerless to alter the status quo, well aware that in the patriarchical society of Pakistan the generals resented having to take orders from a woman of thirty-five.

As for the police, its officers often demanded money from complainants to pursue cases. The lower ranks routinely implemented their superiors' illegal orders to make deals with criminals. In the bandit-infested Sindh province, policemen, who earned £30 a month, were often in cahoots with criminals, who gave them one-fifth of their booty in return for protection.

Tax collectors' earnings were based on commission; and that made it easy for potential taxpayer to bribe them by offering them sums higher than their official commissions. The Water and Power Development Authority was the most corrupt. It was up to its officials to decide who received irrigation water; if bribed, they would transfer the tab for electricity consumed to someone else's invoice. Corruption existed in the private sector as well. 'Intelligence agencies, the government, the opposition, those with political ambitions, and even the President all had journalists in their pay,' reported Christina Lamb, a British journalist and author. 'Those who could pay most or threaten most effectively would get most statements in the papers regardless of their importance.'[5]

Under the circumstances, it came as no surprise when President Ghulam Ishaq Khan dismissed Benazir Bhutto for corruption, graft, mismanagement and nepotism in August 1990.

The ISI intervened directly in the parliamentary poll that followed in October. It brought together nine chiefly right-wing parties, led by Muhammad Nawaz Sharif's Pakistan Muslim League (N) – under the banner of the Islami Jamhoori Ittehad (Urdu, 'Islamic Democratic Alliance'). The alliance was dominated by feudal lords, with a sprinkling of industrialists and emerging import–export houses. It and the party of the Urdu-speaking Indian immigrants, the Muttahida Qaumi Movement (Urdu, 'United National Movement'), trounced Bhutto's PPP, whose strength plummeted to forty-three seats in a house of 217. Nawaz Sharif, a Lahore-based industrialist, became the country's thirteenth prime minister.

Sharif was a protégé of Zia ul Haq. After the non-party elections held in 1985 (boycotted by the PPP) at the urging of Washington, Zia ul Haq appointed him finance minister of Punjab and then promoted him to chief minister. Now, as the country's prime minister, he put Lt General Javid Nasir in charge of the ISI. A committed Islamist, Nasir expanded the ISI's writ in domestic affairs. He allowed the charismatic Maulana Sufi Muhammad to establish the Tehrik-e Nifaz-e Shariat-e Muhammadi (Urdu, 'Movement for the Enforcement of Muhammad's Sharia'; TNSM) in the Malakand district of Khyber Pakhtunkhwa – a seed out of which would grow the Pakistani Taliban a decade later.

In early April 1993, Sharif dispatched his foreign secretary, the highest civil servant in the foreign ministry, to Washington to reassure the newly installed Clinton administration that he would not support terrorism. The ISI drastically reduced direct support for Kashmiri militants but continued it indirectly, through the Jamaat-e Islami (JeI).

Later that month President Ishaq Khan sacked Sharif for maladministration, corruption, graft, and nepotism. When Sharif challenged him, the army chief of staff, General Wahid Kakar, intervened and compelled both man to resign in July. Pressured by Washington, acting prime minister Balakh Sher Mazri got Nasir to retire from the army. Following that, about 1,100 ISI operatives and officers were returned to regular army units.

In the October 1993 parliamentary election, Benazir Bhutto's PPP emerged as the largest group but fell short of a majority by twenty-three seats. As a result, Bhutto ended up leading an unwieldy coalition, which included the Islamist Jamiat Ulema-e Islam (JUeI), led by Fazlur Rahman. Along with the Jamaat-e Islami, the JUeI had been a leading participant in the Afghan jihad. Spurred on by Fazlur Rahman, Bhutto gave the green light to Lt General Pervez Musharraf, then director general of military operations, to dispatch ten thousand new jihadists to Indian Kashmir. Under Bhutto's watch, Islamabad's annual budget for the insurgency in India-held Kashmir spiked to $100 million.[6]

The ISI was busy on the Afghan front as well. The Taliban, its favoured player in that battlefield, captured Kabul in September 1996, and was on an upward trajectory. This raised the morale of the jihadist organizations in Pakistan. The earlier practice of the state allowing extremist factions to collect funds in public had continued. They now redoubled their efforts by appealing for donations in their magazines and pamphlets. The aggregate circulation of the forty publications of the twenty-four jihadist organizations surged to one million.

They were unanimous in encouraging thousands of madrasa students to fight alongside the Taliban in the Afghan civil war.[7] Having rejoiced at the Taliban's capture of Kabul, they started publishing glowing reports of how the Taliban were turning the territory under their control into a Sharia state. By contrast, they ignored the social and economic problems Pakistan had inherited from its long involvement in the Afghan jihad. The country was awash with small arms and narcotics. The drugs trade, at $4 billion a year, exceeded the nation's legal exports.[8] Easy availability of firearms led to a surge in domestic and sectarian violence. The militant publications paid scant attention to the fact that in global surveys Pakistan invariably ranked near the bottom on civil liberties, rule of law, and transparent and corruption-free administration.

In inter-sectarian relations, all were in the Sunni camp. Yet the rabidly Sunni Sipah-e Sahaba (SSP) split in 1996. The radicals, led by Riaz Basra, the party's propaganda chief and a veteran of the anti-Soviet jihad, left to form the Laskhar-e Jhangvi (Urdu, 'Army of Jhangvi'; LeJ). It resorted to terror tactics to press its demands for Shias to be declared as non-Muslims and for an orthodox Sunni Islamic system to be established in Pakistan. The LeJ emerged as the most lethal faction, super secret, with its small cells coming together to stage an operation and then immediately dispersing. Also, unlike similar groups, it had no links with the ISI. As such, the government found it extremely difficult to eradicate it. Though it had only about 500 activists, the LeJ committed 350 acts of terrorism before it was banned in August 2001. Its cadres then either fled to Afghanistan or lent their support to other active terrorist groups.

Orthodox Sunni opposition to Shias rested on the following arguments. While Shias claimed that their imams were infallible, Sunnis regarded only God as infallible, with no exception made even for Prophet Muhammad. Shia clerics' practice of cursing the first three of the four Rightly Guided Caliphs – Abu Bakr, Omar, Uthman and Ali – is un-Islamic: A Muslim must not curse the Companions of the Prophet. The Shia ritual of self-flagellation to commemorate the death of Imam Hussein runs counter to Prophet Muhammad calling on grieving women not to tear their clothes and beat their breasts in grief. In Muslim societies it is patrimony that counts, not the matriarchal line. But Shias trace their descent back to Fatima, the eldest daughter of Prophet Muhammad, who left no surviving son. This is the critical link on which rests Shia leaders' assertion that only a member of Muhammad's family could become a caliph, which led them to recognize only Ali, a cousin and son-in-law of Prophet Muhammad, among the first four caliphs recognized by Sunnis. All the same, to demand that Shias be declared non-Muslim because of these differences was beyond the pale for most ordinary Sunnis.

The rationale behind militant Sunnis' attacks on important Shia individuals or gatherings was to provoke Shias to retaliate. That in turn would make Sunnis at large feel threatened and compel them to discard their complacency – stemming from their majority status – and hit back hard. The net result of the violent and non-violent anti-Shia agitation by the LeJ and the SSP was to escalate inter-sectarian tensions, and add to the already intense hostility between ethnic groups in the country's largest city, Karachi. The Bhutto government found the annual inter-sectarian death toll of eight hundred in the metropolis unbearable, and resorted to blaming India's Research and Analysis Wing (RAW) for the internecine violence. It closed down the Indian consulate in Karachi in 1994. But the mayhem continued.

That did little to counter the increasingly negative assessment of the government by President Farooq Leghari, a PPP stalwart. He dismissed Bhutto in November 1996 on the grounds of maladministration, nepotism and corruption. By now, in Transparency International's index of corruption and graft, Pakistan ranked among the most corrupt nations.[9]

Malfeasance and graft thrived in a society where the majority of its members were rural and illiterate, and where social hierarchy had remained unchanged since medieval times, with a feudal lord at the top served by a multitude of peasants at the bottom. These serfs vied with one another in their servility to the master by bending their knees to kiss the hem of his shirt. Their lords had circumvented the laws about land ceilings passed under General Muhammad Ayub Khan and Zulfikar Ali Bhutto by (nominally) transferring their excess landholdings to their relatives and even, in some cases, to a few ultra-loyal house servants.[10] Indeed, the only significant difference from the medieval era was the adult franchise, introduced in 1970, which required landlords to seek the votes of their underlings at election time.

Landlords understood that their unquestioned overlordship rested on the lack of literacy among their labourers; so they hindered the spread of education. Hence the official figure of 26 per cent literacy in 1990 was widely regarded as exaggerated. According to one Pakistani specialist, only 8 per cent were educated to primary-school standard and only 2 per cent to secondary.[11] The situation hardly improved over the next two decades. In educational terms, Pakistan remained one of the fifteen worst countries on the planet. In 2002, of the 1.7 per cent of GDP that the authorities spent on education, three-quarters came as foreign aid. State schools were too few and underfunded to keep pace with the demand for education. Pakistan's college and university student population of seven per 10,000 people compared poorly with India's eighty-six.[12] In 2010, as the elected National Assembly representative of Mianwali in Punjab, the cricketer-turned-politician Imran Khan revealed that one-fifth of all government schools in his constituency existed only on paper, and that even in half of the actual schools teachers did not turn up regularly.[13]

Winning a seat in a national or provincial assembly brought such material and political returns that feudal lords competed with one another to obtain party tickets which were on sale to the highest bidder. This was true even of the PPP during the lifetime of its founder, Zulfikar Ali Bhutto, who had the distinction of breaking the mould in 1966 by establishing a political party with a wide-ranging programme and whose slogans were 'Power to the people' and 'Power to the peasants'. But within a decade he betrayed his party's early promise to the extent that he fell back on soliciting the support of landlords because of their power to deliver the votes of their farm workers en bloc.

In late 1988, on the eve of the elections for seven hundred seats in the national and provincial assemblies, feudal lords paid up to three million Pakistani rupees (then worth £10,000/$16,000) for a PPP ticket.[14] The going price for the rival Islamic Democratic Alliance was much lower. But, irrespective of party labels, four-fifths of the elected members of the National Assembly were feudal lords.

As an elected representative, a politician acquired more power of patronage than before, and channelled it through the district commissioner, the highest government authority at the local level. The district commissioner was the tax collector, the chief police officer, and the top magistrate in civil cases. In addition, he was empowered not only to issue permits for small arms and the publishing of newspapers and magazines, but also to decide whether a village should be connected to the electricity grid or have a primary school, and where roads should be constructed.[15]

On the eve of the February 1997 general election, there was the same old auction for the tickets of the two leading parties, except that this time Nawaz Sharif's PML (N) was the favourite. The reason for this shift lay with the single most important autonomous group in Pakistan, the twelve corps commanders of the military, who decided to back the PML (N) to weaken Benazir Bhutto. The PML (N) won 66 per cent of the National Assembly seats on a 50 per cent popular vote. Given the two-thirds majority, Sharif had no difficulty in amending the constitution. At his behest, the federal parliament removed the provision that gave discretionary powers to the president to dissolve the National Assembly and thus the government. He then set out to enfeeble or eliminate all opposition, squeeze the press, purge uncooperative civil servants, transfer judges, and manipulate local elections.

The Sharif government's recognition of the Taliban regime in Afghanistan in May 1997 was applauded by the jihadist factions. Their leaders and publications continued to highlight the advance that the Taliban was making towards transforming Afghan society into an ideal Islamic community.

With the detonation of atom bombs in 1998, Sharif's stock rose further. The jihadist organizations were euphoric about the successful testing of the Islamic bomb – a term coined by Zulfikar Ali Bhutto, their bête noire – for two reasons. First, it gave Pakistan a parity in nuclear arms with India, its bigger and more powerful neighbour, that it lacked in conventional arms and manpower. Second, mastering the production and testing of such a weapon was viewed as a triumph of the marriage between Islam and modern technology. This reasoning conveniently overlooked the fact that Pakistan had assembled an atom bomb by pilfering parts and materials from Western sources and obtaining the design from the atheist government of the communist People's Republic of China.

Personally, both Nawaz Sharif and his brother Shahbaz, the chief minister of Punjab, prospered. They possessed four textile mills, a sugar mill, a private hospital, and a street of houses in Lahore, with the largest sugar mill in Asia ready to be opened. Riding a wave of popularity and burgeoning wealth, the overconfident Nawaz locked horns with the military high command. In October 1998, he forced the army chief of staff, General Jahangir Karamat, to resign after he had publicly demanded the formation of the controversial National Security Council. Sharif then promoted Musharraf, who was only third in seniority among the three-star generals. He reckoned that the Urdu-speaking Musharraf, a native of Delhi, chairing the predominantly Punjabi–Pushtun high command, would lack the clout to pressure a civilian government led by a Punjabi. This would turn out to be a dangerously faulty assumption.

Sharif's cordial meeting with his Indian counterpart, Atal Bihari Vajpayee of the Bharatiya Janata Party (BJP), in Lahore in February 1999, and their agreement to engage in an ongoing dialogue and expand trade, alienated him from the Islamist constituency. To divert its criticisms, he resolved to tackle rampant graft in the Water and Power Development Authority by handing over its management to the military, which was considered far less corrupt than the civil service. But the subsequent reduction in bribery raised the prestige not of Sharif but of the armed forces.

This suited the militant factions. For, in the final analysis, what mattered to them was the ISI's policy as determined by the army chief of staff. Aware of Musharraf's earlier involvement in escalating the insurgency in Indian Kashmir, they felt reassured. By the same token, they reviled Sharif's weakness when he succumbed to Washington's pressure and called off the Kargil campaign. As a consequence, they welcomed Musharraf's overthrow of Sharif in October 1999.

BACK TO MILITARY DICTATORSHIP

Musharraf immediately restored the constitutional provision that gave the president (now called the chief executive) discretionary powers to dissolve the National Assembly. The militant groups welcomed too the military dictator's attempts to win the Taliban regime wider international recognition.

The emergence of the breakaway faction of the Harkat ul Mujahedin Islami as the Jaish-e Muhammad (JeM) led by Maulana Farooq Azhar in March 2000 was attributed to the ISI. It had decided to curtail the influence of the parent body, which had taken to acting independently of its progenitor – the ISI. Soon, hundreds of JeM cadre enrolled at the Al Qaida-run training camps in Afghanistan. The organization's periodical, *Zerb-i-Momin* (Urdu, 'Believers' Counterpunch') acted as the semi-official organ of the Taliban government. In line with the Taliban's edict, it refrained from printing images of human faces. It also published reports of Al Qaida's activities.[16] The circulation of its weekly journal, *Ghazwah* (Urdu, 'Battle to Spread Islam'), published in Urdu and English, soared to 250,000, with its daily newspaper, *Islam*, fluctuating around 100,000.[17] By comparison, Pakistan's oldest daily newspaper, *Dawn*, originating in Delhi in 1941 and formerly edited by Muhammad Ali Jinnah, sold 138,000 copies.[18]

Together, these dailies and weeklies, along with the LeT's *Al Dawa* (Arabic, 'The Call'), formed a very substantial proportion of the million copies of jihadist publications sold weekly. Besides the long-established Jamaat-e Islami and Jamiat Ulema-e Islami, the most important jihadist parties were (in chronological order of foundation): Harkat ul Jihad Islami (1980; later morphed into Harkat ul Mujahedin Islami), Sipah-e Sahaba (1984), Lashkar-e Taiba (1987), Hizb ul Mujahideen (1989), Lashkar-e Jhangvi (1996), and Jaish-e Muhammad (2000). They all regarded the Taliban's governance of Afghanistan as a model for a truly Islamic Pakistan to emulate. By disseminating the radical Islam of the majority Sunni sect and anti-Western news and views, the publications of these organizations played a vital role in Talibanizing Pakistani society.

In the wake of 9/11, when Musharraf found himself with the stark choice encapsulated in US president George W. Bush's declaration 'You are with us or you are with the terrorists,' he had no choice but to line up with Washington. After de-recognizing the Taliban regime, he pressured it – unsuccessfully – to hand over Osama bin Laden to the US Jihadist leaders condemned Musharraf's U-turn as an unforgivable betrayal. They and their followers took to the streets, but the protest outside Khyber Pakhtunkhwa was weak.

When the Pentagon mounted an air campaign against the Taliban on 7 October 2001, militant Islamists forecast a bleak scenario for it, referring to the fate that had befallen the former Soviet Union there. Behind the scenes, the ISI predicted that the Taliban would withstand the American onslaught for a year and a half before retreating to the mountains to wage guerrilla warfare. In the event the Taliban fled their stronghold in Kandahar after a month and a half. This left jihadist leaders confounded and depressed. They needed to explain to their followers how and why an organization engaged in setting up God's rule on Earth had been decimated so quickly and so thoroughly by Crusader Christians. It was a task beyond their abilities.

But the wheel of fortune would turn in their favour as they realized that Musharraf and the ISI had decided to differentiate between Al

Qaida, with its global agenda, and the Taliban, with its regional aims that coincided with Islamabad's. 'With one hand Musharraf played at helping the war against terrorism, while with the other he continued to deal with the Taliban,' noted Ahmed Rashid, a Pakistani journalist and author.[19]

MUSHARRAF'S DOUBLE-DEALING

In his landmark speech of 12 January 2002, Musharraf banned five extremist organizations: the Lashkar-e Taiba, Jaish-e Muhammad, Sipah-e Sahaba, (Shia) Tehrik-e Jafaria Pakistan, and Tehrik-e Nifaz-e Shariat-e Muhammadi. But within a year all were back in business under different names. For instance, the Lashkar-e Taiba re-emerged as the Pasban-e Ahl-e Hadith, the Jaish-e Muhammad as the Al Furqaan, and the Tehrik-e Jafaria Pakistan as the Tehrik-e Islami. Moreover, the shadowy ISI paid substantial sums to jihadist leaders such as Saeed of the LeT, Maulana Masud Azhar of the JeM, and Maulana Fazlur Rahman Khalil of Harkat ul Mujahedin Islami to persuade them to keep a low profile for an unspecified period.[20] Since most of their cadres were released from prison within months of their arrest in January, there was only a minor dip in the activities of these and other jihadist groups.

Such behaviour reflected the Pakistani military's traditional doctrine. India is the primary enemy of Pakistan, so it is incumbent on Islamabad to balance Delhi's superiority in defence by following a dual strategy: Build up Pakistan's nuclear arsenal and encourage periodic terrorist acts against targets in India to create a feeling of insecurity there. As for the future, to offset any advantage that India might gain in Afghanistan after the ultimate withdrawal of the US-led NATO forces from that country, Islamabad must sustain and bolster the Afghan Taliban as its proxy. These interlinked strategies of Pakistan underscore the geopolitical arc from Afghanistan to India.

Having allowed the Taliban and Al Qaida rumps to take refuge in

Pakistan's Federally Administered Tribal Agencies (FATA) in late 2001, ISI policy makers mapped out a strategy for the next few years: assist Taliban leaders to establish a base around Quetta by lending them the services of certain generals from the mainstream army. This strategy got political support after elections to the national and provincial assemblies were held as mandated by the Supreme Court. Two months before the poll on 20 October 2002, Musharraf engineered a split in the Pakistan Muslim League (N), with the breakaway faction calling itself the Pakistan Muslim League (Q), denoting Quaid-i Azam.[21] In exchange for the Islamist parties' backing for him to remain army chief of staff while serving as president, he encouraged the formation of a six-party coalition called the Muttahida Majlis-e Amal (Urdu, 'United Council of Action'; MMA), led by Maulana Fazlur Rehman's Jamiat Ulema-e Islam, a leading patron of the Afghan Taliban. In its election campaign, the MMA attributed the events of 9/11 to the machinations of the CIA and the Israeli foreign espionage agency, Mossad, and equated 'war on terrorism' with 'war on Islam'.

The election result was a hung National Assembly, with the PML (Q) emerging as the largest group. (Officially, voter turnout was put at 42 per cent, but the actual figure was 25 per cent, a record low.) However, by gaining a majority in Khyber Pakhtunkhwa's legislative assembly, the MMA formed the government in this strategic province. It allowed jihadist groups to function freely there as well as in FATA, and facilitated the ISI's plan to keep the Afghan Taliban alive. In Baluchistan, another province abutting Afghanistan, the MMA coalesced with the pro-Musharraf PML (Q) to form a government, led by PML (Q) luminary Jam Muhammad Yusuf Khan Ailani. It was during Ailani's watch that the Afghan Taliban, led by its Shura Council based in Quetta, emerged as a major force in Afghanistan. To furnish itself with 'plausible deniability', the ISI outsourced its intelligence, supervisory and logistics tasks to retired officers often working from home.

On the first anniversary of 9/11, President Bush announced that of the 2,700 Al Qaida suspects apprehended in sixty countries, Pakistan stood at the top with a score of 500.[22] This had happened mainly because, pressured by Washington, Musharraf had started sending the army into the semi-autonomous FATA region, starting with the Khyber Agency in July 2002 – an unprecedented move in the histories of Pakistan and British India. Local tribal elders agreed to let in Pakistani forces only after cash payments coupled with promises of development projects. This intrusion would prove to be the thin end of the wedge, culminating five years later in an armed confrontation between the Pakistani state and a coalition of jihadist factions called the Tehrik-e Taliban Pakistan (Urdu, 'Movement of Pakistani Taliban'; TTP).

As the Pakistani troops moved southward from the Khyber Agency to North Waziristan and South Waziristan – believed to be harbouring nearly five thousand local and foreign militants in 2003 – the pressure on local elders to hand over Al Qaida leaders and operatives mounted. But to do so would have violated the centuries-old Pashtun code of protecting guests at all costs. When the elders rejected Islamabad's demand to hand over the fugitives, low-intensity warfare ensued between the local Waziri and Mehsud tribes and the Pakistani soldiers. The two assassination attempts against Musharraf in December 2003 were traced to Waziri leaders. The conflict intensified, with the government suffering unexpectedly high casualties in 2004. Washington joined the fray. The CIA staged its first drone strike in June 2004 and killed Nek Muhammad Wazir, a militant leader, in South Waziristan. His successor, Baitullah Mehsud, continued the fight. Islamabad eventually signed a peace deal with the tribal elders in February 2005. The army withdrew from South Waziristan, with a promise to do the same in North Waziristan in September.

But before the promised pull-back from North Waziristan, Musharraf's attention was diverted to a place very near the heart of the Pakistani state: the Red Mosque – named for the colour of its walls and interior – complex in Islamabad. Containing a mosque, and male and female madrasas and dormitories, it was located about half a mile (1 km) from the headquarters of the ISI and the diplomatic enclave. Founded in 1965 by Maulana Qari Abdullah, the Red Mosque was patronized by General Zia ul Haq. The ISI used it as a transit point for foreign jihadists on their way to Afghanistan during the 1980s. Before his assassination in 1998, Abdullah established a madrasa, called Jamia Hafsa, with separate facilities for boys and girls, on the unauthorized land adjacent to the original site – a violation that was overlooked by the authorities, thanks to his contacts with army commanders who prayed at his mosque.

Abdullah's two sons, the turbaned, bespectacled Maulana Abdul Aziz Ghazi, with a long, uncombed, grey beard, and the younger Abdul Rashid Ghazi, succeeded him. While managing the complex, they maintained contacts with the ISI as well as Al Qaida leaders, including Osama bin Laden, before the Pentagon's attack on Afghanistan.[23] The Red Mosque remained a bastion of radical Islamists. Following the bomb blasts in London on 7 July 2005, carried out by British nationals of Pakistani origin trained in Pakistan, the police tried to raid the mosque as part of an international investigation. They faced female students armed with batons. They retreated.

Three months later, the severe earthquake in Azad Kashmir provided an opportunity for jihadist groups to show their humanitarian side with exemplary efficiency. The JeM and the SSP were the first to offer urgently needed relief to the victims. Also on hand was the TNSM, based in the adjoining area of Malakand and Swat, led by charismatic Maulana Qazi Fazlullah, who had acquired a large following by airing stirring sermons on his radio station.[24] By rushing aid to the earthquake victims, these groups highlighted the weakness of the state. The upsurge in the activities of their cohorts in the Afghan Taliban – reflected in the 1,500 attacks on NATO forces and other targets during the year – heartened Pakistan's militant leaders. Such assaults would shoot up to five thousand in 2006.

SWAT – THE STATUS QUO CHALLENGED

While the focus of Washington remained primarily on FATA, a blueprint for Pakistan as a fully fledged Sharia state, according to the TNSM, was being created in the Swat Valley. Located in the foothills of the Hindu Kush mountain range, this 3,500 square mile (9,070 sq. km) idyllic valley is named after the Swat River. In its upper reaches, the glacier-fed river flows through pine forests framed by snow-capped mountains and clear blue skies. The lower valley, lying in the monsoon belt, is greener than its upper part, with fields yielding bumper crops of wheat and alfalfa. It is home to a rural population of about a million people, living in villages surrounded by apricot orchards, with men in salwar kameez and embroidered caps or silk turbans, and women in colourful, intricately embroidered shirts, baggy trousers, and all-enveloping shawls.

The breathtaking scenes of waterfalls, lakes, and snow-capped mountains – comparable to those in Switzerland – attract wealthy honeymooners, skiers, trekkers, and amateur archaeologists from all over Pakistan. However, the reputation of the upper valley as an ideal skiing area is overblown. In the absence of snowploughs at its prime ski station, Mallam Jabba, a skier often ends up tackling fresh, powdery snow and going off-piste.

Two-thirds of the valley's half a million urban inhabitants live in Mingora, nestled in fruit orchards and scenic mountains, and connected to Islamabad by a snaking 100-mile (160 km)-long road. Like all large Pakistani towns, it has many squares, with the biggest known as Green Square, the meeting place for several potholed roads shared by pedestrians, vendors hawking their wares, donkey carts, honking cars, and pickup trucks adorned with hand-painted scenes of waterfalls, fir trees, and gushing rivers. The square is embellished with billboards advertising not just hotels, Pepsi, tuition classes for university degrees, and Internet cafés, but also the latest movies in a collage of gaudily painted, moustached actors with shaggy hair brandishing kitchen knives menacingly, and amply endowed, but fully covered, actresses with almond eyes looking wonderstruck at the leading protagonists' gestures of bravado.

Mingora has two cinemas. The larger one, with a two-level auditorium and wooden benches, is called Swat. It shows three-hour-long Pushtu films to a predominantly male audience, young and ebullient. Here, the sex-starved callow youths can have the thrill of seeing a group of women dancing or a voluptuous woman in tight clothes displaying her temerity by shouting down the bullying hero – or hearing an expensively dressed woman with a nightingale voice sing ballads of love and longing. Those who cannot afford the 150 Pakistani rupees ($2) ticket have the option of buying DVDs of the movies made in Lahore, Mumbai, or Hollywood in the local bazaar for a quarter of the price of admission to a cinema.

The challenge to this way of life came slowly, innocuously, in 2005 in the form of sermons broadcast on the radio. The speaker was a young but charismatic cleric named Maulana Qazi Fazullah with the de rigueur beard who kept his head covered with a black silk turban. An eloquent speaker, he started airing his sermons on an unauthorized FM 91 channel. At first, he spoke of the basic tenets of Islam. Then, as a qazi, a qualified religious judge, he lashed out at the corruption and lassitude of state judges working in league with venal police and rich landlords under a judicial system dating back to British rule. To rectify the unjust situation, he demanded the promulgation of the Sharia in the district. This resonated with the bulk of the population. All local mosques began relaying his sermons on their loudspeakers.

Fazullah's prestige rose sharply when he responded swiftly to the urgent needs of the victims of the earthquake in Pakistan-held Kashmir. The TNSM's ranks grew as recruits from outside the district volunteered to join. He expanded his appeal further by attacking the feudal lords who owned mansions and vast orchards and fields, but paid only a pittance to their labourers. To remedy the unjust situation, he encouraged his armed partisans to seize the properties of big landlords. When the dipossessed landowners fled to Peshawar, Fazullah redistributed their lands. By so doing, he broke new ground. This was not the policy of any other jihadist organization – or the long-established Islamist parties whose leaders argued that land distribution had occurred according to 'the will of Allah'.

At the same time Fazullah intensified his drive to promote virtue and eradicate sin. That meant getting rid of TV, DVDs, and computers because they transmitted images of human beings. Since God creates humans, interfering with that divine right by drawing or transmitting their images is un-Islamic, he declared. He enjoined men to grow beards and called on women to don the full burqa before appearing in public and not to work outside the home.

THE RED MOSQUE DEFIANCE

The drive towards implementing the Sharia in full was advancing elsewhere in Pakistan as well. By 2006, the growing aggressiveness of the TNSM and other jihadist groups was reflected at the Red Mosque in Islamabad. The government chose to overlook the militants' transgressions such as threatening unveiled women and DVD vendors selling Hollywood films. This was an effective way to convey the message to Western capitals that the alternative to unqualified backing for Musharraf was a fundamentalist regime.

In late March 2007, as part of their anti-vice campaign, female madrasa students made a 'citizens' arrest' of three women for running a brothel and released them only after they had made confessions, apologized, and donned burqas. There were reports of small arms being smuggled into the complex. In early April, Abdul Aziz Ghazi demanded that the Sharia be applied forthwith in Islamabad. After establishing a Sharia court in parallel with state courts, he dared the authorities to close it.

The Musharraf government could no longer ignore such a stark challenge to its authority and responded with force. That unveiled an open warfare between the jihadist groups – founded by the ISI over the past quarter-century – and the Pakistani state, which continues.

On 3 July, army troops and commandos of the Special Service Group mounted Operation Sunrise to clear the Red Mosque and the adjacent Jamia Hafsa of militants. Several deadlines for the evacuation followed. When Abdul Aziz Ghazi was apprehended as he attempted to escape wearing a burqa, some 800 male and 400 female students from Jamia Hafsa surrendered. But that still left more than 100 militants and 300 to 400 students, women and children inside the complex.

After examining the deployment of people inside the complex by using unmanned aerial vehicles, the security forces mounted an assault on 10 July. They faced fire from militants, positioned behind sandbags on the roof, as they tried to disable scores of booby traps to be able to enter Jamia Hafsa. Intense fighting followed, with the armed militants attacking the intruders with incendiary and fragmentation grenades. One of them turned out to be a suicide bomber. Even bloodier combat ensued in the basement, where the extremists, armed with machine guns, assault rifles, and shoulder-fired rockets, used women and children as human shields. In the firefight Abdul Rashid Ghazi was killed. The violence ended only when the resisters in the basement were killed or chose to surrender.

It was only on 11 July that the authorities claimed full control of the devastated complex. At its peak Operation Sunrise saw twelve thousand commandos and army and paramilitary troops engage 100-plus militants surrounded by a few hundred women and children. For eight days, the spectacle of troops manning machine guns behind sandbagged posts and from the top of armoured vehicles, tanks, and helicopter gunships had made the neighbourhood look like a war zone. The cache of weapons discovered by the army included Russian- and Chinese-designed rocket-propelled grenades, anti-tank and anti-personnel mines, suicide-bombing belts, light machine guns, AK47 assault rifles, sniper rifles, pistols, and night vision equipment, and more than fifty thousand rounds of ammunition.

The government put the number of fatalities at 102, including more than seventy extremists and eleven commandos. By contrast, the opposition Muttahida Majlis-e Amal claimed that between 400 and 1,000 people were killed and that they were all students, women, and children. A popular belief took hold that in the Red Mosque siege up to 3,000 died, that most of them were female students at Jamia Hafsa and that their bodies were buried in secret graves. Later, many would attribute the poor performance of the pro-Musharraf PML (Q) party in the February 2008 elections to this bloody episode.[25]

Many of the activists who escaped the Red Mosque headed for their homes in Khyber Pakhtunkhwa and FATA, and reinforced the militant groups there, particularly the TNSM. A suicide attacker struck a military convoy near the Afghan border on 14 July, killing twenty-eight soldiers. The army mounted a major offensive in the tribal area on 19 July. It encountered stiff resistance. Musharraf could not afford to raise the stakes by shifting troops facing India, the primary enemy. Figures released by Washington showed that of the total US aid received by Pakistan in the seven years since 9/11, four-fifths had gone to its military, which had spent most of it on weapons to be used against India.[26]

In August 2007, the fighters of South Waziristan-based Baitullah Mehsud kidnapped 200 Pakistani troops to secure the release of twenty-five militants. A short, portly, bearded man with shoulder-length hair, fleshy mouth, and expressive eyes, Mehsud had fought the Soviets in Afghanistan in the late 1980s, and was with the Taliban when they swept into Kabul in 1996. As such, he was close to both bin Laden and Mullah Muhammad Omar. He used Al Qaida know-how to set up training camps and indoctrinating suicide bombers. Originally supported by the Pakistani military and ISI, he later became autonomous.

After declaring a state of emergency in Pakistan in November, which enhanced his powers, Musharraf struck a deal with Mehsud. He freed the jailed extremists, and in return, Mehsud released all the soldiers except three who were Shia. Their beheadings were recorded on a video which was handed over to Pakistan's envoy. This deal was a one-off. The next month, two suicide bombers blew up a military bus outside the army's general headquarters in Rawalpindi, killing twenty-six officers and soldiers.

In December, Mehsud allied his faction with those of Hafiz Gul Bahadur of North Waziristan, Maulavi Nazir of South Waziristan, Maulana Faqir Muhammad of Bajaur, and Maulana Qazi Fazlullah of the TNSM. The alliance was called the Tehrik-e Taliban Pakistan (TTP) and commanded the loyalty of an estimated 30,000–35,000 fighters. It declared a 'defensive jihad' against the Pakistani military and its intelligence arm, full implementation of the Sharia, and the formation of a united front against NATO troops in Afghanistan. The white flags of the TTP began appearing all over FATA.

Soon the TTP would forge links with the Afghan Taliban and Al Qaida as well as the ultra-militant Punjab-based groups such as the Lashkar-e Jhangvi and LeT. As part of its 'defensive jihad' against Pakistan's army, it started using lethal improvised explosive devices.

The TTP was unmoved by the resignation of Musharraf first as army chief of staff – with ISI head General Ashfaq Parvez Kayani succeeding him – and then as president, following the poor performance of his party in the February 2008 elections. Nonetheless, it remained comparatively quiescent during the transition that saw the PPP's Yusuf Raza Gilani become prime minister in March 2000. The process of forming the new administration ended in September when Asaf Ali Zardari was elected president.

Ignoring the political developments in Pakistan, the Bush White House had kept up its escalation of strikes by CIA-operated drones in FATA. The Predator and the heavier Reaper drones were used either for surveillance or for firing air-to-ground missiles or laser-guided bombs. Launched from local airfields by remote control they could remain airborne for up to thirty hours with top speed of 300 miles (480 km) an hour, and cruise at an altitude of 45,000 feet (13,716 m). They were controlled by satellite by CIA crew based in the US, mostly at the Creech facility in Nevada.

Compared to the four drone raids in 2007, there were six in August 2008 alone. The pace was maintained in September. This provoked the TTP to retaliate, particularly when the Pakistani army also resorted to using heavy artillery and air raids against suspected insurgent hideouts in the hilly, inaccessible terrain of FATA, destroying many homes and shops.

On 22 September (23 Ramadan), the truck bombing of the Marriott Hotel in Islamabad, involving 1,320 pounds (600 kg) of RDX and TNT left a crater 195 feet (59 m) in diameter and 24 feet (7.3 m) deep, killing 53 people. This terrorist act was attributed to the TTP. That evening, following Zardari's maiden speech to both chambers of parliament, the Speaker of the lower house had arranged a dinner for the entire civilian and military leadership at the Marriott, where they would have collectively broken their fast after sunset as required during Ramadan. But a last-minute decision moved the dinner venue to the prime minister's residence. By happenstance, there was a symmetry between this sudden change of plan and what had happened in the case of the attack on the Indian Parliament nearly seven years earlier in Delhi.[27]

Subsequent investigations of the incident showed close coordination between the TTP, Al Qaida, and the Punjab-based radical jihadist groups. The suicide bomber was an Afghan militant trained by the TTP in the Mohmand Agency; an Al Qaida leader, Osama al Kinni, planned and financed the vicious attack; and the jihadist groups in Punjab facilitated the operation.[28]

Later, these organizations drew several upbeat conclusions from the LeT's extremely effective, three-day-long assault on Mumbai on 26 November, widely labelled India's 26/11. LeT leaders had planned and implemented the operation with military precision, and had co-opted the former officers of Pakistan's armed forces.

The jihadist groups' most ambitious goal was to escalate tensions between India and Pakistan to the point of war. Given the troop movements on both sides that followed 26/11, it appeared at one point that hostilities might indeed break out. But Indian leaders wisely settled instead for using the threat of hitting terrorist training camps in Pakistan as a pressure tactic and getting Washington to use its leverage on Islamabad. On a less strategic level, luxury hotels in Mumbai were symbols of India's commercial strength. The focus on the Nariman (Chabad) House pointed at Delhi's close ties with Tel Aviv. This was reinforced by references made by the terrorists to the recent visit of an Israeli general to Indian Kashmir. The liberation of Kashmir was on the agenda of Al Qaida as well as the Pakistan-based jihadist organizations. Thus the attacks in Mumbai signalled the merger of the specific aim of highlighting the oppressed condition of Muslims in Kashmir with Al Qaida's wider goal of taking up the cause of Muslims wherever they are persecuted – be it Palestine, Bosnia, Chechnya, Afghanistan, or Iraq.

The downside of the event for South Asian jihadists was that one of the ten terrorists – twenty-one-year-old Muhammad Ajmal Amir Kasab from a village in Punjab – survived. In his subsequent confession, he admitted to being trained by the LeT widely linked to the ISI. This exposure further strained relations between Pakistan's radical jihadists and the ISI.

In late December 2008, Mullah Muhammad Omar, based in Baluchistan, sent a six-member delegation to South Waziristan to urge the TTP to scale down its attacks in Pakistan and help counter the planned rise in US forces in Afghanistan. That led to the formation of the Council of United Mujahedin in February, coordinated by Sirajuddin Haqqani, son of Jalaluddin Haqqani. However, nothing substantial came of it: Relations between the TTP and the Pakistani government had deteriorated to an irreconcilable degree.

2009, THE MOST VIOLENT YEAR YET

With the foundations of the Pakistani state under attack, its military and paramilitary forces striking back, and the CIA-operated drone strikes spiking to fifty-one – almost one a week, 2009 would prove to be the bloodiest year so far.

From the Washington–Islamabad viewpoint, military attacks had merits as well as demerits. They disrupted communication between top leaders, forcing them to forgo face-to-face meetings with their planners and strategists since gatherings of a dozen or more men were often targeted. Jihadist chiefs were compelled to move house constantly. But such strikes also ended the tribal custom of groups of men assembling in the evening to converse freely, which caused popular resentment against Washington. So in the battle for hearts and minds the tactic was counterproductive. Also, the practice of killing and maiming enemies by remote control led the locals to conclude that Americans lacked the daring and valour required to fight the foe at close quarters. 'If courage is the coin of the realm then courage is what proves to the local Pushtun tribes that you are their allies,' said Peter W. Singer, director of the Washington-based 21st Century Defense Initiative.[29] Lastly, the inevitable 'collateral damage' caused by such strikes, resulting in the deaths of innocent civilians, fed anti-American feeling. Sticking to the centuries-old tradition of 'an eye for an eye', the families of the dead resolved to get even with their killers, as represented by the American forces in Afghanistan. This swelled the ranks of the Afghan Taliban as well as the TTP.

While the Pakistani government disapproved of US drone attacks in public, it cooperated with Washington covertly. It did so in order to ease the pressure from the White House to be more aggressive towards FATA-based insurgents. The clandestine use of Shamsi airfield, 200 miles (320 km) south-west of Quetta, by US Special Operations Force (SOF) troops, going back to the start of the Afghan War on 7 October 2001, had continued. The task of loading drones with missiles and bombs was performed by the employees of US-based Blackwater USA company – as revealed by the *London Times* in February 2009.[30] Moreover, as early as 2006, joint teams of CIA operatives, radio experts and SOF troops were secretly posted inside the Pakistani military bases in FATA.

It was from there that the CIA recruited paid informers, often indigent locals, to help pinpoint targets. The TTP caught many of them and, after video-recording their confessions, executed them. In one such DVD, nineteen-year-old Habib ur Rahman confessed to receiving 20,000 Pakistani rupees ($250) for dropping microchips hidden in a cigarette wrapper at the home of a target. If he got caught he would receive protection, and if the operation succeeded he would receive thousands of US dollars, he was assured by his recruiters. Instead, he ended up dead.[31]

On the other side of the border, Pakistanis were shaken by the daredevil assault on the visiting Sri Lankan cricket team in the heart of Lahore despite its police escort. After detonating bombs to stop the convoy, a dozen gunmen lobbed grenades and rockets and killed seven policemen before quickly disappearing. Such an audacious attack in the country's second largest city undermined citizens' confidence in the authorities' ability to provide them with basic security. Because no group claimed responsibility, it provided a field day for experts on TV chat shows. (Later, the mastermind of the operation would be named as Dr Muhammad Aqeel, aka Dr Usman, of the Lashkar-e Jhangvi.)

But instead of undertaking introspective analyses of how and why the country had descended into such an abysmal condition – or even why Lahore had been targeted – officials and experts did what they had always done. They blamed the malevolent hand of India's RAW. Cabinet minister Nabil Ahmed Gabol rushed to judgement – based on 'evidence' miraculously gathered within a few hours – and asserted that the terrorists had come across the border from India. 'It was a conspiracy to defame Pakistan internationally.'[32]

Summing up the comments made on talk shows on Pakistan's many TV channels, which had sprung up following Musharraf's decision in 2004 to permit private broadcasters to operate,[33] Ali Sethi, a Pakistani journalist, referred to a leader of the PML (Q) who had 'no doubt' that the attack was the work of Indian intelligence agencies. A former ISI director general was also of the same mind.[34] This was the continuation of a standard practice by the ISI, whose briefings were faithfully reproduced by the media. Following the sensational Mumbai attacks in November 2008, the ISI alleged that Indian officials were behind the atrocity, intent on covering up investigation into Hindu extremists. Its version collapsed when the surviving terrorist, Kasab, told a court in Mumbai that he had been trained by the LeT, which had well-established links with the ISI. When Pakistan's jihadists turned violently against the Pakistani state, the ISI put an implausible spin on it, alleging that TTP activists were being armed by India. Indeed, this 'fact' was injected into the minds of the military soldiers and officers to motivate them to fight the TTP. By so doing, they were told, they would be attacking India and its malignant design to bring about the break-up of Pakistan.

As for the attack on Sri Lanka's cricketers, it would be left to an unnamed security official to explain to the BBC's Syed Shoab Hasan why the jihadists had picked Lahore as their target. 'Lahore is the only city in Pakistan which has remained relatively peaceful since the 9/11 attacks,' he said. 'It has been Pakistan's saving grace, and whoever wants to destabilize the country or the government, would go after Lahore.'[35]

Little wonder, then, that Lahore remained in the eye of the storm. On 30 March, about ten gunmen in police uniforms, armed with automatic weapons and grenades, raided the Manawan Police Training School in the city. They seized the main building while 750 unarmed police cadets were assembled on the parade ground. It took the security forces six hours to retake the main building. In the firefight eight cadets and instructors were killed. Three terrorists exploded their suicide belts, four were apprehended, and the rest escaped. In a telephone interview with the BBC, Baitullah Mehsud, carrying bounties of $5 million from the US and $650,000 from Pakistan on his head, claimed responsibility for the operation. He explained that it was in retaliation for the continuing CIA drone strikes – which had escalated after Barack Obama became president on 21 January 2009 – in which the Pakistani government was complicit. The TTP's repeated attempts to hit a drone had failed.[36]

By contrast, its daring and meticulously planned salvos in Lahore, based on the information gathered by its efficient intelligence agency, signalled the start of low-intensity warfare.

After much prevarication, the ISI and army commanders realized the bitter truth: The jihadist organizations they had fostered and nourished since the 1980s had turned into Frankenstein's monster, threatening the existence of Pakistan as a functioning state, with incalculable consequences for the rest of South and South-west Asia. So they decided to discard the policy dating back to the rule of Zia ul Haq, sever ties with their creatures of the past, and engage them in a fight, the length and severity of which they could not forecast. This decision, taken in their own interest, was welcomed by the Obama administration, which placed high hopes in the democratically elected Zardari. As the husband of the assassinated Benazir Bhutto, he was expected to crush jihadists in FATA, Swat, and elsewhere in Pakistan with an iron hand.

However, this was a misreading of the domestic situation in Pakistan. Zardari held the office of president but not its power. Outside of Sindh, his home province, he lacked popularity. He was disliked by the military high command, made up of Punjabis and Pushtuns. As in the past, those aspects of the country's domestic and foreign policies that impinged on national security remained the exclusive domain of the military. So long as General Musharraf was president and army chief, he had the authority to devise and implement a whole range of policies from national security to education. That unique status also allowed him to juggle, successfully, the need to satisfy Washington on the one hand and the corps of army commanders and the ISI on the other. The latter were intent on bolstering the Afghan Taliban and pacifying Islamists at home by blowing hot and cold with the jihadists in FATA and Swat.

Zardari had neither the power of Musharraf nor his cunning. At the same time he craved to make a noticeable difference to the lives of urban Pakistanis, who were rattled by the daring terrorist attacks. Through intermediaries, Zardari worked out a secret deal with Maulana Abdul Aziz Ghazi. After being released from house arrest in mid-April 2009, Ghazi delivered a Friday prayer sermon at the Red Mosque. 'You should be ready to make sacrifices for Islam,' he told an audience of several thousands. 'The day is not far away when Islam will be enforced in the whole of the country.' He qualified his disapproval of suicide bombings against Muslims thus. 'We are a peaceful people, but if our way is blocked, then you have witnessed the scenes in Swat and in FATA.'[37]

Ghazi's reference to Swat was apt. By then, the TTP had established a de facto government in Swat under the leadership of Maulana Qazi Fazlullah, with Sharia courts, Islamic taxes, vigilante patrols, and checkpoints. Its courts dispensed summary justice: lashings for minor offences and beheadings for major ones such as spying. Because of desertions and killings by the militants, the provincial police force had dwindled to the point of non-existence. Its role was taken over by five thousand bearded, Kalashnikov-carrying TTP vigilantes in camouflage vests and running shoes. They emulated the Afghan Taliban by using a black turban as their uniform. Under the circumstances, the Zardari government's agreement to replace the old colonial-era law with the Sharia as part of a ceasefire agreement with the TTP meant little.

To encourage the growing of beards by men, the TTP authorities threatened barbers. Those who continued to shave beards, found their shops vandalized. In its drive to ban music, the TTP shut down more than two hundred music shops. Its threats to local musicians, singers, and female dancers led to a mass exodus. It sealed cinemas in Mingora and elsewhere, arguing that music and dancing aroused lust and led to fornication, a vice.

In December 2008, the TTP authorities announced the closure of girls' schools from mid-January. They argued that the education being imparted there was corrupting young females; only after the educational system had been cleansed of all un-Islamic elements would they allow girls to be educated. They failed to apply this logic to boys, whose schools remained open. To compel obedience to their order, they torched more than 180 girls' schools. That resulted in the voluntary closure of nine hundred schools. All told, this diktat jeopardized the educational future of some 125,000 girls and young women.

The TTP also required that a woman in the street must always be accompanied by a male relative. When TTP vigilantes saw an unveiled woman shopping on her own, they would take down her particulars and arrange for her to be thrashed. The punishment for a woman or teenage girl who was seen in the company of an unrelated man was severe. The circulation in the rest of Pakistan of a two-minute video, shot using a mobile phone, in late March–early April brought home the brutality inflicted on women by the TTP. It showed a burqa-clad woman face down on the ground, with two men holding her arms and feet while a third – a bearded, black-turbaned TTP vigilante – flogged her before a small, silent crowd of men and boys. 'Please stop it,' the hapless young woman beseeched, whimpering. Every time the whip struck her backside, she screamed in pain. 'Either kill me or stop it now,' she pleaded – in vain. 'Hold her legs tightly,' came the order, off-camera. After the prescribed thirty-four lashes had been administered, the wailing woman was dragged to a nearby building. Her crime? 'She came out of her house with another guy who was not her husband, so we must punish her,' said Muslim Khan, the TTP spokesman. 'There are boundaries you cannot cross.'[38]

How did the TTP authorities learn of this minor incident? Through their network of spies and agents. By issuing verdicts favouring tenants and farm workers in their disputes with feudal lords, by parcelling out confiscated land and houses to the landless, and by giving villagers a free hand in cutting down trees for lumber, the TTP had acquired a very substantial body of supporters and sympathizers. Some of them became its eyes and ears, calling at night on the TTP's intelligence chief to report who had spoken favourably of the military or the government in Islamabad or played music behind walls; which barber had taken to shaving his customers' beards at home; and who had committed adultery (for which, however, four witnesses were needed). The worst of all crimes was spying for the federal government. The punishment was beheading. The decapitated corpses were left hanging by their legs, with their heads tied between their feet.

So far such a nightmarish state of affairs – viewed as utopian by TTP activists – existed only in a small valley. But life in Pakistan's mainstream urban centres was far from normal. The Islamabad that Ghazi was allowed to witness in April 2009 was different from the one at the time of the siege of the Red Mosque. The capital now had 40-foot (12.2 m)-high sandbag walls with nests of gun-wielding troops as well as concrete blast walls. The heavily protected area around parliament was called the red zone. To reach the presidential palace, an invited visitor had to go through eight checkpoints, starting 2 miles (3 km) from the final destination. The main avenue outside the bland ISI headquarters was closed. Five-star hotels were fortified like army bases. Many streets were blocked. While cabinet ministers travelled in convoys bristling with armed guards, Western ambassadors journeyed in bulletproof limos. Almost all schools were now equipped with closed-circuit TV and guarded by uniformed men displaying small arms. Such security steps were taken because of a major army offensive in Swat, involving air raids, artillery bombardments, and rocketing by helicopter gunships, to overthrow the TTP's rule. The subsequent battle led to the flight of 200,000 civilians as well as most of the five thousand militants, including Maulana Qazi Fazlullah. The army claimed success in June.

But it would be the end of August before the displaced people felt sufficiently assured by the presence of thirty thousand army troops, backed by Frontier Corps paramilitaries and police, to return to their homes, many of them destroyed or damaged in the violence. Among them was Sher Shah Khan, one of a dozen feudal lords who had fled to Peshawar. During his forced year-long exile, the TTP damaged twenty-three of his houses, razed his orchards, and killed twelve of his relatives and servants. It was not until October that the forty-year-old projector at the Swat cinema in Mingora flickered back to life – to the boisterous cheers of some seven hundred young males who packed the dusty auditorium.

Meanwhile, on 5 August, a drone strike on the village of Zanghra in South Waziristan hit the most prized target for Washington and

Islamabad when it killed Baitullah Mehsud – as well as his wife, in-laws, and eight others. A diabetic, Mehsud had an acute kidney ailment which had reduced his mobility. His assassination reduced the lingering mistrust between the CIA and the ISI, well illustrated by a news item in the London *Sunday Times*. Thanks to the telephone intercepts obtained by the US National Security Agency, the ISI's complicity in the bombing of the Indian Embassy in Kabul in July 2008 by the Haqqani group had been established. During the subsequent visit to Washington by Pakistani prime minister Gilani, CIA chief Mike Hayden showed him a dossier on the ISI's support for the Afghan Taliban. When the Pakistani delegation asked for more information, President Bush said, 'When we share information with you guys, the bad guys always run away.'[39]

After Baitullah Mehsud's death, the TTP's leadership passed to his deputy, Hakimullah Mehsud, then the TTP's commander in the Khyber, Kurram, and Orakzai Agencies. His distinguishing features were his Grecian nose, neatly trimmed beard and penchant for wearing a round hat instead of a turban. He was a cousin of Qari Hussein, who directed the suicide-bombing squads. Hakimullah pledged to avenge Baitullah's death by increasing attacks on Pakistani and American targets.

The orgy of terrorist violence that the TTP – working in collaboration with Al Qaida and the Punjab-based ultra-jihadist groups – unleashed made several other points. It showed the TTP's resilience and resolve to dissuade Pakistan's army from expanding its campaign into South Waziristan. By taking the fight into Pakistani cities, it aimed to intensify the general sense of insecurity, making ordinary citizens wonder what would happen next, and engender a major crisis of confidence in the government. It would also increase friction between the civilian and military authorities, with the former favouring compromise and the latter advocating force. Lastly, by exposing weak links in the country's security apparatus and complacency among top officials, it aimed to undermine ordinary citizens' faith in the military, police and intelligence agencies.

In October, the TTP staged ten major terrorist attacks in Islamabad, Rawalpindi, Peshawar, Kohat, Lahore, and the Swat Valley, almost always targeting these vital agencies. The orgy of violence started on 5 October with an assault by a suicide bomber, wearing a security forces' uniform, who infiltrated the United Nations' World Food Programme office in Islamabad near the navy headquarters and the private residence of Zardari. His explosive device killed five, and caused an exodus of foreign NGOs from the capital. Four days later, a car bomb in the crowded Khyber Bazaar in Peshawar killed forty-nine. Then TTP terrorists blasted a checkpoint outside an army compound, resulting in a firefight. A far more brazen and ambitious attack came on 10 October in Rawalpindi, home to the general headquarters of the military. Ten jihadists, wearing army uniforms and riding in a van with military registration plates and loaded with automatic weapons, mines, grenades, and suicide jackets, penetrated the heavily guarded headquarters at dawn. They went past the first security post. Challenged at the second checkpoint, they engaged in a gun battle, where four of them died. The rest sped ahead and seized the Military Intelligence Directorate building, killing the director general and taking thirty-nine hostages. By the time the Special Service Group's commandos ended the siege after twenty hours, a third of the hostages lay dead – as did five more terrorists. The lone survivor was Muhammad Aqeel (aka Dr Usman). After deserting the Army Medical Corps in 2004, he had joined the banned LeJ. His suicide vest did not work well and left him badly injured and unconscious.

The terrorists had planned on taking senior army commanders hostage and making three demands: release a hundred jihadists; end military cooperation with America; and put Musharraf on trial. Five of the attackers were from Punjab, and the rest from South Waziristan, where TTP commander Wali ur Rahman had planned the operation. As in the case of the Marriott Hotel blast, the troika of Al Qaida (supplying funds), the TTP (logistics and training support), and the Punjabi jihadist organizations (providing manpower) was involved.

This episode shook the confidence of most urbanites. In major cities such as Islamabad, Lahore and Karachi, people reduced their shopping trips to the absolute minimum. Clientele in restaurants fell abruptly. Blast walls rose in front of schools and colleges. Privately run schools employed sharpshooters and armed guards.

The terrorists' demand to end military cooperation with Washington reflected popular opinion. A poll conducted in June 2008 showed 69 per cent of Pakistanis opposed to the Pentagon working with Pakistan's military against Al Qaida and the Taliban, and 52 per cent blaming the violence in their country on the US In a Gallup poll in October, 54 per cent said the US military presence in Afghanistan was a threat to their country.[40]

There was more violence to come. The fifteenth of October 2009 became notable for the number of major assaults – three in Lahore and one each in Peshawar and Kohat. Teams of terrorists in police uniforms hiding suicide vests underneath attacked three police facilities in and near Lahore, including the Federal Investigation Agency office, the Manawan Police Training School, and the Elite Police Academy. The death toll was thirty-eight. The Federal Investigation Agency office and the Manawan site were attacked for the second time in a year, indicating clearly that the jihadists had sleepers among the people working there. The assault on the Elite Police Academy, which trained cadets in counter-insurgency, was especially ironic.

It was obvious that Pakistan was becoming so destabilized that its government was unable to stand on its two feet and was having to depend heavily on America – much detested by ordinary Pakistanis. As cited above, most of them blamed the US for their misfortunes. It was America that had dragged their country into the so-called 'War on Terror', which in reality was a war on Islam, both Iraq and Afghanistan being Muslim countries. It had cajoled and pressured Pakistan's security forces to fight fellow Muslims at home, which had led to deep fissures in society and created unprecedented insecurity. This long-running internecine violence had cost Pakistan twice as much as the aid the United States had given it since 9/11. So, according to this perception, the source of Pakistan's present woes lay not in FATA or Afghanistan but in America. Lastly, the US had not reconciled itself to seeing Pakistan as a nuclear power and was looking for pretexts to de-nuclearize their country to please its long-time ally Israel and its freshly acquired associate, India. This version of events resonated with most Pakistanis. 'Polls show that more Pakistanis believe the US is a threat to their country than India, and any time you outpoll India as the bad guy in Pakistan, you are in deep trouble,' wrote Bruce Riedel, a South Asia specialist at the Washington-based Brookings Institute.[41]

October ended with the most lethal and senseless terrorist outrage of all. It claimed 117 lives, mostly those of women and children, in Peshawar. A truck bomb exploded between the Meena and Koochi bazaars, famous for selling women's dresses, cosmetics, jewellery, and household items. The TTP and Al Qaida tried to distance themselves from the attack. Earlier, shopkeepers had received warnings that the markets had become 'dens of immorality' because they catered for women.

These acts of carnage occurred against the background of a deteriorating national economy. The power cuts during the summer of 2009 were so drastic that for the first time in Pakistan's history there was negative industrial growth. The state-owned power-generating industry suffered from decades of underinvestment and gross mismanagement, including underinvoicing those consumers who paid bribes. It was left to the seventeen-member Supreme Court, led by chief justice Iftikhar Muhammad Chaudhry, to remind people of the corruption at the highest political–administrative level. On 16 December, it nullified the National Reconciliation Order issued by Musharraf in October 2007 to facilitate the return of Benazir Bhutto and Nawaz Sharif to contest the upcoming elections. The order had given amnesty to almost six thousand politicians and civil servants accused of corruption. These included the current interior minister, Rehman Malik, and the defence minister, Ahmad Mukhtar. In addition, the Supreme Court ordered the government to contact the Swiss authorities to reopen proceedings against Zardari concerning the illegal transfer of $50 million of suspect gains to offshore companies in Zardari's name.[42] Zardari's lawyers claimed that as president he enjoyed immunity from prosecution. His prestige hit rock bottom.

This turmoil at the highest political level, exposing the chronic corruption of the elite, encouraged the TTP to maintain its war of attrition against Pakistan and the Americans in Afghanistan. On 30 December, Dr Humam Khalil Muhammad al Balawi, a Jordanian physician ostensibly working for the CIA, exploded a bomb at the CIA station at Forward Operating Base Chapman in Khost near the Pakistani border. Supposedly a base for reconstruction projects, this was a central planning point for drone attacks focused on the North Waziristan-based Haqqani network. Balawi was a double agent for the TTP. His suicide bomb killed seven operators from the CIA's paramilitary Special Activities Division, making it the intelligence agency's biggest loss since the 1983 truck bombing of the US embassy in Beirut, which left eighteen CIA operators dead. The TTP said it had used a turncoat CIA operative to avenge the killing of its leader, Baitullah Mehsud.[43]

By 31 December, the TTP had mounted nineteen assaults on military targets outside FATA and Swat, including eight near the army's general headquarters in Rawalpindi. It had also attacked the ISI premises in Lahore, Peshawar, and Multan, and courts in Peshawar. As a result of the low-intensity warfare between the TTP and the Islamabad government, 3,021 Pakistanis lost their lives – far higher than the toll in war-torn Afghanistan.

2010: VIOLENCE SUBSIDES, RIVERS RAGE

The year 2010 started with a truly ghastly terrorist act when a suicide bomber blew up his vehicle in a crowd as it watched a volleyball game in the village of Shah Hassan Khal, south of Peshawar. The death toll was 105 people. The villagers suffered this fate because they had raised an anti-TTP militia. A peace committee of villagers was in session at a mosque near the venue when 600 pounds (270 kg) of explosives were ignited.

Following a routine condemnation of the vicious assault, the government announced that its military would not mount new offensives against the TTP. This led to a de facto truce, which provided an opportunity for the TTP to regroup and reorganize. It then turned its wrath on Shias, Sufis and Ahmadis as well as on the rallies held by its opponents. For instance, in April a TTP suicide bomber killed forty-three people at a political rally in Khyber Pakhtunkhwa. An attack on two Ahmadi mosques in Lahore in May left ninety-five people dead, while suicide bombers at the city's famed Data Ganj Bakhsh complex claimed more than two score lives. After a lull during August, when floods devastated large parts of the country, the TTP targeted Shias by attacking their religious processions in Karachi and Quetta in September. And in early October a suicide bomber blasted the shrine of Sufi saint Abdullah Shah Ghazi in Karachi.

Important though these violent events were from the viewpoint of law and order, they paled before the monumental task that befell Pakistan's people and leaders as they struggled to cope with the worst floods in eight decades. The persistent monsoon rains that began in late July in Baluchistan, affecting first Khyber Pakhtunkhwa and then Punjab and Sindh, continued unabated for a month. They displaced over twenty million people, about one-eighth of the national population, and covered a fifth of Pakistan, devastating nearly eight million acres of fertile land and millions of livestock as well as roads, bridges, the electricity grid, communications, administrative offices, schools and health clinics.

While Pakistan beseeched the international community for urgent assistance, a TTP spokesman took a contrary position. He said that government officials were keen to get foreign aid 'not for the people affected but to make their bank accounts bigger'. The humanitarian wings of the jihadist organizations were the first to offer relief and succour to the victims. The JeI's Al Khidmat (Urdu, 'The Service') Foundation was in the vanguard, followed by the Jamaat ud Dawa's Falah-e Insaniyat (Urdu, 'Humanity's Release') and the Maymar Charitable Trust, the new name for the banned Al Rashid Foundation.

Over twenty thousand volunteers from these charities started rescuing stranded people in flooded areas, operated ambulances, set up refugee camps, and arranged food, shelter and medical care. The Pakistani media reported widely the humanitarian activities of these groups as well as their efforts to convey a message of Islamic brotherhood. It also gave prominence to the order of the army chief, General Kayani, that his troops should give top priority to the rescue and relief effort. About sixty thousand Pakistani troops, backed by the air force, swung into action, particularly in the volatile Khyber Pakhtunkhwa. Kayani was shown on TV commiserating with the victims. His approval rating soared to over 60 per cent. In contrast, Zardari was shown boarding a helicopter in Paris to fly to his château in northern France.

On the civilian side, ill-managed rescue attempts coupled with poorly handled relief efforts, corruption, and favouritism increased the distrust with which most Pakistanis regarded politicians. Victims and others accused officials of diverting relief to their own party supporters. There were widespread doubts about whether the government administered foreign aid honestly. The opposition leader Nawaz Sharif's proposal to have an independent body supervise the relief effort was summarily dismissed by Zardari.

Later, when General Kayani complained about the ineptitude and corruption of the government to Zardari and Gilani, and urged them to sack some ministers in the overblown sixty-member cabinet, many of them facing graft charges from the past, his interlocutors spurned his recommendation. This happened a few days after a local newspaper's disclosure that Gilani and twenty-five other cabinet ministers, including the finance minister, Hafiz Shaikh, paid no income tax, according to sworn affidavits submitted by the ministers to the Election Commission. Little wonder that Pakistan's tax revenue is among the lowest in the world. Only 1.4 per cent of Pakistani households pay income tax.[44]

Since, according to finance minister Hafiz Shaikh, there was just enough money left in the public treasury to pay two months' salaries to its employees, the government had to redirect the $500 million pledged by the US to improve the nation's infrastructure to cover its own running expenses. Of all the members of the international community, it is America that has the greatest interest in keeping Pakistan afloat financially and otherwise. Hence, it urged the IMF to rescue Pakistan. The IMF responded positively, but only after the Gilani government had agreed to cut subsidies on food and fuel, and to broaden its minute tax base.

Washington's abiding commitment to destroy Al Qaida and the Afghan Taliban rests on its alliance with Islamabad. That relationship starts to fray every time the Pentagon or the US-led NATO in Afghanistan violates Pakistan's sovereignty. This is what happened on 30 September – in a far more provocative manner than ever before. On that day, a NATO helicopter gunship from Afghanistan crossed into Pakistan in hot pursuit of insurgents and accidentally killed three paramilitaries of the Frontier Corps in the Kurram Agency. The government in Islamabad was livid. It calculated that if it overlooked this transgression, India might use the same logic of 'hot pursuit' or 'self-defence' to violate its territory, and stage its instant, multi-prong Operation Cold Start against Pakistan. This very realistic calculation underwrites the archlike structure of the geopolitical relationship between the adjoining countries.[45]

Pakistan therefore protested loudly. It closed the Khyber Pass to NATO trucks carrying supplies, including fuel, from Karachi to Afghanistan. The daily traffic of over five hundred vehicles stopped, and fuel tanks got stranded. This provided a golden opportunity to TTP activists to torch the tankers – an act that seemed to have popular support. Only when the US ambassador in Islamabad and the chairman of the Joint Chiefs of Staff at the Pentagon offered abject apologies did Pakistan reopen the border after ten days.

During the crisis, NATO was compelled to make more use of the Bolan and Khojak Passes near Quetta in Baluchistan. While not as popular as the Khyber Pass to their north, they have been used, in the past, as passages between Afghanistan and the Indian subcontinent.

11

A CORRUPT REGIME, A VENGEFUL TALIBAN

QUETTA WAS ON the receiving end of the exodus caused by the upheaval in Afghanistan in the 1980s. As a result, it expanded into a sprawling, multi-ethnic city of more than a million people, with Pushtuns forming the second largest group after the native Baluchis.

Due to its proximity to Afghanistan and Iran, the British had turned Quetta, endowed with a salubrious mountain climate, into a garrison town. In 1907, they enhanced its military status by establishing the army's Command and Staff College there. That legacy has lasted. Today, as before, the large army base in the cantonment area remains a restricted zone for civilians.

As you leave the city, the neat, precisely built army barracks give way to bustling bazaars and bleating sheep auctions along the crumbling, winding road, incongruously called the Regional Cooperation Development Highway. The sun-bleached terrain is ochre, dotted with dunes, peaks, cliffs, bluffs, and small valleys. In the intermittent craggy plains stand the hamlets of mud-walled houses. In contrast to the desiccated landscape, the large settlements carry such names as Gulistan (Place of Flowers) and Shelabagh (Garden of Shela). Equally, in the absence of a fort, Qila Abdullah (Fort of Abdullah) is a glaring misnomer.

An uphill climb takes the traveller first to the complex of the 55th Pishin Scouts' Light Infantry Regiment, containing a barracks, an armoury, stores and an officers' mess and then to the 7,500-foot (2,750 m)-high Khojak Pass, where a signpost points to 'Solitude Hut' – a perfect place for meditation. The downhill journey ends in the dusty, chaotic border town of Chaman (Urdu, 'Garden') in the midst of a 4,000-foot (1,200 m)-high plain, frequently racked by sandstorms. Of its twenty thousand inhabitants, several thousand are Hindus, often engaged in trade, both legitimate and illicit.

But these Hindus are a minuscule minority among the Pushtuns who inhabit the area in every direction, including across the frontier into Afghanistan, whose border town of Spin Boldak appears after four miles (6 km) of no-man's-land. A high concrete arch and a few dozen rifle-carrying border guards are the first signs of Afghanistan.

For more than a century after its demarcation in 1893, this international frontier remained porous. The Pushtuns belonging to the same tribe but living on opposite sides of the poorly marked Durand Line crossed freely. Given such laxity, it was easy for militant Pushtuns in Pakistan to enter Afghanistan to participate in the jihad against infidel forces and return home during winter when snowfalls hampered mobility. Later, when pressure from Washington on Islamabad led to a strict regime of border checks, tens of thousands of local Pushtuns acquired both a Pakistani national identity card and an Afghan passport.

The illicit trade in drugs, weapons and untaxed, imported consumer durables went on as before, with the smuggling barons continuing to pay prearranged bribes to immigration, customs, and security personnel. As a result, most private Toyota Land Cruisers, SUVs, and trucks were subject to a cursory search by frontier guards.

From Spin Boldak it is a three-hour ride by car to Kandahar, the second largest city in Afghanistan. As an oasis in the midst of a vast desert, Kandahar, ringed by lush green fields and fruit orchards, became the centre of the trade routes connecting the Indian subcontinent with Central Asia, the Persian Gulf region and the

Middle East. As a result, it has always been much coveted by ambitious generals, starting with Alexander of Macedonia.

'Kandahar has been the cusp,' writes Sarah Chayes, an American reporter based in the city since 2002. 'You can see this place as an implacable barrier, or you can see it as the place where the barrier is pierced, a valve that channels a flow of people, ideas, merchandise and wisdom.'[1] The last in a series of ideas channelled through Kandahar was the ideology of the Taliban, who succeeded the Afghan Mujahedin Alliance after the latter's degeneration into warring factions in 1992. So numerous were the sacrifices made by the Mujahedin in their jihad against the Soviets and their Afghan allies that the main square of Kandahar was renamed Martyrs' Square.

To the square's north-east lie the city's most cherished monuments. Foremost among them is the mausoleum of Ahmad Shah Durrani, the founder of present-day Afghanistan. A striking hexagonal structure with an arched entrance, capped by a greenish-blue dome guarded by six slender minarets, the mausoleum is approached through a gateway framed by cypress trees. It was Durrani's singular privilege to receive the Cloak of Prophet Muhammad as a present from the emir of Bukhara, Murad Beg, in 1768, when the two rulers ratified a treaty between their kingdoms. In Kandahar, the Cloak was stored in a trunk inside the main mosque of green marble exterior, tiled surfaces, and gilded archways. Only on rare occasions has it been displayed in public. One such was when a cholera epidemic ravaged the city in 1935.

The Cloak's next exposure came in April 1996, when the Taliban were in the ascendant. When their spiritual leader, Mullah Muhammad Omar, appeared wearing the cloak, a crowd of nearly 1,200 clerics and tribal leaders hailed him as the *Emir al Muminin* (Arabic, 'Commander of the Faithful') as well as the Emir of Afghanistan. Nobody in that gathering would have guessed then that in less than six years their revered luminary, bearing those two weighty titles (the former applying to all Muslims), would become a fugitive in Pakistan, totally dependent on the goodwill of its ISI directorate.

THE CHANGED ROLE OF MULLAH OMAR

What galled these Afghan mullahs and tribal chiefs further, in 2002, was that Omar's tormentor, US president George W. Bush, was brimming with confidence and preparing to oust the leader of another Muslim country, Iraq. On 20 March 2003, the American troops, backed by the British, mounted a fully fledged invasion of Iraq and overthrew the regime of President Saddam Hussein. After Bush had declared 'Mission Accomplished' on 1 May, his consul, Paul Bremer, administered the occupied Iraq until June 2004.

During the two-and-a-half-year period from Omar's flight from Kandahar to the end of Bremer's tenure, the United States was almost totally engaged first in defeating and then in ruling Iraq. This provided the ISI with a golden opportunity to revive the Afghan Taliban under the founding leadership of Mullah Omar. Paradoxically, two diametrically opposed processes got going simultaneously: stabilizing Afghanistan under the guardianship of the US-led NATO, with a nominal United Nations stamp of approval in the form of an International Security Assistance Force (ISAF) to assist in the 'maintenance of security'; and the revival of the Taliban.

The Taliban announced its rebirth dramatically a week before the first anniversary of 9/11 with a bomb explosion in Kabul, which caused fifteen fatalities, and an assassination attempt on Hamid Karzai, acting interim president of Afghanistan since December 2001, in Kandahar.[2] While the Pentagon trumpeted its swift victory in Iraq in March–April 2003, the Taliban staged guerrilla attacks in the southern provinces of Helmand and Zabul adjoining Pakistan – the Taliban's prime source of volunteers, cash and arms, and the site of several training camps. Mullah Omar reconstituted his Shura Council of ten members and revived specialist committees for military, political, financial, and cultural affairs.

By the end of 2003, the Taliban's military and political committees had established their jurisdiction over five of Zabul's seven districts. From there they would extend their control to almost half of Uruzgan,

Helmand, and Kandahar provinces.[3] The Taliban's fighting force of 6,700 was commanded by Mullah Mansour Dadullah. A one-legged veteran of the anti-Soviet jihad, the black-turbaned mullah with thick eyebrows and sensuous mouth was given a seat on the Taliban's Shura Council long before the Pentagon's 2001 air campaign against Afghanistan.

THE FLEDGLING POST-TALIBAN STATE OF AFGHANISTAN

Whatever progress was made in reconstituting the state of Afghanistan was done under the nominal aegis of the UN. The impotence of the Karzai government was embarrassingly obvious. In December 2002, Karzai signed a decree disbanding assorted militias, now 100,000 strong, and announced a one-year deadline for warlords to give up their weapons. Nothing happened for ten months. It was only when ISAF swung into action in October 2003 that the first phase of rounding up tanks and artillery guns began.

A worse fate awaited another decree of Karzai also issued in December 2002. He ordered the immediate formation of the Afghan National Army (ANA) of seven thousand men – expanding to seventy thousand in seven years. No such force came into being then. The powerful regional warlords refused to cooperate, fearing, rightly, that a national army would undercut their authority. Given their strong links with the CIA, the warlords were able to defy Karzai.

Furthermore, well-meaning UN recommendations proved unrealistic since they clashed with Afghan tradition and history. For instance, the UN specified that the newly formed army should reflect the ethnic composition of Afghanistan: 38 per cent Pushtun, 25 per cent Tajik, 19 per cent Hazara, 8 per cent Uzbek, and the rest 10 per cent. However, the UN estimates were inaccurate. Pushtuns formed 46–48 per cent of the population, and Hazaras only 9–10 per cent. In any case, there was no tradition of Hazaras or Uzbeks soldiering. That was the preserve of Pushtuns in the main, with a subsidiary role for Tajiks. As the main supporters of the anti-Taliban Northern

Alliance, Tajiks had emerged as competitors to Pushtuns in the military. Little wonder that the ethnic composition of the army in mid-2004 was Pushtuns 53 per cent of the ranks, and 32 per cent of the officer corps, with Tajiks garnering 37 per cent and 56 per cent respectively. The remaining ethnic groups had a negligible share.[4]

On the political front, it was the UN that had sponsored the emergency Loya Jirga of 1,501 members in Kabul in June 2002 to elect the interim president, agree the structure of the government, and appoint a commission to draft the constitution. At Washington's behest, warlords were put on a par with the thirty-two provincial governors, all of them occupying the front seats at the emergency gathering. This was meant to demonstrate that the notoriously corrupt, rapacious warlords were endorsing the unfolding political process. With seven-eighths of the delegates voting for him, Karzai had his interim presidency confirmed. His twenty-nine-strong cabinet maintained the status quo, with General Muhammad Qasim Fahim as defence minister and other Tajiks retaining, inter alia, the foreign, interior, and intelligence ministries. The job of the National Security Directorate went to Amrullah Saleh, a close aide to the late Ahmad Shah Masoud. As in the past, he kept a suspicious eye on Pakistan and its designs on Afghanistan, and looked benignly on India. His policy of giving equal weight to Pakistan and India thus reflected the interconnectedness of the three leading countries of South Asia.

Since India was one of the three major powers that had backed the Northern Alliance with cash, weapons, and military advisers during the Taliban rule in Kabul, the Tajik ministers returned the favour by awarding government contracts to Indian companies. These included building or rebuilding highways, including the one connecting Kandahar with Spin Boldak. Such highly visible projects helped to create a positive image of India among Afghans. Within two years of the Karzai government assuming office, Delhi began implementing its $500 million reconstruction plan, and initiated training programmes for Afghan civil servants and educationalists. In January 2004, it reopened its consulates in Kandahar, Jalalabad, Mazar-e

Sharif, and Herat, closed since 1979. Delhi's moves were designed to generate goodwill, with the prospect of reaping political dividends later and challenging the dominant influence Islamabad had acquired in Afghanistan.

By contrast, most Afghans were unaware of the large reconstruction projects being funded by America. One example was the reconstruction of the 190-mile (300 km) Kabul–Kandahar section of the national highway, which was completed post-haste at a huge expense of $90 million. Unluckily for Washington, it was widely perceived as a project designed to facilitate safe and swift movement of the Western and Afghan troops rather than to benefit local people.

Pakistan eyed India's activities in Afghanistan with intense suspicion. It viewed Delhi's opening of consulates in January 2004 near its border as a ploy to establish an espionage network masterminded by its intelligence agency, the Research and Analysis Wing (RAW). It believed that RAW had been charged with stoking up the irredentist Baluchi nationalist movement as Delhi's quid pro quo for Islamabad's backing for the separatist movement in Indian Kashmir.

By January 2004, Afghanistan's own intelligence agency, the National Security Directorate, was operational. And the 550-member Constitutional Loya Jirga had endorsed the draft constitution. The Islamic Republic of Afghanistan was adopted as the official title of the country. The constitution outlawed any legislation considered repugnant to Islam, but refrained from describing the Sharia as the sole source of legislation. It specified a strong, centralized government led by a president, assisted by two vice-presidents, with the former authorized to appoint all provincial governors and police chiefs and to act as the commander-in-chief. The bicameral parliament was to consist of the 249-member *Wolesi Jirga* (People's Assembly) and the 102-strong *Meshrano Jirga* (Elders' Assembly), with a third of the latter's members nominated by the president. The People's Assembly was empowered to impeach the chief executive.

In December 2004, Karzai was elected president under the new constitution with a little over 55 per cent of the ballots on an impressive voter turnout of 73 per cent. His vice-presidents were Ahmad Zia Masoud, a Tajik, and Karim Khalili, a Shia Hazara. Khalili had good reason to be proud of the new constitution, which broke new ground by recognizing the minority Shia Jaafari jurisdiction along with that of the majority Sunni Hanafi.

THE TALIBAN PHOENIX RISES

Just as the Constitutional Loya Jirga adopted the new constitution in Kabul, the Taliban began implementing its plan to seize the districts around Kandahar as a prologue to capturing the country's second largest urban centre. By then, the size of the US military in Afghanistan, charged with defeating America's enemies as part of the Pentagon's Operation Enduring Freedom, had risen to ten thousand soldiers from the initial three hundred Special Operations Force (SOF) troops.

Faced with the Taliban's steady advance, the Americans decided to confront the enemy in firefights as and when they could. In one such encounter in late 2003, a battalion of the Taliban engaged with them, and then withdrew to Baluchistan in Pakistan. That is, within two years of their flight from Afghanistan, the Taliban had reacquired enough confidence and clout to engage in an occasional firefight with their foe, secure in the knowledge that they had safe havens in the adjoining Pakistan.

Following the end of Washington's direct rule of Iraq in mid-2004, the Bush administration decided to invest more interest and cash in Afghanistan. As a result, the strength of US troops increased to 17,000. The number of American bases rose to twenty-six from eleven a year earlier, their headquarters being at Bagram airbase. By then, the US National Security Agency unit stationed at Bagram had intercepted communications between the Afghan Taliban commanders and ISI officers in Chaman. Organizing safe passage for the Taliban, who were transported in Pakistani army vehicles carrying civilian registration numbers, with their original dark grey colour masked by paint of a different hue.

As a quid pro quo, the Taliban's supreme Shura Council adjusted its policy to align it with the ISI's. For instance, though it denounced the presidential poll in December 2004, it did not order its cadres to hinder voter registration. Pakistan's ISI, run by General Ashfaq Parvez Kayani, wanted to strengthen Hamid Karzai, a Pushtun, against the powerful Tajik-dominated anti-Pakistan Northern Alliance. Also, field reports to the Shura Council indicated a strong inclination among local communities to participate in the election because it held the promise of being free and fair. Following Karzai's victory, the Taliban took similar stances on the subsequent parliamentary and provincial council polls.

The Pentagon integrated SOF units into the regular army under the new title of Combined Joint Task Force 180 and placed it under a general. This rebranding coincided with the abandoning of the SOF's strategy of hard and soft components. Freed from the rules that apply to regular army and Marine troops, SOF soldiers acted in an arbitrary fashion. They broke into homes in the middle of the night, roughed up suspects, and used gratuitous violence in their pursuit of suspected terrorists and guerrillas. In their soft mode, working in small units, they would spend weeks in a small area to cultivate friendly relations with locals by offering generous bribes but also by funding the building of wells, schools, and clinics while gathering information about the enemy. This method was effective but time-consuming.

Keen to make progress swiftly, the Pentagon's decision makers switched to a strategy of 'clear and sweep'. From now on, they ordered, Combined Joint Task Force 180 would stage sweeps of a large number of districts. In practice, this meant US soldiers descending on a village, lining up all the men and boys, and searching and interrogating them as if they were terrorists – thereby alienating them. In any case, covering Afghanistan fully according to the new plan required 200,000-plus troops, nearly twelve times the present strength. The only way this could be achieved was by expanding the fledgling Afghan army and ensuring that it stayed united and loyal.

Once the CIA had stopped its subsidies to warlords, the Pentagon raised its budget for the creation of the ANA – but only as an auxiliary force to accompany US soldiers in the field. To ensure there was no deviation from its policy, the Pentagon embedded mentors in the ANA down to company (100–150 soldiers) level.

Given the incredibly high illiteracy rate and frequent smoking of hashish, recruitment and retention in the ANA proved problematic. The rates of attrition and desertion were uncommonly high. Initially, the Pentagon barred the ANA from operating on its own above the company level, and denied logistics or communications support to any ANA battalion (average strength: six hundred troops) attached to an American or NATO unit. It was not until the latter half of 2005, when the Americans began pursuing Taliban fighters into their sanctuaries, that they permitted ANA units to operate alone above the company level. Later, when they dispatched ANA troops to battle Taliban partisans, the Afghans suffered a casualty rate of 15 per cent, an unbearably high figure.

As a result, the desertion rate in the ANA went up even higher. Most Afghans signed up because the salary of $240 a month was attractive. But when it came to combat, they did not know what they were fighting for: Was it for the Afghan constitution, President Karzai, or Afghanistan per se? Being mostly illiterate, they could not read the constitution. Loyalty to a weak president at the head of an incompetent and corrupt government was highly unlikely. In any case, the concept of loyalty to an entity above the tribe or ethnic group was alien to most soldiers.

In an interview with a Beirut-based journalist, Ghaith Abdul-Ahad, an Afghan infantryman revealed a common experience: 'When the Taliban attack they are so close that we talk to each other on the radios,' he said. 'They shout "Allahu Akbar, Allahu Akbar". We ask them why they are fighting us – we are Afghans like them. They tell us that we are infidels because we are helping the foreigners occupy our country.' 'What do you tell them?' asked Abdul-Ahad. 'Nothing,' came the reply. 'They are right.'[5]

In the political arena, when Fahim failed to get the vice-presidency or a cabinet seat, thus losing his power of patronage, the eight-year-old Tajik-dominated Northern Alliance disintegrated. In contrast, its nemesis, the Taliban, grew in strength. Between the winters of 2002–03 and 2005–06, the number of Taliban militia trebled to twelve thousand. Learning from the experiences of the Sunni insurgents in Iraq, the Taliban had resorted to using improvised explosive devices (IEDs) against foreign troops, thus adding a lethal dimension to the asymmetrical war they waged. On an average, they detonated ten IEDs a week. Parts were provided by pro-Taliban elements active in the neighbouring Baluchistan and Khyber Pakhtunkhwa provinces in Pakistan, and then assembled by the Taliban in Afghanistan.

This division of labour was one of the several differences between the Taliban, Mark I and the Taliban, Mark II.

THE TALIBAN, MARK II

'We went from the jihad to the government and now we are in the jihad again,' said Maulavi Abdul Halim, a mullah and part-time Taliban fighter in the southern town of Ghazni. 'We have learned from the mistakes we committed. Lots of our leaders have experience in the jihad and in the government. The leaders are the same leaders but the fighters are new and they don't want to be like those who ruled and committed mistakes in the past.'[6] This neatly sums up the difference between the pioneering Taliban and its post-2001 version. In the mid-1990s, the Taliban movement arose on Afghan soil in the midst of a bloody civil war. It gained ground by using a combination of brutal force, aided actively by the ISI, and generous bribes to tribal leaders to switch sides, with the cash coming from the Saudi intelligence agency, Istikhabarat. Now, Taliban leaders could operate only from Pakistan, and had to struggle in an Afghanistan controlled by US-led NATO forces, its anti-Taliban Afghan allies and a plethora of warlords on the CIA's payroll – without any cash from Riyadh. As such, they devised a gradualist strategy of fostering a cadre in Pakistan to be introduced in small batches into the rural areas of Afghanistan's Pushtun-majority region covering twelve provinces.

One salient element common to both versions of the Taliban was the vital role played by Pakistan's ISI. The ISI was all the more indispensable for Mark II of the Taliban. Its recruits came largely from the madrasas based in Baluchistan and Khyber Pakhtunkhwa, and their training occurred in the camps located in these provinces and Pakistan's seven semi-autonomous Federally Administered Tribal Agencies (FATA): (from north to south) Bajuar, Mohmand, Khyber, Orakzai, Kurram, North Waziristan, and South Waziristan.

In a typical madrasa in Pakistan or Afghanistan, a student spent twelve years studying the Quran and various other aspects of Islam. Once he had memorized the holy book and acquired the title of *qari* (Arabic, 'reader' or 'reciter'), he was qualified to join the Taliban movement and be trained to join the jihad against alien infidels and their agents, such as President Karzai. The six-week training programme was as much political as it was military, with the full implications of jihad explained. Those who showed promise were dispatched to war-torn Iraq via Baluchistan and Iran for a further three months' training to qualify as instructors on graduation.

Repeating its practice during the anti-Soviet jihad, the ISI controlled a certain proportion of Taliban commanders directly. Such actions of the Taliban as razing schools would later be attributed to these 'rogue' commanders by loyalists to the Taliban supreme Shura Council. Overall, the ISI gave a free hand to the Shura Council to manage logistics and safe havens, and, if necessary, to make alliances with like-minded organizations.

In the mid- and late 1990s, the Taliban, Mark I had emerged as a singular organization with a self-granted mandate to overpower the warring factions. Now Taliban, Mark II leaders forged an alliance with the Hizb-e Islami of Hikmatyar, with its 1,500 militia based in eastern Afghanistan, and maintained close contacts with the Al Qaida leadership, ensconced in the mountains of FATA and commanding two thousand battle-hardened fighters. Since Al Qaida was deeply involved in fomenting and maintaining the insurgency in Iraq, it became the main channel for passing on the experience and expertise of its partisans in Iraq to the Taliban's cadres. The principal element of this expertise was the production of IEDs and suicide vests. On the strategic level, Taliban leaders came to adopt the view that, since their struggle was part of the broader international jihad, they should focus on gaining the backing of the Islamic community worldwide and pay scant attention to the non-Muslim world. Equally important, they came to share Al Qaida's global jihadist agenda of keeping the Americans and other Westerners engaged in Afghanistan, as they were also in Iraq, and wear them down. Their earlier culturally oriented, ultra-orthodox interpretation of Sunni Islam now became more political and internationalist.

Knowingly or otherwise, the leaders of the Taliban, Mark II ended up pursuing a blend of the strategies of Mao Zedong – infiltrate villages to build up a base in the countryside, then surround urban centres and seize them – and of the anti-Soviet jihadists of the 1980s who deployed all possible means to show their foe's political decision makers that their objectives were either prohibitively expensive and/or unachievable. The latter strategy had involved provoking the Soviets to resort to air strikes which, by causing civilian casualties, had stoked anti-Soviet feeling. Now the US-led NATO forces ended up following in the footsteps of the Soviets.

Applying Maoist tactics, the Taliban cadres, arriving from Pakistan, first sought the permission of village and tribal elders to enter an area dominated by a particular tribe. Once they had obtained this, they had little difficulty getting along with villagers as they shared rural Afghan mores and culture. This approach was remarkably similar to what the US SOF units did. But the differences between American troops – racially apart and totally unfamiliar with the local language and culture, but carrying wads of dollars – and Taliban partisans were stark.

If the Taliban newcomers noticed rivalry between local tribes or leading personalities, they exploited it to their advantage. If concord prevailed, they cooperated with the elders to focus on the grudges of the community that had either not been articulated properly by traditional leaders or ignored by ineffective and corrupt bureaucrats. By being vociferous in their anti-government rhetoric, the Taliban expanded their popular base. The occasional conflicts between the tribes – a leitmotif in Afghan history – weakened the traditional leaders and presented an opportunity for the Taliban, claiming to transcend tribalism, to set up a new base or to consolidate an old one.

All along, they sought suitable places to hide weapons and ammunition. They also set up an intelligence network of informers, spies, and double agents to undermine pro-Kabul and pro-Washington elements. To rid the countryside of anti-Taliban elements, they used the age-old method of delivering written threats distributed anonymously at night. Over time that drove their adversaries to the cities and big towns. The situation deteriorated so rapidly in the Pushtun region that, by 2004, Afghan soldiers had ceased patrolling rural areas and withdrawn to administrative centres in districts and provinces.

Given their dedication to Islam and commitment to enforce the Sharia, the Taliban readily gained the backing of the village mullah, a literate and respected member of the community who depended primarily on voluntary donations for his family's upkeep. The mullah often became a recruiting agent for the Taliban. His criticism of the Kabul government rested on the perception that it was venal and reliant on foreign infidels for its survival.

The Karzai administration was aware of its unpopularity among mullahs in the country's nearly forty thousand villages. One solution was to co-opt rural mullahs by putting them on the state payroll. But it lacked funds to accomplish this. Moreover, any such move would have raised expectations among village and tribal elders of being turned into state employees. That would have been beyond the means of even a moderately prosperous government. Therefore, it was often only in the cities that some clerics publicly spoke out in favour of the president and his administration, For example, they pointed out that Karzai had appointed an ultra-conservative cleric, Maulavi Fazl Haq Shinwari, as head of the Supreme Court, and that he had permitted the Council of Ulema to establish its own television channel.[7]

As the insurgency gathered steam, Karzai decided to placate the religious lobby. He signed a decree in 2006 to establish the Public Morality Police. But lacking adequate funds, this failed to impinge on the popular mind in urban areas. For its part, the Taliban targeted pro-government clerics. At first they intimidated them with the traditional handwritten 'night letters', which were widely distributed or nailed to the door of the target's house or the mosque where he preached. If the cleric continued with his pro-government line despite such warnings, the Taliban assassinated him. Of the twenty clergy killed by the Taliban between mid-2005 and mid-2006, twelve were based in Kandahar.

However, the Taliban were not alone in being violent towards their adversaries. US forces were hardly angels of mercy in their actions in rural Afghanistan. Between June 2004 and May 2005, for instance, there were 113 reported human-rights violations by American troops.[8]

THE REVIVED TALIBAN ENTERS THE IT AGE

The revived Taliban's resort to the age-old method of night letters contrasted sharply with their adoption of the latest information technology and its lifting of the ban on music and photography with which its earlier incarnation was closely, and scandalously, associated.

In their propaganda, the Taliban, Mark II made much use of music and songs which have always been hugely popular with Afghans, rural or urban. Having abandoned their proscription on photography and human images, they hooked up with pro-Taliban businessmen and technicians in Pakistan to churn out hundreds of audio cassettes,

CDs and DVDs. These were sold in bazaars at affordable prices. In addition, the Taliban set up a website to disseminate their ideas and news stories, not to mention their own Voice of Shariat Radio with mobile transmitters in three provinces.

The Taliban's website was updated hourly by Lukman, a multilingual Pushtun student of Kabul University, with a finely trimmed moustache, who was a member of the Taliban's culture committee. 'We monitor the situation and when we see any issue that can provide propaganda to the Taliban, we raise it and create awareness amongst the people: issues like the occupation and how they terrorize the people, the corruption of the government, anything that can help the cause of the Taliban,' he said in a rare interview to a visiting Arab journalist. He was too young to have been with the Taliban when they wielded power. 'Lots of my university friends are with the Taliban not because they are Taliban but because they are against this government and the occupation,' explained Lukman. 'No one expected the Taliban to be back, but when the normal people saw the corruption of the government, when they saw that the warlords are back, people started supporting the resistance.' He claimed that the Taliban had informers 'even in the streets'. His friend, Abdul Rahman, was a recruiter for the Taliban. 'I convince friends inside and outside the university that the Taliban are coming. We use all the facilities we have, our words and our pens to recruit for the movement, in the university, the bazaar and everywhere in the city.' Rahman added. 'We work cautiously, we talk to the people as if we are talking about [general] political and daily issues. The government is too weak to follow us or monitor us.'[9]

In the countryside, it soon became standard practice for Taliban commanders to send a video camera or a mobile phone equipped with a camera with any unit assigned to carry out an operation – be it an ambush, detonating an IED, or the killing or injuring of enemy soldiers. The cameraman was instructed to focus on the foe's faltering performance or desperate cries for help. Such images were then incorporated into DVDs containing commentaries and sermons, urging the faithful to join the anti-foreigner jihad.

A study of a batch of DVDs, picked at random, showed that the Taliban, Mark II were pursuing a multipoint agenda. They addressed issues affecting Muslims at both macro and micro levels, and focused on moulding Afghan and Muslim popular opinion, which stood far apart from public opinion in the West. Their basic argument was that America's invasion of Afghanistan was similar to the Soviet Union's, and that the response should be the same: the staging of a jihad. But unlike the Soviet action, America's aggression against Afghanistan was part of a global Christian war against Islam. Surveys showed that, by 2006, many Afghans had come to believe that the presence of Western troops was part of 'an attempt to dominate the Muslim world'.[10] It was the Christian world that had installed the Karzai government in Kabul, which was a mere puppet. In their search for a legitimate authority, true Muslims should turn to the ulema, particularly in villages.

To imprint viewers' minds with unforgettable visuals, some DVDs displayed stomach-churning images of the devastation that the Pentagon's relentless bombing in Afghanistan and Iraq had inflicted on human beings, animals, and the economic infrastructure. They also highlighted the throwing of the Holy Quran into the toilets at the Guantánamo Bay detention centre by American soldiers as well as the denigration of Prophet Muhammad in cartoons in Danish and other Western newspapers. Turning to Afghanistan, they claimed that, instead of burying the corpses of the Taliban mujahedin, US troops desecrated them by burning them, and that the soldiers in the US-commanded and funded ANA were barred from praying.

Another set of DVDs highlighted the resistance by the Taliban in Afghanistan, and by other jihadist organizations elsewhere in the world, to the depredations being inflicted on the Muslim world by the Christian powers. Reports on the jihads in Iraq, Palestine, South Lebanon, and Pakistan's tribal belt were replete with powerful images. Next came upbeat accounts of successful guerrilla operations by the Taliban mujahedin interspersed with interviews with the perpetrators. Far more focused were the farewell speeches by prospective suicide bombers, who reiterated that those who die in a jihad will be looked after by Allah in heaven. The purpose of such DVDs was to gain recruits for further suicide bombings.

The overarching message of these DVDs was this: Since we, the resisting mujahedin, know the terrain and the people, and the enemy does not, and since we are deploying low-technology tactics against the enemy's hi-tech weaponry, we will outlast him. Because our faith in Islam is deep, our resolve unshakable, and time is on our side, we are destined to prevail in the long run.

This message seems to have been grasped widely in the Pushtun countryside, where most people did not want to alienate the Taliban, reckoning that they would return to power, albeit in moderated form. So if there were three sons in a rural family, the parents assigned one to the jihad while the others continued to work in the fields. It was an insurance policy that many households in the countryside came to adopt over the years. Even in towns and cities, a growing number of residents became reluctant to ally themselves with the weak and graft-ridden authorities, thinking that the Taliban might win ultimately.

THE WEAKNESSES OF NATO AND THE KARZAI GOVERNMENT

As for the NATO forces in Afghanistan, they had nothing to match the Taliban's audio cassettes, CDs and DVDs. Their 'Psychological Operations (Psy-Ops)' campaign consisted mostly of billboards and leaflets. Their propagandists printed wicked-looking cartoon poppies with fanged teeth to illustrate the evils of opium production, and concocted mangled pictures to warn the locals of the hazards of planting IEDs or interfering with them. In the Taliban-controlled areas, NATO resorted to dropping leaflets from the air. In other zones, its fortnightly publication, *Voice of Freedom*, printed in Pushtu, Dari, and English, on glossy paper and given away free, highlighted the progress the Kabul government was making in many fields – it came in handy as wrapping paper to the vendors of fatty kebabs.

More seriously, NATO and US troops, being ignorant of Afghan culture and history, showed scant sensitivity to such local norms as treating women's quarters as no-go areas and refraining from mishandling men in front of their wives and children. Their disdainful ways alienated local communities and dispirited anti-Taliban elements. They operated in an environment where the central authority lacked sufficient civil servants, policemen, and informers to provide public services to the scattered rural communities and to receive reliable information on security and other matters. The quality of state employees was poor.

A policeman is the most visible and authoritative symbol of any government. In post-Taliban Afghanistan, the new Afghan National Police (ANP) consisted of the warlords' militias dressed in Western uniforms and trained first by the German officers and then Dyncorp, an American security company. Given the 90 per cent illiteracy rate among recruits, most could not even read a car licence plate number. They received only three to eight weeks of training, which was focused on dealing with insurgents rather than maintaining law and order. Hired locally, recruits were trained nationally and then returned to their home base. It was therefore very likely that a typical policeman had a brother, cousin, or uncle with the Taliban. As such, before any anti-insurgent operation, a local cop would often call his close relative by mobile phone and warn him that the police were planning a raid. The size of the ANP was small. In a typical district in the south, there would be no more than forty policemen, with only fifteen available for patrol duties. Even before harassment by the Taliban, they rarely visited rural communities.

On the other side, the cadres of the Taliban, Mark II were different from their predecessors. In contrast to the harsh manner in which the Mark I administration had implemented its puritanical decrees and the brutality with which it had treated its adversaries, the new cadres were required to follow the code of conduct set down by Mullah Omar in his *Layeha* (Pushtu, 'Rules'). He distributed this pamphlet to the thirty-three members of the supreme Shura Council. It listed thirty rules. The salient ones were: Former mujahedin with bad reputations will not be permitted to rejoin; harassing of innocent persons is prohibited; any dispute with the local people must be resolved either by senior commanders or the Council of Ulema or elders; searching houses and confiscating arms without the specific permission of a senior commander is forbidden; captured arms must be distributed equitably; selling weapons and other equipment is forbidden; prisoners must be passed on to the commanders; suspected spies must be given a fair trial before being punished; and a jihadist can move to another district only after securing the permission of his current commander.[11]

The strict application of the Layeha enhanced the Taliban's popular standing. They were also helped, inadvertently, by an abrupt switch in the Pentagon's counter-insurgency strategy. Initially, the Pentagon had opted to counter the enemy's infiltration and consolidation in rural areas with aggressive actions, which made villagers curse the Americans and turn against them. Realizing its mistake, it now adopted a policy of providing economic development and assistance to tackle poverty, which it considered the root cause of the insurgency. The downside of this change was that, once US troops stopped raiding suspected villages, the Taliban got the chance to consolidate their hold there.

Following their consolidation in four southern provinces, the Taliban, Mark II set up their parallel administration there. At the top, each province had its own Taliban governor, military leader, and Shura Council. Below them were district commanders, with each dividing his force into smaller units of five to fifty men. Later, the supreme Taliban Shura Council divided Afghanistan into five military zones, each under a senior commander, with two others, located in Quetta and Peshawar, charged with supervising logistics in Afghanistan and Pakistan, respectively.

The provincial leadership followed the guidelines laid out by Mullah Omar and his council. But within the general framework the leaders of a province or district were given latitude to exploit the enemy's weakness – the ultimate criterion for any adopted tactic being the end result. Knowing the lie of the land, local leaders were in the best position to decide what to do and how. As in any insurgent force, whether secular or religious, ideology and commitment trumped professional skills, with enthusiastic but inexperienced recruits having a greater say than their counterparts in a traditional armed force.

If a Taliban unit was operating near a highway, it focused on setting up IEDs or staging ambushes against the enemy rather than engaging in firefights. The mountainous terrain and the absence of railways helped insurgents. All NATO supplies had to be transported by road across deserts and treacherous mountain passes. To stop a long convoy, all an insurgent unit had to do was to hit the first and last vehicles. For helicopter-borne NATO forces, it was difficult to spot small groups of guerrillas moving swiftly in the craggy mountains, with individuals hiding behind rocks or inside caves.

Motorcycles became a vital element in the Taliban strategy, deployed as a fast, easy-to-manoeuvre means of transportation, reconnaissance, communication, and battlefield coordination. Their role remained unaltered as the war dragged on. That was not the case with satellite phones, first used in 2003 alongside field radios. Their combined use enabled a commander to coordinate the activities of his company, which his predecessor in the 1990s had been unable to do. But, equipped with sophisticated radio-monitoring devices, NATO forces were able to pinpoint Taliban positions and target them with artillery or air strikes. This forced the Taliban to discard satellite phones and revert to coded messages and torch signals, and to use Icom scanners to monitor NATO's radio and telephone communications.

By 2005, Taliban partisans had learned to assemble in large numbers and disperse swiftly in fours and fives, heading for mountainous terrain or taking cover in ditches when NATO soldiers called for air strikes by warplanes or helicopter gunships. Taliban commanders had procured copies of the Russian-made Strela 1 and 2 shoulder-fired missiles, and trained their men to fire them. However, these weapons proved virtually useless against the high-flying unmanned aerial vehicles that were increasingly deployed by the CIA.

Nonetheless, the Taliban scored a hit against a low-flying helicopter on 30 May 2007 in Helmand province. But, sticking to its blanket statement that insurgents did not possess heat-seeking missiles, a NATO spokesman attributed the insurgents' success to a strike by rocket-propelled grenades. The lie was exposed in one of the classified field reports leaked by the anti-secrecy organization WikiLeaks in July 2010.[12]

The Taliban's armed resistance to foreign occupation went hand in hand with their administration of the areas they held. They focused on providing services to the people. Banditry and land disputes were the major problems in rural areas. The Taliban enhanced their popularity by targeting criminal bands who routinely gained a free hand by bribing the police.

Corruption was rife in the poorly paid, undisciplined police force. With monthly salaries varying between $20 and $70, policemen resorted to extracting money from the public through illegal means, the most common being road tolls at checkpoints.[13] A classified US field report, leaked to leading publications in America, Britain, and Germany, provided a telling illustration of such practices. An American investigator working with the local police investigator in Paktia province detained all checkpoint policemen accused of extortion. 'While waiting, I asked the seven patrolmen we detained to sit and relax while we sorted through a problem without ever mentioning why they were being detained,' wrote the American. 'Three of the patrolmen responded by saying that they had only taken money from the truck drivers to buy fuel for their generator.' Two days later when the American followed up, he was told by the Afghan police officers that the case had been dropped because the witness reports had all been lost.[14]

Police commanders imposed taxes on crops of poppies, hashish, and marijuana, and exempted poppy fields from eradication if their owners bribed them. In unsafe areas, they demanded a bribe to let a convoy of fuel trucks pass; otherwise, they informed the Taliban. Most commanders filched salaries of non-existent lawmen fraudulently listed on their roll-call – an easy exercise because most policemen, being illiterate, signed receipts for their salaries with their thumb prints. (Only a forensic expert could distinguish one thumb print from another.) Since police had maximum opportunities for graft, the posts of district and provincial police chiefs were highly prized, with the going price for securing one being upward of $100,000 – especially in border provinces. There, the appointees soon recovered such sums illicitly by skimming off customs duties and taking bribes from smugglers.

According to the classified US field reports leaked by WikiLeaks, the police chief of Paktia province openly extracted cash from his subordinates, and allowed the police commander of the capital, Gardez, to set up illegal checkpoints around the town. By reporting falsely that his men had engaged in a firefight, the police chief in Zurmat, Paktia, received thousands of rounds of ammunition, which he then sold on to a bazaar merchant. Another provincial police commissioner purloined food and uniforms, leaving his men cold and underfed during the winter.[15]

A citizen needed to grease the palms of government or public sector employees to acquire an electricity connection or get a relative out of jail often arrested on trumped-up charges. Obtaining a driving licence required fifty-one steps, with that many bureaucrats to be bribed. When the interior ministry reduced the number of steps, the 'tip' for each shot up.

If an Afghan found himself in a dispute about the legal possession of his house, he would probably be required to pay the judge $20,000 to $30,000, depending on the value of the property, to have it resolved in his favour. The judicial system as a whole was rotten. 'If you take your case to a government court it will take you four to five years to finish because the longer the case goes the more bribes you pay,' said Shirjan, a village elder with a wispy goatee near Kunduz. 'So the officials don't want you to finish. Whereas if you take your case to the Taliban court they will give judgment in one day and according to God's ruling [the Sharia]. So the people go to the

Taliban.'[16] It is noteworthy that the majority of people in the Kunduz area belong to non-Pushtun ethnic groups.

There was yet another source of embezzlement – financial aid provided by foreign governments and NGOs. To reach its target, this had to pass through the hands of government officials and/or village and tribal elders. It was estimated that up to half of all economic aid disappeared into the pockets of these intermediaries, turning the upper crust of society, rural as well as urban, into parasites.

Another major source of kickbacks originated in the funds dispensed by the Pentagon. These were spent on transporting supplies of water, food, fuel, and other basic necessities to more than four hundred US-led ISAF camps, forward operating bases and combat outposts in Afghanistan – not to mention the three hundred ANA and ANP bases. In its report 'Warlord Inc.', released in June 2010, the US House Subcommittee for National Security alluded to the $2.16 billion annual contract, called 'Host Nation Trucking', for ferrying supplies to American bases in Afghanistan.[17] This sum was divided equally among six major transport companies. 'The principal private security sub-contractors are warlords, strongmen, commanders and militia leaders who compete with the Afghan central government for power and authority,' the report noted. The Pentagon left it to the contractors to protect supply convoys. They in turn hired the services of warlords, the three most important being Commander Ruhullah, Matiullah Khan and Abdul Razziq. Commanding six hundred gunmen, Ruhullah worked for Watan Risk Management (WRM) owned by Rashid and Ratib Popal, cousins of President Karzai. Matiullah Khan's 2000-strong militia controlled the insurgent-infested 71-mile (115 km)-stretch between Kandahar and Tarin Kowt. And Abdul Razziq was the border police commander in Spin Boldak. If a transport contractor refused to pay, the gunmen of these warlords targeted its convoys.[18]

The reality was that almost all the contractors had to use the Kabul–Kandahar corridor to deliver supplies to the south and south-east, the major areas of fighting, and the west. Over this stretch of the highway only WRM could provide security. And it worked with Commander Ruhullah, who charged $1,500 per truck for safe passage. Ruhullah would wait until there were hundreds of trucks ready to move south. Then he would put his fighters, armed with AK-47 assault rifles and rocket-propelled grenades, in four-wheel drives and pickups to serve as escorts. Even the NCL Logistics Company, owned by Hamed Wardak, a son of defence minister General Abdul Rahim Wardak, depended on WRM for the Kabul–Kandahar corridor and loaded its cargo in WRM trucks. Ruhullah reportedly worked both sides. A well-informed US military official in Kabul estimated that overall 10–20 per cent of the amount that the Pentagon spent on 'Host Nation Trucking' ended up with the Taliban.[19] In their direct dealings, the Taliban charged a quarter to a third of the $3,500 paid per truck by the Pentagon or NATO to private transport companies ferrying supplies to the troops for safe passage. These payments went directly to the central treasury, which paid modest salaries to the Taliban's policemen and judges.

The rural folk could not help comparing the spartan lifestyle of Taliban employees and leaders with the extravagant ways of the predatory, venal government officials. As it was, housing provincial and district government offices in the fortified compounds serving as American military bases inhibited free communication with citizens. This created a wide gulf between ordinary Afghans and the Karzai government.

The Taliban, Mark II had also acquired an external source of income. It received donations from the Afghan diaspora working in the oil-rich Gulf States, where sympathetic local businessmen also contributed funds. In addition, there was an assorted collection of donors in Pakistan – a vast pool of an estimated five million Pushtuns living in Karachi, rich Pushtun businessmen in Peshawar and Quetta, and the pro-Taliban jihadists in the armed forces and intelligence agencies.

In due course, the growing of poppies and the trade in their derivatives would become one of the major sources of revenue for the Taliban.

POPPIES, CORRUPTION AND THE TALIBAN

Once the United Nations and US-backed anti-drug campaigns in Turkey, Pakistan, Myanmar, Thailand, Vietnam, and Laos had virtually halted the growing of poppies in the early 1980s in those countries, Afghanistan became the pre-eminent producer of raw opium derived from poppies.

Drugs are prohibited in Islam. But since most of the opium was being exported to the non-Muslim world and consumed there, the Taliban regime turned a blind eye to the narcotics trade. It was only after Mullah Omar came under greater influence from Osama bin Laden that he banned the growing of poppies, in July 2001. That curtailed the annual output of raw opium from 4,600 tonnes to 400 tonnes. The annual revenue of only $25–$50 million in taxes on poppies and opium was a negligible part of the Taliban regime's Budget.[20]

Poppies are grown in the arid southern and north-eastern zones of Afghanistan because they need little water and, as a cash crop like cotton or tobacco, they yield a good return. After the downfall of the Taliban, the growing of poppies mushroomed. This caused concern in Western capitals. They pressured the Karzai administration to act. But it lacked the political will as well as effective means to do the job properly. So its poppy eradication programme became an amalgam of high-flown rhetoric, periodic reiteration of its commitment, and scant or lopsided action. It ended up affording lucrative opportunities to the police to enrich themselves and to the Taliban to finance its insurgency.

The first half-baked push for poppy eradication came in 2002. Initially, it focused on small growers, promising them adequate compensation. When the government extended the programme to better-off farmers, they bribed policemen not to destroy their crops or do only token damage. As for the promised compensation, the money sent by Kabul disappeared into the pockets of provincial and district officials. That left the compliant growers penniless and indignant, and encouraged them to back the emerging Taliban.

When pressured again by Western nations, the Karzai government launched another poppy-eradication campaign in 2005. By then, the Taliban had put down roots in the poppy-growing region. Openly opposing the programme, they offered protection to those farmers who wanted to plant poppy seeds in return for paying 10 per cent Islamic tax on the produce, called ushur, collected in kind after the crop had been harvested. During the next two years, the area under poppy cultivation in Helmand increased fivefold. From that beginning, the Taliban graduated to taxing those who produced raw opium (aka opium paste) and heroin, and those who transported the goods. They charged the Islamic zakat tax of 10 per cent on traders and transporters. They always gave receipts and never charged extra or took bribes.

By the late 2000s, the number of Afghans engaged in opium cultivation and trade ballooned to 3.3 million – that is, one out ten Afghan men, women and children. Thus growing of poppies became a very substantial part of Afghanistan's economy. At $1,700 a year, the per capita income of the Afghans engaged in poppy-related activities was five-and-a-half times the national average. At an estimated $2–$2.5 billion farm value, opium accounted for one-quarter to one-third of national GDP.[21]

A symbiotic relationship had developed between poppy farmers, government officials, and the Taliban. In the words of an unnamed opium trader of twenty years: 'If Afghan farmers don't plant opium then smugglers don't make money. If we [the smugglers] don't make money the Taliban and police don't make money. The Taliban and the officials have a very strong relationship – if they don't then how can we do so much trade and travel to so many districts?' He added: 'The Taliban benefit from the poppy because the farmers pay them taxes. And when the government destroys the fields, the people support the Taliban. The government also benefits from the poppy – we pay officials so they won't destroy our crop.'[22]

The Taliban's rationale for taxing the opium industry was that they were waging a jihad, and that it was the religious duty of the faithful to contribute to their organization in cash or kind. Doing so was tantamount to participating in the jihad. The Taliban military commander charged a separate fee for safe passage to vehicles carrying narcotics to the borders of Pakistan, Iran or Tajikistan. Depending on the amount of opium he was carrying, a trader used a motorcycle, taxi or Toyota Land Cruiser. For larger consignments, an armed convoy was arranged, with half a dozen gunmen assigned to three vehicles.

The smugglers' bribe for the police was also fixed at 10 per cent. So, a drugs dealer, smuggling 100 kg of opium or heroin, would give 10 per cent to the Taliban and another 10 per cent to the police and other government functionaries. Once Afghan officials had been bribed, they would contact their counterparts across the border in Pakistan, Iran or Tajikistan. Finally, the smuggler had to pay the border police commander before his convoy would be allowed to leave the country.

As the area under poppy cultivation grew at a rapid pace, so did the incidence of graft. According to the Berlin-based Transparency Internatinal, which monitors corruption in government, Afghanistan's ranking among 180 countries plummeted from 117th in 2005 to 176th in 2008.

When, in the late 2000s, the fighting in the south became more intense, traders scouted the northern route to Tajikistan across the three-quarter-mile (1 km) wide Oxus. They selected Ishkashim, a sparsely populated frontier town in the province of Badakhshan, with a settlement of the same name in Tajikistan. It soon became the base of thirty smugglers who exported heroin and imported assault rifles. The border police commander was himself a smuggler, and was therefore privy to inside information about fellow smugglers. He charged $100 for 1 kg of heroin, and a modest $1 for 1 kg of hashish.

A typical smuggler, dealing with 50 kg a week, worth $12,500, soon discovered that it was better to bribe the lawmen in advance. Because if he got caught by them he would end up paying a hefty sum on the spot.

The area was full of heroin laboratories. There were ten between Ishkashim and Baharak, the capital of the adjoining district to the west, 60 miles (100 km) away. Each laboratory refined 12 kg of raw opium into 3 kg of heroin, to be sold for $2,500 a kilo. Once it reached Tajikistan's capital Dushanbe, its value doubled; and in Moscow the price rose tenfold to $50,000. If smuggled to Greece and Turkey via Pakistan, its value jumped from $5,000 a kg in Pakistan to $20,000–$30,000 a kg.

Among the incoming goods from Tajikistan, the latest, lighter and deadlier model of the Kalashnikov was most in demand. Because it could pierce body armour, it was popular with the Taliban. Bought at $700 a piece in Dushanbe, they sold for $1,100 in Ishkashim, a profit margin of 50 per cent, allowing for bribes and transportation costs. The Taliban's central military committee welcomed the addition of these lethal assault rifles as it tried to bolster its armoury following the setback it had suffered in mid-2006 with the failure of its attempt to capture Kandahar.

THE BATTLE OF PASHMUL

For the Taliban's primary enemy, the United States, the year 2006 started badly in Iraq. The bombing of the Askariya Mosque in Samarra – one of the holiest Shia shrines – in February by Sunni extremists triggered a low-intensity war between the majority Shias and minority Sunnis. The Pentagon's 170,000 troops proved inadequate to dampen hostilities rooted in the early days of Islam.

The news from Afghanistan was equally bleak. The Taliban controlled twenty districts in the south, and had a fighting force of seventeen thousand, a third of it posted in Pakistan, with Maulavi Jalaluddin Haqqani as commander-in-chief. A white-turbaned member of the Jadr tribe from Paktia province, with a long unkempt beard, deep-set eyes, and bushy eyebrows, Haqqani was a veteran of the anti-Soviet jihad. Now, under his command, the Taliban had refined their tactics relating to suicide bombings carried out by recruits from the students of Pakistan-based madrasas. At the start of 2004, two out of every three suicide-bombing attempts failed due to amateurish assembling of the explosives. By early 2006, however, the failure rate had fallen to one out of seven. This led NATO troops to suspect every unidentified Afghan civilian of being a bomber – just what the Taliban wanted them to believe. By 2006, the insurgents had also mastered the stacking together of anti-tank mines to be used as IEDs, sharpened their skills at hitting moving vehicles, and set up field hospitals near NATO outposts. (Later, while maintaining a close alliance with Mullah Omar, Haqqani would take command of the Taliban partisans in the south-eastern provinces of Paktia, Paktika, Khost, Logar and Ghazni, leaving the jihad in the southern provinces to Mullah Omar.)

On the opposing side, the auxiliary ANA was now 18,000-strong. The 'official' figure, though, was 37,000, since it included 19,000 soldiers who existed only on paper. Yet, facing escalating inter-sectarian violence in Iraq, all US defence secretary Donald Rumsfeld could do was to add a mere 5,000 American troops to the existing 17,000.

During the spring, the Taliban, numbering 1,500–2,000, mounted guerrilla assaults on NATO units, dominated by Canadian forces, from the Pashmul area between Bazaar-e Panjwai, the capital of the Panjwai district, and Zhare, 12 miles (20 km) south of Kandahar city. Mullah Dadullah chose the Pashmul–Panjawi area as his forward base for the following reasons. It was close to the strategic east–west highway linking Chaman with Herat via Kandahar. The local orchards, vineyards with drainage ditches, high-walled compounds and network of tunnels and 10-foot (3 m)-deep trenches constructed during the anti-Soviet jihad of the 1980s offered security from heavy air raids as well as shelter from air reconnaissance. Lastly, by willingly taking in the Taliban as family guests, the local farmers helped to make them safe from air strikes.

Between mid-May and mid-June, NATO soldiers had thirty-seven running fights with groups of Taliban, each 30–40 strong. To minimize casualties, NATO made excessive use of air strikes, averaging twenty-five a day in May. The resulting death toll of 400 in that month included civilians. The killing of non-combat Afghans received wide publicity, creating popular indignation at the bombers and NATO. In contrast, following the orders issued by Mullah Omar, Taliban partisans left civilians unharmed, and focused on Afghan policemen and army troops.

In late June, when firefights with the Taliban ended, NATO commanders concluded that they had defeated the enemy. They therefore reduced the troop presence in the area, whereupon, like the Afghan Mujahedin Alliance in the 1980s, the Taliban moved back in. In the summer, the Taliban acted boldly, driving around in the very Ford Ranger pickup trucks that the Pentagon had supplied to the ANA and ANP. They showed overt signs of penetrating the nearby Kandahar district with the ultimate aim of capturing its capital. This caused much nervousness among officials in Kandahar and Kabul. NATO's high command bolstered its forces to nearly 10,000, with 3,300 Britons, 2,300 Americans, and 2,200 Canadians, as well as soldiers from Denmark and Estonia.

Though air strikes dropped to an average of twelve a day, the number of civilian casualties mounted. Continued violence created insecurity which was exploited by bandits. The NATO high command decided to stage a major offensive, codenamed Operation Medusa, to clear the Panjwai district of Taliban influence. Before staging this operation on 2 September, NATO called on the villagers to leave the area. But most stayed. Yet NATO went ahead with its massive air strikes, which included 2,000-pound bombs. Unable to battle properly while being bombarded non-stop, Taliban fighters tried to retreat, only to find themselves attacked by American Special Forces units. In the ground battles that ensued, NATO pressed ill-trained Afghan soldiers into combat. In hand-to-hand fighting, Taliban insurgents often used their local hosts as human shields.

In the fortnight-long hostilities, the Taliban fired 1,000 mortar shells, 2,000 rocket-propelled grenades, and 400,000 rounds of ammunition, according to NATO. (That still left one million rounds of unused ammunition, to be discovered later by NATO.) After initially claiming to have killed 512 Taliban, NATO more than doubled the figure to 1,100.[23] It did not release the figures for the fatalities suffered by its own forces or the ANA, but a perusal of the dead soldiers listed by the Canadian Defense Ministry alone showed the figure to be twenty-one. The Taliban claimed that for each of the fighters they had lost, they had killed two members of the Afghan National Security Forces (ANSF) – the collective term used for army troops, policemen, and border guards. The success of Operation Medusa led NATO members to dispatch more soldiers to Afghanistan, raising the total NATO strength to 47,000 troops.

Overall, the Taliban suffered a serious tactical defeat in Pashmul. It was a battle that NATO simply could not afford to lose. It was incumbent upon it to demonstrate its will and to stand and fight. Taliban leaders should have taken this factor into account. Instead, they blundered by putting too much faith in what had happened during the 1980s, when the Soviets decided to leave the orchards and vineyards of Pashmul alone, considering the area of little strategic value. In any case, it was unrealistic of the leaders of an insurgent organization, lacking tanks, artillery, and warplanes, to think they could seize a major city and hold it. Given such heavy odds, why did the Taliban Shura Council try to capture Kandahar and engage in a stand-up fight with NATO? The most likely answer is that it wanted to maintain a certain momentum in its campaign, which had started modestly four years earlier. It felt an urgent need to boost the morale of its ranks with a high-profile victory.

In retrospect, however, the Battle of Pashmul emerged as a defining moment in the post-2001 history of Afghanistan. It secured the Taliban, Mark II a place in the Afghan equation, which until then had consisted of two elements with different identities but the same goal: the Karzai government and NATO forces. Now, faced with a vigorous, highly motivated enemy, Kabul and Brussels had no option but to engage in a full-blown counter-insurgency campaign.

The episode also provided indisputable evidence of the wholehearted backing given to the Afghan Taliban by the ISI led by General Kayani. During Operation Medusa, a besieged battalion of the Taliban called for reinforcements from Baluchistan, which soon arrived. Such an armed force could not have existed in Pakistan without the cooperation of the ISI.

By the summer of 2006, NATO intelligence had obtained irrefutable proof of the ISI's alliance with the Afghan insurgents, covering recruitment, training, arming and dispatching of partisans as well as overseeing their leadership. Islamabad's strategy was based on the assumption that America would not linger in Afghanistan for years on end, and that a revived but moderated Taliban would be a prize asset in post-US Afghanistan. Pakistan's president, General Pervez Musharraf, had adopted this as an undeclared official policy.

This was the background to the dinner that President Bush hosted for Musharraf and Karzai in Washington on 28 September 2006. When Karzai complained bitterly about Pakistan's policy, Musharraf accused him of basing his allegations on 'outdated' intelligence and kowtowing to India. By so doing, Musharraf highlighted the intimate linkage that exists between his country and its neighbours to the east and the west. Actually, by virtue of the partitioning of the Indian subcontinent, and the disputed Durand Line frontier with Afghanistan, Pakistan inherited this relationship at birth. Afghans feel so strongly about the inequity of this international border that even the Taliban government, though heavily dependent on Islamabad for its survival, refused to accept it. Mullah Omar proved immune to repeated appeals from Musharraf and the ISI to approve the Durand Line in writing.

Despite the many billions that the US treasury had poured into Afghanistan since 2002, and the $5.5 billion given to the Pakistani army to assist the Pentagon's operations in Afghanistan, the American president found himself at his wits' end as he tried to reconcile his quarreling guests. Yet there was no escaping from the hard fact that the fates of their countries were inseparable. To mount a successful counter-insurgency campaign against the Afghan Taliban, Islamabad and Kabul needed to cooperate fully under the aegis of Washington.

THE COUNTER-INSURGENCY CAMPAIGN

Ideally, foreign soldiers should act as auxiliaries to local security forces in order to defeat insurgents. But in Afghanistan the roles were reversed, with the ANA serving as an auxiliary to NATO forces. As for the casualties – dead and injured – the ratio between NATO troops and insurgents remained roughly the same: 1:3 in guerrilla actions and 1:15 in conventional combat.[24] The comparable figures for guerrilla actions in earlier long-running wars in Algeria, Malaya, and Vietnam were respectively: 1:4, 1:2, and 1:1.

The inherent weaknesses of the non-Afghan troops remained unchanged: the shortness of their tours of duty, resulting in the almost total absence of institutional memory and experience; over-reliance on air power, with its concomitant civilian casualties; and ignorance of local terrain, people, and their language and culture. All in all, despite several attempts, NATO failed to maintain control of the population and make them feel safe – a vital element in any counter-insurgency campaign.

Preconditions for success in a counter-insurgency campaign are: effective, locally recruited police and military forces and intelligence agencies, and a well-conceived and consistent strategy. In 2006, neither of these conditions existed to the degree necessary for victory. The basic strategy, devised by Washington, shifted from one pole to another, thus inadvertently letting the Taliban strike roots in the rural south and south-east. One school of thought advocated confronting the symptoms – the insurgents' ideology and tactics – head-on, whereas the other proposed tackling the underlying causes – the poverty and economic backwardness of the rural communities. The former, requiring an assault on the enemy's bastions to frustrate his plan to upgrade the insurgency, could be implemented forthwith. In contrast, the latter, involving the investment of money and effort to build up the economic infrastructure and public services, was a medium- to long-term project.

Within two years of implementing the policy of furnishing the countryside with infrastructure while doling out cash for information about the insurgents, US officials had gathered enough evidence to be able to assess its effectiveness. In the augural year of 2004, American commanders paid $40 million in cash to village elders and others for intelligence while unveiling development projects relating to health, education and drinking water. But since the schools were built without local involvement, the Taliban encountered little resistance, when, following the Americans' departure from the area, they arrived and burned them down. In addition, they seized and destroyed all the goods and propaganda literature US troops had left behind. By 2006, the word had spread through the Pushtun countryside that the Taliban would punish anybody who provided information to the Americans.

The failure of its carrots policy led Washington to revert to sticks. But by now the Taliban were so well organized and spread over a large territory that their commanders moved men and weapons from the area under NATO pressure to somewhere less threatening. NATO did not have enough armed personnel to saturate all of the disturbed south – much less all of Afghanistan – the situation the Kremlin had faced twenty years before. Also, during the winter months, Taliban leaders resorted to sending suicide bombers to large cities to remind their friends and foes alike that their organization was alive and kicking.

Meanwhile, what the US could, and did, do was to accelerate its programme of equipping the ANA with tanks and artillery, introduced on the eve of the Battle of Pushmal. The Pentagon, which bore the full cost of training, equipping, and maintaining the Afghan military, raised the Afghan soldier's monthly salary from $50 to $70. This compared poorly with the $1,300–$2,500 a month earned by his American counterpart.[25] It cost the US treasury $800,000 a year to maintain a single American soldier in Afghanistan. By contrast, the Pentagon estimated that the annual running cost of the 60,000-strong ANA would be $1 billion, or $16,000 per Afghan soldier – 2 per cent of the figure for his American counterpart.[26] The Taliban's budget in 2006 was believed to be $3 million a month, or $36 million a year – equivalent to the expense to the Pentagon of maintaining 45 American troops in Afghanistan. In 2005, it cost the US $16 million to kill each Taliban partisan; in 2006, that figure halved because the Taliban took to mounting large-scale attacks on urban centres.[27]

The ANP continued to be a weak member of the national security apparatus. It suffered from an incredibly high turnover of personnel. Of the 6,000 policemen trained in Kandahar during 2003–06, half had left the force by the time NATO mounted Operation Medusa. This was part of a national trend. Instead of a steady increase in the ANP's size, as visualized by NATO, its overall strength fell in 2006.

The following spring, the ANP behaved in a way that shocked many citizens. In late March, NATO launched a major offensive, codenamed Operation Achilles, to clear the northern part of Helmand province, a leading producer of poppies, of the well-entrenched Taliban. Its 4,500 troops were supplemented by a thousand members of the ANSF. After offering token resistance, the Taliban withdrew from the area because they wanted to avoid damage to the poppy crops which were ready to be harvested. NATO, assisted by the ANSF, retook the important town of Sangin. While jubilant NATO commanders celebrated, attributing (wrongfully) their success to the hard line adopted by the Washington-led alliance, the townspeople expressed anger at the bombings and troops' indiscriminate barging into homes to carry out searches. Far worse, Afghan policemen went on reckless looting sprees in shops in Sangin. 'This is the first time . . . I saw armed men in uniform come and begin to rob the bazaar,' said Gul Agha, the owner of a clothing shop. 'They also came to my shop, and took away some very expensive fabrics.' Nisar Ahmad, another store owner, said, 'Men in uniforms stole everything . . . took goods worth 1.4 million [Pakistani] *kaldars* [$23,000].'[28]

During the winter lull, the Taliban carried out two daring suicide bombings in Kabul and Kandahar. The one in the capital in January 2008, accompanied by a gun assault, rocked the luxury Kabul Serena Hotel, located a short distance from the Presidential Palace. By causing the deaths of a hundred people, the Kandahar attack in February became the deadliest in the city since the Taliban's overthrow seven years before. In both instances, the insurgents arrived in official uniforms in the security forces' standard Ford pickups. Four months later, the Taliban carried out a massive jailbreak in Kandahar, freeing at least 350 incarcerated comrades. The car bombing of the Indian embassy in Kabul on 7 July killed fifty-eight people. The conclusion drawn by US intelligence agencies – that the ISI was involved – dovetailed with the findings of Afghanistan's National Security Directorate. This was part of the ISI's agenda to reduce India's influence in Afghanistan in collusion with the Haqqani group based in Pakistan's North Waziristan Agency.

The Indian embassy attack strained Afghanistan–Pakistan relations to breaking point. A few weeks earlier President Karzai had told Pakistan that if it did not repress the jihadists in FATA, he would dispatch Afghan troops to Pakistan to accomplish the task. This warning came in the wake of two major border skirmishes between the Afghan and Pakistani forces, which were revealed two years later through WikiLeaks. Nearly 150 paramilitaries from Pakistan's Frontier Corp crossed into Afghanistan near Khost on 25 April 2008 and exchanged fire with Afghan border guards. Later that day, two separate groups of Afghan soldiers, each thirty strong, retaliated by targeting Pakistani border posts. The firefights ended only when the tribal elders from both sides met at the frontier and resolved the dispute.[29] In mid-May, there was a three-day-long fight between the Afghan and Pakistani troops in the Aryub Zazai district of

Afghanistan's Paktia province. It left seven Pakistanis and eight Afghans dead. The incident was triggered by the demolition of Afghan security checkpoints by Pakistanis who wanted to build their own posts.[30]

Such clashes had a fairly long history, dating back at least to 2005. They were routinely concealed from the public – as could be deduced from the classified US cables published by WikiLeaks. For instance, during an armed confrontation in September 2005, precipitated by the posting of a Pakistani national flag inside Afghanistan, 120 Afghan soldiers gathered on the border in Khost province. They threatened to attack Pakistani troops if the latter did not abandon a disputed checkpoint. It required the intervention of an American officer to calm the disputants.[31]

These skirmishes are rooted in what happened in 1893. In that year Britain pressured King Abdur Rahman to accept the Durand Line as the border between Afghanistan and British India. Having done so, the British went on to reinforce the Khyber Pass with a string of forts for its garrisons – aware that the Afghans would bristle at this delineation being thrust upon them and make periodic attempts to get the border altered in their favour.

12

AFGHANISTAN: A SECOND VIETNAM

OF THE SIXTEEN gates of the historic walled city of Peshawar (derivative of *Purushapura*, meaning 'town of men', in Sanskrit), the best known is the Kabuli Gate. It leads to Kabul via the famous Khyber Pass. Over the past half-century, though, the picturesque Old City with its artistically patterned red stone façades has been dwarfed by sprawling growth in all directions. But the westward expansion cannot go farther than 12 miles (20 km) beyond the city limits, which is where Khyber Pakhtunkhwa ends.

Jamrud, the last stop in mainland Pakistan, opens onto the semi-autonomous Federally Administered Tribal Agencies (FATA). The border is marked by a striking stone archway – with a fluttering Pakistani flag pinned at its centre – supported by robust stone turrets flanking the N5 national highway. To drive farther along the N5, a foreign visitor needs a special permit. An uphill climb then ensues, past crumbling watchtowers and the insignia of several regiments dating back to the days of the British rule, until the traveller reaches Landi Kotal, a garrison town. Standing at an altitude of 3,500 feet (1,075 m), Landi Kotal marks the peak of the Khyber Pass. It is the main shopping centre for the area, with a maze-like bazaar where store owners display pistols, hand grenades and Kalashnikovs. A drive through the cantonment area presents the contrasting sight of precisely laid-out barracks as well as the officers' mess of the Khyber Rifles, a paramilitary force of local Afridi tribesmen. The primary task of the Khyber Rifles – part of the Frontier Corps, an auxiliary to the regular Pakistani army – is to safeguard the pass.

With the international border town of Torkham only 4 miles (6 km) away, the traffic builds up, with giant tanker trucks carrying fuel for NATO forces in Afghanistan muscling their way forward speedily. Cars travel in one lane, and trucks and pickup vans in another. Medium-sized private trucks provide a moving feast of eye-catching red, yellow and green-blue hand-painted images of flying pigeons and partridges, snow-capped meadows, and brooks of gushing glacial water – as well as Quranic verses to counter any evil force.

Torkham is a settlement of breeze-block houses, its border post a beehive of round-the-clock activity. More than half of the goods required by NATO troops in Afghanistan pass through Torkham. Between it and the Afghan border post there is a mile of no-man's-land. In that short distance a driver must do the mental switch-over from driving on the left, as in Pakistan, to driving on the right, as required in Afghanistan. Until the Battle of Pushmal in the spring of 2006, the Afghan border police were relaxed about checking the travel documents of the ethnic Pashtuns of the region. After that, at the behest of Washington, border controls tightened.

The mountains on both sides of the road rise to a crescendo of jagged peaks dusted with snow even in summer. The zigzag descent down the Khyber Pass through a moonscape of dung-coloured hills is spectacular and stomach-churning in equal measure. The adrenalin rush subsides only when the highway levels off at an altitude of 1,800 feet (550 m). A cruise along a smooth highway, well maintained at the Pentagon's expense, can induce in the traveller's mind a recreation of history – with invaders and conquerors marching in the opposite direction, starting with Cyrus of Iran (r. 550–529 BC) and ending with Babur, in the first quarter of the sixteenth century, equipped with cannons – through Alexander of Macedonia (336–

323 BC), Mahmoud of Ghazni, Genghis Khan and Tamerlane. Men, armour, horses and, above all, indomitable resolve.

As the car nears the provincial capital of Jalalabad at the confluence of the Kabul and Kunar Rivers near the Laghman Valley, the honey colour of the mountains gives way to the lush green of the fields of wheat, mustard seed, and watermelons. The Afghan National Army is in charge of security here while the Pentagon has several military bases in the area, the largest being at the airport. As the social and cultural centre of eastern Afghanistan, Jalalabad greeted the fall of the Taliban in 2001 with greater glee than any other city of comparable size. Men rushed to shave off their unkempt beards, others began trading in TV sets and buying Indian and Pakistani music cassettes. Thriving businesses sprang up in the bazaar located underneath a busy road. Now, a foreign visitor's inquiries are likely to be drowned out by Bollywood pop songs blaring from the loudspeakers of a shop selling Pushtu, Indian, and Western music.

After Jalalabad, the dust-coloured, brown-turning-to-grey barren landscape returns. On both sides of the road lie gravel and bits of clay. In the distance are small settlements of mud houses with high walls to keep the cattle in and protect females from the gaze of male strangers. Here and there, children in tattered clothes wave at speeding vehicles before running back to their mud-brick homes.

KABUL: A WAR ZONE

Before reaching Kabul, you see a white blimp hanging above the city. Launched by NATO, this is a tethered surveillance balloon equipped with an enormously powerful camera capable of monitoring vast swathes of the capital. On approach roads into the city, large security cameras on giant metal poles record the traffic as it enters and exits. At checkpoints, soldiers examine car boots for drugs, weapons and other contraband.

A city of dust and pollution, Kabul greets the visitor with the stench of uncollected garbage, and the sight of plastic detritus shining in the sun, piled up at the margins of rutted streets. Even in the upscale residential neighbourhoods, black sewage flows through drains partially covered with broken cement grates. Old-style shops carry large signs in Persian but also in English. Important streets display billboards showing a young unveiled woman wearing make-up holding a mobile phone to her ear. In the streets there are more unveiled women than the ones in burqas. Younger women sometimes appear in jeans and long skirts with their heads covered by a shawl.

Opposite the Kabul Serena Hotel, the leading haunt for foreigners, stands the multistorey maroon-coloured Central Bank of Afghanistan. Beyond it lies the quarter-mile (0.4 km) radius of forbidden territory around the Presidential Palace. The second most guarded premise is the US embassy. Locals invited to a meeting there have to clear five checkpoints to reach their final destination. All important private establishments employ armed security guards. If you want to eat at a Western-style restaurant or meet someone at one of the several spacious Western-style cafés, you must first undergo a body search and deposit any small arms (which foreign diplomats and some others are allowed to carry) with the sentry at the guard room.

'In 2003, the talk was about mopping up a few pockets of resistance,' said Anouhita Mojumdar, an Indian journalist resident in Kabul since 2003.

> Security has grown worse since 2006. It has become difficult to move around Kabul. Razor-wire fences over high walls all over; checkpoints, watchtowers, bunkers, concrete bollards, metal barriers, concrete barriers, bunkers with armed soldiers sitting behind sandbags. All government offices are protected by concrete blast walls. More streets are blocked by red-striped poles. We have more kidnappings, more gun blasts. Kabul is a city under siege. Since 2006 there has been much less mixing between locals and foreigners.[1]

The situation remained unchanged when Barack Obama succeeded George W. Bush as US President in January 2009. His election campaign slogan, 'Change We Can Have', did not apply to the Pentagon's war in Afghanistan. In February, he ordered the dispatch of 17,000 combat troops and 4,000 trainers to Afghanistan, raising the total of United States soldiers to 68,000 – much higher than the combined strength of non-US NATO forces at 55,100.

For the Americans and others familiar with the history of the Vietnam War (March 1965–January 1973), there was a strong sense of déjà vu. Presidents who choose to expand armed conflicts find their options hopelessly narrowed if their initial sunny scenario does not play out as envisaged and the situation continues to worsen. Their generals then ask for more soldiers and funds. The commander-in-chief obliges even when public opinion is turning against the war. This is what happened in Vietnam. And history began repeating itself in Afghanistan. Obama and his senior aides became addicted to the application of escalating force while emulating their predecessors in the White House – vacillating between prioritizing providing protection for the population and going all out to smash the Taliban, no matter how severe the 'collateral damage'.

Like two poker players, the Taliban and the Pentagon raised their bids. There was a wide chasm between how these warring parties were viewed by ordinary Afghans. Whereas most Americans considered the Taliban as terrorists allied with Al Qaida and Osama bin Laden, most Pushtun Afghans regarded the Taliban as a resistance movement against a corrupt regime in Kabul propped up by infidel foreign troops. Moreover, a large majority of rural Afghans seemed to believe the Taliban's assertion that the Western Christian troops were in their country because of their animosity to Islam. Many non-Taliban Afghans subscribed to the view that America and its allies had deliberately allowed bin Laden and Mullah Muhammad Omar to go free and were covertly backing the Afghan Taliban to provide themselves with a pretext for staying in the region and dominating it. No wonder the violence escalated.

THE TALIBAN'S DEADLIER TACTICS

According to the United Nations Assistance Mission in Afghanistan, at 2,118, the number of civilian fatalities in 2008 was about 40 per cent higher than in 2007. By the middle of 2009, of the 378 districts, 43 per cent were categorized 'highly unsafe', according to the latest UN security map. Nationally, the Taliban had established a permanent presence in 54 per cent of territory.[2] By all accounts, they enjoyed high popularity in the dozen Pushtun-majority provinces, home to 55 per cent of the population.

Among the five of the six provinces around Kabul with a significant Taliban presence were Logar and Wardak. In areas such as Salar in Wardak, US troops were wary of arriving at a destination by tank since the whole area was heavily mined. Nor did they use armoured personnel carriers. Rather, they travelled by helicopter. 'When I started in this area, three years ago [in 2005], I had six fighters, one RPG [rocket-propelled grenade] and two machine guns like these,' Taliban commander Qomendan told Arab journalist Gaith Abdul-Ahad during his clandestine visit to a Taliban base in the mountains of Wardak. 'Now I have more than 500 fighters, 30 machine guns and hundreds of RPGs. The hundreds of Afghan policemen the Americans have deployed patrol the area all the time, but they can't control it.'[3]

In August 2008, there were major assaults in the Kabul region. These included attacks on government buildings, including the Afghan military headquarters, suicide bombings outside the NATO mission and a NATO convoy on the Kabul–Jalalabad road, and the assassinations of Logar's provincial governor and police chief. As a result, the number of private security companies operating in and from Kabul shot up to forty-seven.

An unmistakable indicator of the Taliban's growing presence was the frequent appearance of 'night letters' calling on Afghans not to cooperate with infidel foreigners. More dramatic signs included the series of craters along the main Highway 1 going south caused by improvised explosive devices (IEDs), and the charred remnants of NATO supply vehicles and containers, which began appearing within 15 miles (24 km) of Kabul's southern boundary.

At 3,250, the number of IEDs in 2008 was three times the figure for the previous year. In 2009, it would jump to 7,228, a record. Attacks on US and NATO supply vehicles in the first three months of 2009 destroyed 300 vehicles. The standard Mine-Resistant Ambush-Protected (MRAP) vehicle provided protection against IEDs, but since it had to travel by road it was still susceptible to ambush.

By the end of 2009, the Taliban's supreme Shura Council supervised well-organized channels of revenue which had enabled it to extend the organization's presence to all the provinces except one. Estimates of the annual income from drugs ranged from $70 million to $400 million. Taliban fighters helped harvest the poppy crop, for which they got paid. At the top of the trade were the drug barons who contributed directly to the Taliban's Shura Council in Quetta. The Taliban also garnered some of the funds that the Pentagon paid six local contractors to transport civilian and military supplies, including MRAPs and High Mobility Multipurpose Wheeled Vehicles, called Humvees, from the Bagram air base to the several hundred NATO bases and posts across the country. Those Afghans operating beyond the Pentagon's loop had direct dealings with Taliban leaders in the south. As for the organization's income from sources outside Afghanistan, one CIA estimate put the total at $106 million a year. But these sums were dwarfed by the $65 billion that the Pentagon spent in Afghanistan in fiscal 2009.

The Taliban's improved financial condition led to their militia sharpening their fighting skills. The American officers with combat experience in Iraq noted the difference. In Iraq, the insurgents attacked US troops and then fled. By contrast, in Afghanistan one unit of the Taliban would fire enough ammunition to force the Americans to keep their heads down while another Taliban unit manoeuvred around their target to kill as many soldiers as they could. This was a carbon copy of the tactic US Marines are taught. Also, once the Taliban realized that US soldiers were listening in to their two-way radio communications, they deliberately described phony locations of roadside bombs and ambushes.

Taliban commanders showed an acute sense of when and where to retreat to be able to fight another day. When four thousand US Marines moved into Helmand province (area: 6,000 sq. miles/15,540 sq. km) along with Afghan troops on 2 July 2009 as part of Operation Khanjar, (Dari, 'Sword') the Taliban vanished. That allowed the Marines to proceed southward and recapture the town of Khan Neshin, the capital of Rig district. Here they learned of a series of failures by the government of President Karzai: for instance, district governor Masoud Ahmad Rasouli Baluch had received only fifty of the promised 120 policemen and only one-sixth of the promised 180 Afghan soldiers. He lacked advisers, doctors, teachers, and all other professionals. The governor bluntly told the American troops that two out of three locals supported the Taliban. They did so because of their religion, their objection to the presence of foreign troops, and their dependence on growing poppies – to make a living – a vital activity protected by the Taliban. The Marine commander found the accompanying Afghan policemen and soldiers so unreliable that he deployed two-thirds of his troops to do policing jobs such as manning checkpoints and outposts circling the town.[4]

Just as they did for their revenue, Taliban leaders continued to depend on outside assistance to maintain or increase their military capabilities. The ISI remained their sole benefactor. Based on analyses of its ongoing electronic surveillance and fresh information received from its paid agents, the Pentagon noticed that when Taliban partisans needed fuel or ammunition to keep up their assaults on foreign soldiers, they approached the ISI's 'S' section. And when the Taliban's supreme Shura Council found it necessary to replenish its ranks, ISI agents tapped Pakistan-based radical madrasas for volunteers.

Washington protested anew. Islamabad merely recycled its earlier rationale: It needed a strong lever to exercise in Afghanistan to frustrate Delhi's designs to fill the political vacuum in the aftermath of the American withdrawal by reviving the Tajik-dominated anti-Taliban Northern Alliance. As before, Islamabad resisted pressure from Washington to move against Afghan Taliban leaders based in Baluchistan. It pointed out that its military was already overstretched, engaged as it was in ongoing counter-insurgency operations in FATA and the Swat Valley. Moreover, public opinion was opposed to opening up yet another front. Such a move, it added, would also risk inciting widespread anger in Baluchistan, which had a long history of tense relations with the federal government.

Islamabad reiterated its policy of differentiating between the Taliban fighters staging cross-border attacks into Afghanistan and the Pakistani Taliban staging lethal attacks on the state's vital organs. At the same time it had no objection to being bracketed with Afghanistan by the policy makers of the new US administration.

OBAMA'S COUNTER-INSURGENCY STRATEGY

On assuming the American presidency, Obama described the Afghan conflict as a war of necessity. He appointed Richard Holbrooke, a sixty-eight-year-old top-ranking diplomat, as his special envoy to Afghanistan and Pakistan. Treating the two countries as a joint entity, Holbrooke coined the term 'AfPak'. All this was widely publicized.

What was not known to the general public was the Obama White House's decision to expand the list of Afghan targets to be killed or captured. Henceforth, those Afghan drug traffickers believed to have links with the Taliban were to be treated as if they were Taliban leaders. That meant adding fifty people to Washington's Joint Integrated Prioritized Target list of 367 names. Since such a step violated international law and the conventional rules of military engagement, there was resistance from other NATO members. Subsequently, however, they acquiesced under pressure. In the first half of 2009, the Pentagon reportedly killed several suspected traffickers and arrested others, claiming that it informed President Karzai before staging targeting missions.[5]

Refreshingly, Obama stopped using the term 'War on Terror', the oft-repeated phrase of George W. Bush, and refrained from his predecessor's policy of creating fear among Americans – except where Afghanistan was concerned. 'Those who attacked America on 9/11 are plotting to do so again,' he said. 'If left unchecked, the Taliban insurgency will mean an even larger safe haven from which Al Qaida would plot to kill more Americans.'[6] The truth, however, was that Al Qaida leaders were ensconced in Pakistan, an ally of the US, which was supporting it militarily and financially. Obama's statement was therefore inherently wrong. An insurgent organization whose leading figures were themselves operating from outside Afghanistan were in no position to provide sanctuary to other leaders there. Neither of the two culprits, Umar Farouk Abdulmuttalab and Faisal Shahzad, who would attempt to hit American targets by respectively triggering explosive devices aboard a plane over Detroit on Christmas Day 2009 and on 1 May 2010 in Manhattan, was linked to Al Qaida proper. Abdulmuttalab was trained in Yemen by its affliate, Al Qaida in Arabian Peninsula, and Shahzad in FATA by *Pakistani* Taliban operatives.

Then there was the more fundamental issue regarding wars of necessity and choice. The war of necessity classification applies only to those cases where crucial national interests are at risk, and no other option exists except military force. Such was the case for America in World War I, World War II, the Korean War (1950–53) and the First Gulf War (1991). In Afghanistan, the US had the viable alternative of helping to mobilize Afghanistan's neighbours – the Central Asian republics, China and Russia along with Pakistan – to devise a regional counter-terrorism strategy, and to complement it by improving its own domestic security apparatus. But, boxed into their mantra of war of necessity – primarily to distinguish it from the war of choice in Iraq – Obama and his close aides made no attempt to develop this alternative idea into a practical strategy and debate its pros and cons.

Instead, in March 2009, Obama declared that the US would now take the fight to the Taliban in the south and south-east for two reasons: to provide time and space for the Kabul government to build up its security forces, and to convince the Taliban that resistance did not pay. The first of the two reasons was eerily reminiscent of the 'Vietnamization' of the war in Vietnam by US president Richard Nixon, who decided to build up the military of the corrupt and ineffectual government in South Vietnam to fight the Vietcong guerrillas after the US troop withdrawal. His policy failed.

Whatever the rationale, Obama's decision made America a fully fledged party to the long-lasting civil war in Afghanistan which dated back to the split in the People's Democratic Party in 1978. This is precisely what US president Lyndon Johnson did in March 1965 when he dispatched Marines to South Vietnam, so embroiling America in an eleven-year-old civil war. Johnson argued that he had no option but to escalate the war in Vietnam to contain international communism, now Obama presented his decision as an essential step in the fight against international Islamist terrorism.

In May 2009, Obama decided to shift the leadership of the US military and the NATO-led International Security Assistance Force (ISAF) from generals imbued with traditional army thinking and strategy to those favouring all-out counter-insurgency tactics as practised by the commanders of US Special Operations Forces (SOF). So out went General David McKiernan for his alleged 'underperformance', and in came General Stanley McChrystal as commander of the NATO-led ISAF and US Forces Afghanistan.

In his specialized field, McChrystal's credentials were impressive. From March 2003 to August 2008, he led the Pentagon's super-secret Joint Special Operations Command in Iraq. This virtual executive assassination wing acted out of the office of the hawkish Republican vice-president Dick Cheney. His team had its own clandestine interrogation and detention centre near Baghdad, Camp Nama, where Task Force 6-26 followed the policy: 'If you don't make them bleed, the authorities cannot prosecute you.'[7]

Before his transfer from Iraq to the Pentagon to serve as director of the Joint Staff – to assist the chairman of the Joint Chiefs of Staff in coordinating the operations of the four wings of the armed forces – McChrystal proposed deploying American commandos to strike at the Afghan Taliban's sanctuaries in Pakistan. Approved later by President Bush, this plan was implemented. Pakistan protested the violation of its sovereignty vehemently. As a result, the programme was stopped after two cross-border raids, in one of which civilians were killed. These events only came to light after Bush's presidency had ended, and were part of a long-concealed chain of events stretching back to 2003. According to Anthony Shaffer, author of *Operation Dark Heart*, published in mid-September 2010, McChrysal led an SOF unit, operating from Bagram air base, much earlier – in 2003. Calling itself Jedi Knight, the unit specialized in 'black ops', including 'striking at the core of the Taliban' inside the border region of Pakistan. The details in the book, initially cleared by the US army, were later judged by intelligence agencies to be so damaging to American interests that at the last moment the Defense Department rushed to buy up all ten thousand copies of it from the publisher.[8]

Later, in September 2010, the renowned *Washington Post* journalist Bob Woodward, in his book *Obama's Wars*, revealed that the CIA had raised a clandestine 3,000-strong Afghan paramilitary force for covert cross-border 'black ops', including assassinations, in the Afghan Taliban and Al Qaida sanctuaries in Afghanistan *and* Pakistan.[9] This deeply embarrassed the Pakistani government and lowered its standing among its self-respecting citizens.

As the freshly appointed military chief in Afghanistan, charged with implementing a revised strategy, McChrystal was required to submit his assessment of the current security situation. But by the time he did so, on 30 August 2009, Afghanistan was caught up in a debilitating scandal about the blatant rigging of the presidential poll on 20 August. (There were simultaneous elections to 420 provincial council seats.) This illustrated graphically how politics in Afghanistan operated through a system of tribal, factional and ethnic networks in which power brokers organized support for a parliamentary or presidential candidate in return for money, power and position.

THE 2009 AFGHAN PRESIDENTIAL ELECTION

Describing the election as part of the 'programme of the Crusaders', the Taliban called for a boycott. On the eve of the poll, they successfully hit high-profile targets – a military convoy travelling along the Kabul–Jalalabad highway and a location next to the main entrance to NATO headquarters in the capital. Of the thirty-four provinces, the twelve Pushtun-majority ones remained classified as 'high risk' – meaning there was limited or no government presence – according to the interior ministry.

On the polling day for the presidency and the provincial councils, the Taliban fired hundreds of rockets in the Pushtun-majority areas. As a result, voter turnout in the south and south-east was only 5–10 per cent. Kandahar province was hit by 120 rockets, with twenty directed at its capital. In the whole province only 25,000 people voted whereas the officials put the number at 350,000. In some areas the ballots cast exceeded the actual voters. Piles of ballot papers carrying the names and symbols of forty-four presidential candidates had not been folded – an unmistakable sign that they had not been put through a ballot-box slot.

Furthermore, to the great disappointment of Washington and London, of the 80,000 people living in the Helmand River Valley area recently liberated by the American and British troops, only 150 voted. In Gardez, a town of 70,000 Pushtuns and Tajiks, Karzai's campaign headquarters bribed each of Paktai province's village elders to the tune of $8,000–$10,000 to deliver votes. In the end Pushtuns voted for Karzai, and Tajiks for a fellow Tajik, Abdullah Abdullah, a former foreign minister.

Voting required only a registration card which carried the person's name, photograph, and address but no signature or thumb print. Those tribal leaders who had been appointed polling officers started collecting these cards several weeks before 20 August under the guise of helping their owners to register for receiving material assistance from the government. These cards were then sold on the black market for $10 each. Even then, nationally, the voter turnout was only around 30 per cent, with most of the ballots cast in the non-Pashtun north. Poor turnout suited the tribal chiefs acting as polling officers. If, for instance, eighty people actually voted at a polling station for 500, at the end of the day the polling officer was free to cast the remaining 400-odd ballots for his favourite candidate.

This poll set a new record for bribery, corruption of election officials, ballot stuffing, and doctoring of the count. The Electoral Complaints Commission (ECC), the UN watchdog, was inundated with 2,615 complaints. Of these, fifty-four were categorized as high priority. But the authority to authenticate the final result rested with the all-Afghan Independent Election Commission (IEC), appointed by Karzai. Its declaration of victory for Karzai, gaining 54.6 per cent of the vote, was challenged. A recount ensued.

Daily reporting of the electoral shenanigans by the media in the US led to a noticeable drop in American support for the Afghan war. A *New York Times*/CBS News survey showed that 57 per cent felt that the war was going badly for America, compared to 33 per cent who thought it was going well.[10] With the US economy in the doldrums – home foreclosures at a record level and unemployment hovering around 10 per cent – American taxpayers began complaining about spending $100 billion a year to maintain almost 100,000 troops in Afghanistan. The Pentagon's contribution was far higher than the 65,000 troops provided by the other forty-three members of the International Security Assistance Force.

Each soldier in Afghanistan now cost the US treasury almost one million dollars a year. 'Whatever the national colors flying above each provincial "forward operating base", the food is always the same: American,' reported Julian Borger, a British journalist.

> That's because it's provided by KBR (previously, Kellogg, Brown & Root), a former subsidiary of Dick Cheney's old mega-firm, Halliburton. In every base it puts on a staggering buffet spread for the troops, of which most hotels would be proud. There is a choice of half a dozen desserts including ice cream at every meal, and every last scrap of food

> is imported. No wonder it costs so much to keep the International Security Assistance Force (ISAF) in the field – an estimated $2,000 per soldier per day.[11]

Due to higher salaries and other upkeep expenses, the cost of posting an American soldier in Afghanistan exceeded that for a European.

It was mid-October by the time IEC officials had discarded a third of the votes as bogus, and Washington had corralled Karzai behind the scenes to accept the audited result. The IEC released its certified figures: Karzai, 2.28 million votes, 49.67 per cent; Abdullah, 1.4 million, 30.6 per cent. By failing to secure more than 50 per cent, Karzai had to face a run-off. This was set for 7 November. But a week before, Abdullah withdrew his candidacy because his demands for changes to the IEC, including the resignation of its chairman, were rejected, damaging the chances for a transparent poll.

Karzai commenced his second term as president on 19 November. His two vice-presidents were General Muhammad Qasim Fahim, a Tajik former vice-president and a bête noire of Pakistan, and Karim Khalili, a pro-Tehran Hazara. In his inaugural speech, Karzai said it would be five years before the Afghan forces were able to secure the whole country. His statement seemed overly optimistic. Several months later, General David Petraeus, commander of the NATO-led ISAF and US Forces Afghanistan, would tell the Senate Armed Forces Committee that it would be 'a number of years' before Afghan forces could manage on their own. 'Helping to train and equip host nation forces in the midst of an insurgency is akin to build an advanced aircraft while it is in flight, while it is being designed, and while it is being shot at,' he remarked.[12]

CORRUPT TO THE CORE

Karzai also pledged to fight corruption. It was about time. According to Transparency International, Afghanistan was the second most corrupt country of the 180 it rated, with only Somalia being worse. That signified deterioration in Afghanistan's sixty-third position among 178 countries in 2005. Transparency International defined corruption as 'abuse of entrusted power [in the public sector] for private gain'.

Along with the Ministries of the Interior (specifically police) and Justice (judges), the Ministry of Public Works (development projects) was at the top of the graft league table. Overall, half of foreign aid was lost due to corrupt or fraudulent practices, with 90 per cent of the US Agency for International Aid's $7 billion annual development grant being diverted aid. A survey by Integrity Watch Afghanistan, focusing on petty or administrative corruption that impacted directly on citizens, produced a disturbing estimate. 'The Afghan population as a whole paid twice as much in 2009 as it had paid in 2006,' it concluded. 'Bribery today represents a burden of $1 billion on the Afghan GDP [of $12 billion]. One adult in seven experienced direct bribery in Afghanistan while 28 per cent of Afghan households paid a bribe to obtain at least one public service.'[13] The amount involved in bribes equalled the total national tax revenue.

Corruption was rife in the top stratum of society. This came to light with the near-collapse, in September 2010, of the privately owned Kabul Bank, which handled the salaries of 250,000 civil servants as well as members of the security services. The ruin on the nine-year-old bank became so severe that the only option left to the government was nationalization. It could not afford to let a bank handling the salaries of soldiers and policemen go bankrupt. The bank had given massive unsecured loans to its largest shareholders. These included the bank's chairman, Sher Khan Farnood (owning 28 per cent of the equity), the chief executive officer, Khaliullah Frozi (28 per cent), Mahmoud Karzai, a brother of the president (7 per cent), and Muhammad Haseen, a brother of vice-president Muhammad Qasim Fahim (7 per cent). At Farnood's behest, the bank lent $65 million to Haseen, who financed Hamid Karzai's re-election campaign to the tune of $14 million. Farnood himself borrowed at least $140 million to buy 39 multimillion-dollar villas on Palm Jumeirah, a luxury man-made peninsula in Dubai. The root of the Kabul Bank crisis was the collapse of the Dubai real-estate market in 2008. The subsequently appointed government investigators said that the bank was also linked to their inquiry into New Ansari, a money-transfer company suspected of transferring billions of dollars out of Afghanistan on behalf of politicians, drug barons, and Taliban leaders.

An investigation into the bank's affairs by the Afghan Threat Finance Cell at the US embassy in Kabul – consisting of the agents of the FBI, Drug Enforcement Administration, Treasury Department, and Pentagon – gathered wide-ranging evidence of bribes to silence parliamentarians and others to let top bank executives indulge in fraud and embezzlement. According to some Afghan officials, Kabul Bank came to function as an unofficial agent of the Karzai administration and bribed parliamentarians to get its legislation passed.[14]

Classified diplomatic cables sent by the US embassy in Kabul, published by WikiLeaks in December 2010, contained extraordinary tales of graft and embezzlement. One referred to reports of Afghan vice-president Ahmad Zia Masoud arriving in Dubai in October 2009 – towards the end of his tenure in office – with $52 million in cash in suitcases and being waved through by airport officials.[15] Reports about Juma Khan Hamdard, governor of Paktia province, were shocking and alarming in equal measure. Citing 'credible sources', one US embassy cable referred to Hamdard's practice of dispatching armed goons to take construction contractors hostage until they paid bribes. Through his business in Dubai, he maintained multifarious contacts – from the insurgents in Parwan, Kunar and Kabul provinces to the ISI and the Iranian intelligence service.[16]

Along with sleaze and extortion went unabashed nepotism, with the Karzais and other politically well-connected families benefitting massively from the billions of dollars Washington had poured into Afghanistan since 2002. Following the elevation of the once obscure Hamid Karzai to the presidency, his clan members, long settled in the suburbs of Washington as restaurateurs and retail traders, rushed home to bécome important government officials, highly successful property developers or transporters with lucrative contracts from the Americans. The riches of the president's younger brother and his personal representative in the south, Ahmad Wali Karzai, based in Kandahar, were the talk of the town. A US embassy cable sent in June 2009 (and published by WikiLeaks) summarized his activities thus: He profited from trucking contracts, private security companies, and real estate, including the Ayno Mina development, a suburb on the edge of Kandahar built on land obtained at a rock-bottom price from the government. He used state institutions to protect and enable legal and illegal enterprises. Another super-affluent brother, Mahmoud Karzai, was put under electronic surveillance by US prosecutors as part of a corruption investigation into his insider dealings in real estate, cement and other industries.[17]

He had locked horns with the military high command by developing a profitable residential real-estate project on thousands of acres of valuable land in Kandahar that the army claimed as its own. As the ultimate institution that trained, equipped, and paid the Afghan army, the Pentagon had a valid interest in the case.

McCHRYSTAL, IN THE SHADOW OF WESTMORELAND

'The weakness of state institutions, malign actions of power brokers, wide-spread corruption and abuse of power by various officials and ISAF's own errors have given Afghans little reason to support their government,' said McChrystal in his report on 30 August. He also faulted NATO for its poor configuration for counter-insurgency and its lack of knowledge of the local languages and culture. Instead of putting the Afghan people first, continued McChrystal, NATO had relied overly on 'force protection and on fire power.' While it should be seen to be confronting Al Qaida and the Taliban, it should also show that it was defending the Afghan people.[18]

But the prerequisite for defending citizens was that they should want this service to be provided by foreign troops. That was hardly the case in Afghanistan. Most people were sitting on the fence, refusing to take sides, on balance unwilling to alienate the Taliban – an integral part of the Afghan society – by lining up with the transient Americans.

Unlike the freshness of his perspective on NATO, which included the Pentagon, McChrystal's reading of the Taliban covered familiar ground. Its leaders, he said, had appointed shadow governors in most provinces and levied taxes. Based in Pakistan, they were linked with Al Qaida, and were being helped by 'some elements' of the ISI. McChrystal wanted a minimum of forty thousand more US troops to tackle the problem. They would be deployed to expel the Taliban from their bastions, then hold the captured areas using primarily Afghan soldiers, as a prologue to the final goal – constructing roads, bridges, schools, clinics and police stations. On the political track, the aim would be to bring about defections of moderates among the Taliban ranks. This power-point presentation – tailored to brief foreign journalists and officials in Kabul – had little in common with reality.

With the joint total of US and NATO-led ISAF troops already at 133,000 – a shade lower than the Soviet peak (140,000) – more and more Afghans saw the American soldiers and their allies as hostile invaders rather than friendly forces. An ABC News poll in Afghanistan showed that 82 per cent were opposed to an increase in US and other NATO forces.[19]

While controversy about the rigged presidential poll raged in Afghanistan, Obama held a succession of meetings in the White House's Situation Room (now nicknamed Seminar Room) to debate McChrystal's requirements. President Johnson too consulted widely when General William Westmoreland, the US commander in South Vietnam, requested more troops in early 1965. Obama found his civilian and military advisers sharply divided, with uniforms mostly on one side and business suits largely on the other. The infighting was intense. General James Jones, the national security adviser, referred to the president's political advisers variably as 'the water bugs', 'the Politburo' and 'the Mafia', simply because they opposed dispatching more troops to Afghanistan. At the same time, Obama needed to pay heed to public opinion. A substantial and vocal section of his Democratic Party wanted a pull-out from Afghanistan.[20] So he compromised. On 1 December, he announced a dual-track plan: dispatching thirty thousand more troops, including three thousand trainers, within the next six months, while simultaneously declaring that the US would start withdrawing its forces from July 2011.

The decision to bolster the US forces led many American historians and veteran politicians to see parallels with Vietnam. 'Iraq and Afghanistan stand in the shadow of Vietnam,' said Robert Dallek, a biographer of President Johnson and the author of *Hail to the Chief: The Making and Unmaking of American Presidents*. 'It becomes inescapable that people are going to have doubts and questions about the wisdom of trying to control so distant and foreign a place.' The declassified White House tapes of telephone conversations showed that Johnson himself had shared those doubts. In his election campaign in 1964, he had maintained that the Vietnam conflict was not an American war. Yet on being elected, he decided to shore up the unpopular government in South Vietnam. While most of those participating in the debate following Westmoreland's request for more troops favoured granting it, one of the president's close friends, Clark Gifford, disagreed. 'We send in 100,000 troops, they'll match us with a hundred thousand of their own,' he said. 'I see nothing but catastrophe for our country.'[21]

Among politicians, George McGovern had stood out for his opposition to the Vietnam War since his election as senator in 1962. His consistent stance helped him to secure the 1972 Democratic nomination for the presidency against the incumbent Richard Nixon. Commenting on Obama's decision decades later, McGovern said, 'We're headed down the same road. We are not going to come out in 2011 . . . It's a no-win proposition. And in Afghanistan, nobody has ever been able to prevail in that deserted and mountainous country.'[22] Sure enough, towards the end of 2010, top officials of the Obama administration tried to downgrade the July 2011 deadline by insisting that any withdrawal of US troops would be minimal and that 2014 was the date when US-led NATO would start passing on responsibility for security to the Afghan forces.

In the American context, the major difference between Vietnam and Afghanistan was conscription. Since it was in force (from 1950 to 1973), many young middle- and upper-middle-class men mounted vigorous street protests against the Vietnam War. In the case of Afghanistan, those engaged in combat were all volunteers. As such, any opposition to the Afghan conflict, even when backed by a majority, remained muted.

By striking a balance between doves and hawks among his aides, Obama attempted to satisfy opposing domestic and foreign constituencies. By setting out a date for the beginning of the withdrawal, he fell in line with the view of nearly 60 per cent of Americans who, according to the latest *New York Times*/CBS News poll, did not want US troops to remain in Afghanistan beyond two years.[23] The announcement was also meant to shake up the incompetent Karzai administration and make it accelerate the build-up of its military and police. On the other hand, the immediate bolstering of US troop numbers in Afghanistan was designed to reassure Islamabad that the Obama administration was intent on winning the war. 'Winning' in this case had come to mean degrading the Afghan Taliban, and disrupting, dismantling and defeating Al Qaida and preventing its return to Afghanistan.

Critics of the Obama plan argued that, pressured by the Pentagon's surge in the south and south-east, the Taliban would decamp to the north and west, continue to receive clandestine assistance from Pakistan's ISI, and wait out the Americans. Hence the scenario of an attenuated Taliban in Afghanistan seemed unrealistic. That in turn would confirm the view of Pakistan's policy makers that it was against their national interests to antagonize the Afghan Taliban just when their chances of regaining power in the near future had improved.

A major drawback in the Pakistani perspective was that it lacked nuance. The Taliban, supported almost exclusively by Pushtuns, were unlikely to monopolize power in the future, and would have to share it with non-Pushtun groups, particularly their arch-rivals, the pro-India Tajiks. Fahim, one of the two Afghan vice-presidents, was a Tajik and a former leader of the Northern Alliance with a history of strong ties with Delhi. And the chairman of the seventy-member High Peace Council, appointed by President Karzai in September 2010 to find a peaceful solution to the conflict, was Burhanuddin Rabbani, another Tajik and a Northern Alliance stalwart.

'GOVERNMENT IN A BOX'

Building up the Afghan army and police was proving to be a Herculean task. The average annual desertion rate for the two forces was 24 per cent. At any given time 20–30 per cent of troops were absent without leave (AWOL). A soldier had to be for sixty AWOL days before any disciplinary action could be taken against him. Engendering supra-tribal loyalty in the troops remained a challenge – particularly after all the publicity given to the rigged presidential election and the brazen embezzlement at the bank that handled their salaries. As and when troops start getting their pay cheques from the government in Kabul rather than the Pentagon, there is a chance they will start harbouring unqualified loyalty to their paymaster. But such a day remains far away. Meanwhile, they have become part of the experiments being conducted by the Pentagon to devise an effective counter-insurgency campaign.

As Karzai was swearing in his freshly appointed cabinet at the Presidential Palace on 19 January 2010, the capital was rocked by audacious terrorist acts. Two men detonated suicide bombs near Pushtunistan Square, not far from the Palace, while five of their fellow militants headed for the Central Bank and the five-storey Faroshqa supermarket. They also targeted the finance and justice ministries. By the time they were killed by the security forces, they had succeeded in creating blood-splattered mayhem in the heart of Kabul. The Taliban leadership's message was clear: We can strike anywhere, any time we like, and the Karzai government and its American masters can do nothing about it.

A few days later at a press conference in Islamabad, US defense secretary Robert Gates took a softer position on the Taliban. 'Political reconciliation ultimately has to be a part of settling the conflict,' he said. 'The Taliban we recognize are part of the political fabric of Afghanistan at this point.'[24] Karzai had come to the same conclusion, surreptitiously, long before. He went public with it at the international conference on Afghanistan on 28 January 2010 when he said he would invite Taliban leaders to the Loya Jirga. Indeed, a month earlier, he had already moved in that direction when an electronic copy of the Reconciliation and General Amnesty Law, passed by parliament by a slim majority in March 2007, was discovered by a Kabul-based news agency. This law gave immunity from prosecution to all warlords, former factional leaders, and Taliban fighters and leaders. But, after its passage the government did not gazette it immediately – that is, send hard copies to judges and make an electronic version available online.[25]

The Afghan president had started conducting super-secret talks with the Taliban's number two, Mullah Abdul Ghani Baradar, through trusted intermediaries. Born in 1968 in Weetmak in Uruzgan province, Baradar supervised day-to-day operations, appointed military commanders and shadow governors, secured finances and supplies, and directed the Taliban's parallel administration in the south and south-east. As a comparative moderate, he advocated the organization narrowing its aim to liberating Afghanistan and not getting involved in a global jihad, as favoured by the younger neo-Taliban leaders who were ideologically close to Al Qaida. For security reasons he refrained from meeting Mullah Omar and received his general instructions through couriers. The increased US drone attacks and Pakistan's offensives in the Afghan border region compelled him to move to Karachi in January 2010. It was in that city's industrial neighbourhood, Loni Kot, that he was arrested on 8 February by an ISI team accompanied by CIA agents.[26] The ISI targeted him because he was one of the two dozen Taliban leaders they suspected of talking to Karzai through Afghan intermediaries and excluding it from the process. The ISI was resolved to abort any attempt at negotiations that precluded it.

Mullah Omar moved fast to appoint Baradar's successor – thirty-seven-year-old Mullah Abdul Qayum Zakir (aka Abdullah Ghulam Rasul), then commander of southern Afghanistan. Captured on the battlefield in Afghanistan in November 2001 by anti-Taliban forces, he was held at the Guantánamo Bay detention centre until 2007. On his release, he rejoined the Taliban and emerged as a tough commander.

In the opposite camp, true to his reputation as a tough commander, McChrystal mounted Operation Moshtarak (Dari, 'Together') in the poppy-growing belt of Helmand in late January 2010. He had assembled a combined force of fifteen thousand, consisting of the Afghan security agencies and troops from America, Britain, Canada and Estonia. Their target was Marja, a Taliban stronghold of 85,000 people.

To distinguish it from previous offensives, McChrystal announced that NATO and Afghan officials had assembled a large team of Afghan civil servants, backed by 1,900 police officers, who would move into the liberated Marja. 'We've got a government in a box, ready to roll in,' he declared. This was a new model war being unveiled by a heroic commander with imagination. Soon after, the phrase 'government in a box' would come to haunt him.

Faced with such overwhelming armed might, the Taliban disappeared after a few days of fighting. On 18 February, Afghan troops raised the national flag over the damaged bazaar. But instead of eradicating the drugs trade, one of the publicized reasons for the offensive, US and NATO commanders decided to overlook the production of opium in Marja because most residents were dependent on it for their livelihood.

More disappointingly, the security situation in Marja deteriorated within weeks despite the disbursement of hundreds of thousands of dollars in the local 'Afghanis' currency by US Marines as compensation for property damage or as wages to those who worked on their projects. One battalion alone distributed $150,000 a week. And, the Taliban found ways of accessing the American cash to be used against the Pentagon. Citing his local informants, Colonel Ghulam Sakhi, an Afghan National Police commander, revealed that at least thirty Taliban had visited one US Marine Corps outpost to take money as compensation for property damage or family members killed during the offensive. 'You shake hands with them, but you don't know they are Taliban,' Sakhi said. 'They have the same clothes and the same style [as others]. And they are using the money against the Marines. They are buying IEDs and buying ammunition, everything.'[27]

By late May the situation had worsened to the point where the Americans were in control by day but found themselves challenged by the gun-wielding Taliban at night. Instead of the blueprint for the future in Afghanistan, Marja had become, in the words of McChrystal, 'a bleeding ulcer'.

The admission did little to temper McChrystal's propensity to boast, which had been augmented by his habit of surrounding himself with unquestioning acolytes. Stuck in Paris in April due to the cancellation of air traffic as a result of volcanic eruption in Iceland, and feeling uninhibited after many rounds of drinks, McChrystal and his team garrulously criticized the Obama administration's top officials to Michael Hastings of *Rolling Stone* magazine. They were scathing about the way the White House was directing the war in Afghanistan, accusing the US ambassador to Afghanistan, Retired General Karl Eikenberry, of undermining the war. They called General James Jones, the national security adviser, a 'clown', and mocked Vice-President Joe Biden. There was also indirect criticism of President Obama for appearing 'uncomfortable and intimidated' by senior generals at their first meeting at the Pentagon in January 2009. The interview was published in the magazine on 22 June. It caused a firestorm.

By criticizing the commander-in-chief in public, McChrystal violated a cardinal principle of the American constitution which specifies civilian control of the military. Disagreement with or criticism of the commander-in-chief was allowed in private, but never in public. After holding a meeting with McChrystal to hear his side of the story, Obama dismissed him as the commander of the NATO-led ISAF and US Forces Afghanistan, and replaced him with General David Petraeus.

However, there was no change in the policy that McChrystal had devised. Petraeus confirmed that the long-postponed offensive to expel the Taliban from Kandahar would be launched in July. When this failed to happen, he explained that the strategy of securing the areas around the city was taking longer than expected. Moreover, neither he nor his commander-in-chief, Obama, had a strategy to handle the unprecedented and extraordinary exposure of tens of thousands of classified raw field reports in Afghanistan that would become available on the Internet in late July.

AN AUTHENTICATED, UNVARNISHED VIEW OF WAR

By publishing a summary of over ninety thousand documents – covering US military incidents and intelligence reports from January 2004 to December 2009 – on 25 July 2010, the *New York Times*, the *Guardian* and the Hamburg-based *Der Spiegel* performed unmatched public service. They were given access to this rich treasure trove by the anti-secrecy organization, called WikiLeaks, run by Julian Assange, an Australian citizen.

It was the first time in history that ordinary citizens became privy to an unvarnished, blow-by-blow account of an ongoing war. Thus, among other things, they could see how the highly efficient public-relations machine of the United States had withheld many vital facts and had spun others to serve its employer's political ends. For example, it had denied the successful use of ground-to-air missiles by the Taliban, and it had made no mention of any of the nearly 150 instances when NATO forces killed or injured civilians.

The salient points made by the voluminous reports can be summarized as follows. The Taliban has proved to be a cunning foe. It combines its armed attacks with sabotage and trickery, often fighting briefly before slipping away. To neutralize their Afghan opponents and widen their own base, they deploy a mixture of threats, violence, charm, cash, populist demands, and Islamic zeal. The Afghan police force is unreliable, with numerous examples of its officers defecting and taking with them the arms and trucks captured during previous successful raids. The US-funded provincial reconstruction teams have failed due to rampant corruption and cultural misunderstandings. The tensions and rivalries between different groups of power brokers plague the Afghanistan administration all the way to the top, including the presidency. The scores of instances of Afghan civilians getting killed in small numbers when their vehicles mistakenly got too close to checkpoints or military convoys had left the population fearful of, and alienated from NATO forces. The expanded activities of US SOF units created resentment among Afghans due to their exemption from accountability, lack of coordination with local security forces, and the resulting civilian casualties. The list of incidents of 'friendly fire' – NATO troops harming one another or fellow Afghan soldiers – was far too long. As for the Pakistani ISI, its collusion with the Afghan Taliban goes beyond the widely known parameters. Islamabad allows ISI officers to meet Taliban leaders in clandestine strategy sessions to orchestrate militant networks fighting the US forces in Afghanistan. Maintaining such an intimate relationship with the Afghan Taliban also ensured that Pakistan would have a powerful tool in hand to destabilize any pro-India government that might emerge in Kabul in the post-America era.

Predictably, US defense secretary Robert Gates denounced the WikiLeaks disclosures, claiming, inter alia, that they endangered

Afghan lives. But on 16 August, in reply to a query from Senator Carl Levin, chairman of the Senate Committee on the Armed Services, he said that a review by the Pentagon showed that these disclosures 'had not revealed any sensitive intelligence sources and methods'.[28] As expected, Karzai's Presidential Palace also lambasted the leaks, which came against a background of escalating violence. In August, the number of Taliban attacks, including bombs, small-arms fire and shelling, soared to 4,919 – a year-on-year increase of 50 per cent. After some hesitation, the president decided to delay the upcoming election to the 249-member People's Assembly until after the fasting month of Ramadan, ending on 10 September, to allow proper campaigning.

FLAWED PARLIAMENTARY ELECTIONS

The average of twenty candidates vying for each parliamentary seat looked impressive. But the explanation for this lay in the monthly salary of $2,200, a princely sum, not to mention the power of patronage that parliamentarians wielded. The rising insecurity forced the government to reduce the number of polling stations from 6,300 to 5,800. Even then, a tenth of these remained closed on the polling day, 18 September.

The Taliban spokesman, Zabiullah Mujahid, told the Associated Press in Kabul by telephone: 'The election is only to the benefit of foreigners who want to maintain their existence in the country by holding such a process. That is why we announced to the local people that all Afghan people should boycott this election.'[29] The effectiveness of this message could be judged by examining what happened in Marja, the town liberated by NATO in February. Only about a thousand men registered to vote there.

As in the presidential poll, voters' registration cards were available for sale, at an average price of $6. The demand for real as well as fake cards was high. Among other things that explained the 626 per cent voter turnout in Paktia province. Due to this and other malpractices, one-third of the 5.4 million ballots cast would be invalidated – the same proportion as in the presidential poll.

True to its word, the Taliban fired three hundred rockets on polling day, the principal target being the traditional Pushtun-majority areas. 'The streets and bazaars were largely empty when polls opened at 8 a.m., and by noon there were reports that fewer than 100 people had cast ballots in Marja,' reported Elisabeth Bumiller from the town.[30] So, McChrystal's 'bleeding ulcer' remained just that under the watch of his successor. Aware of the review that Obama had planned on making in December 2010, Petraeus, now went into overdrive to show concrete results.

HARSH TRUTH VERSUS ROSY REPORTS

Under Petraeus's command, the number of bombs and missiles fired at the Taliban rose by half. More importantly, the SOF's helicopter-borne night raids shot up fivefold, from forty a month in 2009 to two hundred. But they were proving less effective. The Taliban responded by having two people in every village in the Pushtun region keep watch at night. They were instructed by the local Taliban commander to alert fellow villagers, as soon as they heard a helicopter approaching, to prepare to fight or flee. Likewise, anyone spotting a spy plane alerted the rest of the villagers.

Those insurgent commanders who got captured or killed were replaced by younger men educated and indoctrinated in the madrasas of Pakistan. So here was another parallel with the American military involvement in Vietnam. Communist leaders were able to replenish their guerrilla forces rapidly as there was no dearth of volunteers in South and North Vietnam. In Afghanistan, the Taliban's supreme Shura Council could, and did, match any increase in US troops with volunteers drawn from Afghanistan as well as the twenty-eight million ethnic Pushtun inhabitants of Baluchistan, FATA and Khyber Pakhtunkhwa. It was therefore hard to see how Petraeus was going to achieve his strategic aim of convincing the Taliban's supreme Shura

Council that it could not win and so should declare a ceasefire and enter into talks with the Karzai government openly.

As it was, the Afghanistan NGO Safety Office (ANSO), whose system for collecting information around the country was unmatched, offered statistics and analysis which contradicted the statements by NATO's public-relations department. Unlike NATO and the Presidential Palace, ANSO had no military or political agenda to advance. According to ANSO, between July and September 2010, Taliban attacks grew 59 per cent compared to the same period in 2009. The record number of 1,600 assaults staged in a week of September was five hundred higher than in any previous week of the conflict. In the non-Pushtun north there had been a significant rise in violence. 'The sum of the Taliban's activity presents the image of a movement anticipating authority and one which has already obtained a complex momentum that NATO will be incapable of reversing,' it concluded.[31]

In an on-the-record interview with Bob Woodward for the latter's book, *Obama's Wars*, Petraeus summarized his view. 'I think you keep fighting,' he said. 'You have to stay after it. This is the kind of fight we're in for the rest of our lives and probably our kids' lives.'[32] It seemed Petraeus had less grasp of American history and the national psyche than the prime minister of North Vietnam in the 1960s, Pham Van Dong. 'Americans do not like long, inconclusive wars, and this [Vietnam War] is going to be a long, inconclusive war,' he had said. 'Thus we are sure to win in the end.'

13

FIGHTING EXTREMISM

THE ONGOING WAR in Afghanistan, pitting United States-led NATO forces against the Taliban, is the most destabilizing element in South Asia. It was that country's transformation into a front-line state in the Cold War in 1979–80 that became the primary factor in shaping the subsequent history of the region. The prize in the conflict is ending Afghanistan's civil war, dating back to 1978, and establishing a stable regime, recognized by all its neighbours and other United Nations member states. Achieving such an outcome eluded the mightiest of nations. The Soviet Union, a superpower until 1991, failed. And failure now seems to be in the offing for the remaining superpower, the United States of America.

In his interview with Bob Woodward, General David Petraeus said, 'You have to recognize also that I don't think you win this war.'[1] Equally remarkably, when Woodward asked President Barack Obama, 'You can't lose a war or be perceived to lose one, can you?' Obama replied: 'I think about it [the Afghan War] not so much in the classic [sense], do you lose a war on my watch? I think about it more in terms of, do you successfully prosecute a strategy that results in the country being stronger rather than weaker at the end of it?'[2]

In late October 2010, Petraeus confirmed that the NATO-led International Security Assistance Force (ISAF) had provided 'safe passage' for 'top Taliban leaders' to fly into Kabul from Quetta for talks with Afghan president Hamid Karzai. It turned out that only one such 'leader' was involved, and that ISAF had provided him with the transport. Later, to the great embarrassment of the US and Afghan governments, that 'leader' turned out to be a trader based in Quetta. How he managed to con a whole raft of American and Afghan officials and spooks remains a mystery. The upshot of the meeting was that Karzai gave him some money from a slush fund, which he has publicly acknowledged maintaining, in order to secure defections from the Taliban.

Given Obama's commitment to start withdrawing US soldiers from Afghanistan from July 2011, no matter how minimally, there is no incentive for the Taliban's supreme Shura Council to confer legitimacy on the despised Karzai government by talking to him, even through intermediaries. It knows too that neither Karzai nor his Western sponsors will accept its demand that all foreign forces must leave before it negotiates with the president in Kabul.

For their part, Karzai and his Western benefactors will also insist that their preconditions are met. One: The Taliban must accept the present constitution – a demand it will reject summarily. Two: It must sever any links it has with Al Qaida and agree upfront never to give sanctuary to its leaders or ranks in Afghanistan. No progress on this subject can be made without the overt or covert involvement of Pakistan's ISI directorate. The ISI has been and will continue to be a vital factor in this complex equation. The issue of delinking with Al Qaida is likely to divide the Taliban's supreme Shura Council. The ISI will most likely side with the comparative moderates to help move the process towards a peaceful solution.

This is the best-case scenario. The worst-case scenario is all attempts to get the adversaries to talk to one another fail, and a much weaker Afghan government with reduced Western backing finds itself having to fight a foe who is stronger than before. 'Victor takes all' will be the rule of this confrontation. To abort an outcome that invests the Taliban with total power, Afghanistan's neighbours will intervene, thereby intensifying the civil war. The resulting crisis will prove even more intractable than any of the previous ones.

To return to the best-case scenario: Given the political will on both sides, a compromise can be struck whereby all foreign troops withdraw to their bases within a period of, say, eighteen to twenty-four months. That could prepare the ground for sharing power with the Taliban. This could take the form of the Taliban getting a share in government jobs at all levels and/or control of the Pushtun-majority provinces. Working out the details of such an agreement would be a long, tortuous exercise stretching over many months at the very least. The tenure of the resulting transitional authority would have to be decided upfront. Its main task would be either to set out a procedure for convening a Loya Jirga to draft a new constitution, or holding elections under United Nations supervision for the resulting representative body to produce a fresh constitution.

Given the history of glacial progress in inter-Afghan negotiations, it is hard to imagine either a Loya Jirga or a new constituent assembly materializing before the late 2010s – particularly when the rabidly anti-Taliban forces, led by pro-Delhi Tajiks, would be only too ready to play the role of a spoiler. In all multilateral negotiations, it takes only one party to take an uncompromising stance to wreck the process.

Assuming positive progress, the Loya Jirga or the constituent assembly will have the option of creating a centralized or federal state. The federal arrangement will enable the Taliban to be the supreme authority, with a popular mandate, in the Pushtun-majority provinces, while the Tajiks, Hazaras, and Uzbeks will have the option of living under a less regimented system. If this drawn-out process ends successfully, the Taliban would morph, knowingly or inadvertently, into a religious–political party like the Jamaat-e Islami in Pakistan.

What about Al Qaida and its partisans? If, as and when they find the pressure by the freshly reconciled Afghan factions, backed by the regional powers and America, unbearable in the tribal areas of Pakistan, they will decamp in small groups to Karachi and small ports along Baluchistan's coast on their way to Yemen and/or Somalia. This is what happened after the fall of the Taliban regime in late 2001. Already, due to US drone attacks and Pakistani military's offensives in the Federally Administered Tribal Agencies, many Al Qaida and Tehrik-e Taliban Pakistan activists have left the border area and found a haven among the large Pushtun community in Karachi.

To facilitate the realization of the best-case scenario, the introverted policy pursued so far by the US and its Western allies needs to be rectified. Driven by the trauma of 9/11, Western nations have monopolized policy making and execution in Afghanistan. By so doing, they have overlooked a stark geopolitical reality. The ultimate outcome in Afghanistan is of greater strategic consequence to its regional neighbours – Iran, Turkmenistan, Uzbekistan, Tajikistan, Russia, China, Pakistan, and India – who will face a more menacing threat from Afghanistan, if the Taliban acquires a monopoly on power or even a dominant role there, than will America.[3]

Indeed, during his meeting with British prime minister Gordon Brown in September 2008, Pakistani president Asif Ali Zardari presented a paper in which he proposed Pakistan convening a conference of the representatives of Afghanistan, Iran, China, Russia, and India along with Turkmenistan, Uzbekistan, and Tajikistan to debate how to overcome the current crisis in the region – with the US and Britain attending as observers. The aim was twofold: to dispel the popular belief among the region's Muslim-majority countries that America was using the War on Terror as a pretext to attack and destabilize Muslim states, and to demonstrate that this campaign was now being owned by the regional countries themselves. Brown did not consider the proposal seriously; nor did President George W. Bush. For his part, Zardari lacked the intelligence and political savvy to press his proposal.

Zardari's other major weakness was – and is – that responsibility for foreign policy that impinges on national security rests exclusively with the military. Even in domestic affairs the armed forces high command continues to play a crucial behind-the-scenes role. The US embassy cables leaked by WikiLeaks in December 2010 revealed that Zardari's future hung in the balance during the first half of March. The opposition leader, Muhammad Nawaz Sharif, rallied his supporters in Lahore to march on Islamabad to force Zardari to honour his promise to reinstate chief justice Iftikhar Chaudhry, who had been sacked by President Pervez Musharraf. General Ashfaq Parvez Kayani, the army chief, met US ambassador Anne Patterson four times in a week. In the last meeting he hinted that he might have to 'persuade' Zardari to resign and go into exile if the situation deteriorated – to be replaced by Afsandyar Wali Khan of the regional National Awami Party. He conveyed to Patterson the 'disquiet' of his corps commanders about the corrupt Zardari's failure to meet Pakistan's 'economic and security challenges'.[4] Yielding to pressure, Zardari reinstated Chaudhry, and thus saved his own office, now shorn of any meaningful power even in internal affairs.

However, Pakistan's corps commanders were so obsessed with countering India's potential influence in Afghanistan that they failed to notice that Iran and China were set to become major players in Kabul. In 2009, the Congjiang Copper Group, a Chinese corporation, obtained the right to mine copper ore in Afghanistan from one of the richest deposits on the planet. It offered $3.4 billion for the licence – $1 billion more than the highest bid by a Western metallurgy company. The following year, Karzai publicly admitted receiving cash from Tehran to meet 'the expenses of my office'. Of course, nobody expected him to say outright that Iran was trying to buy influence in Kabul.

While Western governments and NGOs are trying to build up a modern, functioning state in Afghanistan, an uphill task, they are worried by the prospect of neighbouring Pakistan ending up as a failed state. Such a development, or even the disintegration of Pakistan, will create a host of intractable problems not only for the region but the world at large.

PAKISTAN: KEYSTONE OF THE SOUTH ASIAN ARCH

Pakistan is the pivotal country in the region, the keystone in the arch with war-torn Afghanistan at one end and stable India at the other. It is also beset with all the major problems of the modern world: population explosion, rising inequality, maladministration, ethnic and sectarian tensions, breakdown of law and order, a thriving drugs trade, religious fundamentalism, home to the largest number of Islamist extremists in the world, and possession of nuclear arms. Because of police incompetence in gathering solid evidence, and judges' fear of being murdered by violent jihadists, most cases against suspected Islamist militants result in acquittal. Journalists shy away from criticizing judicial rulings for fear of being punished for contempt of court. They resort to self-censorship when writing about the armed forces and the ISI. Reflecting the anti-American sentiment that prevails at the popular level, most of the mass media has taken to pushing a nationalist and pro-Islamist line. Pakistan's civilian institutions remain feeble and its major political parties stuck in feudal loyalties. Its military commanders, trained in conventional warfare, are untutored in leading counter-insurgency campaigns effectively to tackle the jihadist insurgency at home.

Its economy is weak, with its already crumbling infrastructure further being damaged by devastating floods in 2010. This disaster wiped 2 per cent off its GDP growth, leaving just enough to match population growth. Official statistics show that animal dung and leftover waste from crops provide over 80 per cent of Pakistan's energy, and that two out of five rural households lack electricity. The gap between the affluent and the indigent is widening. There is high unemployment among uneducated or poorly educated young men imbued with Islamic fervour. The country suffers from a top-heavy bureaucracy which is inept and steeped in graft. The easy availability of small arms has undermined law and order. Karachi, the nation's largest city with eighteen million inhabitants, has become a haven for weapons smugglers, drug barons, and extortionists. Violence rooted in ethnicity and crime now claims a hundred lives a month in this seaside city – far more than the fatalities caused by the Pakistani Taliban's suicide bombings in the whole country.

Pakistan – the Next Generation, a report on young Pakistanis, commissioned by the British Council and published in November 2009, presented a bleak picture of the country's future. It was based on interviews with 1,226 Pakistanis, aged 18–29, from varied backgrounds. Because of the ongoing Pakistani Taliban violence, almost 80 per cent believed that their country was headed in the 'wrong direction'. But the 23 per cent annual inflation rate, which pushed 7 per cent of Pakistanis below the poverty line, was the interviewees' topmost concern, far above terrorism. Over 90 per cent agreed that better-quality education was a priority. The same proportion also complained that the present system was corrupt. 'Here a [typical] student struggles day and night but the son of a rich man by giving money gets higher marks than he does,' said a young man in Lahore. Only a fifth of the interviewees had permanent full-time jobs. Another 50 per cent said they lacked sufficient skills to join the regular workforce. Whereas 10 per cent were 'very interested' in Pakistani politics, 35 per cent were not interested at all. At 60 per cent, the military was the most trusted institution, followed by the madrasas at 50 per cent, with the national government at the bottom, on 10 per cent. More remarkably, 75 per cent identified themselves as Muslim first, and then Pakistani, with only 14 per cent describing their identity in the reverse order. Last but not least, only a third believed democracy to be the best system of governance, another third preferring the Sharia, and 7 per cent dictatorship.[5]

The findings of this extremely significant report – commissioned by a foreign cultural organization without any political agenda to advance in Pakistan – show that a military campaign focused on targeting the leaders and commanders of radical jihadist groups defuses the crisis only partially. The root of the problem lies deeper – in the national identity that was imprinted on young Pakistanis through relentless Islamist propaganda and education (for those who acquired it) in the 1980s under General Muhammad Zia ul Haq. It is that generation that has now come of age. It is the one that by and large identifies itself primarily as Muslim and is divided evenly between supporting democracy and Sharia rule. Such a large body of young citizens cannot be simply captured or killed.

An episode that unfolded during November 2010–January 2011 furnished a stark profile of society as a whole and indicated the most likely future scenario. On 8 November, a court in Lahore, acting under the Blasphemy Law of 1986, sentenced Aasia Bibi, a Christian mother of four, to death for insulting Prophet Muhammad during a dispute with some Muslim women in her village. Salman Taseer, the liberal governor of Punjab, criticized the law and signed a mercy petition addressed to the president. A ministerial review ordered by Zardari concluded that the verdict was unsound and recommended a presidential pardon. The government announced its intention to amend the 1986 law, which had been manipulated in such a way as to make a Christian sixteen times more prone to its application than a liberal Muslim. Islamists of various hues mounted a vocal protest. The government caved in and ruled out any amendment. Two fiery clerics offered a bounty to anyone who killed Taseer. An umbrella organization called Tehrik-e Tahaffuz-e Namoos-e Risalat (Urdu, 'Movement for Protecting the Dignity of Prophethood') organized countrywide demonstrations on 31 December, a Friday (the Muslim holy day of the week), against any changes to the Blasphemy Law.

On 4 January, Malik Mumtaz Hussein Qadri, one of Taseer's police bodyguards, assassinated the provincial governor in Islamabad. Since Qadri, a hefty, bearded man of twenty-six, had briefed other bodyguards in the unit about his intentions, they watched passively as he pumped twenty-seven sub-machine-gun shots into the back of Taseer. 'Salman Taseer deserved to be killed because he had called the Blasphemy Law a black law,' Qadri declared. The cold-blooded murder and its aftermath showed fissures in society on several levels.

Within hours, a Facebook page praising the assassin attracted more than two thousand followers. While leaders of moderate religious parties like the Jamaat-e Islami said Taseer 'deserved' to be killed, five hundred clerics of the hardline Jamaat Ahle Sunnat (Urdu, 'Society of People of Sunna') forbade their followers to pray for the deceased or attend his funeral. They lauded Qadri as a 'hero of the Muslim world'. On TV discussion programmes many commentators justified the murder. Random interviews with people in the street showed that they thought Taseer was killed because *he* had insulted Prophet Muhammad.

The next day, prior to Qadri being presented before a magistrate and charged with murder and terrorism, over two hundred lawyers garlanded the smiling defendant, showering him with rose petals.[6] They were among the thousand attorneys from the twin cities of Islamabad and Rawalpindi who gave their signed support to Qadri's defence. In contrast, fearing for his life, the public prosecutor did not turn up at the hearing. Nor did Zardari show up at the funeral of Taseer, a luminary of his Pakistan People's Party. The opposition leader, Nawaz Sharif, also stayed away. Corps commanders were likewise conspicuous by their absence. The retreat of the civilian and military power elite in the face of murderous intimidation heartened Islamists and their jihadist cohorts.

This episode was a dramatic illustration of the triumph of street power over electoral authority. In Pakistan, the electoral system is weighted in favour of feudal lords since a large majority of voters live in villages, whereas day-to-day politics are played out in urban centres. There Islamist groups enjoy wide support among the lower-middle and working classes who fill the ranks of the security and intelligence services as well as the civil service. Taseer's assassination and its aftermath also revealed the true extent of the Islamization of society introduced by Zia ul Haq.

It remained to be seen if, jolted by this landmark episode, the political elite would close ranks and mount a concerted campaign to seize the initiative away from Islamists and their radical allies. That would require devising and implementing a multi-pronged strategy combining the use of the state's repressive organs to curb violence with education, information and propaganda provided via government-run electronic media as well the mosques run by moderate clerics. A simple but effective point could be made that the Islamic invocation of '*Bismillah al Rahman al Rahim*' ['In the name of Allah, the Merciful, the Compassionate'], the stress is laid on God's mercy and compassion – not on his harshness and spite.

Proactive steps taken to counter the influence that radical jihadist organizations have acquired through terror and intimidation should also include rallying the practitioners of Sufism, which is popular in Pakistan's heavily populated provinces of Punjab and Sindh. Actually, a half-hearted move was made in that direction by Musharraf in October 2006 – not as an antidote to extremism but as a means to counter the poor image Pakistan had in the West. He established a National Council for the Promotion of Sufism under the chairmanship of Chaudhary Shujat Hussain, leader of the pro-Musharraf Pakistan Muslim League (Q). It announced an ambitious programme. But after holding a Sufi music festival in Lahore, and printing calendars in its name, the council soon became dormant.

It was not until June 2009, when the Pakistani Taliban went on the offensive against the state, that the civilian government set up a seven-member Sufi Advisory Council to combat extremism and fanaticism by spreading Sufism. But it has proved as toothless and unimaginative as the National Council before it, despite the devastating attacks on revered Sufi shrines continuing unabated. It has yet to realize the urgent need to establish a coordinating centre for the Sufi network – the first essential step to tapping the full potential of the Sufi way of life as a strong counter-force to the violence of radical Islamists.

In any war, a protagonist should look for a chink in the armour of his antagonist and target it. To their list of enemies, starting with the Western nations and the West-backed Muslim regimes, radical jihadist organizations have added not only crusader Christians and pantheistic Hindus but also Shias, Ahmadis, and Sufis. Opening so many fronts simultaneously is a strategic error that their adversaries have so far failed to exploit.

The best-case scenario is for Pakistan's military and civilian leaders to formulate a comprehensive plan encompassing these ideas and to implement it if only to maintain the integrity of Pakistan's territory and administrative apparatus. The worst-case scenario is for the current low-intensity warfare between the state and the jihadist groups to continue, with the Punjab-based extremists – fortified by the defiant support given to Governor Taseer's assassin by a constituency that spans all classes – creating mayhem in the heartland of Pakistan. This would further damage the country's economy and future.

So far there is no sign of an effective strategy being devised partly because the Pakistani establishment is divided and is following inconsistent policies. While it aids the Afghan Taliban, it confronts the Afghan movement's ally, the Pakistani Taliban. And its abiding hostility towards India, encapsulated in the Kashmir dispute, has led it to cooperate actively with such jihadist bodies as the Lashkar-e Taiba (LeT).

THE KASHMIR DISPUTE

Among the possible solutions to the Kashmir issue, the earliest one, contained in UN Security Council resolution 47 in 1948, required a plebiscite in all of Jammu and Kashmir as it existed under British rule. Today, it would be virtually impossible to implement that resolution. The Aksai Chin region, forming nearly one-sixth of the area of Jammu and Kashmir, is controlled by China, which has no intention of relinquishing its jurisdiction. The same is true of the Trans-Karakoram Tract, part of the pre-1947 state which Islamabad transferred to China as stipulated in the 1963 Sino-Pakistani border agreement.

The Khunjerab Pass in the Karakoram mountain range on the northern border of the federally administered Gilgit–Baltistan of Pakistan is of vital strategic importance to China's Xinjiang Autonomous Province. The road across this pass was completed in

1982. Now there are plans to build a railway to link up with Gwadar, the Chinese-built deep-water port in Baluchistan. The chief purpose of this project would be to transport petroleum from the nearby Persian Gulf region to China, thus drastically cutting the distance that tankers have to travel to deliver oil to energy-hungry China.

A poll of 2,369 people in Indian Kashmir by the Delhi-based *Hindustan Times* in September 2010 showed that only 6 per cent wanted 'a complete merger of entire Jammu and Kashmir into Pakistan'. The figures for 'a complete merger of the state into India' were 76 per cent in Jammu and 70 per cent in Ladakh. In the Kashmir Valley, 66 per cent wanted 'complete freedom to entire Jammu and Kashmir as a new country'.[7] An independent Kashmir implies both Pakistan and India withdrawing their troops from the areas they control. The mistrust on both sides is so deep that working out the modalities of such a phased pullout will tax the best brains, particularly when Delhi steadfastly refuses the involvement of a third party. And even if, against all odds, an independent Kashmir comes into existence, it will be a weak, landlocked country surrounded by powerful neighbours with clashing agendas.

When anti-India protests led to widespread demonstrations and strikes in the Kashmir Valley in the summer of 2010, Pakistan's ISI refrained from accentuating the agitation. Deeply engaged at home in fending off a grave security threat to the Pakistani state from radical jihadist groups, it lacked the men and money to intensify protest in the Kashmir Valley. As for the future, there will be periodic upsurge in Kashmiri Muslims' indignation at Delhi which will boil over into street protests and strikes. The Indian government will continue to do what it has done before: use a mixture of carrots (increased subsidies to the state government) and sticks (use of paramilitaries and army troops). It will continue to violate human rights as it has done in the past. Actually, the history of wide-scale violation of human rights by the Delhi government goes back as far as the mid-1950s in the north-eastern region, which is far removed from the gaze of the foreign media.

Since Delhi has ruled out any alteration to India's current border in Kashmir, the only viable solution is the one that Musharraf was in the process of thrashing out secretly with the Indian government: transforming the present Line of Control into the international border but keeping it porous in the way Pakistan did its Afghan border until 2006. Even though Musharraf conducted these negotiations while he was also army chief, there was still no guarantee that if and when the covert talks progressed to a signed agreement all his corps commanders would have fallen in line.

To the all-powerful military in Pakistan, Kashmir represents more than a territory. It has become the symbol and substance of the idea on which Pakistan was founded – namely, that a Muslim minority among Hindus will never get a fair deal and must therefore have a sovereign state of its own. On top of that, Zia ul Haq wrapped up the issue in Islamic terms. Kashmir has provided the armed forces with their most effective argument for their huge budget which remains exempt from scrutiny by the government or parliament. So, though the generals in Pakistan would not say so publicly, they would be loath to see this dispute settled peacefully.

PAKISTAN'S NUCLEAR ARSENAL

It was the issue of Kashmir that drove Zulfikar Ali Bhutto to launch a nuclear arms programme, and a military ruler, Zia ul Haq, to advance it by all means – an enterprise in which rabidly anti-Soviet US president Ronald Reagan became his accomplice. The end result is a Pakistan with a nuclear arsenal of almost one hundred atom bombs as of 2010. Unlike India, it has refused to announce that it would not be the first to use atom bombs in a war. The Pakistan-based Al Qaida leaders have publicly expressed their wish to acquire weapons to bring about a nuclear 9/11.

Both Delhi and Washington were therefore alarmed by the four (known) terrorist attacks staged during October 2007–October 2009 on Pakistani army bases storing nuclear weapons as well as by infiltrations made by extremists into other military facilities. These included an assault in November 2007 on the country's principal airbase at Sargodha, Punjab, where nuclear-capable F16 jet aircraft are parked. The following month, a suicide bomber struck at Pakistan's nuclear airbase at Kumra, 55 miles (88 km) north-west of Islamabad, home to the Pakistan Aeronautical Complex. In August 2008, the gates to the factory engaged in assembling Pakistan's nuclear weapons in the military city of Wah Cantonment – the twin town to Kumra – were blown up by a group of suicide bombers. The Kumra defence equipment complex experienced an assault in October 2009.[8]

It is quite likely that among the 8,000–12,000 Pakistanis involved in the nuclear weapons programme there are sympathizers of jihadist groups who may facilitate some kind of attack or pilfering. All that is needed is radicalization of a key player within the nuclear establishment. In August 2001, Bashiruddin Mahmood, a pro-Taliban head of Pakistan's plutonium reactor until 1999, and Chaudhry Abdul Majeed, one of the pioneers of Pakistan's nuclear programme, met Osama bin Laden. According to Majeed, bin Laden asked them to build a radiological bomb, adding that he could obtain smuggled uranium from Uzbekistan. Majeed explained that they were nuclear engineers, not weapons designers. Both Pakistanis were involved in running an Islamic charity organization in Afghanistan. When news of their meeting leaked, the Pakistani government arrested them on 23 October. Two months later, Mahmood was released from jail and put under house arrest. The still-imprisoned Majeed died of a heart attack in January 2006.

At present, Pakistan's nuclear weapons are well guarded, thanks partly to the $100 million worth of technical assistance provided by the Pentagon. Islamabad has explained its vetting system to Washington. Its Strategic Plans Division, in charge of nuclear security, runs a personal-reliability programme for all those who enter the high walls of the nuclear facilities. This is designed to screen out Al Qaida spies, Taliban sympathizers and Islamic extremists. The Strategic Plans Division also ensures that bomb components are stored at different sites. But that makes them susceptible to hijacking in transit. The US fears that someone working in the facilities could gradually smuggle out enough material to build a bomb eventually.

Since Americans are denied access to most nuclear sites, the US does not have a full list of the storage facilities. To leave nothing to chance, US army has trained a commando unit to retrieve Pakistani nuclear weapons if extremists, possibly from inside Pakistan's security apparatus, get hold of a nuclear device or materials to build one.[9] It would be unsurprising to learn that Israel too had trained such a commando unit or was in the process of doing so – or that India had done so.

THE JIHADIST TRAJECTORY IN INDIA – DECLINING

The Congress party government of Lal Bahadur Shastri (1964–66) initiated India's nuclear arms programme, followed by an underground test in 1974 under Indira Gandhi, before the right-wing Bharatiya Janata Party (BJP)-led government carried out a series of nuclear explosions in 1998. As the political arm of the fundamentalist Hindu paramilitary organization, Rashtriya Swayamsevak Sangh (RSS), which vehemently opposed the partition of British India, the BJP is uncompromising on maintaining the current frontiers of the Republic of India, including Kashmir.

Though only a minor force in Indian politics at its establishment in 1980, the BJP built up its popular base by advocating Hindu chauvinism with a strong anti-Muslim bias so effectively that it succeded in heading a coalition government less than two decades later.

The BJP's victory came at the cost of the Muslim minority. Even under the secular rule of the Congress party, Indian Muslims had much to complain about. It was during its rule in Delhi that the historic Babri Mosque in Ayodhya was demolished by the Hindu zealots of the RSS and the BJP. The pogrom of Muslims in 2002 in Ahmedabad, capital of BJP-governed Gujarat, marked a nadir for the community.

Reaction followed. The Pakistan-based LeT set out to create an India-based jihadist organization – and succeeded. By the autumn of 2005, the Indian Mujahedin (IM) became operational. It carried out terrorist attacks in many Indian cities, culminating in a series of bombings in Delhi in September 2008. Two months later came the sensational attacks in Mumbai, orchestrated by the LeT in Pakistan, in which the IM apparently played no role. After a long lull, a café in Pune popular with foreigners got hit in February 2010.

These violent incidents have done nothing to assuage the problems of the Muslim community. If anything, by providing fuel to Hindu-chauvinist organizations, they have worsened the lot of Muslims. Organizations such as the LeT and IM would very much like to see this trend continue so that Muslims grow increasingly disillusioned with the democratic system and peaceful ways of solving socio-political problems. They can point out that, though the discrimination suffered by Muslims was documented in the report by a commission headed by Rajinder Sachar, former chief justice of the Delhi High Court, in 2006, none of its recommendations has been implemented.[10] That gives them ammunition in urging fellow Muslims to abandon peaceful means to achieve redress for their grievances.

However, two major factors are preventing aggrieved Indian Muslims from reaching the boiling point. First, their leaders are aware that, though 165 million-strong, they are a minority in a country of 1.2 billion. Any resort to violence would rebound badly on the community. The second factor is the tradition of block voting by the Muslim electorate, which enables local leaders to gain some amelioration for their fellow believers by bargaining with the competing candidates at polling time. This reduces the chance of young disaffected Muslims inflating the shrunken ranks of the likes of the IM.

At the same time, backing for the IM from Pakistan has declined sharply. The ISI has its hands full meeting the jihadists' violent challenge at home. Also, the arrest of David Coleman Headley in October 2009, followed by his detailed confession of his activities on behalf of the ISI and LeT, provided the Indian intelligence agencies with a cornucopia of actionable information and helped the authorities to improve security and thwart the IM's plans – so far.[11]

14

OVERVIEW AND CONCLUSIONS

WITH A WAR in progress in Afghanistan, the events in that country regularly make the news headlines throughout the region and the West. By comparison, Pakistan, nominally at peace, is less newsworthy. Yet it is in extremis. The remark, 'May God give us the strength to save Pakistan,' penned by the country's president, Asif Ali Zardari, in the visitors' book at the mausoleum of the republic's founder, Muhammad Ali Jinnah, aptly sums up the dire situation.[1]

Pakistan faces a multitude of grave problems: Its economy is faltering, its civil administration remains incompetent and corrupt, its judicial system is untrustworthy, its educational system is underfunded, and its major political parties are dominated by feudal interests. The only state institution that functions well, and enjoys high prestige among the people, is the military. It is holding the multi-ethnic country together territorially, while aid from Washington and its allied multilateral financial institutions – the IMF and World Bank – keep Pakistan afloat economically.

As a rule nothing motivates armed forces better than having a sharply defined foe. Pakistan has one. India has been, is, and will continue to be *the* enemy. That has been the abiding creed of the Pakistani military. To prove its point, its leaders refer to a series of major events, starting with the independent India's deliberate delay in dividing up the assets of British India and refusing to transfer money to the fledgling state of Pakistan in 1947. It was Delhi's complicity with Bengali nationalists that led to the loss of East Pakistan in 1971. Then there is the running sore of the Muslim-majority Kashmir shackled to India. And there is India's adoption of the Cold Start strategy in 2004, which involves eight division-size Integrated Battle Groups – each consisting of infantry, artillery, armour and air support – primed to penetrate Pakistan quickly at unexpected points to disrupt its military command-and-control networks as a response to terrorist attacks from Pakistani territory. Furthermore, India is all set to become a power broker in Afghanistan once the Americans have left. These two elements are an integral part of Delhi's strategy to crush Pakistan in a pincer movement intented to bring about its disintegration. Therein lies the logic behind the sustained support given by Islamabad's ISI directorate to the Afghan Taliban as a counter-force to frustrate India's aims in South Asia.

ISLAM, THE LEITMOTIF OF AFGHAN HISTORY

Though the ISI played a crucial role in fostering and boosting the Afghan Taliban in 1994, conservative Sunni Islam, which underscores the militant movement, has a long history in Afghanistan. As early as 1888, Afghanistan's staunchly Sunni ruler, Abdur Rahman, rallied his fellow Sunni subjects – Pushtun, Uzbek and Turkmen tribes – to subdue Shia Hazaras inhabiting the Hazarajat mountains in central Afghanistan.

The idea of merging politics with religion in the person of an emir-sultan in Afghanistan also originated with Abdur Rahman. He declared that only 'divine guidance' could ensure that the people would choose a true and legitimate ruler (*sultan*). He thus gave himself the twin task of furthering the cause of Islam (*fi sabil al Islam*) and liberating the Afghan soil from the domination of the infidel foreign forces. In 1896, he published a treatise on jihad in which he supported his argument that the demands of jihad overrode those of family, clan or tribe by citing twelve verses from the Quran.

When Amanullah Khan offered the nation its first written constitution in 1923, it declared Islam to be the official religion of Afghanistan. Whereas the special Loya Jirga he convened accepted his proposal for a representative government based on universal suffrage and military conscription for men, it opposed modern education for girls and age limits for marriage. When he persisted in his drive for gender equality and allowed women to discard the veil, he ended up losing his throne.

The constitution promulgated by Muhammad Nadir Shah in 1931 narrowed the official religion to the Hanafi school of Sunni Islam and decreed that all civil and criminal laws should be based entirely on the Sharia. The king consulted senior clerics on all important social, educational, and political issues; they disenfranchised women.

In 1953 Muhammad Daoud Khan, commander of the Central Forces and a cousin of King Muhammad Zahir Shah, staged a coup with a nod from the palace. He then set up an authoritarian regime under which senior clerics found themselves on the defensive. He succeeded in introducing social reforms because he had the backing of a loyal, professional army, built up with the assistance of Moscow.

The new constitution promulgated by Zahir Shah in 1964 ruled out any law 'repugnant to the basic principles of the sacred religion of Islam'. Yet when Daoud Khan seized supreme power in 1973 and abolished the monarchy, he claimed that he did so to return the country to 'Islamic values'. After his success in co-opting moderate Marxists and severely weakened nationalist centrists, Daoud Khan found himself opposed only by Islamists. He therefore suppressed them. Then, to monopolize power, he turned against the Marxists. His unremitting repression drove the leaders of the Marxist People's Democratic Party of Afghanistan (PDPA) – acting against the wishes of the Kremlin – to activate the network they had built up in the army and overthrow Daoud Khan in 1978.

Once in power, the PDPA's moderate and radical factions began quarrelling about the place of Islam in society and the pace of socio-economic reform at the expense of vested interests. These differences became irreconcilable while opposition from the traditional centres of power, backed by illiterate, conservative, and religious villagers, gathered momentum. Afghan Islamists, calling themselves mujahedin, set up bases in the Pakistani city of Peshawar. In July 1979, the US administration of President Jimmy Carter began channelling money and arms to these groups in collusion with the military government of General Muhammad Zia ul Haq in Pakistan. The general had overthrown the democratically elected government of Zulfikar Ali Bhutto, leader of the Pakistan People's Party, in July 1977. Washington hoped that growing Islamist resistance in Afghanistan would tempt the Kremlin to intervene militarily and get bogged down in the way the US had been in Vietnam.

To Washington's delight, the rising Islamist challenge did not lead the PDPA's two factions to close ranks. Instead, the power struggle turned violent, claiming the lives of the leaders of both factions. This paved the way for the entry of the troops of the Soviet Union whose leaders envisaged a stay of about six months to normalize the situation. The US got what it wanted.

Ironically, it was the split in a leftist, secular party that sparked a civil war in Afghanistan in late 1978, which has raged since then with varying intensity and in which Islam along with ethnic rivalries between the leading groups – Pushtun and Tajiks – has been a major factor.

In the final analysis, the blame for pushing Afghanistan into civil war lies with the excesses committed by the PDPA's radical wing. Equally, it was the trumping of the pragmatic approach of negotiations with Moscow advocated by US Secretary of State Cyrus Vance by the hawkish stance of the national security adviser Zbigniew Brzezinski – adopted by President Carter – that put the US on the path that led twenty-two years later to 9/11. That in turn opened a new chapter in the Afghan civil strife.

PAKISTAN'S GAIN AND LOSS

The Kremlin's military intervention in Afghanistan turned Pakistan into a front-line state in the Cold War and strengthened Zia ul Haq's grip on power. There had been military coups in Pakistan before but this one was different. It was carried out by a diehard Islamist who turned Pakistan into an ideological state and remoulded civil society and the military like no other leader before or since. His thorough Islamization of state institutions, including schools and colleges which were equipped with revised textbooks, has produced a generation where a third of the 18–29-year-old Pakistanis want immediate imposition of the Sharia. A larger proportion of older Pakistanis, who experienced Zia ul Haq's rule as adults, is believed to be even more supportive of the Sharia. That became clear during the Aasia Bibi episode, involving the assassination of Punjab's governor, Salman Taseer, and the showering of praise on his assassin, Malik Mumtaz Hussein Qadri, by many citizens belonging to different classes.

Until Zia ul Haq's coup, Pakistan's rulers had used Islam haphazardly, often as a tactical tool to defuse an incipient crisis or a pressing challenge from the street. This was true of the founder of Pakistan, Muhammad Ali Jinnah, a successful British-trained lawyer who practised in London and led a secular life. But Jinnah found that in electoral politics the cry of 'Islam in danger', was a winner. And his assertion that Muslims in the subcontinent were a people apart from the Hindu nation helped him and his All India Muslim League to create a feeling of unity among their disparate constituents, who did not share a common race, culture or language.

Now, in the three-decades-old Pakistan, Zia ul Haq's stress on Islam helped him to encourage Pakistanis to transcend the ethnic differences between Punjabis, Pushtuns, Baluchis, Sindhis and the Urdu-speaking immigrants from India, called Muhajirs. But his introduction of the Islamic tax of zakat, to be collected directly by the government, exposed a deep schism between majority Sunnis and minority Shias, who were enjoined to pay *khums*, one-fifth of their annual profits, to the grand ayatollah of their choice. Faced with peaceful protest, Zia ul Haq exempted Shias from paying zakat. Since then Sunni–Shia relations have been strained, made worse by repeated attacks on Shia gatherings by radical Sunni jihadist factions.

Zia ul Haq's upgrading of the status and importance of the nominated Council of Islamic Ideology (CII), charged with offering legal advice on Islamic issues to the government and parliament, has adversely affected pragmatic decision making. One glaring example concerns family planning – declared un-Islamic by the council in 1984, a ruling that has proved detrimental to the economic well-being of Pakistan.

The Zia ul Haq government's deep involvement in furthering the anti-Soviet jihad in Afghanistan during 1980–88 left Pakistan with acute problems: easy availability of small arms and narcotics, and the imbibing of radical Islam by many ISI and other military officers who worked closely with the Afghan Mujahedin Alliance.

On the other hand, in exchange for critical assistance in its Cold War with the Kremlin, Washington virtually suspended its non-proliferation policy on nuclear arms. It turned a blind eye as Islamabad, actively aided by Beijing, forged ahead with its nuclear weapons programme, testing its atomic bomb at a Chinese site in March 1984. The success of this programme gave Pakistan a parity with India that it lacked in conventional weaponry and manpower. That, followed by the first withdrawal of the Soviet troops from Afghanistan in October 1986, led Zia ul Haq to formulate his policy of weakening India by stoking up disaffection in Indian Kashmir.

By blatantly rigging the elections in Kashmir in March 1987, the Indian government inadvertently provided an exceptional opportunity for Pakistan's ISI and Islamist organizations to advance their seccessionist agenda. The separatist insurgency took off in 1989, once all Soviet troops were out of Afghanistan and the victorious Mujahedin were free to pursue jihad elsewhere in the neighbourhood.

Delhi responded as it had done to similar insurgencies in north-east India: repression sweetened with injections of funds. But there were major differences this time. The sanctuaries of militants active in Indian Kashmir were in Pakistani Kashmir and adjoining areas in Pakistan. Also, unlike the predominantly Christian ethnic minorities of the Mongoloid race in the north-eastern region, those engaged in an armed struggle against the Indian security forces in Kashmir were Muslim and of the same racial stock as northern Indians and Pakistanis. India's security forces set a new record with their violations of human rights, devising new and more horrific ways of torture not deployed elsewhere in the world.

Pakistanis seethed with anger as jihadist factions called for action to liberate Kashmir from the clutches of Hindu India. Senior Pakistani generals, including Pervez Musharraf, planned a military move in Indian Kashmir, reportedly without even informing the elected prime minister, Muhammad Nawaz Sharif. The campaign started in May 1999 in the Kargil region of Indian-controlled Kashmir. The offensive caught the Indians by surprise. But they recovered. An intense battle ensued. To defuse the escalating crisis, US president Bill Clinton intervened publicly. He invited Nawaz Sharif and his Indian counterpart, Atal Bihari Vajpayee, to an urgent meeting in Washington. Intent on keeping Kashmir a strictly bilateral issue, Vajpayee declined, citing prior commitments. Following his meeting with Clinton on American Independence Day 1999, Sharif agreed to withdraw troops from Kargil – without first consulting the military high command.

He thus violated the cardinal principle guiding Pakistan since the deaths of its founding figures, Jinnah in 1948 and Liaquat Ali Khan in 1951, that the ultimate authority for forming and implementing policies on national security lies exclusively with the corps commanders. By breaching this code, Sharif sowed the seeds of his downfall, which came in October 1999 when General Musharraf staged a coup against him.

THE KNOCK-ON EFFECT ON INDIA

Like Nawaz Sharif before him, Musharraf had to deal with Vajpayee, leader of the Hindu nationalist Bharatiya Janata Party (BJP). Established in 1980, the BJP had gained popularity so rapidly that by 1998 it had become the leading member of a coalition government in Delhi. Its two-track strategy focused on criticizing the centrist, secular Indian National Congress for 'appeasing' Muslims to gain their votes, and transforming the generally laidback majority Hindus into militant Hindu chauvinists.

The BJP was a creature of the Rashtriya Swayamsevak Sangh, formed in 1925 and modelled along the lines of the Italian Fascist Party. It defined a Hindu as someone who lived between the Indus and the vaguely defined 'seas on the east', and regarded this territory as both fatherland *and* holy land. Since Muslims and Christians belonged to religions whose roots lay outside this holy land, their presence enfeebled the Hindu nation. Lal Krishna Advani, who joined the RSS at the age of fifteen, became the BJP's president in 1986, at a time when Islamic fundamentalism was on the rise in Afghanistan and Pakistan. That galvanized the BJP to mount a campaign to revive Hindu militancy, and underlined the interconnectedness of the three South Asian neighbours. To capture the popular Hindu imagination, Advani focused on the sixteenth-century Babri Mosque in the northern Indian town of Ayodhya, claiming that it had been built on the site where the Hindu deity Lord Rama was born.

Starting in September 1990, Advani undertook a thirteen-month journey of 6,300 miles (10,100 km) by a motorized chariot decorated with saffron-coloured pennants – a replica of the battlefield vehicle used by Hindu warriors in ancient times – to arouse the Hindu masses to right the wrong at Ayodhya. This was a prologue to the demolition of the historic mosque in December 1992 by thousands of militants of the BJP, RSS and allied organizations.

It set off a cycle of Hindu–Muslim violence and counter-violence in which Muslims suffered. Among other things, the Babri Mosque episode intensified the insurgency in Kashmir and encouraged Pakistan-based jihadist groups to mount audacious terrorist attacks in India. That in turn helped bolster the electoral base of the BJP and placed it at the head of coalition governments in 1998 and 1999. This impacted on Delhi's foreign policy, particularly with respect to Israel.

THE INDIA-ISRAEL-AMERICA ALLIANCE

The anti-Muslim bias of the BJP-led coalition governments brought about strong intelligence, security and defence links with Israel, which had secured full diplomatic recognition from India in 1992 – before the Israel–Palestine Liberation Organization Accord of 1993. By the end of the decade, close ties between India and Israel had become a fixture in the Delhi-Washington-Tel Aviv nexus. Delhi's embrace of Israel is hugely unpopular with the Pakistani public and politicians as well as militant organizations. The stories of India and Israel colluding to hit Pakistan's nuclear facilities kept reappearing periodically in the Pakistani media, reminding readers and viewers of the abiding hostility that these countries harboured towards Pakistan. The Delhi–Tel Aviv ties figure prominently in the narratives of the jihadist groups in Pakistan. It was significant that the targets chosen by the Pakistan-based Lashkar-e Taiba in its attacks on Mumbai in November 2008 included a Jewish outreach centre – run by a religious organization with a strong presence in Israel – which catered primarily for young Israelis on holiday after finishing their conscription.

In the international arena, the disintegration of the Soviet Union in 1991 made it inevitable that Delhi would strengthen its relations with the US, the remaining superpower. Not that independent India, following its policy on non-alignment in external affairs, had stayed aloof from America previously. Indeed, at the outbreak of the Sino-Indian War in 1962, Indian prime minister Jawaharlal Nehru, the apostle of non-alignment, made a frantic plea to the White House for urgent military assistance. As for the other superpower, once its relations with the regime in Beijing soured in 1960, the Soviet Union had started assisting India militarily and strengthened its earlier commercial links. Thus, for two decades, both the Kremlin and the White House had bolstered Delhi as a counter-force to Beijing. It was only during the presidency of Ronald Reagan in the 1980s that relations between India and the US chilled. That had to do with Afghanistan. Delhi refused to condemn the Kremlin publicly for its military intervention while it watched apprehensively Pakistani generals pilfer US-supplied arms – meant exclusively for the Afghan Mujahedin – to replace their old weaponry.

India's consternation returned when 9/11 once again turned Pakistan into a front-line state – this time in the 'global War on Terror' with generous American aid, military and civilian, flowing into Islamabad.

Yet in December 2001, a daring attack on the parliament in Delhi by Pakistan-based jihadist groups put India and America in the same column: 'Victims of Terrorism'. The resulting reinforcing of security, military and intelligence links between India and America had a knock-on effect in the commercial area: Indo-American trade thrived. Since Israel claimed to have been a victim of Palestinian terrorism for much longer, an Indian-Israeli-American alliance firmed up.

WASHINGTON'S FLAWED POLICY-MAKING PATTERN

A fatal flaw in the Bush administration's strategy for countering terrorism was that it treated Islamist terrorism perpetrated by non-state actors as if it were the communism of the Soviet bloc. The latter existed as the ideology of several functioning states, led by the Soviet Union, a vast country equipped with thousands of nuclear weapons. Thus the Cold War was waged by two sets of legitimate states following well-defined rules of hot war and cold peace. That was not the case with Al Qaida or any of its allied or friendly jihadist factions in Pakistan. True, the Afghan Taliban administered almost all of Afghanistan. But in the international community the Taliban regime was recognized only by three countries, the most important being Pakistan. The conventional military strength of the Taliban regime was minuscule. So the Bush government ended up rallying its massive conventional military might to confront an entity engaged essentially in an asymmetrical warfare.

This was the latest in a series of missteps taken by the US in this region. The basic problem characterizing a long series of actions taken by successive US administrations, whether Republican or Democrat, is this: At key points, the White House opts for expedient policies with little attention paid to their medium- and long-term consequences. For instance, following the flight of the Taliban from Afghanistan in December 2001, instead of strengthening the hand of the central government in Kabul, the Bush government decided to work with the warlords in the provinces, thus maintaining the status quo albeit without the presence of Taliban in the capital. Because the provincial warlords were in cahoots with the drug barons, the growing of poppies and the consequent narcotics trade became embedded in the administrative system of Afghanistan, much to the hand-wringing disappointment of Washington and its NATO allies.

Other examples date as far back as 1979. Fired by the typically American 'can do' spirit, and resolved to settle the long-running Cold War in its favour, President Carter intervened clandestinely in Afghanistan in order to induce intervention by the Soviet Union – a trap into which the Kremlin fell. In 1981, the CIA had the option either of assisting a group of three moderately Islamic, nationalist, pro-monarchy Afghan parties along with a few secular, anti-Marxist factions, or a collective of three fanatical Islamist groups. Bill Casey, director of the CIA, backed the zealots. Why? The leading faction, the Hizb-e Islami of Gulbuddin Hikmatyar planned to cap the expulsion of the Soviets from Afghanistan with forays into Soviet Tajikistan to start undermining the communist system in Central Asia. Casey eagerly bought into this half-baked, ill-conceived scenario.

Had Casey backed the moderate Islamic nationalist parties, the history of the region and the world would have been starkly different. Since these factions respected the Afghan traditions in religion and governance (by a king), they enjoyed far more popular support than did the anti-royalist, fundamentalist groups who were far too radical for conservative, traditionalist Afghans. Deprived of the CIA's largess, the extremist Afghan factions would have been reduced to a subsidiary role, and the world would have been spared the rise of Frankenstein's monsters in the form of Al Qaida and the Taliban.

Equally, the condoning of Pakistan's nuclear programme by the Reagan White House has led to a situation where a country with an arsenal of some 110 atomic bombs is exposed to attacks on its sensitive military facilities by fanatical teams of suicide bombers drawn from a pool of several thousand jihadists. This poses an extreme danger, not just to the region but to the world at large. The jihadists organizations' failure so far to hijack a Pakistani atom bomb or vital parts in transit or storage does not rule out the chance of their success in the future. Nor has it persuaded them to abandon their overarching aim of souring relations between Islamabad and Delhi to the point of hot war. The fact that the two nuclear-armed neighbours came to the brink of all-out war at the time of the Kargil battle in the spring of 1999 and again three years later makes jihadist leaders feel that their objective is realistic.

This pattern of expedient policy making persists. Consider the strategy of NATO commander General David Petraeus in 2010 to target Taliban commanders in night raids. This is designed to force the Taliban's supreme Shura Council to come to the negotiating table on NATO's terms: acceptance of the present constitution, severance of links with Al Qaida, and a cast-iron guarantee never to give sanctuary to Al Qaida in Afghanistan. The chances of such a scenario materializing are minimal. The reality is that killed Taliban commanders soon get replaced by younger fighters, more hardline than their predecessors. That reduces, rather than enhances, the chances of the Taliban seeking talks with the Karzai government.

The disjunction between the short- and medium-term outcomes is obvious.

Moreover, the critical point is not the number of Taliban commanders killed but the size of the recruiting pool. Besides the thirteen million Pushtuns in Afghanistan, there are more than twice as many Pushtuns in Pakistan. There is no way to distinguish Afghan Pushtun from Pakistani Pushtun. That was the case in Vietnam too, where there was nothing to differentiate a South Vietnamese from a North Vietnamese.

VIETNAM, ALL OVER AGAIN

Indeed, there are so many parallels with America's earlier, long-running involvement in Vietnam that they need elaboration. In 1961, US president John F. Kennedy inherited 900 American military advisers posted in South Vietnam, then ruled by President Ngo Dinh Diem. He immediately increased their number to 2,000 and ratcheted up the figure to 16,500 by the time he was assassinated on 22 November 1963 – three weeks after Diem was killed in a military coup. During the next two years there were several coups and short-lived governments while the US increased its financial aid to South Vietnam. As a result of the incompetence and corruption of the Diem government and its successors, between 1959 and 1964, the number of South Vietnamese guerrillas rocketed from 5,000 to 100,000. By comparison the strength of South Vietnam's military rose marginally, from 850,000 to almost one million.

Kennedy's successor, Lyndon Johnson, defeated his Republican rival, Senator Barry Goldwater, partly on the basis of arguing that Vietnam was *not* an American war. But after being elected as president, he dispatched 3,500 Marines to South Vietnam in March 1965 to engage in combat. Successive South Vietnamese governments remained unpopular. While desertions from the South Vietnamese military increased and morale nosedived, the commander of US troops in that country, General William Westmoreland, promised victory by the end of 1967. His promise failed to materialize. Indeed, in 1968, the Pentagon found itself in such dire straits that it asked for 200,000 more troops. President Johnson refused, and decided not to run for re-election. His Republican successor, Richard Nixon, came up with the concept of the 'Vietnamization' of the war, with South Vietnamese soldiers taking complete charge of the country's security.

To get a snapshot of the current state of US-led NATO troops in Afghanistan, all one has to do is to replace 'Vietnamization' with 'Afghanization'. That is the point President Barack Obama, following the script written by General Petraeus, reached by December 2010, agreeing with Petraeus's claim that the Taliban's momentum had been arrested, but adding the caveat that the gain was 'fragile and reversible'. Washington's NATO allies were coached to say that Obama's earlier mention of July 2011 as the date for the Pentagon's withdrawal from Afghanistan was really the start of 'transition' and that US-led NATO soldiers would engage in combat until the end of 2014. It was left to Mark Sedwill, NATO's civilian head in Afghanistan, who worked alongside Petraeus, to explain that 2014 was simply 'an inflection point', and that it too was not guaranteed.

A chronological narrative of the US war in Afghanistan should start with Bush, having a mere three hundred personnel of the Special Operation Force there in December 2001, refer to his leaving the White House in January 2009 with 47,000 regular troops in Afghanistan, and then see that number double in a year and a half under his successor. To reinforce the parallel with the Vietnam War, the narrative should point out that the Pentagon's increased use of drone strikes, ground incursions, and targeted killings in Pakistan's tribal belt is eerily reminiscent of its attacks on Cambodia to secure South Vietnam.

THE JIHADISTS' APOCALYPTIC VISION

What distinguishes the present situation in Afghanistan–Pakistan from Vietnam in the 1960s is the dramatic change in international affairs caused by the lethal attacks on New York and Metropolitan Washington on 11 September 2001 – namely, the launching of the global War on Terror by the United States. Since the perpetrator of 9/11 was Al Qaida operating from Taliban-administered Afghanistan, the US-led war, unleashed on 7 October 2001, targeted Afghanistan and then – purportedly as a result of dubious intelligence from the CIA – the Iraq ruled by Saddam Hussein, a secular leader. What Iraq had in common with Afghanistan was its almost wholly Muslim population. That fact provided Bush's many critics with evidence that under the rubric of 'War on Terror' he was waging a war on Islam. Their analysis was in line with the view held by most Muslims in South Asia.

This in turn led to widespread anti-Washington feeling in the region, particularly Pakistan and Afghanistan. It prevailed as much among the general public as it did among the civil service and lower ranks of the military of the two nations. The governments of these neighbouring countries face a formidable task: how to take into account popular anti-American sentiment while being cravenly dependent on largess from Washington and the US-backed international financial institutions to keep their polities solvent. The resulting governmental fragility allows the jihadist movement to grow.

In Pakistan, this movement exists legally, participating in national politics, and clandestinely (as the Pakistani Taliban) engaged in low-intensity warfare with the state. The two elements come together at critical moments such as when the controversy about the Blasphemy Law gripped the nation and led to the assassination of Governor Taseer in January 2011. Together they put their adversaries on the defensive – with the powerful army chief General Ashfaq Parvez Kayani declining to condemn Taseer's murder, or even to commiserate with his family publicly. He later explained to a group of Western ambassadors that too many soldiers sympathized with the assassin and any statement of sympathy for Taseer from him could have imperiled the army's unity.[2]

Despite the huge sums spent by Washington and countless Western NGOs to bolster the government of President Hamid Karzai over the past many years, the Afghan Taliban has grown in strength and extended its influence into non-Pushtun areas. On the other side, opinion polls show that the public in the Western world, including the United States, are getting tired of waging wars in distant Muslim countries like Afghanistan. This is happening at a time when a growing number of policy makers in the West are conceding, in private, that at some point in the future the Taliban will have to be accommodated into the power structure of Afghanistan if that hapless country is ever to return to a normal existence. No matter how gradually this is accomplished, such an eventuality will give a fillip to Islamist elements in the Central Asian states of Tajikistan and Uzbekistan. Continued repression by the Tajik and Uzbek governments has driven Islamist groups underground but failed to annihilate them, particularly in the populous Fergana Valley.

It would also mean the realization of General Muhammad Zia ul Haq's dream of Pakistan becoming primus inter pares among Muslim countries in South, West, and Central Asia as it inspires and aids Islamist movements elsewhere in the sprawling region. The Islamist dictator had taken into account Pakistan's large Muslim population, then second only to Indonesia's; its straddling of Central, West, and South Asia; the size of its military, the sixth largest in the world; and its arsenal of nuclear weapons.

Zia ul Haq is gone, but the geopolitical and military reasons underlying the scenario he visualized for his country remain unchanged, while the Islamizing forces continue to make strides. Indeed, building on Zia ul Haq's vision, the Pakistani Taliban has cast Pakistan as the core of a revived Islamic caliphate, extending over vast swathes of Asia, where the Sharia would rule supreme.

Overall, this apocalyptic vision is driving jihadist leaders in Pakistan and Afghanistan to continue their programme of destabilizing the present regimes as a prelude to setting up Sharia states there.

EPILOGUE

THE WIKILEAK REVELATIONS published by the *New York Times*, *Guardian*, *Hindu* and *Dawn* between November 2010 and May 2011 provided many nuggets of significance about South Asia. And yet there was hardly any mention of the search for Osama bin Laden. So when US President Barack Obama, in his TV address on 1 May at 10.30 p.m. Eastern daylight, announced that bin Laden had been killed by an American force after 'a brief fire fight', it astonished the world.

THE KILLING OF BIN LADEN AND ITS AFTERMATH

Following several months of meticulous planning and preparation, based on CIA intelligence gathered over years, on the night of 1 May 2011, five military helicopters took off from Bagram air base in Afghanistan, carrying seventy-nine commandos of the US Naval Special Warfare Development Group, called SEALs (Sea, Air, Land). (The acronym is derived from the fact that they could operate anywhere on sea or land, or in air.) That marked the launching of Operation 'Neptune Spear'. Aware of the ISI's repeated leaks of information supplied by the CIA to jihadists during the second administration of President George W. Bush, Obama had decided against co-opting, or even informing, Pakistan of his plan.[1]

Three of the aircraft, the Chinook heavy lift helicopters, landed in the desert near the Afghan-Pakistan border to act as back-ups while two specially modified stealth Black Hawk helicopters, carrying twenty-four commandos, flew to Abbottabad – a garrison city of 300,000 which hosted the Pakistan Military Academy, 35 miles (56 km) north of Islamabad. Their mission was to capture or kill bin Laden living in a safe house in the Bilal Town suburb of the city.[2]

The original plan for one of the two teams to fast rope onto the roof of the targeted three-storey house inside a compound went awry when a Black Hawk suffered a malfunction which was aggravated by high compound walls and above-average air temperature, resulting in a damage to its rotor blade. Though bin Laden's men blew up the damaged Black Hawk, its rotor did not break up in pieces.[3] However, the crash landing did not injure anybody seriously. A back-up Chinook arrived to replace the loss. The other Black Hawk landed outside the compound and its commandos scaled the walls to get inside.

Together, the heavily armed SEALs, wearing night-vision goggles, blew their passage through walls and doors with explosives. They killed bin Laden's courier, Abu Ahmad al Kuwaiti, and al Kuwaiti's wife as well as his male relative. Bin Laden's adult son, Khalid, was shot dead as he rushed down the stairs of the main house.

As the commandos moved up the stairs just before 1 a.m. local time on 2 May, they saw bin Laden peering over the third-floor ledge and then retreating to his room. They followed him. A shot fired by one of the commandos hit bin Laden in the chest, with another bullet hitting him just above the left eye.

Following this fifteen-minute-long military operation, the SEALs scooped up all the documents, computer hard drives, DVDs, thumb drives, and other electronic equipment. They arrested the women and children in the safe house, using plastic handcuffs or zip ties to immobilize them, and left them in the courtyard for easy discovery by the Pakistani authorities.

The US night raiders returned to Bagram airfield with bin Laden's corpse. By the time Obama made his dramatic announcement in Washington, the corpse had been flown to the aircraft carrier *The Carl Vinson* in the North Arabian Sea. Following the Islamic funeral rite, he was given a sea burial at 11 a.m. local time on 2 May.

Within minutes of Obama's statement, thousands of people gathered outside the White House to celebrate the demise of the globe's most notorious terrorist, who had remained free for almost ten years after masterminding the attacks in New York and Metropolitan Washington on 11 September 2001. Hundreds of flag-waving New Yorkers assembled at the Times Square in a jubilant mood while others visited the old site of the World Trace Centre.

There were public celebrations in Delhi and other Indian cities. More than 40 million people across the country watched the news of bin Laden's death on TV, a record. An unsigned article in the *Times of India*, the most popular English-language daily, asked why India could not do to Dawood Ibrahim and Hafiz Muhammad Saeed, the alleged masterminds of the carnages in Mumbai in 1993 and 2008 respectively, what the US did to bin Laden. (Unlike bin Laden, neither Ibrahim nor Saeed had owned up the terrorist act attributed to him.) In response, the Indian Air Force chief, Marshall P.V. Naik, said that India had the capability to stage such surgical strikes against terrorists. But military capability was not enough. It needed to be complimented by an intelligence network on the ground built up over a long period. The Pentagon's raid was the result of several years of CIA activity in Pakistan, culminating in setting up a safe house for its agents in Abbottabad. By comparison, the reach of Delhi's Research and Analysis Wing into Pakistan was limited. The Indian Home Minister P. Chidambaram conceded this by pointing out, 'We don't have our forces on the Pakistani soil. We don't have any support from Pakistan.'[4]

Unsurprisingly, the Bharatiya Janata Party latched on to the fact that bin Laden had been hiding in a safe house with three wives and several children in a Pakistani city for five years. It described Pakistan as 'the epicentre of global terrorism'[5] while one of its senior leaders, Sushma Swaraj, called bin Laden 'enemy number one of humanity'.

In stark contrast, leading his followers in prayers in Lahore, Saeed, leader of the nominally banned Lashkar-e Taiba (LeT) – operating as the Jamaat ud-Dawa – praised bin Laden as a 'great personality' who had awaken the Muslim umma and who would continue to be a source of strength and encouragement for Muslims around the globe. Lahore was one of the several Pakistani cities and towns where special prayers for 'martyr' bin Laden were held by the LeT.[6]

Overall, though, the focus in Pakistan was more on how bin Laden was killed rather than on his death. It was humiliating for the government, particularly its military, to see foreign commandos using three helicopters violate its airspace, kill bin Laden and four others, and depart without being detected.[7] Pakistan's army chief of staff, General Ashfaq Parvez Kayani, described the US action 'a misadventure' and vowed that no further raids would be tolerated. In retribution, he announced that the number of US military personnel in Pakistan will be reduced to the minimum essential.

At the popular level, the US raid was condemned widely. A poll by YouGov-Cambridge University showed that 75 per cent of Pakistanis disapproved of it.[8] At home, public anger was directed primarily at the military for its failure to safeguard the country's sovereignty. This was mirrored by the media. As a result, the parliament summoned five top military officers, led by General Kayani, for questioning.

They appeared before a joint session of the National Assembly and the Senate on 13 May behind closed doors. The sitting lasted eleven hours. Admitting failure, ISI director deneral, Lt Gen Ahmad Shuja Pasha, revealed that he had offered to resign but was persuaded by Kayani to change his mind. Air Marshal Muhammad Hassan, Deputy Chief of Air Staff Operations, explained that highly sophisticated stealth technology enabled Black Hawk helicopters to evade radar. 'By the time the air force learned about the raid from ground reports at Abbottabad and launched fighter jets, the [U.S.] helicopters had completed their mission and flown out of Pakistan,' he said. In answer to a question, he acknowledged for the first time that Pakistan allowed the United States to fly its drones out of Shamsi air base in Baluchistan.[9] So far, Islamabad had maintained that it did not condone Washington's drone campaign. It now emerged that the Pakistani government spoke with a forked tongue not only to its ally, America, but also to its own citizens.

By all accounts, Pasha was the star performer. Having conceded his failure at the start, he ended up rallying the chamber across partly lines by being scathingly critical of Washington's policies toward Islamabad. 'We are at a point in our history where we have to decide whether to stand up to America now or have [the succeeding] generations come to deride us.'[10] Inspired partly by Pasha's passionate rhetoric, the Parliament unanimously passed a resolution condemning Washington's unilateral attack on bin Laden as a violation of Pakistan's sovereignty, threatened to close US military supply routes to Afghanistan if the CIA's drone strikes in the tribal areas did not cease, and called for a review of the relationship with America to ensure full respect for Pakistan's national interests.[11] In practice, this resolution meant nothing more than the ISI barring the CIA from conducting operations in Pakistan without its knowledge.

While Pakistani officials acted as the injured party, politicians and commentators in the US wondered aloud as to how the world's most wanted terrorist could live comfortably in a spacious house with his wives and children within three-quarter mile of the Pakistan Military Academy. The most plausible explanation was that this could happen only with the complicity or incompetence of some powerful figures in the Pakistani military and/or intelligence.

The third possibility of deliberate oversight was not aired much. But it acquired credibility when the *Guardian* reported on 10 May that according to serving and retired US and Pakistani officials, including General Tommy Franks, CENTCOM commander, and Eric Edelman, undersecretary of Defence for Policy Administration during the Bush presidency, Pakistan's President General Pervez Musharraf and Bush reached a secret agreement in 2002: Pakistan would allow US forces to conduct a unilateral raid inside its borders in search of bin Laden and four other Al Qaida leaders. The two presidents also agreed that, for record, the Pakistanis would protest against such an incursion. This pact was renewed by Kayani during the transition to democracy – between February 2008, when Musharraf resigned as the army chief of staff, and August 2008, when a full civilian government was sworn in.[12] If so, by protesting vehemently, the Pakistani authorities merely performed the role written for them in the secret deal.

As expected, there was a spate of minor and major attacks by the Tehrik-e Taliban Pakistan (TTP), primarily in Khyber Pakhtunkhwa, to avenge the killing of bin Laden. On 13 May, two TTP suicide bombers attacked a Frontier Corps training academy in Charsadda, killing ninety-eight men, most of them cadets boarding buses for home. Five days later, about seventy armed militants assaulted a security post in a suburb of Peshawar. At the end of a four-hour gun battle, seventeen persons lay dead. On 25 May, an attack on a police station in Peshawar by extremists ramming a car packed with explosives killed eleven persons and reduced the building to a rubble.

Far more serious was the storming of the Mehran naval air station in Karachi on 22 May by ten armed attackers belonging to Al Qaida's 313 Brigade. They managed to blow up two US-made P3 naval surveillance aircraft, and engaged in a sixteen-hour battle that left ten military personnel dead. This was the biggest assault on a military facility since the attack on the army headquarters in Rawalpindi in October 2009. The meticulously planned, audacious attack, occurring a few weeks after the dismal failure of the country's army and air force on 2 May, humiliated further the armed forces' top brass.

In his report published in the *Asia Times Online* on 27 May, the newspaper's bureau chief in Islamabad, Syed Saleem Shahzad, revealed that Al Qaida cell members at the Mehran base furnished the attackers with maps showing entry and exit routes during day and night, the location of hangers and the details of probable reaction from external security forces. Thus armed, the militants entered the heavily guarded facility at night, with one group targeting the surveillance planes, another engaging the military's strike force, and the remaining group of six escaping while the rest provided them covering fire.[13] The attack on the base was a riposte to the naval authorities' ongoing efforts to weed out Al Qaida cells.

Two days later, while on his way to a TV studio for an interview, Shahzad disappeared in central Islamabad. On 30 May his severally beaten dead body was found about 100 miles (160 km) from his abandoned car. A specialist on security and terrorism, he had received threatening calls from the ISI, telling him to stop reporting on these issues.

On 7 July, in an extraordinary move, US chairman of the joint chiefs of staff Admiral Mike Mullen publicly said that the Pakistani government 'approved' the Shahzad murder. 'I have not seen anything that would disabuse that report that the government knew about this,' Admiral Mullen told journalists in Washington. 'It was sanctioned by the government, yeah.'[14] The Pakistani government called his statement 'extremely irresponsible'.

This exchange of remarks aptly summed up the gravely strained relations between Islamabad and Washington. The opinion in the American media and Congress had turned hostile to Pakistan. Reflecting this sentiment, the Obama administration withheld $800 million out of more than $2 billion military aid to Islamabad. The sum covered military equipment worth $500 million and cash payment. Retaliating against Islamabad's expulsion of US trainers, the Pentagon stopped the dispatch of rifles, ammunition and body armour to the Pakistani troops that were being trained by them. And when Islamabad refused visas for the Americans assigned to set up and operate military equipment – radios and helicopter spare parts – the Pentagon withheld shipment. Washington held back the payment of $300 million in cash to Islamabad to reimburse part of its expense of keeping 100,000 Pakistani soldiers along the Afghan border, the amount originating in the Coalition Support Funds of the US. According to Congressional sources, the United States had paid Pakistan $8.9 billion in its Coalition Support Funds since 2001, with the total military and civilian financial assistance to Islamabad amounting to $21 billion.[15] Pakistan's spokesman said that its armed forces did not need military aid from the US. Civilian and military leaders of Pakistan resented the use of repeated leaks critical of their country almost daily in the American media as pressure tactics to do exactly what the Obama administration wanted. Many Pakistani commentators argued that their country had suffered a loss of $40 billion as a consequence of waging the US-led 'war on terror', and that up to 15,000 Pakistani soldiers and paramilitaries had been killed in that conflict compared to 6,163 American soldiers lost by the Pentagon in Afghanistan and Iraq until mid-2011.[16]

Despite public bickering, the two sides knew well that they were too dependent on each other to even consider a break. Pakistan's economy was in dire straits, with power outages closing factories, and spiralling food and fuel prices causing street protest. The country was kept afloat by loans from the International Monetary Fund sanctioned at the behest of the US. Civilian politicians needed Washington's backing in order to deter the generals from removing them from power; and military corps commanders were dependent on the advanced weaponry from the Pentagon to enable them to present a credible deterrence to India. On its part, Washington needed active cooperation of Islamabad to capture or kill Ayman Zawahiri, the successor to Bin Laden, and other Al Qaida leaders as well as Mullah Muhammad Omar, believed to be hiding mostly in the tribal agencies. This area also provides safe haven to an ally of the Afghan Taliban, the Haqqani group, which is fighting the forces of NATO and the government of President Hamid Karzai in Afghanistan. Furthermore, the US has scant chance of engaging the Afghan Taliban in serious peace negotiations without the assistance of the ISI.

THE AFGHANISTAN IMBROGLIO

ISI officials found news from Afghanistan encouraging. According to the Afghanistan NGO Safety Office, attacks by insurgents during April–June 2011 grew 42 per cent over the corresponding period in the previous year, and 119 per cent since the US military surge started in June 2009.[17] Also, once Taliban leaders realized that they could not match the firepower and organizational superiority of US and British troops in Helmand and Kabul provinces, they switched to a two-track policy of assassinating officials and staging daring terrorist attacks in urban areas. Their overall aim was to demoralize the Afghan security forces being prepared to take over from NATO troops as announced by Karzai on 22 March. The first in the line were the Hazara-majority central province of Bamiyan and the predominantly Tajik province of Panjshir along with the capitals of Laghman, Helmand, Herat and Balkh provinces.

On 19 May, Taliban insurgents staged multiple assaults on the checkpoints in the Helmand capital of Lashkar Gah before lobbing rockets at their targets. A week later, they attacked the compound of the provincial governor, Gulab Mangal. Only when an American drone appeared in the skies did they flee. In early June, Lashkar Gah was rocked by the detonation of numerous improvised explosive devices (IEDs), with many attached to police vehicles and others hidden in crates.[18]

Ignoring the escalating violence, Washington and its allies kept pouring money into civilian and military development programmes. Their annual contributions in 2010 equalled Afghanistan's GDP of $14 billion. A little over half of that amount was spent by the US on Afghanistan's military, police and border guards. Its civilian development projects cost nearly $4 billion a year. One such project funded by the State Department authorized up to $100,000 a month payment to provincial officials, thus fuelling corruption.[19] In the case of the mayor of Lashkar Gah, the embezzlement of American and British aid became so blatant that he was sacked.

Such reports turned US lawmakers against their country's involvement in Afghanistan. In May, a resolution in the House of Representatives calling on Obama to set out a timetable for complete pullback of American troops fell only by eleven votes. And in mid-June, a CNN poll found that 62 per cent of the respondents disapproved of war in Afghanistan, up from 51 per cent in January 2009 when Obama became president. With the death of bin Laden, an increasing number of Americans found it futile to be engaged in Afghanistan. Even Republican presidential candidates supported calls for a withdrawal.

This was the backdrop to President Obama's TV address to the nation on 22 June. He said that the mission of the 33,000 troops he ordered to Afghanistan in December 2009 was threefold: re-focus on Al Qaida, reverse the Taliban momentum, and train the Afghan security forces to defend their country. 'We are fulfilling that commitment,' he asserted. 'We are meeting our goals.' Therefore, he added, there would be a withdrawal of 33,000 soldiers from Afghanistan by the summer of 2012 or latest by September, with the first 5,000 to return in July, and another 5,000 by December. That would still leave 90,000 US troops in Afghanistan, more than half of the Afghans enrolled in their armed forces.[20] Obama's timing had to do with his re-election campaign scheduled to take off after Labour Day holiday on 3 September 2012.

Most Afghan and Pakistani commentators along with the Taliban and the ISI interpreted Obama's decision as a sign of Washington's weakness. Attacks by the fighters of the Taliban and its ally, the Haqqani group in North Waziristan, became more lethal. The assault on the 200-room Inter-Continental Hotel on a hilltop in western Kabul by eight heavily armed insurgents, wearing suicide vests, on 28 June was a telling example. It was masterminded by Badruddin Haqqani, deputy chief of the Haqqani network, and supervised by the leader of the group's Kabul cell. The hotel was to be the venue of a conference on NATÓ's handover of security to the Afghans on 29 June, and many officials had checked in.

When the insurgents, armed with sixteen rocket-propelled grenades, heavy machineguns, assault rifles and grenade launchers arrived at the perimeter of the hotel at 10.30 p.m., a police guard, who had been bribed, cut a hole in the perimeter wire. He then led the terrorists to the kitchen. Meanwhile, a co-conspirator – a bodyguard of a senior Afghan official staying at the hotel – chatted with security guards to keep them occupied. In the kitchen, the attackers met the third co-conspirator, a translator hired for a visiting group of foreign businessmen. His task was to lead the attackers to the rooms occupied by the aliens. But, somehow, things went awry. Instead of killing the foreigner hotel guests – as the terrorists in Mumbai had done in November 2008 – these intruders ended up firing rockets from the windows of the hotel when, three hours later, NATO troops arrived in sport utility vehicles. Much shooting followed. Then came a platoon of Afghan soldiers on foot.

The gun battle ended only after four US Black Hawk helicopter gunships appeared and, aided by their searchlights, shot three terrorists dead on the roof. Altogether, nine civilians, two policemen and one foreigner lost their lives. The surviving five insurgents committed suicide. Summarizing the dramatic episode, Karzai claimed, wrongly, that Afghan police and an army commando unit had handled the situation on their own, later receiving some help from a NATO gunship.

Karzai got no chance for spinning when his regime suffered a string of high-profile assassinations in the second half of July. The victims included his forty-nine-year-old half-brother, Ahmad Wali Karzai, dubbed 'King of Kandahar'; Jan Muhammad Khan, a grandee of the Karzais' Popalzai tribal confederation, a former governor of Uruzgan, and a close ally of the president; and the mayor of Kandahar, Ghulam Haidar Hamidi, a childhood friend of the president.

The mainstay of Hamid Karzai's support in Kandahar, Ahmad Wali exercised influence in all five southern provinces. He helped the CIA to run a clandestine paramilitary called Kandahar Strike Force. He cobbled together a pan-tribal alliance with money, secured by monopolizing NATO's contracts and receiving kickbacks from drug barons. Always flanked by a posse of bodyguards outside his heavily fortified home, he was shot dead by his own security chief, Sardar Muhammad, who used a small pistol hidden in the papers to be signed by Ahmad Wali. By contrast, Jan Muhammad Khan was killed by two gunmen, wearing suicide vests, who stormed his home in Kabul. And Hamidi died in the garden compound of his complex when he left his office to meet a group protesting against the bulldozing of their illegally built houses, and found himself grabbed by one of the protestors who detonated a bomb hidden in his turban.

All assassinations were claimed by the Taliban. Their leaders wanted to show the public that the Karzai regime was incapable of safeguarding even its highest officials and that self-preservation should motivate them to abandon the government or at least distance themselves from it. This applied also to businesses which were increasingly unwilling to alienate the Taliban. For the first time, the Taliban had success in intimidating mobile phone companies in Kandahar to shut their networks for two nights in a row in mid-July so that they could carry out their activities unhindered. Earlier they had managed this only in rural areas.

On the eve of the handover of security in Bamiyan province from NATO to Afghan forces on 17 July, Ashraf Ghani, the Afghan official supervising the transition, conceded that the security situation in the east had deteriorated.

Given this, the US–Taliban talks are set to reflect the character of the war: an excruciatingly slow and complicated process, hobbled by interference not only by Pakistan but also Iran, India, Russia, Uzbekistan and China.

Signs of this emerged at the 10th annual summit of the Beijing-based six-member Shanghai Cooperation Organization (SCO) in the Kazakh capital of Astana on 14-15 June. Besides the leaders of China, Russia, Kazakhstan, Kyrgyzstan, Tajikistan and Uzbekistan, the meeting was attended by top officials of the observer nations: India, Iran, Mongolia and Pakistan. Also present was Hamid Karzai as president of Afghanistan with the status of a guest nation.

Karzai sought an observer status for his country which was promised after his declaration of neutrality in the region. 'In our bilateral and multilateral discussions with the United States and NATO, we are mindful of the regional dimensions, as well as the concerns of our neighbours,' he said in his address. 'We will not enter into a partnership if we have reason to believe that it might jeopardize the security of our neighbours or that of our region. Over the past decade, we have focused on expanding our bilateral relations with each of the SCO member states."[21] Karzai made this statement against the background of reports that the US had offered to safeguard Afghanistan's neutrality by setting up military bases there after the December 2014 deadline for the withdrawal of all foreign troops – a proposition unacceptable to the SCO's member states as well as its observer nations, including India.

Among SCO leaders, Russia's president Dmitry Medvedev was foremost in proposing an active integration of Afghanistan into SCO structures, arguing that the security of Central and South Asia depended on that country. He claimed to have the backing of other SCO members who realized the significance of political stabilization in Afghanistan.[22] Among the observer status nations, his views were shared by Iran and Pakistan as well as India.

In sum, with the approach of the departure of the US-led NATO forces from Afghanistan, regional nations were getting ready to have a growing input in shaping the destiny of that country with which India has had historic links.

NOTES

1. THE SUFI CONNECTION

1. Devotees aspire to be buried near the tombs of the saints because they believe that on the Day of Judgement the holy sage will intercede on their behalf with Allah.
2. Today, at least one Sufi woman, Bibi Pak Daman, is honoured as a saint and has her shrine in Lahore, Pakistan.
3. Basharat Peer, *Curfewed Night*, Random House India, Noida, 2009, p. 183.
4. Interview in Delhi, February 2010.
5. The Qalandars claim to be seized by an intoxication arising out of the love of God, to such a degree that they reject social pleasantries.
6. The star attraction is the dhamal dancing by a group of prostitutes from Lahore or Karachi near the mausoleum's golden gate.
7. Nelofar Bakhtyar and Fasih Ahmed, 'Save Our Shrines', *Newsweek Pakistan*, 15 November 2010, http://www.newsweekpakistan.com/index.php?option=com_content&view=article&id=107&Itemid=54.
8. In the Pushtu language, Pushtun is called 'Pakhtun', and Peshawar 'Pekhawar'.

2. AFGHANISTAN AND PAKISTAN

1. Dilip Hiro (ed.), *Babur Nama*, Penguin Books, London, 2007, p. 128.
2. Ibid., p. xxiii.
3. See Arthur J. Arberry, *The Koran Interpreted*, Oxford University Press, Oxford and New York, 1964, p. 107.

4. 'President Karzai's Wife Zinat: Invisible and Subjugated,' http://atlasshrugs2000.typepad.com/atlas_shrugs/2009/08/president-karzais-wife-zinat-invisible-and-subjugated.html.
5. Following Amanullah's abdication in favour of his brother Inayatullah, Kalakani had called on the latter to surrender or fight. Inayatullah decided to abdicate in favour of Kalakani.
6. His vast mausoleum, atop the Seesing Hill in eastern Kabul, provides a panoramic view of the sprawling capital.
7. Husain Haqqani, *Pakistan: Between Mosque and Military*, Carnegie Endowment for International Peace, Washington DC, 2005, pp. 164–65. Moscow also provided economic and industrial aid. By 1973, there were 3,000–4,000 Soviet technicians working in Afghanistan.
8. See Arberry, *The Koran Interpreted*, pp. 355–56.
9. Haqqani, *Pakistan*, p. 171.
10. Of the 113,000 tourists in Afghanistan in 1971, more than half were Western: Dilip Hiro, *War without End: The Rise of Islamist Terrorism and Global Response*, Routledge, London and New York, 2002, p. 445, note 6.
11. Haqqani, *Pakistan*, p. 168.
12. Sayyid Abul Ala Maududi, *Purdah and the Status of Women in Islam*, Islamic Publications, Lahore, 1979, p. 23.
13. Haqqani, *Pakistan*, op. cit., p. 127.
14. Washington's ban on the sale of weapons and parts to Pakistan after the 1965 India–Pakistan War was lifted three years later.
15. Cited in Haqqani, *Pakistan*, p. 176.
16. See Hiro, *War without End*, p. 446, note 13.
17. The anti-usury Quranic verses are: 'O believers, fear for God;/ And give up the usury that is outstanding, if you are believers' (2:278); 'O believers, devour not usury,/ doubled and re-doubled, and fear your God;/ happily so you will prosper' (3:125).
18. Anthony Hyman, *Afghanistan under Soviet Domination*, Macmillan, London, 1984, p. 90.
19. Dilip Hiro, *Between Marx and Muhammad: The Changing Face of Central Asia*, HarperCollins, London, 1994, p. 240.
20. Robert M. Gates, *From the Shadows: The Ultimate Insider's Story of Five Presidents and How They Won the Cold War*, Simon & Schuster, New York, 1997, pp. 143–44.

21. Christina Lamb, *Waiting for Allah: Pakistan's Struggle for Democracy*, Hamish Hamilton, London, 1991, p. 221.
22. David Loyn, *Butcher & Bold: Two Hundred Years of Foreign Engagement in Afghanistan*, Hutchinson, London, 2008, p. 187.
23. Hiro, *War without End*, p. 446, note 15.
24. Victor Sebestyen, 'West Ignores Lessons of Soviet Humiliation in Afghanistan', *Sunday Times*, 19 July 2009, http://www.timesonline.co.uk/tol/news/world/europe/article6719240.ece. See also Sebestyen, 'Transcripts of Defeat', *New York Times*, 29 October 2009. http://www.nytimes.com/2009/10/29/opinion/29sebestyen.html?_r=1&scp=1&sq=Victor+Sebestyen&st=nyt.
25. Mark Franchetti, 'Can the West Avoid Russia's Fate in Afghanistan?', *Sunday Times Magazine*, 3 January 2010, pp. 21–29,http://www.timesonline.co.uk/tol/news/world/afghanistan/article6971683.ece.
26. Cited in Mark Urban, *War in Afghanistan*, Macmillan, London, 1988, p. 56.
27. Sabwoon Online, http://www.sabawoon.com/articles/index.php?page=Moment_changed_afg. Also, Wikiquote, http://en.wikiquote.org/wiki/Zbigniew_Brzezinski.

3. THE AFGHAN TRAP

1. *Kabul New Times*, 1 January 1980.
2. Cited in Dilip Hiro, *The Essential Middle East: A Comprehensive Guide*, Carroll and Graf, New York, 2003, p. 103.
3. 'The CIA's Intervention in Afghanistan: Interview with Zbigniew Brzezinski', *Le Nouvel Observateur*, Paris, 15–21 January 1998, posted at http://www.takeoverworld.info/brzezinski_interview_short.html.
4. Cited in Adrian Levy and Catherine Scott-Clark, *Deception: Pakistan, the United States, and the Global Nuclear Weapons Conspiracy*, Atlantic Books, London, 2008, p. 18.
5. India's 1974 budget for its nuclear programme was $140 million; by 2008 it had spent $1 billion.
6. http://archives-trim.un.org/webdrawer/rec/425418/view/Items-in-Visits%20of%20heads%20of%20states%20and%20foreign%20ministers.PDF.

7. http://www.nti.org/e_research/profiles/Pakistan/Nuclear/chronology_1979.html. 'We know that Israel and South Africa have full nuclear capability,' wrote Bhutto. 'The Christian, Jewish and Hindu civilizations have this capability. The Islamic civilization was without it, but that situation is about to change.' p. 158.
8. A separate arrangement was made for Pakistan's purchase of forty F-16 fighter aircraft manufactured in the US.
9. The Saudi intelligence agency's full title is *Riasat al Istikhbarat al Amah*: 'General Intelligence Presidency'.
10. David Loyn, *Butcher & Bold: Two Hundred Years of Foreign Engagement in Afghanistan*, Hutchinson, London, 2008, p. 216. Bahauddin Majrooh was later assassinated by Hizb-e Islami hoodlums.
11. Peter L. Bergen, *Holy Wars: Inside the Secret World of Osama bin Laden*, The Free Press, New York/Weidenfeld and Nicolson, London, 2001, p. 60.
12. http://www.nti.org/e_research/profiles/India/Nuclear/chronology_1982.html.
13. Research by the Center for Non-proliferation Studies, at the Monterey Institute of International Studies. See Humayun Akhtar, 'China Fully Supports Pakistan Nuclear Plan', 7 September 2000; and in http://www.globalsecurity.org/wmd/world/pakistan/nuke.htm, see Pakistan Nuclear Weapons.
14. 'Pakistan Special Weapons–A Chronology', http://www.fas.org/nuke/guide/pakistan/nuke/chron.htm.
15. Stephen Kinzer, 'How We Helped Create the Afghan Crisis', *Boston Globe*, 20 March 2009, http://www.boston.com/bostonglobe/editorial_opinion/oped/articles/2009/03/20/how_we_helped_create_the_afghan_crisis/.
16. Levy and Scott-Clark, *Deception*, p. 105. See also 'Adrian Levy Interviewed By Amy Goodman', 19 November 2007, http://www.democracynow.org/2007/11/19/deception_british_reporter_andrew_levy_on.
17. Cited in ibid.
18. Anthony Hyman, *Afghanistan under Soviet Domination*, Macmillan, London, 1984, p. 204.
19. Lamb, *Waiting for Allah*, p. 223.
20. Ibid.

21. Loyn, *Butcher & Bold*, p. 299.
22. Levy and Scott-Clark, *Deception*, p. 128.
23. Muhammad Najibullah did not use his Ahmadzai tribal identification although his brother Shahpur did.
24. Levy and Scott-Clark, *Deception,* p. 148.
25. Victor Sebestyen, 'West Ignores Lessons of Soviet Humiliation in Afghanistan,' *Sunday Times*, 19 July 2009, http://www.timesonline.co.uk/tol/news/world/europe/article6719240.ece.
26. Ahmed Rashid, *Taliban: The Story of the Afghan Warlords*, Pan Books, London, 2001, p. 129.
27. Global Security Organization, 'Pakistan Nuclear Weapons', http://www.globalsecurity.org/wmd/world/pakistan/nuke.htm; and http://www.fas.org/nuke/guide/pakistan/nuke/chron.htm.
28. Loyn, *Butcher & Bold*, p. 208.
29. http://www.fas.org/nuke/guide/pakistan/nuke/chron.htm.

4. THE RISE AND RISE OF THE TALIBAN

1. *The Economist*, 1 February 1992, p. 66.
2. Hiro, *Between Marx and Muhammad*, p. 262; and John K. Cooley, *Unholy Wars: Afghanistan, America, and International Terrorism,* Pluto Press, London and Sterling, Virginia, 2000, p. 109.
3. Hiro, *Between Marx and Muhammad*, p. 262.
4. Ibid.
5. Abdul Salam Zaeef, *My Life with the Taliban*, Hurst & Company, London, 2010, p. 65; and *News* (Islamabad), 2 February 1995.
6. Sultan Amir Tarar was popular among the Afghan Mujahedin because he adopted Afghan culture and was deeply religious. When Mullah Muhammad Omar was wounded and lost an eye, Tarar sent him to a hospital in Karachi.
7. A few weeks after this event, Mullah Omar's aides met Robin Raphel, US assistant Secretary of State, in Kandahar during her tour of the region – a meeting that implicitly recognized the Taliban as a significant element in the Afghan imbroglio.
8. Ahmed Rashid, *Taliban: The Story of the Afghan Warlords*, Pan Books, London, 2001, p. 45.
9. *Observer*, 29 September 1996.

10. Later, Mullah Muhammad Rabbani was promoted to president of the Islamic Emirate of Afghanistan, but real power rested with Mullah Muhammad Omar.
11. Latifa, *My Forbidden Face: Growing Up under the Taliban, a Young Woman's Story* (trans. Lisa Appignanesi), Virago, London, 2001, pp. 31–32, 36.
12. Cited in *Middle East International* (London), 25 October 1996, p. 6.
13. *Financial Times*, 29–30 September 2001.

5. TARGET KASHMIR

1. See pp. 9–10.
2. Altaf Hussain, 'Kashmir's Flawed Elections', BBC News, 14 September 2002, http://news.bbc.co.uk/1/hi/world/south_asia/2223364.stm.
3. Rajmohan Gandhi, *Understanding the Muslim Mind*, Penguin Books India, New Delhi, 2000, pp. 181–82.
4. http://en.wikipedia.org/wiki/Sheikh_Abdullah.
5. The Muslim Conference continued to exist as a minor political force.
6. Cited in Lamb, *Waiting for Allah*, p. 25.
7. http://kashmir.ahrchk.net/mainfile.php/after1947/9/.
8. Victoria Schofield, *Kashmir in Conflict: India, Pakistan, and the Unending War*, I.B. Tauris, London and New York, 2010, p. 145.
9. Peer, *Curfewed Night*, pp. 10–11.
10. Hussain, 'Kashmir's Flawed Elections'.
11. The Kashmiri jihadists were financed by the ISI with the drugs money. Farzana Shaikh, *Making Sense of Pakistan*, Hurst and Company, London, 2009, p. 169.
12. Balraj Puri, *Towards Insurgency*, Sangam Books, London, 1993, p. 60.
13. From then on, 5 February became the Kashmir Solidarity Day in Pakistan and Azad Kashmir.
14. Peer, *Curfewed Night*, p. 17.
15. The Armed Forces (Special Powers) Act was first passed in 1958 to cover the 'disturbed' areas in the north-east of India. It remains in force there.
16. Peer, *Curfewed Night*, p. 143.
17. Ibid., p. 146.
18. Ibid., p. 144.

19. The cleric who leads the Friday prayer at the main mosque of Srinagar carries the title of Mirwaiz.
20. Some of the former guerrillas ended up as fully fledged soldiers of the Border Security Force or Central Reserve Police Force.
21. India Times Television, News, /http://www.timesnow.tv/Pak-paid-separatist-Bilal-Lone/articleshow/4334242.cms.
22. Safe in Pakistani-administered Kashmir, Mast Gul held a press conference on 26 May 1995.
23. Schofield, *Kashmir in Conflict*, p. 172.
24. Ibid., pp. 176, 177 and 183.
25. Cited in ibid., p. 194.
26. Hiro, *War without End*, p. 379.
27. Tom Wright, 'India Considers Limits on Forces in Kashmir', *Wall Street Journal*, 23 June 2010, http://online.wsj.com/article/SB10001424052748704123604575322770886841554.html, citing South Asia Terrorism Portal.
28. G8 statement on regional issues, http://www/usia/gov/topical/econ/g8koln/g8region.htm.
29. 'Pakistan Warns of Kashmir War Risk', BBC World, 23 June 1999, http://news.bbc.co.uk/1/hi/world/south_asia/376052.stm.
30. Sultan Shahin, 'Back on the Brink of War', *Asia Times*, 18 May 2002, http://www.atimes.com/ind-pak/DE18Df05.html.
31. Hiro, *War without End*, p. 285.
32. Ibid., p. 374.
33. Ibid., p. 382; and Ahmed Rashid, *Descent into Chaos: How the War against Islamic Extremism Is Being Lost in Pakistan, Afghanistan, and Central Asia*, Allen Lane, London, 2008, p. 146.
34. Shashank Joshi, 'India and the Four Day War', Royal United Services Institute, http://www.rusi.org/analysis/commentary/ref:C4BBC50E1BAF9C.
35. Cited in Rashid, *Descent into Chaos*, pp. 119–120.
36. Cited in *Muslim News* (Harrow, UK), 30 January 2009.

6. INDIA, ISRAEL AND AMERICA

1. Besides the seven members of the Arab League and India, China, Cuba, Greece, Iran, and Yugoslavia opposed the resolution, which was passed by 33 votes to 13, with 10 abstentions.

2. 'India-United States Relations', http://en.wikipedia.org/wiki/India_%E2%80%93_United_States_relations.
3. Dilip Hiro, *Inside India Today*, Routledge & Kegan Paul, London, 1976, p. 250.
4. Neville Maxwell, *India's China War*, Penguin Books, Harmondsworth, 1972, pp. 448–49.
5. Manoj Joshi, 'Military Diplomacy: Uniform to Pinstripes', *India Today International*, 6 April 1998, http://www.india-today.com/itoday/06041998/defence.html.
6. Ibid.
7. B. Raman, *Kaoboys of R&AW: Down Memory Lane*, Lancer Publishers, New Delhi, 2008, p. 127.
8. Nicolas Blarel, 'Indo-Israeli Relations', in Sumit Ganguly (ed.), *India's Foreign Policy: Retrospect and Prospect*, Oxford University Press, Delhi, 2010, p. 161.
9. The vote for resolution 3379 on 10 November 1975 was 72 to 35, with 32 abstentions. Among those who voted in favour was Iran, then ruled by the shah, Muhammad Reza Pahlavi, closely allied with the US.
10. Seymour M. Hersh, *The Price of Power: Kissinger in the Nixon White House*, Summit Books, New York, 1983, p. 450.
11. That remains the Indian government's main concern even today.
12. Adrian Levy and Catherine Scott-Clark, *Deception: Pakistan, the United States, and the Global Nuclear Weapons Conspiracy*, Atlantic Books, London, 2008, p. 104.
13. Ibid., pp. 104-05.
14. P.R. Kumaraswamy, *India's Israel Policy*, Columbia University Press, New York, pp. 231–32.
15. Ibid., p. 230.
16. Manoj Joshi, 'Military Diplomacy: Uniform to Pinstripes', *India Today International*, 6 April 1998.
17. As a teacher at the King Abdul Aziz University in Riyadh, Hafiz Muhammad Saeed had come under the influence of Wahhabi ulema.
18. India was then one of the ten non-permanent members of the UN Security Council.
19. Cited in James Chinyaankandh, 'India and Israel: Converging Hostilities?', *Olive Stone* (Birmingham, UK), August 1998, p. 4.

20. A.K. Pasha, 'India and Israel: Growing Cooperation', *World Focus* (Delhi), August 1993, p. 22. Shimon Peres arrived in Delhi accompanied by the chief executive officers of Israel's industrial–military complex.
21. 'India and Israel in a Joint Venture to build an Anti-Aircraft Missile', Agence France Press, 27 February 2008. In one of its early acquisitions from Israel, the Indian navy bought Barak-1 vertically launched surface-to-air missiles to intercept anti-ship cruise missiles. This was to meet its need to counter Pakistan's P3-C II Orion maritime strike aircraft and twenty-seven Harpoon sea-skimming anti-ship missiles supplied by the Pentagon. Sushil J. Aaron, 'Straddling Fault Lines: India's Foreign Policy toward the Greater Middle East', Centre de Sciences Humaines Occasional Paper, 2003, http://www.csh-delhi.com/publications/downloads/ops/OP7.pdf.
22. Christopher Walker and Michael Evans, 'Pakistan Feared Israeli Raid: Missiles Were Put on Alert to Counter Strike at Nuclear Sites', *The Times* (London), 3 June 1998.
23. At $36 billion, Pakistan's foreign debts were 72 per cent of its GDP. With its foreign exchange reserves reduced to $1.3 billion, the government used the state of emergency to freeze all private foreign exchange accounts, totaling $11 billion.
24. Raj Chengappa and Zahid Hussain, 'Bang for Bang', *India Today*, 8 June 1998.
25. Robert Lee Hotz, 'Tests Were Exaggerated by India and Pakistan', *Los Angeles Times*, 17 September 1998.
26. Joshi, 'Military Diplomacy: Uniform to Pinstripes'.
27. A report in an Israeli daily, *Haaretz*, cited by Ashok K. Mehta, 'India, Israel Developing Strategic Partnership', *Observer*, 25 July 2000 – posted on India's Ministry of External Affairs website at http://www.meadev.nic.in/opn/2000july/25obs.htm.
28. Rahul Bedi, 'The Tel Aviv Connection Grows', 26 July 2002, http://www.indiatogether.org/govt/military/articles/isrlbuy02.htm.
29. Ed Blanche, 'Mutual Threat of Islamic Militancy Allies Israel and India', *Jane's Terrorism and Security Monitor*, 14 August 2001.
30. Zahid Hussain, *Frontline Pakistan: The Struggle with Militant Islam*, I.B. Tauris, London/ Columbia University Press, New York, 2007, p. 58.

31. Interview with Zahid Hussain in January 2001: *Frontline Pakistan*, p. 53 and p. 58.
32. Sheela Bhatt, 'New R&AW Chief Is First to Be Trained in Israel', Rediffusion News, 2 April 2003, http://www.rediff.com/news/2003/apr/02raw.htm.
33. Ministry of External Affairs, India, http://meaindia.nic.in/speech/2003/05/o8spco1.htm.
34. Director General of foreign trade, India, http://dgft.delhi.nic.in.
35. These agreements specified joint exercises between their air forces in 2006 and their navies in 2007. In the latter year, bilateral trade between India and America in merchandise stood at $39 billion, up from $5.6 billion in 1990.
36. Haroon Mirani, 'Israeli Rifles Appear in Kashmir', *Kashmir News*, 1 March 2008, http://www.kashmirnewz.com/n000336.html.
37. Cited in Ninan Koshy, 'India-Israel Defense Nexus Deepens', *Mainstream* (Delhi), 2 May 2009, http://www.mainstreamweekly.net/article1350.html.

7. LIBERATING INDIAN KASHMIR

1. See pp. 9–10.
2. Abdul Sattar, *Pakistan's Foreign Policy 1947–2005: A Concise History*, Oxford University Press, Karachi, 2007, p. 16.
3. However, that did not stop Azad Kashmir from adopting a flag of its own.
4. Cited in Farzana Shaikh, *Making Sense of Pakistan*, Hurst & Company, London, 2009, p. 160.
5. Lal Bahadur Shastri died of a heart attack the day after signing the agreement.
6. Ashok Raina, *Inside RAW: The Story of India's Secret Service*, Vikas Publishing House, New Delhi, 1981, pp. 53–54.
7. Cited in Ramchandra Guha, *India after Gandhi: The History of the World's Largest Democracy*, Macmillan, London, 2007, p. 453, quoting a secret report by RAW in January 1971 entitled 'Threat of Military Attack or Infiltration Campaign by Pakistan'.
8. Cited in ibid., p. 452.
9. Husain Haqqani, *Pakistan: Between Mosque and Military*, Carnegie Endowment for International Peace, Washington DC, 2005, p. 71.

10. Hamdoor Rahman, http://en.wikipedia.org/wiki/Hamoodur_Rahman.
11. Christina Lamb, *Waiting for Allah: Pakistan's Struggle for Democracy*, Hamish Hamilton, London, 1991, p. 84.
12. Haqqani, *Between Mosque and Military*, p. 273.
13. Ibid., p. 288.
14. Ibid., p. 295, citing his notes of the meeting at the prime minister's residence on 18 May 1992.
15. Harinder Baweja, 'Get America Out of the Way and We'll Be OK', http://www.tehelka.com/story_main37.asp?filename=Ne020208understanding_pakistan.asp).
16. Cited in Zahid Hussain, *Frontline Pakistan: The Struggle with Militant Islam*, I.B. Tauris, London/Columbia University Press, New York, 2007, p. 105.
17. Adrian Levy and Catherine Scott-Clark, *Deception: Pakistan, the United States, and the Global Nuclear Weapons Conspiracy*, Atlantic Books, London, 2008, p. 323.
18. Cited in Haqqani, *Between Mosque and Military*, p. 261.
19. Sattar, *Pakistan's Foreign Policy 1947–2005*, pp. 271 and 274.
20. Jyoti Malhotra, 'Kashmir: Is Solution in Sight?' BBC News, 7 December 2006, http://news.bbc.co.uk/1/hi/world/south_asia/6217734.stm.
21. Jason Burke, 'Mumbai Spy Says he Worked for Terrorists – Then Briefed Pakistan', *Guardian*, 18 October 2010. http://www.guardian.co.uk/world/2010/oct/18/david-headley-mumbai-attacks-pakistan. The ISI also instructed David Coleman Headley to recruit Indian agents to inform them about Indian troop movement and levels. In December 2007, Headley's Moroccan wife, Faiza Outalah, informed the US embassy in Islamabad of her husband's LeT links. The embassy noted the information but did not consider it 'actionable intelligence'.
22. Steve Coll, 'The Back Channel', *The New Yorker*, 2 March 2009; reposted at New America Foundation http://newamerica.net/publications/articles/2009/back_channel_11191.
23. Helene Cooper and Eric Schmitt, 'US Tries to Calm Pakistan Over Airstrike', *New York Times*, 6 October 2010, http://www.nytimes.com/2010/10/07/world/asia/07diplo.html?ref=eric_schmitt.
24. Ayesha Siddiqa, *Military Inc: Inside Pakistan's Military Economy*, Pluto Press, London and Ann Arbor, MI, 2007, p. 98.

25. See http://hr5.blogspot.com/2008/09/president-zardaris-note.html and http://www.reallyvirtual.com/my-new-found-respect-for-zardari/.

8. ZIA UL HAQ: THE ISLAMIST DICTATOR

1. Jamil-ud-din Ahmad (ed.), *Speeches and Writings of Mr Jinnah*, Vol. II, Shaikh Muhammad Ashrag, Lahore, 1964, p. 403; and Haqqani, *Pakistan*, p. 12, citing *Quaid-i-Azam Mohammad Ali Jinnah's Speeches as Governor General of Pakistan, 1947–48,* Government of Pakistan, Karachi, 1964; also Hector Bolitho, *Jinnah*, Greenwood Press, Westport, Connecticut, n.d., p. 197.
2. 'Jinnah's Speech to Sind Bar Association, Karachi', *Dawn* (Karachi), 26 January 1948, cited in Farzana Shaikh, *Making Sense of Pakistan*, Hurst & Company, London, 2009, p. 60.
3. Cited in Shaikh, *Making Sense of Pakistan*,, p. 85.
4. See pp. 12–18.
5. Haqqani, *Pakistan*, p. 40.
6. Ahmadis are the followers of Mirza Ghulam Ahmad (1835–1908), born in the village of Qadian in Punjab. Their belief that Ahmad was the Messiah in succession to Lord Krishna, Jesus Christ and Prophet Muhammad contradicts mainstream Muslims' tenet that Muhammad is the last and final prophet. They form 2.3 per cent of Pakistan's population.
7. Cited in Haqqani, *Pakistan*, p. 127.
8. Zia ul Haq's Islamization: http://en.wikipedia.org/wiki/Zia-ul-Haq's_Islamization.
9. The Tablighi Jamaat follows the Deobandi interpretation of Sunni Islam's Hanafi jurisprudence.
10. Cited in Shahid Javed Burki and Craig Baxter (eds), *Pakistan under the Military: Eleven Years of Zia ul Haq*, Westview Press, Boulder, Colorado, 1991, p. 5.
11. Cited in Lamb, *Waiting for Allah*, p. 85.
12. Cited in Haqqani, *Pakistan*, pp. 149–50.
13. Yvette Rosser, 'Pakistani Textbooks: Politics of Prejudice', http://www.thesouthasian.org/archives/2004/pakistani_textbooks_politics_o.html.
14. Lamb, *Waiting for Allah*, p. 85.

15. Tariq Rahman, 'Madrassas: Religion, Poverty, and the Potential for Violence in Pakistan', http://ipripak.org/journal/winter2005/madrassas.shtml.
16. Kate Clark, 'UN Quake Aid Went to Extremists', BBC News, 5 October 2006, http://news.bbc.co.uk/1/hi/world/south_asia/5402756.stm.
17. Tariq Rahman, 'Tolerance and Militancy in Schoolchildren', *Dawn* (Karachi), 23 February 2003, cited in Stephen Philip Cohen, *The Idea of Pakistan*, Brookings Institution, Washington DC, 2004, p. 184.
18. Hussain, *Frontline Pakistan*, pp. 8–9. Between 1986 and 2007, half of the 647 Pakistanis charged with offences under these laws were Christian. While none of them was hanged, twenty were murdered by Islamist vigilantes. 'Blasphemy Law in Pakistan', http://en.wikipedia.org/wiki/Blasphemy_law_in_Pakistan.
19. Khaled Ahmed, 'The Secular Mussalman', *Indian Express*, 23 May 1998, http://www.indianexpress.com/res/web/pIe/ie/daily/19980523/14350814.html.
20. The Council of Islamic Ideology's final report appeared in December 1996.
21. See http://www.scribd.com/doc/20467531/Malik-Quranic-Concept-of-War-Original. The capital letters appear in the original text.
22. Sabrina Tavernise and Waqar Gillani, '70 Murders, Yet Close to Going Free in Pakistan', *New York Times*, 5 August 2009, http://www.nytimes.com/2009/08/06/world/asia/06justice.html.
23. The Sipah-e Sahaba Pakistan later split along ethnic lines, with its Punjabi and Pushtun sections going their separate ways.
24. An increase of 2 per cent – from 11.2 to 13.2 per cent – in forty years was hardly a cause for alarm.

9. INDIAN MUSLIMS AMIDST HINDU REVIVALISM

1. My subsequent inquiry revealed that several policemen were charged with manslaughter. But so lethargic is the pace of justice in India that – twenty-eight years on – the case remained unfinished. 'Meanwhile, some of the accused policemen are dead,' said my well-informed source.
2. *Economic and Political Weekly* (Bombay), July 1969, p. 1150.

3. Hiro, *Inside India Today*, p. 236, citing Donald E. Smith, *India as a Secular State*, Princeton University Press, Princeton, NJ, 1963, p. 389.
4. Hiro, *Inside India Today*, p. 236.
5. *Hindutva* is a compound of the words Hindu and *tattva*, meaning 'principles' in Sanskrit. Vinayak Damodar Savarkar, *Hindutva: Who is a Hindu?* Hindi Sahitya Sadan, Delhi, 2003.
6. Madhavrao Golwalkar, *We, or, Our Nationhood Defined*, Bharat Publications, Nagpur, 1939, p. 37.
7. Ibid., p. 62.
8. 'The aims and objects of the Sangha [i.e., RSS] are to weld the diverse groups within the Hindu samaj [i.e., society] and to revitalize and rejuvenate the same on the basis of its *dharma* [i.e., ethics] and *sanskriti* [i.e., culture] so that it may achieve an all-sided development of Bharatvarsha [Sanskrit, "India"],' stated its constitution in 1949.
9. Hiro, *Inside India Today*, p. 188, citing Motilal A. Jhangiani, *Jan Sangh and Swatantra*, Manaktalas, Bombay, 1967, p. 14.
10. Cited in David James Smith, *Hinduism and Modernity*, Blackwell Publishing, Oxford, 2002, p. 189.
11. Hiro, *Inside India Today*, p. 236.
12. *Economic and Political Weekly* (Bombay), January 1970, pp. 187–88.
13. *The Times* (London), 13 October 1969.
14. *Seminar* (Delhi), August 1970, p. 27; and Hiro, *Inside India Today*, p. 232.
15. Asghar Ali Engineer, 'Islam and Muslims in India – Problems of Identity and Existence', *Indian Muslims*, 16–31 December 2000, http://www.indianmuslims.info/articles/asghar_ali_engineer/islam_and_muslims_in_india_problem_of_identity_and_existence.html.
16. 'Digging Up the Past: A Historian's View', http://www.cpiml.org/liberation/year_2003/April/interview.htm.
17. Ram Sharan Sharma, http://en.wikipedia.org/wiki/Ram_Sharan_Sharma#Select_bibliography_of_works_in_English.
18. Haqqani, *Pakistan*, pp. 291–92.
19. Arundhati Roy, *Listening to Grasshoppers: Field Notes on Democracy*, Hamish Hamilton, London, 2009, p. 147. See also 'Analysis: RSS Aims for a Hindu Nation', BBC News, 10 March 2003, http://news.bbc.co.uk/2/hi/south_asia/655722.stm.
20. Mridula Mukherjee and Aditya Mukherjee, 'Communalisation of

Education: The History Textbook Controversy: An Overview', http://www.sacw.net/HateEducation/MridulaAditya122001.html.

21. 'UK reads the riot act to Narendra Modi', *Times of India*, 22 March 2005. http://timesofindia.indiatimes.com/articleshow/1058718.cms; and 'Gujarat Riot Death Toll Revealed', BBC News, 11 May 2005, http://news.bbc.co.uk/1/hi/world/south_asia/4536199.stm.
22. Cited in Roy, *Listening to Grasshoppers*, p. 151.
23. Celia W. Dugger, 'Religious Riots Loom Over Indian Politics', *New York Times*, 27 July 2002, http://www.nytimes.com/2002/07/27/world/religious-riots-loom-over-indian-politics.html.
24. Transcript: Babu Bajrangi. 'After Killing Them, I Felt Like Maharana Pratap,' *Tehelka* (Delhi), 1 September 2007, http://www.tehelka.com/story_main35.asp?filename=Ne031107After_killing.asp. Great Prince Partap of Rajasthan was known for his resistance against the Muslim emperors of Delhi.
25. Interviews in the eighteen-year-old Muslim slum of Seelampur in Greater Delhi, with a population of 55,000, in February 2010 revealed that the settlement had so far produced only two university graduates.
26. See Badri Raina's ZSpace Page, http://www.zcommunications.org/sachar-committee-report-on-indian-muslims-by-badri-raina?toggle_layout=yes).
27. For the complete text of the email relating to the Indian Mujahedin's Ahmedabad blasts, see http://deshgujarat.com/2008/08/02/full-text-of-indian-muajahideens-ahmedabad-blasts-email/.
28. 'The Rise Of Jihad, Revenge of Gujarat', *Outlook* (Delhi), 29 July 2008, http://www.outlookindia.com/article.aspx?238039.
29. Damien McLeroy, 'Indian Youth Joining Terror Groups', *Sunday Telegraph* (London), 14 December 2008, http://www.jihadwatch.org/2008/12/hyderabad-scores-of-young-muslims-have-disappeared-to-pakistan-for-jihad-training.html.
30. Praveen Swami, 'Politics of Hate Gave Birth to Top Terror Commander', *The Hindu*, 23 February, 2009, http://www.hindu.com/2009/02/23/stories/2009022355351000.htm.
31. Hetal Vyas, Deeptiman Tiwary, and Anand Holla, '18-Year-Old IM Man Spilled the Beans on Terror Outfit', *Bangalore Mirror*, 18 February 2009,http://www.mumbaimirror.com/index.aspx?page=article&sectid=15& contentid=2009021820090218031615268b90eeff4.

32. See 'Liberhan Commission,' http://en.wikipedia.org/wiki/Liberhan_Commission. In his book *Open Secrets: India's Intelligence Unveiled*, Maloy Krishna Dhar, former joint director of the Intelligence Bureau, revealed that the plan to demolish the Babri Mosque was conceived at a meeting of the extremist Hindu groups in February 1992.

10. PAKISTAN'S JIHADISTS

1. From 1994 onward, the Jamaat-ud Dawa started opening Ahle Hadith madrasas elsewhere with the ultimate objective of preparing students for jihad.
2. Harinder Baweja, 'Into the Heart of Darkness', *Tehelka*, 20 December 2008, http://www.tehelka.com/story_main41.asp?filename=Ne201208 coverstory.asp.
3. Lamb, *Waiting for Allah*, pp. 178–79.
4. Ibid., p. 187.
5. Ibid., pp. 172 and 285.
6. Levy and Scott-Clark, *Deception*, p. 240.
7. The Pakistani volunteers were often puzzled and intrigued by the way Afghan Taliban fighters would at every opportunity take out pocket mirrors or mirrored snuffbox lids to snip nostril hair, apply eyeliner, and grease their moustaches.
8. Lamb, *Waiting for Allah*, p. 195.
9. Philip Cohen, *The Idea of Pakistan*, p. 89.
10. Acting as virtual magistrates or judges, some of these feudal lords maintained their own prisons.
11. Cited in Lamb, *Waiting for Allah*, p. 187.
12. Cohen, *The Idea of Pakistan*, pp. 247 and 244.
13. Jemima Khan, 'A Dying Man Trusted You to Save His Baby – Don't Let Him Down', *Sunday Times*, 15 August 2010, http://www.thesundaytimes.co.uk/sto/public/article370378.ece.
14. Lamb, *Waiting for Allah*, p. 52.
15. In the 1977 elections, it was district commissioners who, out of excessive loyalty to Zulfikar Ali Bhutto, boosted votes for the Pakistan People's Party, and abducted certain candidates.
16. The banning of the Jaish-e Muhammad by the Pakistani government in January 2002 left the *Zerb-i-Momin* untouched.

17. Hussain, *Frontline Pakistan*, p. 66.
18. See www.dawn.com/fixed/group/publicat.htm).
19. Rashid, *Descent into Chaos: How the War Against Islamic Extremism Is Being Lost in Pakistan, Afghanistan, and Central Asia*, Allen Lane, London, 2008, p. 289.
20. Haqqani, *Pakistan*, p. 306, citing his interview with an ISI official in Islamabad in January 2005.
21. Being president of the republic, Pervez Musharraf did not join the PML (Q).
22. Rashid, *Descent into Chaos*, p. 225.
23. The search of the Red Mosque complex after its takeover by the army would reveal letters from Ayman Zawahiri, the number two in the Al Qaida hierarchy, to the Ghazi brothers directing them and other extremists to wage jihad against the Musharraf government. Dean Nelson and Ghulam Hasnain, 'Bin Laden's Deputy behind the Red Mosque Bloodbath', *Sunday Times*, 15 July 2007, http://www.timesonline.co.uk/tol/news/world/asia/article2076013.ece.
24. Maulana Qazi Fazlullah was the son-in-law of the TNSM's founder, Sufi Muhammad, who was jailed as an extremist.
25. Saeed Shah, 'Deadly suicide bombing marks Red Mosque anniversary', *Guardian*, 7 July 2008, http://www.guardian.co.uk/world/2008/jul/07/pakistan.
26. The US aid to Pakistan between September 2001 and March 2009 amounted to $11.9 billion. Eric Schmitt, 'Pakistan Injects Precision into Air War on Taliban', *New York Times*, 29 July 2009, http://www.nytimes.com/2009/07/30/world/asia/30pstan.html?_r=2.
27. See p. 126.
28. Ismail Khan and Sabrina Tavernise, 'Pakistan Says Feud Kills a Top Militant', *New York Times*, 8 August 2009, http://www.nytimes.com/2009/08/09/world/asia/09pstan.html?_r=1.
29. Cited in Mark Mazzetti, 'The Downside of Letting Robots Do the Bombing,' *New York Times*, 21 March 2009, http://www.nytimes.com/2009/03/22/weekinreview/15MAZZETTI.html.
30. Jeremy Page, 'Google Earth Reveals Secret History of US Base in Pakistan', *The Times* (London), 19 February 2009, http://www.timesonline.co.uk/tol/news/world/asia/article5762371.ece.
31. Declan Walsh 'Mysterious "Chip" Is CIA's Latest Weapon Against al-

Qaida Targets Hiding in Pakistan's Tribal Belt', *Guardian*, 31 May 2009, http://www.guardian.co.uk/world/2009/may/31/cia-drones-tribesmen-taliban-pakistan.

32. 'Gunmen Shoot Sri Lanka Cricketers', BBC News, 3 March 2009, http://news.bbc.co.uk/1/hi/in_depth/7920260.stm.
33. By ending the state's monopoly on broadcasting, General Pervez Musharraf followed the lead of India, which had done so in 1995, and thereby tried to burnish his image as a 'liberal' dictator, prepared to allow diverse views to be expressed.
34. Ali Sethi, 'Lahore Murder Mystery', *New York Times*, 4 March 2009, http://www.nytimes.com/2009/03/04/opinion/04iht-edsethi.1.20584940.html?_r=1.
35. Syed Shoab Hasan, 'Analysis: Why Attack Lahore?', BBC News, 15 October 2008, http://news.bbc.co.uk/1/hi/world/south_asia/7972565.stm.
36. So far the Tehrik-e Taliban Pakistan had managed to down just one drone, on 7 March 2009.
37. Salman Masood, 'Cleric Who Led Militants in Pakistan Is Released', *New York Times*, 17 April 2009, http://www.nytimes.com/2009/04/18/world/asia/18pstan.html?_r=1&adxnnl=1&ref=maulana_abdul_aziz&adxnnlx=1287338548-Scd67DqnqABNQKbig2BiQw; and idem, 'Hard Line Cleric Returns with Bold Call for Islamic rule', *International Herald Tribune*, 18 April 2009.
38. Declan Walsh, 'Video of Girl's Flogging as Taliban Hand Out Justice', *Guardian*, 2 April 2009, http://www.guardian.co.uk/world/2009/apr/02/taliban-pakistan-justice-women-flogging.
39. Christina Lamb, 'Rogue Pakistan Spies Aid Taliban in Afghanistan', *Sunday Times*, 3 August 2008, http://www.timesonline.co.uk/tol/news/world/article4449330.ece.
40. 'Pakistan Public Polls', June 2008, http://www.unitedstatesaction.com/blog/pakistan.html; and Gallup Poll, 29 December 2008, 'Opinion Briefing: U.S.-Pakistan Policy', http://www.gallup.com/poll/113584/opinion-briefing-uspakistan-policy.aspx.
41. Bruce Reidel, 'Pakistan: The Next Nuclear Nightmare?', http://www.brookings.edu/opinions/2009/1012_pakistan_riedel.aspx.
42. Jane Perlez, 'Pakistan Strikes Down Amnesty for Politicians', *New*

York Times, 16 December 2009, http://www.nytimes.com/2009/12/17/world/asia/17pstan.html; and Declan Walsh, 'Pakistan denies coup as court ruling rocks Zardari government', *Guardian*, 18 December 2009, http://www.guardian.co.uk/world/2009/dec/17/pakistan-exit-ban-corruption.

43. Before his suicide mission, Dr Humam Khalil Muhammad al Balawi made a video in the company of TTP leader Hakimullah Mehsud.
44. Jane Perlez, 'Generals in Pakistan Push for Shake-Up of Government', *New York Times*, 28 September 2010, http://www.nytimes.com/2010/09/29/world/asia/29pstan.html.
45. See p. 129.

11. A CORRUPT REGIME, A VENGEFUL TALIBAN

1. Sarah Chayes, 'Drawing Hope from History', *New York Times*, 1 August 2006, http://chayes.blogs.nytimes.com/.
2. Rashid, *Descent into Chaos*, 2008, pp. 143–44.
3. Prominent among those who noticed the reassembling of the Taliban in their old bastions was the younger half-brother of Hamid Karzai, Ahmed Wali, governor of Kandahar city.
4. Antonio Giustozzi, *Koran, Kalashnikov, and Laptop: The Neo-Taliban Insurgency in Afghanistan*, Hurst & Company, London, 2007, p. 187.
5. Gaith Abdul-Ahad, 'Heroin, Schools and the Heart of the Insurgency', *Guardian*, 22 December 2008, http://www.guardian.co.uk/world/2008/dec/22/heroin-opium-poppies-afghanistan.
6. Gaith Abdul-Ahad, 'Face to Face with the Taliban,' *Guardian*, 15 December 2008, http://www.guardian.co.uk/world/2008/dec/14/afghanistan-terrorism.
7. Giustozzi, *Koran, Kalashnikov, and Laptop*, p. 229.
8. Ibid., p. 164.
9. Abdul-Ahad, 'Face to Face with the Taliban,' http://www.guardian.co.uk/world/2008/dec/14/afghanistan-terrorism.
10. Giustozzi, *Koran, Kalashnikov, and Laptop*, p. 194.
11. 'New *Layeha* for the Mujahideen', http://www.signandsight.com/features/1071.html.
12. C.J. Chivers, Carlotta Gall, Andrew W. Lehren, Mark Mazzetti, Jane Perlez and Eric Schmitt, 'View Is Bleaker Than Official Portrayal of

War in Afghanistan', *New York Times*, 25 July 2010, http://www.nytimes.com/2010/07/26/world/asia/26warlogs.html?_r=1.
13. It was only in May 2007 that a policeman's salary was raised to $100 a month.
14. C.J. Chivers *et al*, 'View Is Bleaker Than Official Portrayal of War in Afghanistan'.
15. Ibid.
16. Cited in Abdul-Ahad, 'Face to Face with the Taliban', http://www.guardian.co.uk/world/2009/aug/18/taliban-committee-kunduz-afghanistan.
17. The report also referred to hundreds of unregistered security companies employing seventy thousand largely unsupervised gunmen.
18. Dexter Filkins, 'U.S. Said to Fund Afghan Warlords to Protect Convoys', *New York Times*, 21 June 2010, http://www.nytimes.com/2010/06/22/world/asia/22contractors.html?_r=1&fta=y.
19. Cited in Aram Rostam, 'How the US Army Protects Its Trucks – by Paying the Taliban', *Guardian*, 13 November 2009, http://www.guardian.co.uk/world/2009/nov/13/us-trucks-security-taliban.
20. Hiro, *War without End*, p. 292.
21. Abdul-Ahad, 'Heroin, Schools, and the Heart of the Insurgency'.
22. Ibid.
23. Rashid, *Descent into Chaos*, p. 363.
24. Giustozzi, *Koran, Kalashnikov, and Laptop*, p. 163.
25. It was not until 2009 that the salary of a trained soldier was raised to $120 a month.
26. Rashid, *Descent into Chaos*, p. 203.
27. Giustozzi, *Koran, Kalashnikov, and Laptop*, pp. 97–98.
28. Institute for War & Peace Reporting Trainees, 'Afghanistan: Operation Achilles Heel?', *APR Issue 250*, 27 April 2007, http://iwpr.net/report-news/afghanistan-operation-achilles-heel.
29. Mark Mazzetti, Jane Perlez, Eric Schmitt, and Andrew W. Lehren, 'Pakistan Aids Insurgency in Afghanistan, Reports Assert', *New York Times*, 25 July 2010, http://www.nytimes.com/2010/07/26/world/asia/26isi.html.
30. 'Seven Pakistani Troops Dead as Border Clash Continues', *Nawaaye Afghanistan*, 15 May 2008, http://nawaaye-afghanistan.net/spip.php?article4054.

31. Declan Walsh, 'Afghanistan War Logs: Secret War along the Pakistan Border', *Guardian*, 26 July 2010, http://www.guardian.co.uk/world/2010/jul/25/afghanistan-war-pakistan-border-taliban.

12. AFGHANISTAN: A SECOND VIETNAM

1. Interview, March 2010.
2. Christina Lamb, 'Afghans Look Beyond Bickering Leaders', *Sunday Times*, 26 July 2009, http://www.timesonline.co.uk/tol/news/world/middle_east/article6727734.ece.
3. Abdul-Ahad, 'Face to Face with Taliban', *Guardian*, 15 December 2008, http://www.guardian.co.uk/world/2008/dec/14/afghanistan-terrorism.
4. Richard A. Oppel Jr, 'Marines Face Lonely Fight in a Taliban Stronghold', *New York Times*, 27 July 2009.
5. James Risen, 'US to Hunt Down Afghan Drug Lords Tied to Taliban', *New York Times*, 9 August 2009, http://www.nytimes.com/2009/08/10/world/asia/10afghan.html.
6. 'Remarks by the President in Address to the Nation on the Way Forward in Afghanistan and Pakistan', http://www.whitehouse.gov/the-press-office/remarks-president-address-nation-way-forward-afghanistan-and-pakistan.
7. Tom Engelhardt, *The American Way of War: How Bush's War Became Obama's*, Haymarket Books, Chicago, Illinois., 2010, p. 141.
8. The book was published by St Martin's Press, New York.
9. Bob Woodward, *Obama's Wars*, Simon & Schuster, New York and London, 2010, p. 355.
10. A survey by *Stern* magazine in April 2010 showed that two out of three Germans opposed the war in Afghanistan. Judy Dempsey, 'Merkel Tries to Beat Back Opposition to Afghanistan', *New York Times*, 22 April 2010, http://www.nytimes.com/2010/04/23/world/europe/23iht-germany.html?_r=1&ref=europe.
11. Julian Borger, 'In real terms, NATO is losing', *Guardian*, 20 March 2009, http://www.guardian.co.uk/world/2009/mar/20/afghanistan-nato.
12. Ian Black, 'Petraeus Warns It Could Be Years before Afghan Troops Can Manage on Their Own', *Guardian*, 30 June 2010, http://

www.guardian.co.uk/world/2010/jun/29/david-petraeus-obama-afghanistan.

13. Integrity Watch Afghanistan, http://www.iwaweb.org/.
14. Dexter Filkins, 'The Afghan Bank Heist', *New Yorker*, 14 February 2011, http://www.newyorker.com/reporting/2011/02/14/110214fa_fact_filkins.
15. It was only later that Ahmad Zia Masoud was questioned by US and United Arab Emirates officials investigating money laundering. Apparently, the matter ended there.
16. Jonathan Steele and Jon Boone, 'WikiLeaks: Afghan Vice-President "Landed in Dubai with $52m in cash"', *Guardian*, 2 December 2010, http://www.guardian.co.uk/world/2010/dec/02/wikileaks-elite-afghans-millions-cash.
17. Michael Tennant, 'The Karzai Fortune, Courtesy of US Taxpayers', *New American*, 6 October 2010, http://www.thenewamerican.com/index.php/usnews/foreign-policy/4794-the-karzai-family-fortune-courtesy-of-us-taxpayers.
18. Eric Schmitt and Thom Shanker, 'General Calls for More US Troops to Avoid Afghan Failure', *New York Times*, 20 September 2009, http://www.nytimes.com/2009/09/21/world/asia/21afghan.html.
19. Cited in 'Anti-war Leaders Blast Escalation of Afghanistan War', http://www.fightbacknews.org/2009/12/1/anti-war-leaders-blast-escalation-afghanistan-war.
20. Of the 255 Democrats in the House of Representatives, 120 would go on to vote against sanctioning funds for the Afghanistan War for the next fiscal year.
21. Michael A. Lindenberger, 'Obama's Afghanistan Decision Evokes LBJ's 1965 Order on Vietnam Buildup', *Dallas Morning News*, 6 December 2009, http://www.dallasnews.com/sharedcontent/dws/news/nation/stories/DN-afghanlbj_06met.ART.State.Edition2.4ba1fa7.html).
22. Ibid.
23. Adam Nagourney and Dalia Sussman, 'US Plan for Afghanistan had Weak Support in Poll', *New York Times*, 9 December 2009, http://www.nytimes.com/202009/12/10/world/asia/10poll.html?_r=1.
24. Craig Whitlock, 'To Gates, Taliban Is Both a "Cancer" and Part of Afghan "political fabric"', *Washington Post*, 23 January 2010, http://

www.washingtonpost.com/wp-dyn/content/article/2010/01/22/AR2010012204395.html.

25. Jon Boone, 'Kabul Quietly Brings in Taliban Amnesty Law', *Guardian*, 12 February 2010, http://www.guardian.co.uk/world/2010/feb/11/taliban-amnesty-law-enacted.
26. Abdul Ghani Baradar's predecessors – Mullahs Akhtar Osmani and the one-legged Mansour Dadullah – were killed respectively in December 2006 and May 2007 by NATO forces.
27. Richard Oppel Jr, 'Violence Helps Taliban Undo Afghan Gains', *New York Times*, 3 April 2010, http://www.nytimes.com/2010/04/04/world/asia/04marja.html?_r=1&adxnnl=1&adxnnlx=1288375397-sPzyL4xiSwYgxHUac8jT9w.
28. 'US: Limited Damage from Leak of Afghan War Logs', Associated Press, 16 October 2010, http://www.jpost.com/International/Article.aspx?ID=191557&R=R1.
29. Associated Press, 5 September 2010.
30. Elisabeth Bumiller, 'In Marja, Violence and Intimidation Depress Vote', *New York Times*, 18 September 2010, http://atwar.blogs.nytimes.com/2010/09/18/in-marja-violence-and-intimidation-depress-vote/.
31. Michael A. Cohen, 'Petraeus versus Obama: What's Lurking Behind the Pentagon's Overly Optimistic Spinning of the Afghan War?', *Foreign Policy*, 29 October 2010, http://www.foreignpolicy.com/articles/2010/10/29/petraeus_versus_obama.
32. Woodward, *Obama's Wars*, pp. 332–33.

13. FIGHTING EXTREMISM

1. Woodward, *Obama's Wars*, p. 332.
2. Ibid., p. 376.
3. It is worth noting that, during the Taliban rule from 1996 to 2001, the six immediate neighbours of Afghanistan plus Russia and America used to meet periodically to review the situation. The practice stopped when Washington attacked the Taliban regime and started monopolizing international policy on Afghanistan.
4. Declan Walsh, 'WikiLeaks Cables: Pakistani Army Chief Considered Plan to Oust President', *Guardian*, 1 December 2010, http://

www.guardian.co.uk/world/2010/nov/30/wikileaks-cables-pakistani-leadership-wrangle.

5. Sabrina Tavernise, 'Survey of Pakistan's Young Predicts "Disaster" if Their Needs Aren't Addressed', *New York Times*, 21 November 2009, http://www.nytimes.com/2009/11/22/world/asia/22pstan.html?_r=1.
6. Showering rose petals is a ritual performed to welcome a bride to the groom's household.
7. 'Two Thirds in Kashmir Want Independence: Poll', *Dawn* (Karachi), 12 September 2010, http://news.dawn.com/wps/wcm/connect/dawn-content-library/dawn/news/world/04-kashmir-independence-poll-qs-06; citing the *Hindustan Times* poll.
8. It was not until August 2009 that a six-strong terrorist group was arrested in Sargodha. Christina Lamb, 'Elite Troops Ready to Combat Pakistani Nuclear Hijacks', *Sunday Times*, 17 January 2010, http://www.timesonline.co.uk/tol/news/world/asia/article6991056.ece.
9. Ibid.
10. See p. 229.
11. See p. 180.

14. OVERVIEW AND CONCLUSIONS

1. See p. xxx.
2. General Ashfaq Parvez Kayani reportedly showed a group of Western ambassadors in Islamabad a sheaf of pictures of police officers hailing Governor Salman Taseer's assassin, Malik Mumtaz Hussein Qadri, as a hero. Ahmed Rashid, 'An Army without a Country', *New York Review of Books* blog, 4 March 2011, http://www.nybooks.com/blogs/nyrblog/2011/mar/04/army-without-country/.

EPILOGUE

1. See p. 270. After Operation 'Neptune Spear', US officials reportedly confronted Pakistan's generals twice that the insurgents had been warned of impending American strikes.
2. To be on the right side of international law, the Obama Administration temporarily transferred the military personnel involved in the mission to the civilian CIA since the United States was not at war with Pakistan.

3. This would later lead to speculation that the Pakistanis had allowed the Chinese military attaché and his staff to examine the damaged rotor for its stealth technology.
4. *Times of India*, 3 May 2011, 'Why can't India do a US to the likes of Dawood, Saeed?'; http://articles.timesofindia.indiatimes.com/2011-05-03/india/29499048_1_indian-intelligence-special-forces-anti-india; and *Express Tribune*, 5 May 2011, Aditi Phadnis, 'After Bin Laden, Can India hunt down terrorists in Pakistan?', http://tribune.com.pk/story/162161/taking-a-lesson-from-the-us-raid-can-india-hunt-down-terrorists-in-pakistan/.
5. *New Kerala News*, 2 May 2011, 'Osama's killing proves Pakistan is epicenter of terrorism: BJP', http://www.newkerala.com/news/world/fullnews-200733.html.
6. Reuters, 3 May 2011, 'LeT holds prayers for Bin Laden in Pakistan', http://tribune.com.pk/story/160762/let-holds-prayers-for-bin-laden-in-pakistan/.
7. The Pakistani government wanted to demolish Osama bin Laden's safe house which had become a symbol of national humiliation but refrained form doing so when Washington insisted on its intelligence agents doing a thorough check-up of the walls and the ground for any buried weapons or documents.
8. *Guardian*, 6 May 2011, Matt Wells and Mark Tran, 'Osama Bin Laden's death: Aftermath and Reactions', http://pul.se/Osama-bin-Ladens-death-aftermath-and-reaction_Guardian-Osama-bin-Laden-World-news-3TxKuODcnHW,1I3Ti5SO6w0E.
9. *New York Times*, 13 May 2011, Jane Perlez, 'Denying Links to Militants, Pakistan's Spy Chief Denounces U.S. Before Parliament', http://www.nytimes.com/2011/05/14/world/asia/14pakistan.html. In the first quarter of 2011, the CIA carried out 27 drone attacks which caused 159 deaths.
10. *Time*, Omar Waraich, 'Berating General Pasha: Pakistan's Spy Chief Gets a Tongue-Lashing', http://www.time.com/time/world/article/0,8599,2071412,00.html.
11. Significantly, General Kayani remained silent throughout the long session, thus sparing himself the humiliation of having to answer questions by civilian politicians.
12. *Guardian*, 10 May 2011, Declan Walsh, 'Osama bin Laden mission agreed in secret 10 years ago by US and Pakistan', http://

www.guardian.co.uk/world/2011/may/09/osama-bin-laden-us-pakistan-deal.

13. *Asia Times Online*, 27 May 2011, Syed Saleem Shahzad, 'Al Qaida had warned of Pakistan strike', http://www.atimes.com/atimes/South_Asia/ME27Df06.html. Shahzad specialized in delving deep into the underworld of Islamist militancy, and had interviewed Sirajuddin Haqqani as well as Ilyas Kashmiri, who commanded Al Qaida's operational arm Brigade 313.
14. BBC News, 8 July 2011, 'Pakistan "approved Saleem Shahzad murder" says Mullen', http://www.bbc.co.uk/news/mobile/world-south-asia-14074814.
15. *Guardian*, 11 July 2011, Saeed Shah, 'U.S. suspends Pakistan military aid as diplomatic relations worsen', http://www.guardian.co.uk/world/2011/jul/10/us-suspends-pakistan-military-aid. In 2010–11 fiscal year, the US provided Pakistan with $4.5 bn in aid.
16. See http://icasualties.org/.
17. Afghanistan NGO Safety Office: Quarterly Report, 21 July 2011, http://afghanistan101.blogspot.com/2011/07/quarterly-report-afghanistan-ngo-safety.html.
18. In all of Helmand province, there was only one trained Afghan IED expert.
19. *New York Times*, 8 June 2011, Elisabeth Bumiller and Brian Knowlton, 'Ambassadorial Nominee Warns of Risk if the U.S. Abandons Afghanistan', http://www.nytimes.com/2011/06/09/world/asia/09Diplo.html?pagewanted=all.
20. Germany said it would pull out all of its remaining 4,500 troops before December 2011, with France planning to withdraw 1,700 of its 4,000 soldiers by that date. *The Times*, 24 June 2011, Jeremy Starkey, Michael Evans and Roland Watson, 'British troops "at risk" from US withdrawal').
21. Karzai's statement at SCO summit in Astana 14-15 June 2011, http://www.gmic.gov.af/english/index.php?option=com_content&view=article&id=241:statement-by-hamid-karzai-at-the-10th-summit-of-the-heads-of-state-of-the-shanghai-cooperation-organization-sco&catid=47:features&Itemid=84.
22. *Trend*, 15 June 2011, A. Maratov, 'Russian president proposes multi-aspect cooperation with Afghanistan', http://en.trend.az/news/politics/1891811.html.

SELECT BIBLIOGRAPHY

Ahmad, Jamil-ud-din (ed.), *Speeches and Writings of Mr Jinnah*, Vol. II, Shaikh Muhammad Ashrag, Lahore, 1964

Ali, Tariq, *The Duel: Pakistan on the Flight Path of American Power*, Scribner, New York/ Simon & Schuster, London, 2008

Arberry, Arthur J. (trans.), *The Koran Interpreted*, Oxford University Press, Oxford and New York, 1964

Bergen, Peter L., *Holy Wars: Inside the Secret World of Osama bin Laden*, The Free Press, New York/Weidenfeld and Nicolson, London, 2001

Bhutto, Zulfikar Ali, *If I Am Assassinated*, Vikas Publishing House, Delhi, 1979

Burki, Shahid Javed and Craig Baxter (eds), *Pakistan under the Military: Eleven Years of Zia ul Haq*, Westview Press, Boulder, COLO, 1991

Cohen, Stephen Philip, *The Idea of Pakistan*, Brookings Institution, Washington, DC, 2004

Cooley, John K., *Unholy Wars: Afghanistan, America and International Terrorism*, Pluto Press, London and Sterling, VA, 2000

Dhar, Maloy Krishna, *Open Secrets: India's Intelligence Unveiled*, Manas Publications, New Delhi, 2005

Engelhardt, Tom, *The American Way of War: How Bush's War Became Obama's*, Haymarket Books, Chicago, ILL., 2010

Gandhi, Rajmohan, *Understanding the Muslim Mind*, Penguin Books India, New Delhi, 2000

Ganguly, Sumit (ed.), *India's Foreign Policy: Retrospect and Prospect*; Oxford University Press, Delhi, 2010

Gates, Robert M., *From the Shadows: The Ultimate Insider's Story of Five Presidents and How They Won the Cold War*, Simon & Schuster, New York and London, 1997

Giustozzi, Antonio, *Koran, Kalashnikov and Laptop: The Neo-Taliban Insurgency in Afghanistan*, Hurst & Company, London, 2007/ Columbia University Press, New York, 2007

Golwalkar, Madhavrao, *We, or, Our Nationhood Defined*, Bharat Publications, Nagpur (India), 1939

Guha, Ramchandra, *India After Gandhi: The History of the World's Largest Democracy*, Macmillan, London, 2007/ Ecco Press, New York, 2007

Haqqani, Husain, *Pakistan: Between Mosque and Military*, Carnegie Endowment for International Peace, Washington, D.C., 2005

Hiro, Dilip, *Inside India Today*, Routledge & Kegan Paul, London, 1976/ Monthly Review Press, New York, 1977

——, *Between Marx and Muhammad The Changing Face of Central Asia*, HarperCollins, London, 1994

——, *War Without End: The Rise of Islamist Terrorism and Global Response*, Routledge, London and New York, 2002,

——, *Timeline History of India*, Barnes and Noble, New York, 2006

Hussain, Zahid, *Frontline Pakistan: The Struggle with Militant Islam*, I.B. Tauris, London/ Columbia University Press, New York, 2007

Hyman, Anthony, *Afghanistan under Soviet Domination*, Macmillan, London, 1984

Kumaraswamy, P.R., *India's Israel Policy*, Columbia University Press, New York, 2010

Lamb, Christina, *Waiting for Allah: Pakistan's Struggle for Democracy*, Hamish Hamilton, London, 1991

Latifa, *My Forbidden Face: Growing up under the Taliban, a Young Woman's Story* (Trans. Lisa Appignanesi), Virago, London, 2001

Levy, Adrian and Catherine Scott-Clark, *Deception: Pakistan, the United States and the Global Nuclear Weapons Conspiracy*, Atlantic Books, London, 2007/ Walker & Company, New York, 2007

Loyn, David, *Butcher & Bold: Two Hundred Years of Foreign Engagement in Afghanistan*, Hutchinson, London, 2008

Peer, Basharat, *Curfewed Night*, Random House India, Noida, India, 2009

——, *Curfewed Night: One Kashmiri Journalist's Frontline Account of Life, Love, and War in His Homeland*, Scribner, New York, 2010

——, *Curfewed Night: A Frontline Memoir of Life, Love and War in Kashmir*, HarperPress, London, 2010

Puri, Balraj, *Towards Insurgency*, Sangam Books, London, 1993

Raina, Ashok, *Inside RAW: The Story of India's Secret Service*, Vikas Publishing House, 1981

Raman, B., *Kaoboys of R&AW: Down Memory Lane*, Lancer Publishers, New Delhi, 2008

Rashid, Ahmed, *Taliban: The Story of the Afghan Warlords*, Pan Books, London, 2001

——, *Taliban: Militant Islam, Oil and Fundamentalism in Central Asia*, Yale University Press, New Haven, CT, 2001

——, *Descent into Chaos: How the War against Islamic Extremism Is Being Lost in Pakistan, Afghanistan and Central Asia*, Allen Lane, London, 2008/ Viking, New York, 2008

Roy, Arundhati, *Listening to Grasshoppers: Field Notes on Democracy*, Hamish Hamilton, London, 2009/ Haymarket Books, Chicago, ILL., 2009

Abdul Sattar, *Pakistan's Foreign Policy 1947–2005: A Concise History*, Oxford University Press, Karachi, 2007

Savarkar, Vinayak Damodar, *Hindutva: Who is a Hindu?* Hindi Sahitya Sadan, Delhi, 2003

Schofield, Victoria, *Kashmir in Conflict: India, Pakistan and the Unending Conflict* , I.B. Tauris, London and New York, 2010

Shaikh, Farzana, *Making Sense of Pakistan*, Hurst & Company, London, 2009/ Columbia University Press, New York, 2009

Siddiqa, Ayesha, *Military Inc. Inside Pakistan's Military Economy*, Pluto Press, London and Ann Arbor, MI, 2007

Smith, David James, *Hinduism and Modernity*, Blackwell Publishing, Oxford, 2002

Urban, Mark, *War in Afghanistan*, Macmillan, London, 1988

Woodward, Bob, *Obama's Wars*, Simon & Schuster, New York and London, 2010

Zaeef, Abdul Salam, *My Life with the Taliban*, Hurst & Company, London, 2010/ Columbia University Press, New York, 2010

Zahab, Mariam Abou and Olivier Roy, *Islamist Networks: The Afghan-Pakistan Connection*, Hurst & Company, London, 2004/ Columbia University Press, New York, 2007

INDEX